THE ENCYCLOPEDIA OF
Coloured Pencil
TECHNIQUES

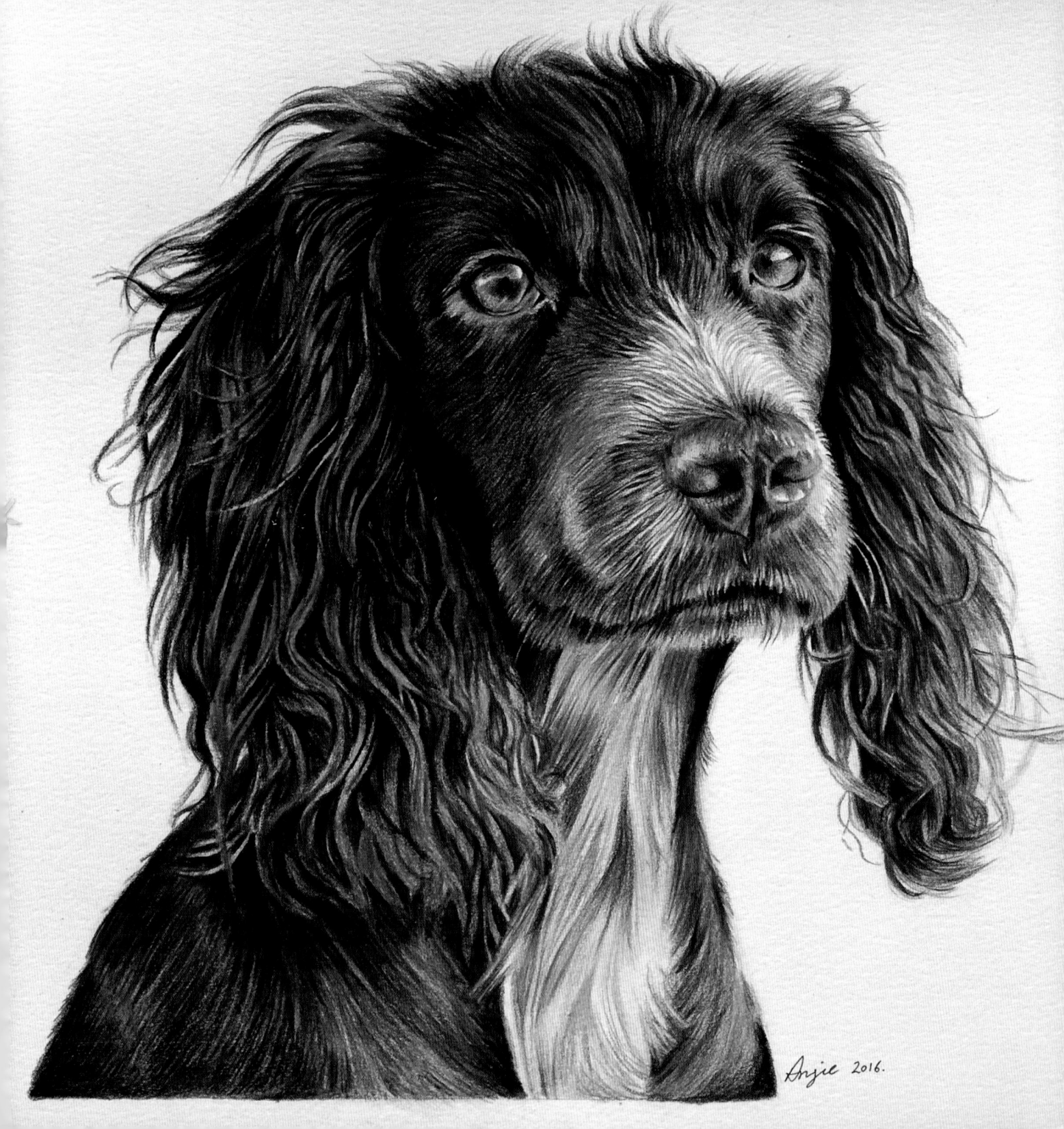

Anjie 2016.

THE ENCYCLOPEDIA OF
Coloured Pencil
TECHNIQUES

Judy Martin

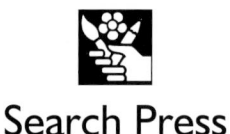

Search Press

A QUARTO BOOK

Published in 2016 by
Search Press Ltd
Wellwood
North Farm Road
Tunbridge Wells
Kent TN2 3DR

Reprinted 2017

ISBN: 978-1-78221-477-9

Conceived, designed and produced by
Quarto Publishing plc
The Old Brewery
6 Blundell Street
London N7 9BH
www.quartoknows.com

QUAR.CPE2

Assistant Editor: Georgia Cherry
Art Director: Caroline Guest
Designer: Julie Francis
Indexer: Helen Snaith
Creative Director: Moira Clinch
Publisher: Paul Carslake

Printed in China by 1010 Printing
International Ltd

Credits: page 2: Tilly by Angie
Hedgecock; page 4: Sanctuary (detail) by
Gretchen Parker; page 5: Train in
Budapest by Wilfrid Barbier, Order/Chaos
by Gary Greene

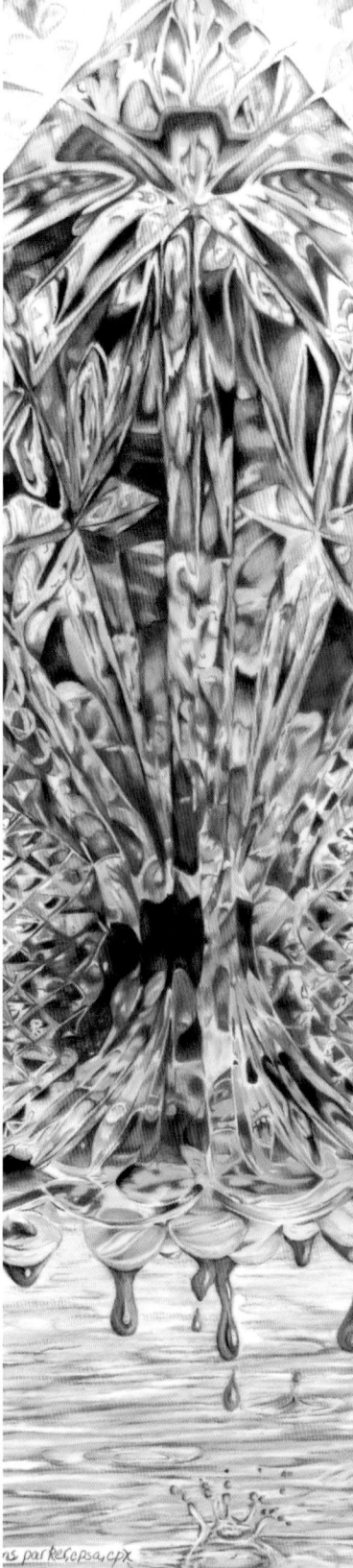

Contents

Foreword   6
Materials   8

TECHNIQUES   10

HANDLING PENCILS   12
PAPER GRAIN EFFECTS   14
COLOURED PAPERS   16
TEXTURED GROUNDS   18
LINEAR MARKS   20
SHADING   22
BLENDING   26
HATCHING   28
BLOCKING IN   30
FILLING IN   32
STIPPLING   33
GRADATION   34
DASHES AND DOTS   36
BURNISHING   38
OVERLAYING COLOURS   40
MIXING PENCILS   42
LINE QUALITIES   44
HIGHLIGHTING   46
CONTOUR DRAWING   48
SKETCHING   50
ERASER TECHNIQUES   52
SOLVENTS   54
IMPRESSING   56
WHITE LINE   58
SGRAFFITO   60
FROTTAGE   62
MASKING   64

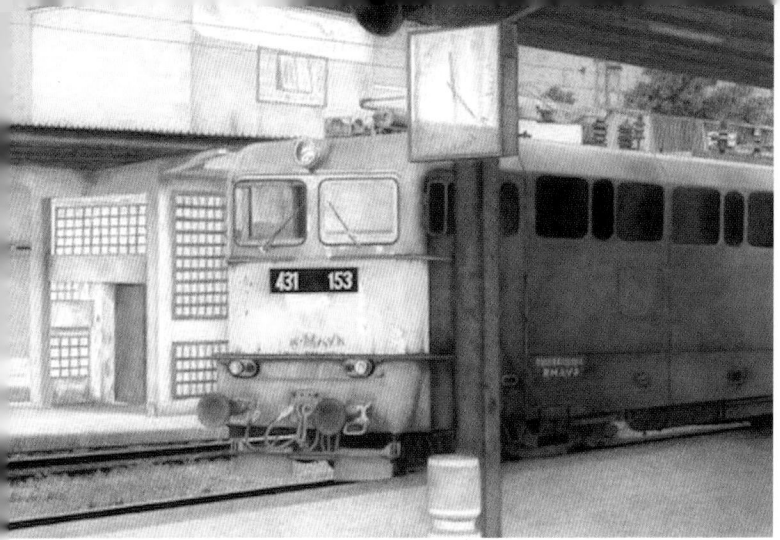
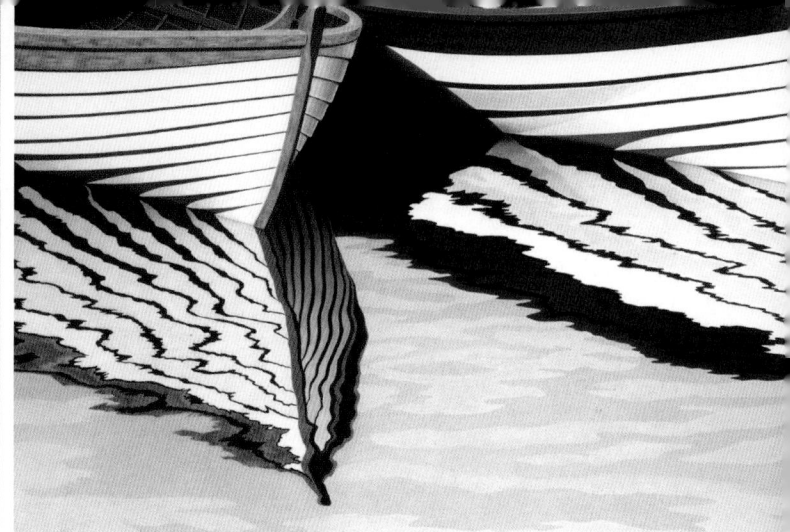

GRAPHITE PENCIL 66

INK AND PENCIL 68

LINE AND WASH 69

PASTEL AND PENCIL 70

WATERCOLOUR AND PENCIL 72

COLLAGE 74

TRACING 76

SQUARING UP OR DOWN 78

FIXING 79

PATCH CORRECTION 80

TRANSPARENT SUPPORTS 82

THEMES 84

Landscape and Townscape 86

SPACE AND DISTANCE 88

COLOUR STUDIES 90

SHAPES AND TEXTURES 92

LIGHT AND ATMOSPHERE 94

BUILDINGS 96

FACADES 98

TOWNSCAPES 100

DEMONSTRATION: Space and light 102

Objects 106

DOMESTIC OBJECTS 108

DECORATIVE OBJECTS 110

TOYS AND EPHEMERA 112

GROUPS 114

FRUITS 120

TABLE SETTINGS 122

DEMONSTRATION: Form and surface detail 124

Nature 128

FLOWERS AND FOLIAGE 130

CONTAINER PLANTS 136

ANIMAL STUDIES 138

PATTERN AND TEXTURE 144

ANIMAL MOVEMENT 146

DEMONSTRATION: The fresh beauty of flowers 148

People and Portraits 152

INDIVIDUALS 154

CHILDREN 156

LIFE STUDIES 158

MOVEMENT 160

ENVIRONMENT 162

EXPRESSIVE PORTRAITS 164

FULL-LENGTH PORTRAITS 166

DEMONSTRATION: Two approaches to the same subject 168

INDEX 172

CREDITS 176

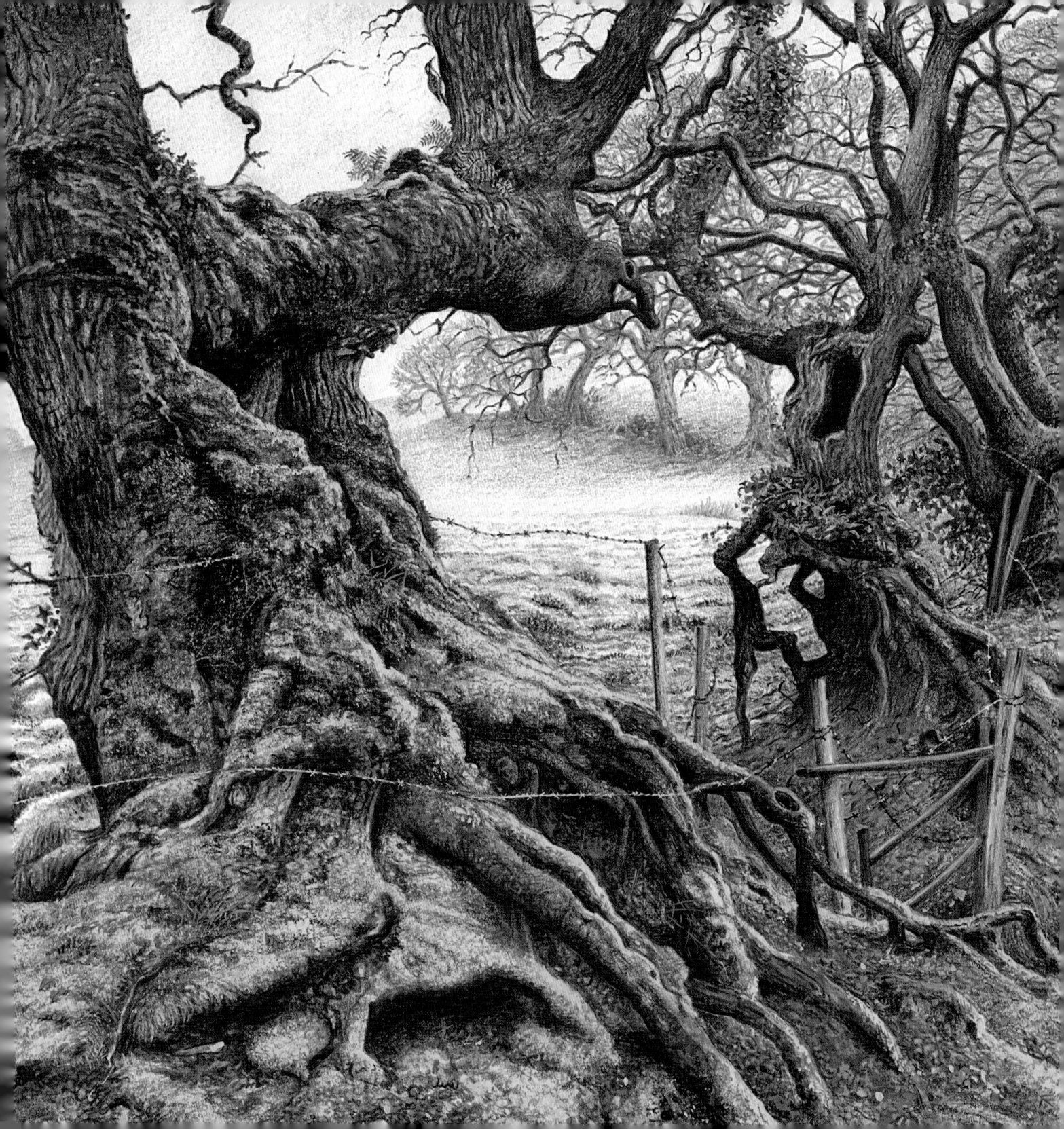

Foreword

Coloured pencils are an excellent medium for the newcomer to drawing and painting. Clean, portable, easy to handle and relatively inexpensive, they can be used any time and in any location. No supplementary materials or equipment are required, contrasting markedly with paints. All you need to get going are the pencils themselves and some drawing paper or a sketchbook.

Many different brands of coloured pencils are on the market and each have their own special qualities of colour and texture. They are very different from the cheap and cheerful crayons of the schoolroom that you may have used for your first ventures in drawing. Artists' pencils with waxy and chalky leads can be stroked onto the page almost like paint – the velvety, malleable textures are a pleasure to handle and the colour ranges are inspirational.

Mastering only one or two basic techniques can enable you to produce a surprisingly sophisticated result, which is encouraging to the beginner. There is a great deal more to discover in this simple but versatile medium however. This book provides you with the means to explore fully the potential of coloured pencils through the examples set by practised artists and through experimentation of your own. Remember too, as with any artist's medium, learning a new skill is a challenge but it should not be a chore. There is no absolutely right or wrong way to use coloured pencils, and the only essential aim is to enjoy both the progress and results of your work.

JUDY MARTIN

GRAHAM BRACE
**ENCHANTED
EMBANKMENT**

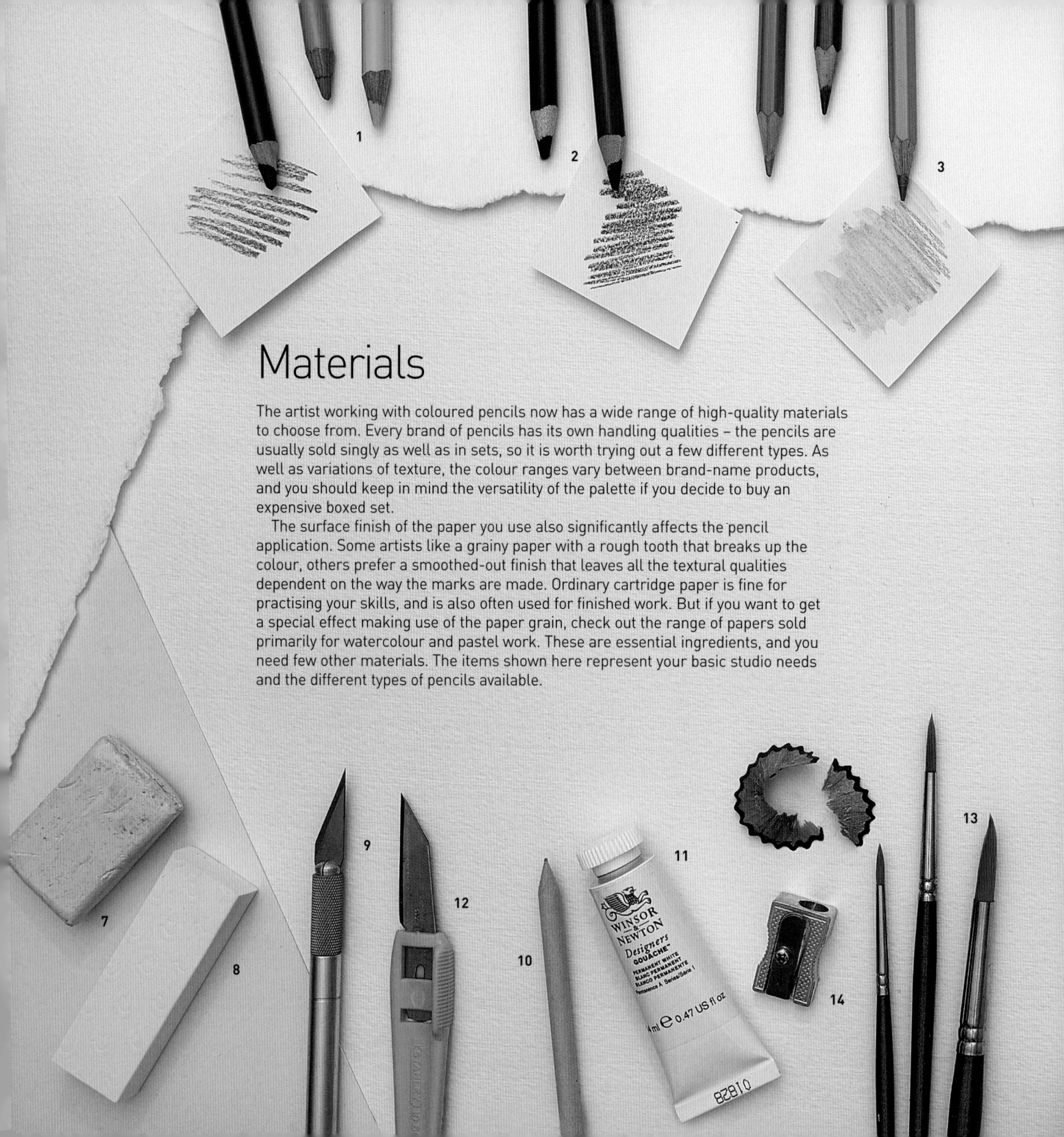

Materials

The artist working with coloured pencils now has a wide range of high-quality materials to choose from. Every brand of pencils has its own handling qualities – the pencils are usually sold singly as well as in sets, so it is worth trying out a few different types. As well as variations of texture, the colour ranges vary between brand-name products, and you should keep in mind the versatility of the palette if you decide to buy an expensive boxed set.

   The surface finish of the paper you use also significantly affects the pencil application. Some artists like a grainy paper with a rough tooth that breaks up the colour, others prefer a smoothed-out finish that leaves all the textural qualities dependent on the way the marks are made. Ordinary cartridge paper is fine for practising your skills, and is also often used for finished work. But if you want to get a special effect making use of the paper grain, check out the range of papers sold primarily for watercolour and pastel work. These are essential ingredients, and you need few other materials. The items shown here represent your basic studio needs and the different types of pencils available.

1

2

3

7

8

9

10

11

12

13

14

WINSOR & NEWTON
Designers
GOUACHE
PERMANENT WHITE
BLANC PERMANENT
BLANCO PERMANENTE
Permanence A. Series/Série 1
4 ml 0.47 US fl oz

01828

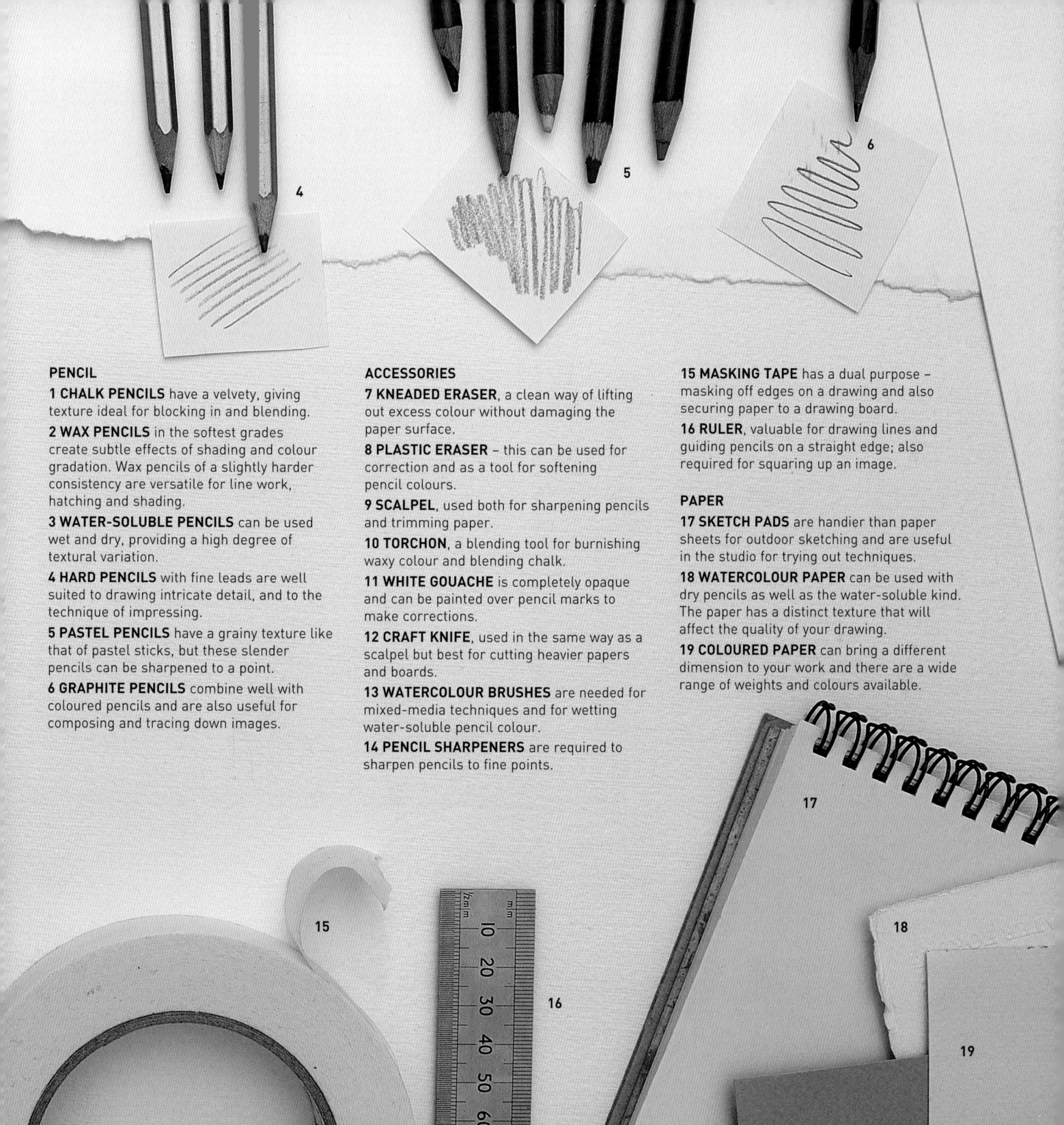

PENCIL

1 CHALK PENCILS have a velvety, giving texture ideal for blocking in and blending.

2 WAX PENCILS in the softest grades create subtle effects of shading and colour gradation. Wax pencils of a slightly harder consistency are versatile for line work, hatching and shading.

3 WATER-SOLUBLE PENCILS can be used wet and dry, providing a high degree of textural variation.

4 HARD PENCILS with fine leads are well suited to drawing intricate detail, and to the technique of impressing.

5 PASTEL PENCILS have a grainy texture like that of pastel sticks, but these slender pencils can be sharpened to a point.

6 GRAPHITE PENCILS combine well with coloured pencils and are also useful for composing and tracing down images.

ACCESSORIES

7 KNEADED ERASER, a clean way of lifting out excess colour without damaging the paper surface.

8 PLASTIC ERASER – this can be used for correction and as a tool for softening pencil colours.

9 SCALPEL, used both for sharpening pencils and trimming paper.

10 TORCHON, a blending tool for burnishing waxy colour and blending chalk.

11 WHITE GOUACHE is completely opaque and can be painted over pencil marks to make corrections.

12 CRAFT KNIFE, used in the same way as a scalpel but best for cutting heavier papers and boards.

13 WATERCOLOUR BRUSHES are needed for mixed-media techniques and for wetting water-soluble pencil colour.

14 PENCIL SHARPENERS are required to sharpen pencils to fine points.

15 MASKING TAPE has a dual purpose – masking off edges on a drawing and also securing paper to a drawing board.

16 RULER, valuable for drawing lines and guiding pencils on a straight edge; also required for squaring up an image.

PAPER

17 SKETCH PADS are handier than paper sheets for outdoor sketching and are useful in the studio for trying out techniques.

18 WATERCOLOUR PAPER can be used with dry pencils as well as the water-soluble kind. The paper has a distinct texture that will affect the quality of your drawing.

19 COLOURED PAPER can bring a different dimension to your work and there are a wide range of weights and colours available.

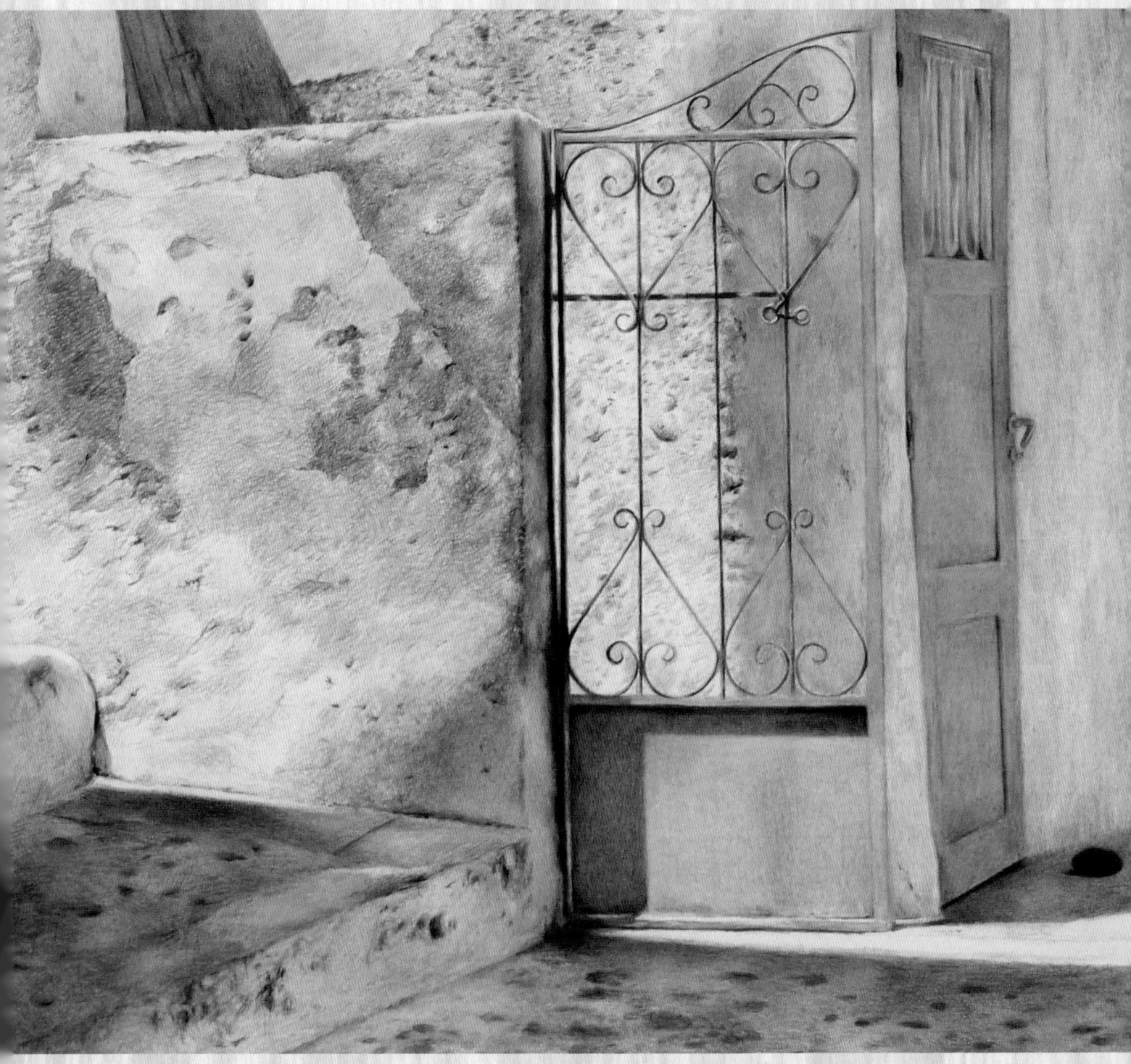

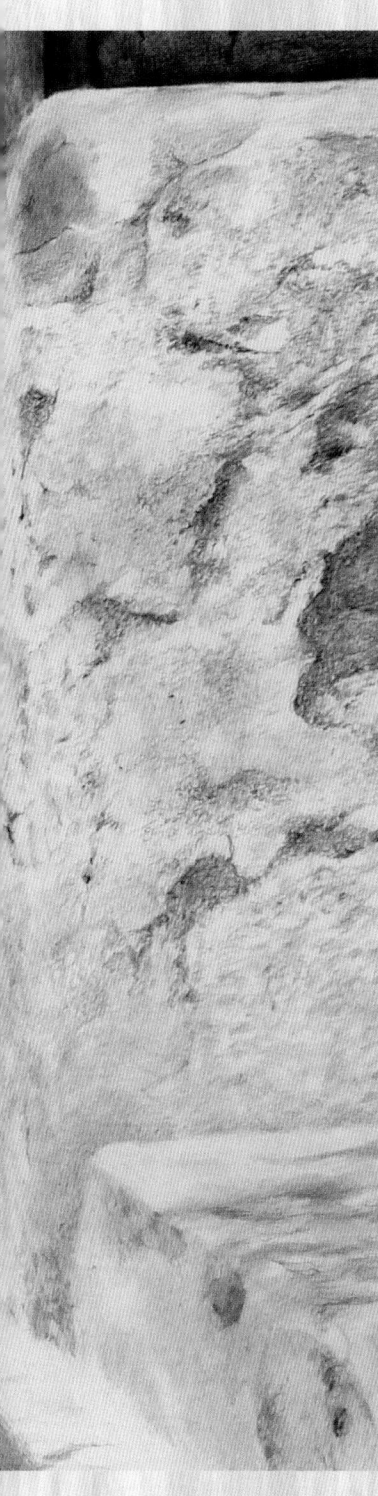

Techniques

■ ■

Coloured pencil "leads" consist of particles of coloured pigment mixed with an inert white filler that gives opacity, such as kaolin or talc, a binding medium that holds the materials together and enables shaping of the colour sticks, and waxes, which give the pencils smooth handling properties. It is the varying proportions of these substances that produces the variations in quality, texture and strength of colour.

Some coloured pencils are hard and translucent, some very waxy and giving, others chalky and opaque. Most pencils are classically shaped with the slender coloured lead encased in wood. These can be sharpened to a fine point for detailed line work, or can be used blunt to create broader, smooth strokes. You can also obtain square-sectioned colour sticks that resemble hard pastels but have a waxy texture like that of coloured pencils.

The techniques demonstrated in the following pages are equally effective with all types of coloured pencils unless otherwise stated. The only type designed to be handled differently is the water-soluble coloured pencil, whose colour medium is formulated to dissolve and spread like watercolour paint when brushed over with clean water. However, even this can be used dry in the same ways as other kinds of pencil.

SUSAN BRINKMANN
GATE IN OIA SANTORINI

Handling Pencils

There is no right or wrong way to hold a coloured pencil – any grip that is comfortable and gives you control of the pencil movement is right for you. However, the surface effects you obtain can vary subtly in response to the way you handle this simple drawing tool. They are affected by the pressure and direction of the marks you apply and their range and extent.

The conventional grip in which the shaft of the pencil rests in the curve of the thumb, with the tip guided by your thumb and first two fingers, gives tight control. You can make very delicate marks, firm lines and even shading by small movements of the fingers, wrist and hand. For more open, scribbled or hatched textures, you can use more sweeping movements of your hand and arm.

Alternatively, you can grip the pencil with your hand curled over or under the shaft. These grips give less subtle control but encourage free gestural movements of the hand and arm. For instance, shading with an underhand grip can be very light and quick, while linear marks made with the overhand grip can be heavy and vigorous.

If you are experimenting with a change of scale or textural variations in your work, it is always worth trying different ways of physically manipulating your medium.

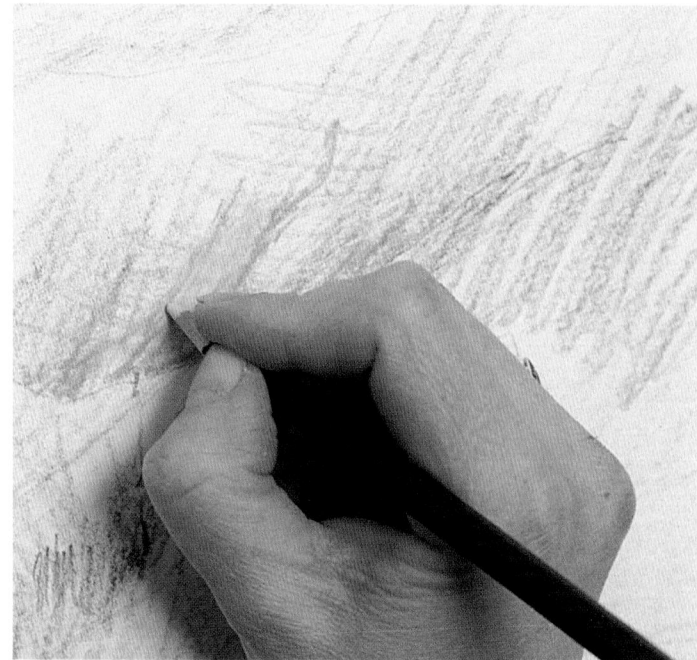

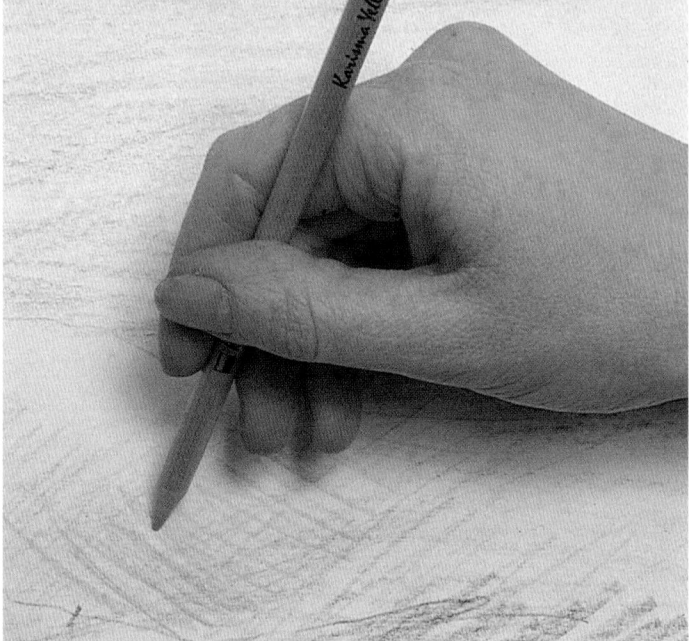

Conventional grip
The common method of holding a pencil, similar to the grip used for writing, gives tight control over line work and shading (top). Holding the pencil higher up the shaft (right) gives you a freer handling method for loose shading and hatching, and you can also approach the drawing from different angles.

Overhand grip

If you hold the pencil with your forefinger over the shaft, rather as if you were stabbing something with a fork, this tends to encourage firmer pressure. It is a good way to develop dense shading (right), or to produce a strong line quality (far right).

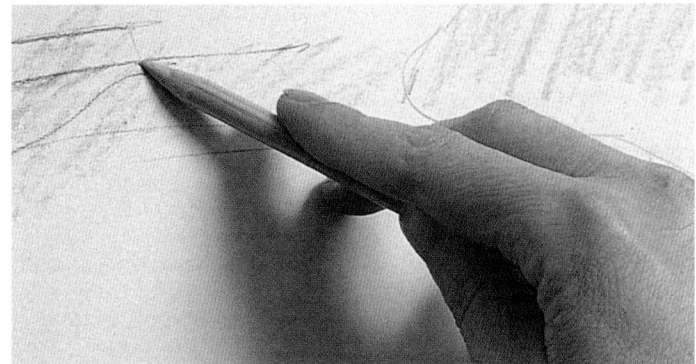

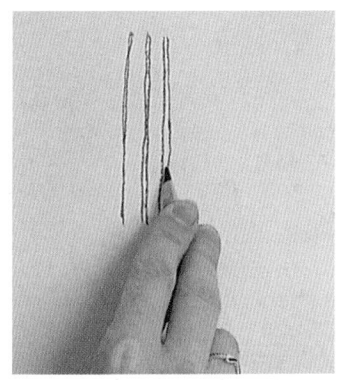

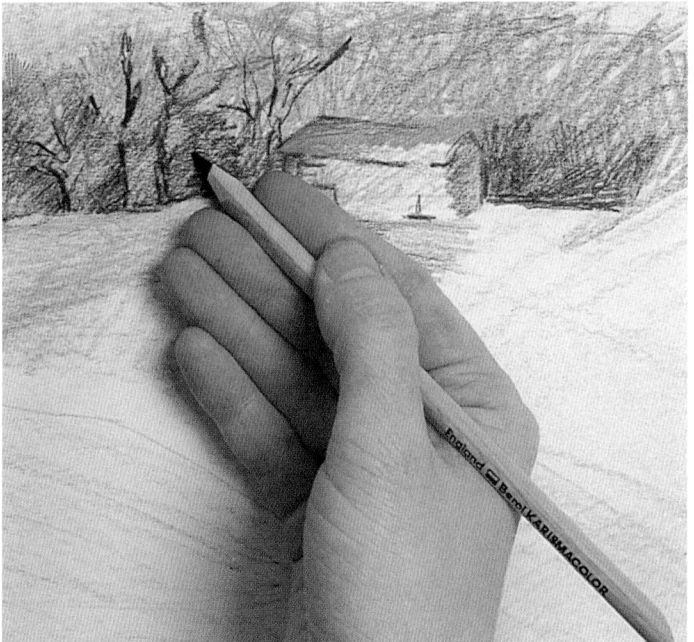

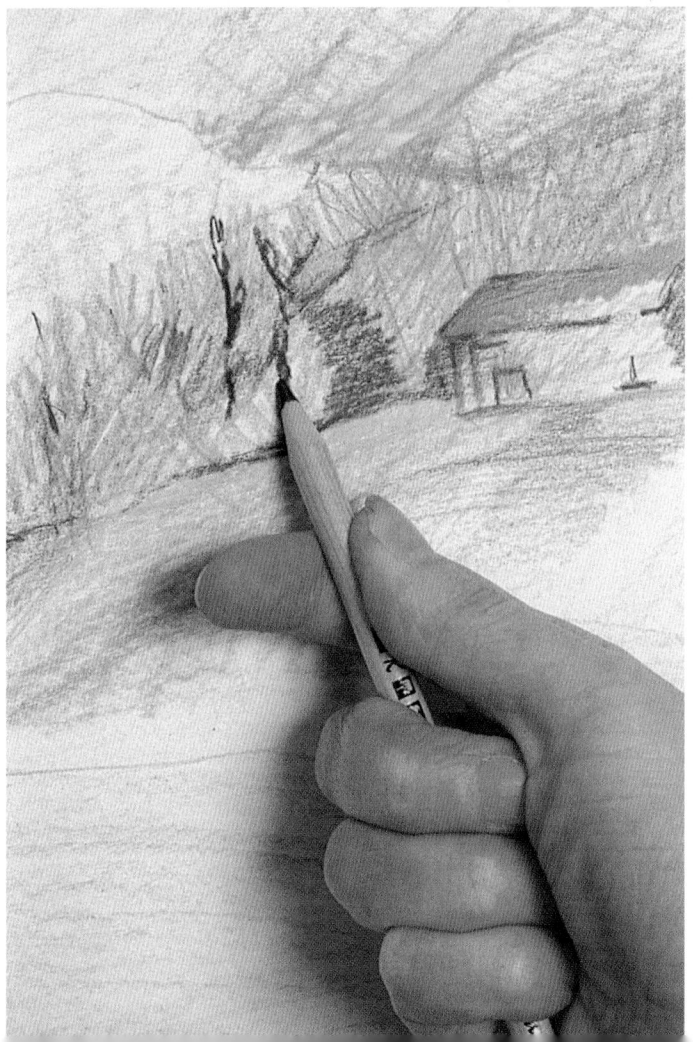

Underhand grip

This method in which you cradle the pencil in the palm of your hand, confines the movement of the pencil tip. Applying pressure with thumb and forefinger (right), you can produce a heavy but sensitive line quality; to make the line your whole hand moves, not just the wrist and fingers. Underhand shading has a lighter touch (above) and you can vary the pressure by simply lifting your fingers slightly.

Paper grain effects

To build up the colour density in a coloured pencil drawing, you need a surface with sufficient tooth to create some friction with the pencil point – otherwise the texture of the pencil lead rapidly produces a smooth, compacted finish that resists further applications.

The degree of tooth in a drawing paper depends on the papermaking ingredients and the method of finishing. Cartridge paper, for instance, is relatively smooth, although it has an excellent tooth for pencil drawing. Pastel papers have pronounced grain intended to grip the loose pigment particles laid down by soft pastels. Watercolour papers come in a variety of weights and finishes, the heaviest having a visibly "pitted" surface texture.

The more heavily textured the paper grain, the longer the surface stays open and workable, an important consideration if you are depending on colour overlays for your effect. However, on very grainy paper, it is difficult to get a fine, sharp line, because the surface breaks up the pencil mark, and tiny glints of the paper colour will show through even densely worked areas of shading. Varying the kind of paper that you use can bring an extra dimension to your work. Try different weights and textures to find out if they are comfortable to work on and produce qualities that suit your own technique and drawing style.

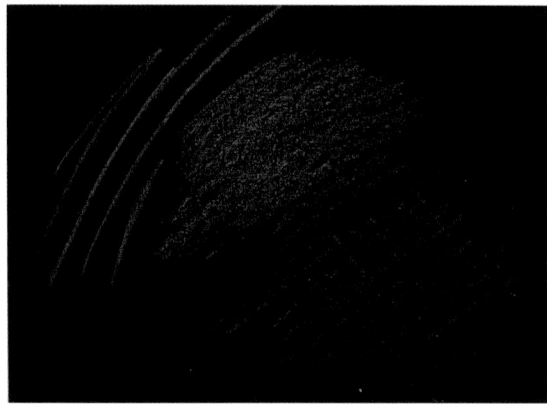

Textured papers
Smooth, laid and heavily textured papers – whatever you choose will affect the quality of your drawing.

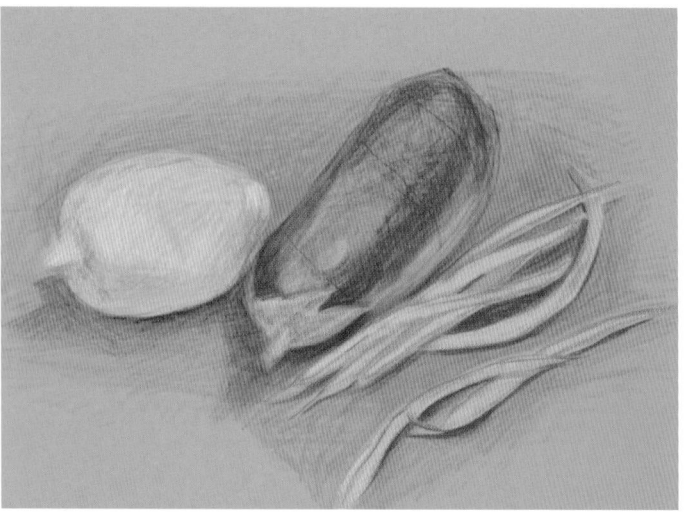

◄JANE STROTHER
FRUIT
There is an almost luminous quality to this vignette in dry pencil on bright pink paper. Full use of complementaries is seen in the use of the cool pink with the green of the beans and warm yellow lemon. The paler colours have a greater opacity than the others and so are less affected by the ground colour, thus adding to the vibrancy.

Coloured papers
There are many types of coloured papers and the kind that you choose depends on how much you want the paper colour to influence the applied pencil colours. The heavier the grain, the more of the paper colour shows through. A medium-toothed, fairly even-surfaced paper, like this black sheet, gives the pencil marks a pleasing soft texture, but allows the colours to build up cleanly.

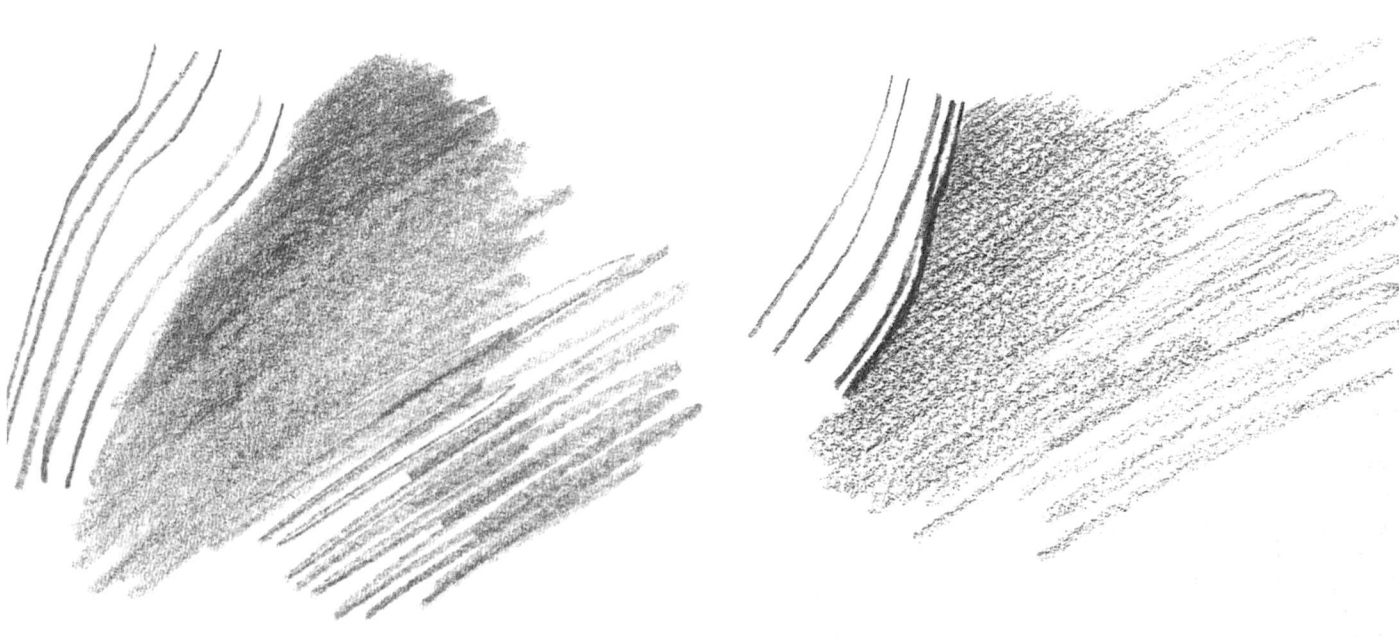

Cartridge paper

A relatively smooth surface with a slight tooth, like ordinary cartridge paper, gives a soft grainy quality to light pencil strokes, but as the pressure of the pencil increases, the grain of the paper is likely to be "ironed out" and has less effect.

Pastel paper

Papers made specially for work in pastel have quite a pronounced grain intended to grip the loose colour. With coloured pencils, the grain shows up as a lightly pitted pattern within the coloured strokes.

Watercolour papers

Heavy watercolour papers sometimes prove too resistant for coloured pencils. The more giving types still have a distinctive grain pattern that leaves white flecks showing through the colour. The grain may be heavy (right), roughening the pencil texture, or it may have a mechanical pattern (far right) that breaks the marks into a mesh-like texture.

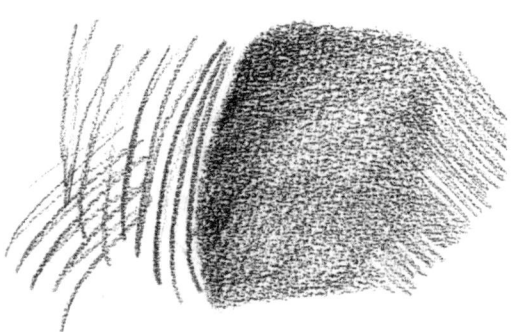
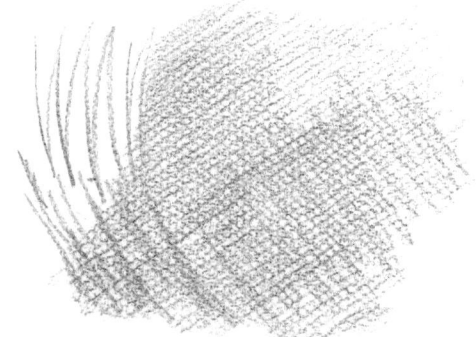

Coloured Papers

The small area of contact that the pencil tip has with the paper means that it can take a lot of time and effort to build up areas of solid colour. Depending on the nature of your subject and the style of your drawing, working on coloured paper can have distinct advantages. The colour of the ground can be used in two particular ways. Firstly, it can act as a mid-tone which enables you to key the range of tones and hues in your applied colours. Secondly, it can form a unifying element of the composition, perhaps standing for a specific element of your subject – for instance, blue for sky and seascape, green or terracotta for a landscape, a warm beige or buff background for an interior or still life.

Coloured pencils are often slightly translucent, so the paper colour modifies the pencil colours, especially the lighter tints. You may wish to make a tint chart trying out the effect of coloured lines and areas of shading on the ground you intend to use. This enables you to predict modifications and make use of the harmonies and contrasts that the paper colour can introduce.

It is best to select low-key or neutral tones and colours – very brightly coloured papers can make it difficult to handle your range of pencil colours, although on occasions you might require a dramatic colour effect to suit the mood of the subject.

If you want to include subtleties such as blended background colours or light textural effects, you can prepare a coloured ground by putting a watercolour wash over stretched white paper.

There is little advantage to using a coloured ground if you eventually cover it completely, so experiment with pencil techniques that give an open surface texture, allowing the paper colour to contribute, such as dashes and dots or hatching (see pages 28–29 and 36–37).

A range of coloured papers
A coloured paper will be closer to the average tone of the final picture, making it easier to key the range of tones and hues in your applied colours.

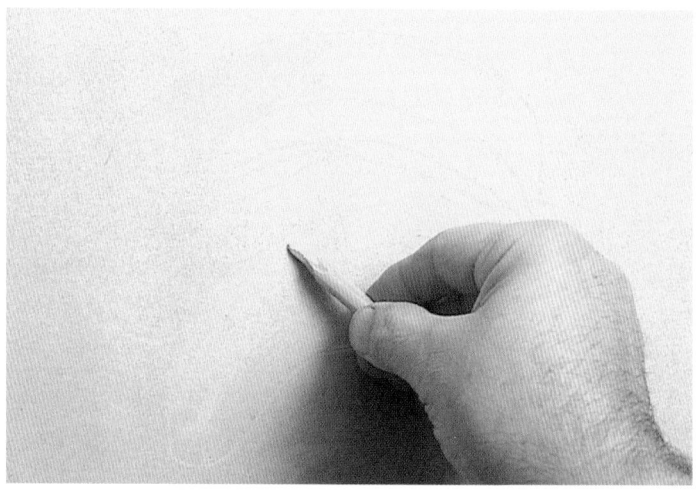

Drawing on coloured paper
1 Select a paper colour that harmonizes with the basic colours of your subject, as here, or one that will create a dramatic opposition. If you wish to begin with an outline, sketch it in lightly and begin blocking in the main colour areas.

2 Build up the shading gradually at first, introducing as many colours as you need to match the variations in the subject.

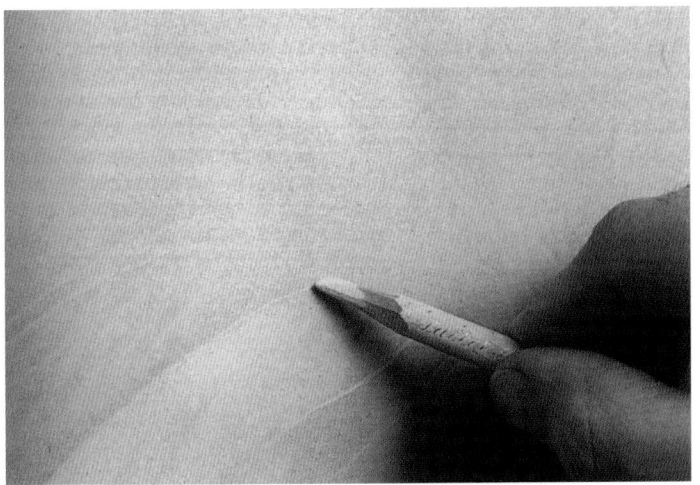

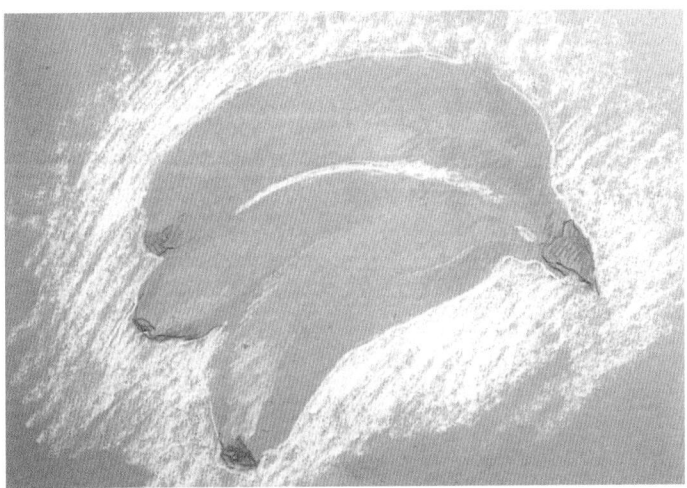

3 As you begin to shade more heavily, you can obliterate the paper colour in certain areas, while retaining it in others to help with the modelling of colour and tone.

4 The muted paper colour here acts as a mid-tone against the brighter yellows and white highlighting and background. Lightweight linear marks in brown define the banana stalks and tips.

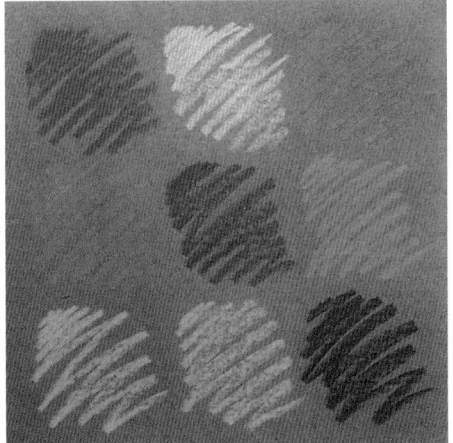

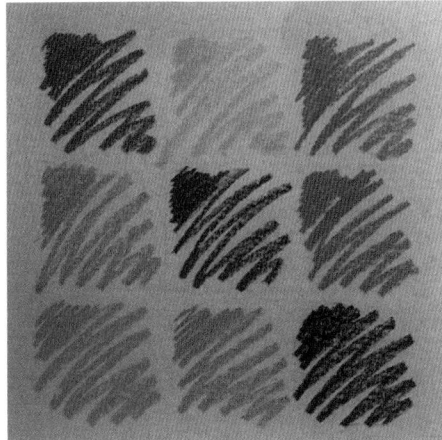

Making colour charts

The paper colour affects the appearance of your pencil colours, especially those which are light-toned or translucent. You may find it helpful to make quick colour charts to check the variations. Notice, for example, how the warm brown ground and cold blue one create a significant difference in the effect of the cool grey and yellow ochre pencils (bottom left and centre). The orange (middle right) appears lighter on brown than on blue. The translucent bright yellow (centre top) is diminished in intensity by the underlying blue but the red (top left), which is a naturally dense, strong hue, is less influenced by different background colours.

Textured Grounds

Purpose-made drawing papers provide a wide range of textures (see paper grain effects, pages 14–15), but there are many interesting materials you can draw on that provide distinctive surface qualities, giving variety to your coloured pencil renderings.

Stationery materials such as brown wrapping paper, large manila envelopes and cardboard packaging provide rough-textured surfaces with a pleasant, warm mid-tone. Abrasive papers such as fine glasspaper and sandpaper have a gritty tooth, and come in colours ranging from charcoal black to natural sandy yellows – but remember that a highly abrasive surface uses up the pencil leads very quickly. For a fine "woven" ground, you can use the prepared canvas boards sold for oil and acrylic painting.

Some artists like to work coloured pencil over brushed textures, in which the rhythmic movement of the brush has created fine ridges and hollows that counterpoint the pencil strokes. The quality of a painted ground varies from the light texture of a watercolour or gouache wash to the dense opacity of acrylic emulsion or gesso. An extra advantage is that you can choose to apply a white ground or a tint of your own mixing.

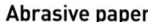

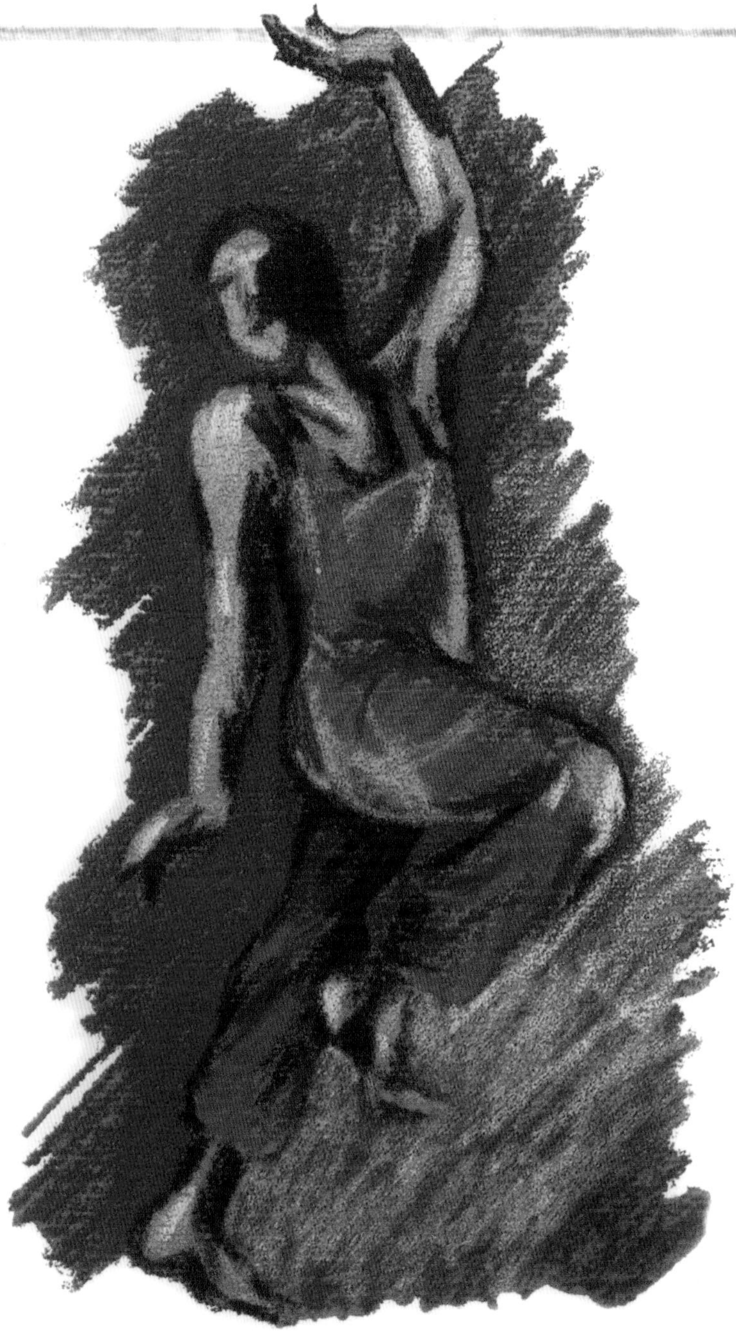

Abrasive paper
A fine abrasive sandpaper or glasspaper grips the colour very firmly, enabling you to build up rich, vibrant hues and patterns of light and shade.

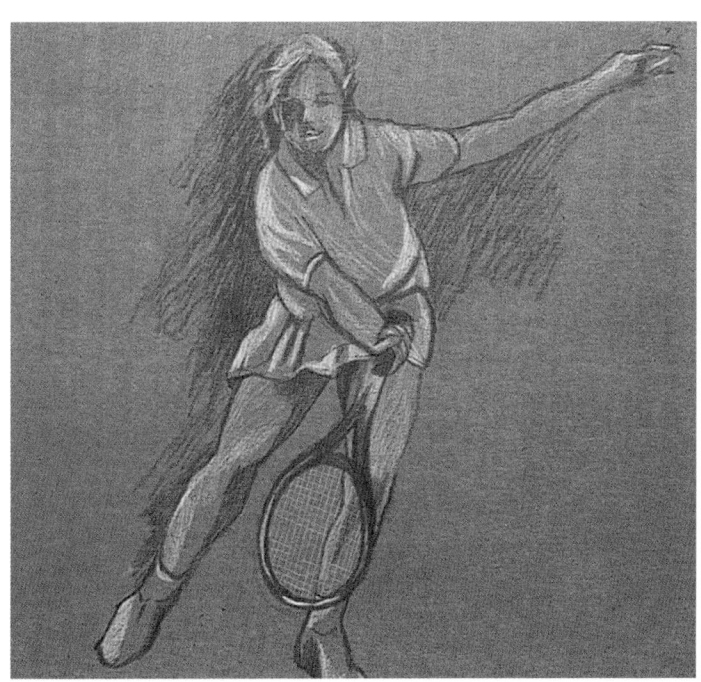

Cardboard

A section cut from an ordinary cardboard carton has pale brown colouring with a faint striated texture. This acts as a warm mid-tone for a monochrome drawing. The thickness of the cardboard provides a soft, giving surface.

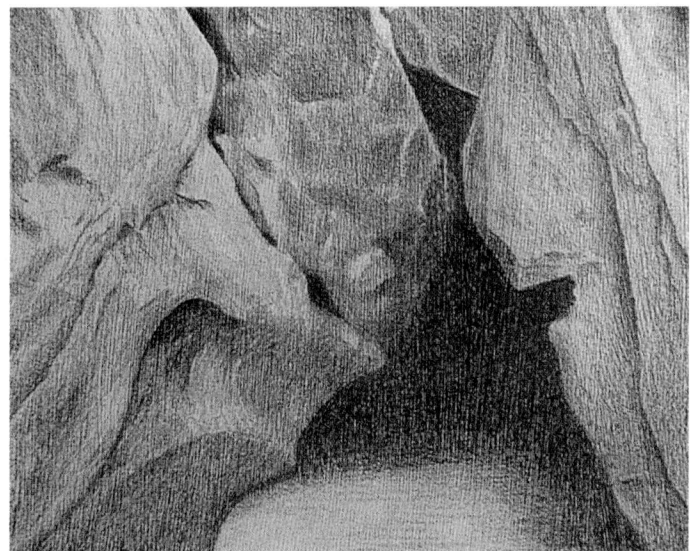

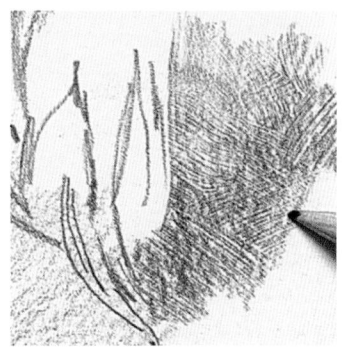

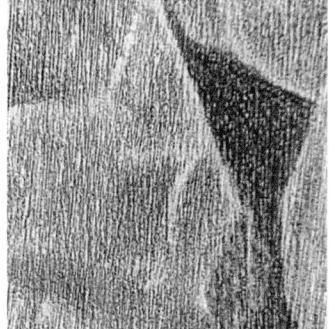

Drawing on gesso

1 Apply acrylic gesso ground freely and thickly to drawing paper or board and allow it to dry completely.

2 Brushmarks in the gesso ground affect all kinds of marks that you can make with your pencils. It gives broken linear textures and strong grain patterns in areas of shading.

BARBARA SCHOEMMER
CAPE KIWANA II

The texture of the ground can act as a significant element of your subject. In this drawing, the brushed gesso ground corresponds to the rough surface texture of natural rock.

Linear Marks

Because pencil is a point medium, the kind of marks you make with it are basically linear in character. Standard techniques of pencil drawing employ this characteristic – for instance, hatching – but the tool is capable of making many different kinds of marks, which are less easily defined. These vary according to the way you push or pull the pencil across the paper as well as to whether the pencil tip is sharp or blunt, chisel-edged or rounded. You can produce finely "spattered" slashes and trails, decisive hooks and ticks, curling flourishes or angry scribbles, linear patterns that are loose and randomly formed or neat and regimented.

Through experiment you can build a repertoire of linear marks that may stand for different elements of your subjects – such as man-made or natural patterns and textures or atmospheric effects – and also enliven the surface qualities of your drawing. In this way you can introduce discreet variety even in areas that from normal viewing distance read as continuous flat colour or tone.

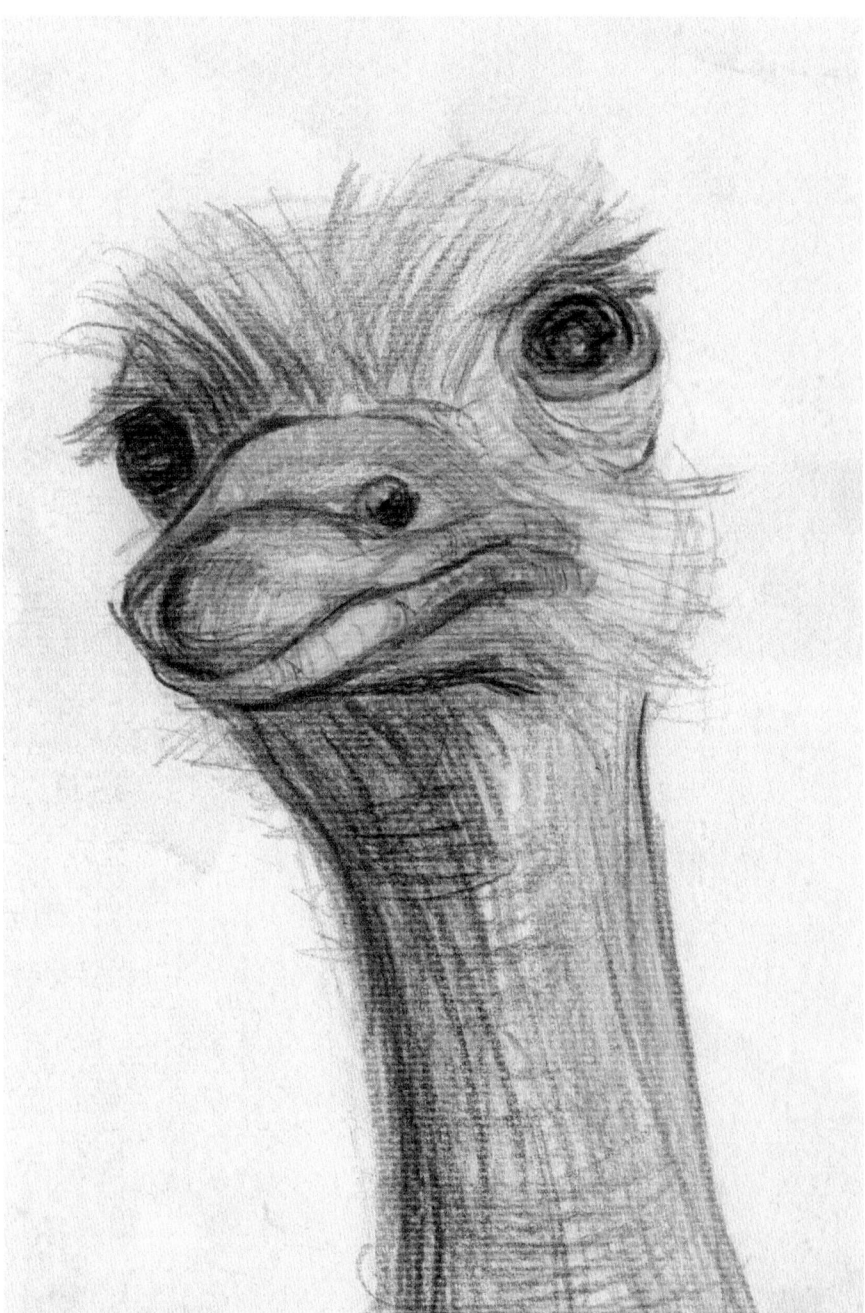

ANONYMOUS ▶

OSTRICH

Lines, hatching and shading are used to give form to this artwork. The marks are denser in the shadow areas.

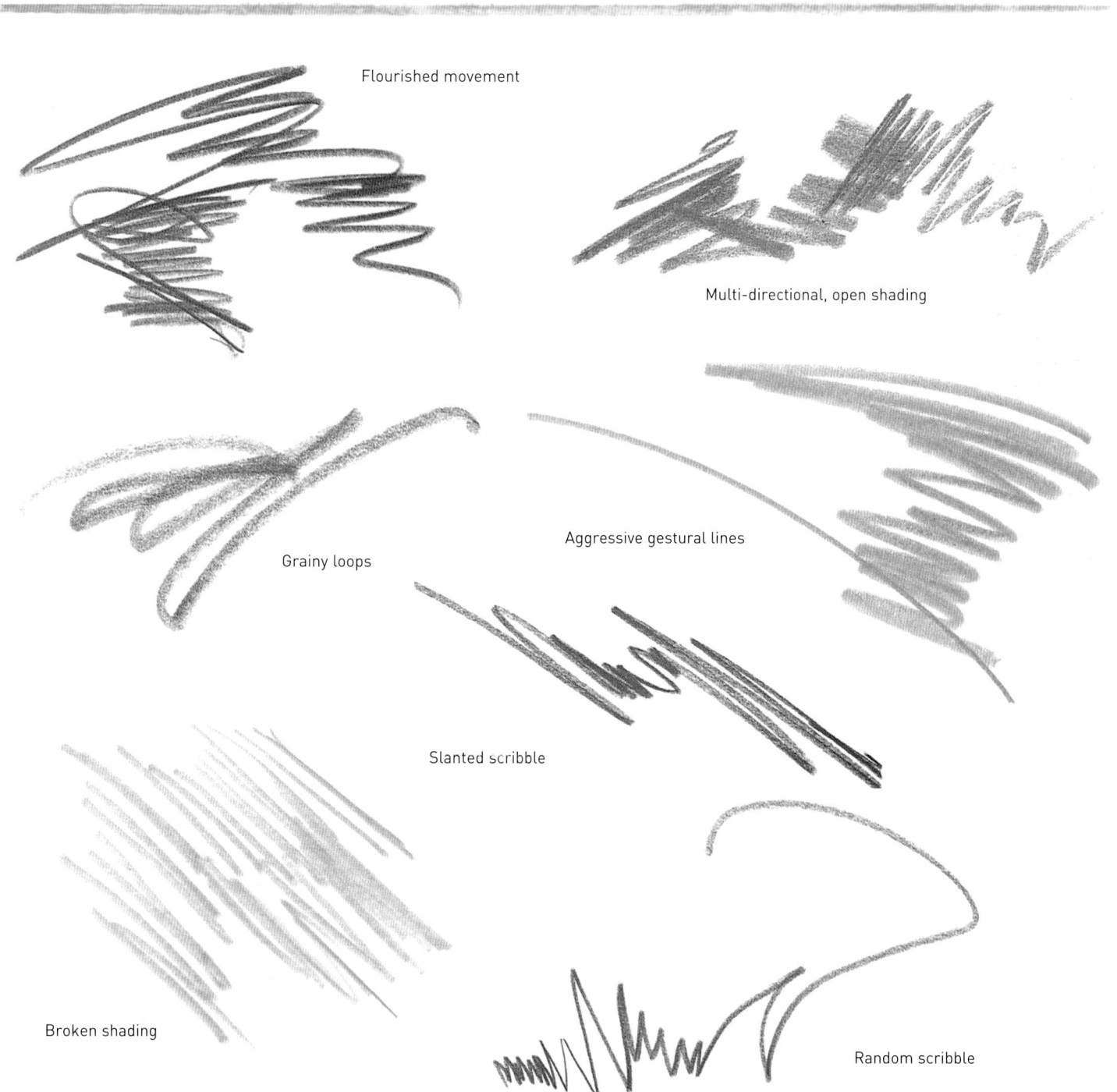

Flourished movement

Multi-directional, open shading

Grainy loops

Aggressive gestural lines

Slanted scribble

Broken shading

Random scribble

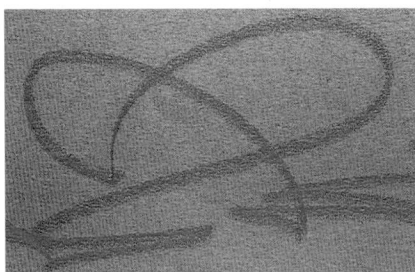

Playful freehand curves

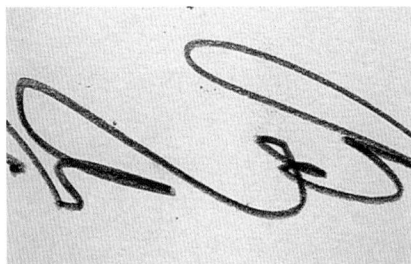

Calligraphic sequence

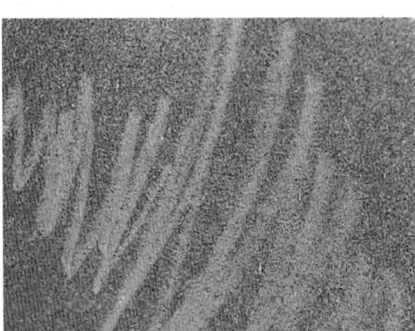

Whole hand movement

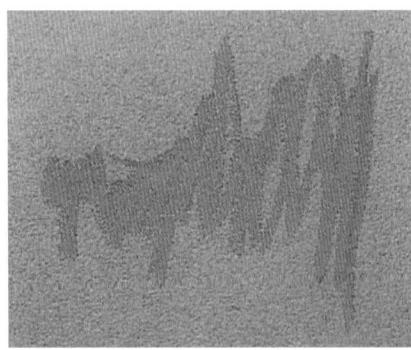

Layered, open shading

Shading

Shading is the classic method for achieving effects of continuous tone and colour. You simply move the pencil point evenly back and forth across the paper, gradually increasing the surface coverage.

Shading typically has a directional "grain", reflecting the movement of your hand and the pencil tip. You can choose to emphasize this linear quality or to eliminate it, depending on the pressure you apply and the angle you work from. Heavy pressure and a consistent angle create directional emphasis. To achieve non-directional shading, build up the colour in lightweight layers and alter the angle of the strokes frequently. An alternative is to keep turning the paper.

Shading is used both to build up colour areas and to model form through gradations of tone and hue. The strongest colour you can obtain is the actual colour of the pencil lead; lighter tones of the same hue are formed by easing the pressure on the pencil tip.

To create soft colour "glazing", aim to use the side rather than the point of the pencil lead and maintain consistent but gentle pressure.

PAT AVERILL▶
EAGLE CREEK
Pat Averill started by tinting the sky and background trees so they would look distant. Pencils were applied lightly and blended with a rag and/or cotton bud. The sunlit areas on branches and trees were blocked in and dark colours were layered for the shaded foreground. Pat used a warm dark green with a cool red and overlaid it with more of the warm dark green and, eventually, black, before burnishing with the complement of surrounding colours.

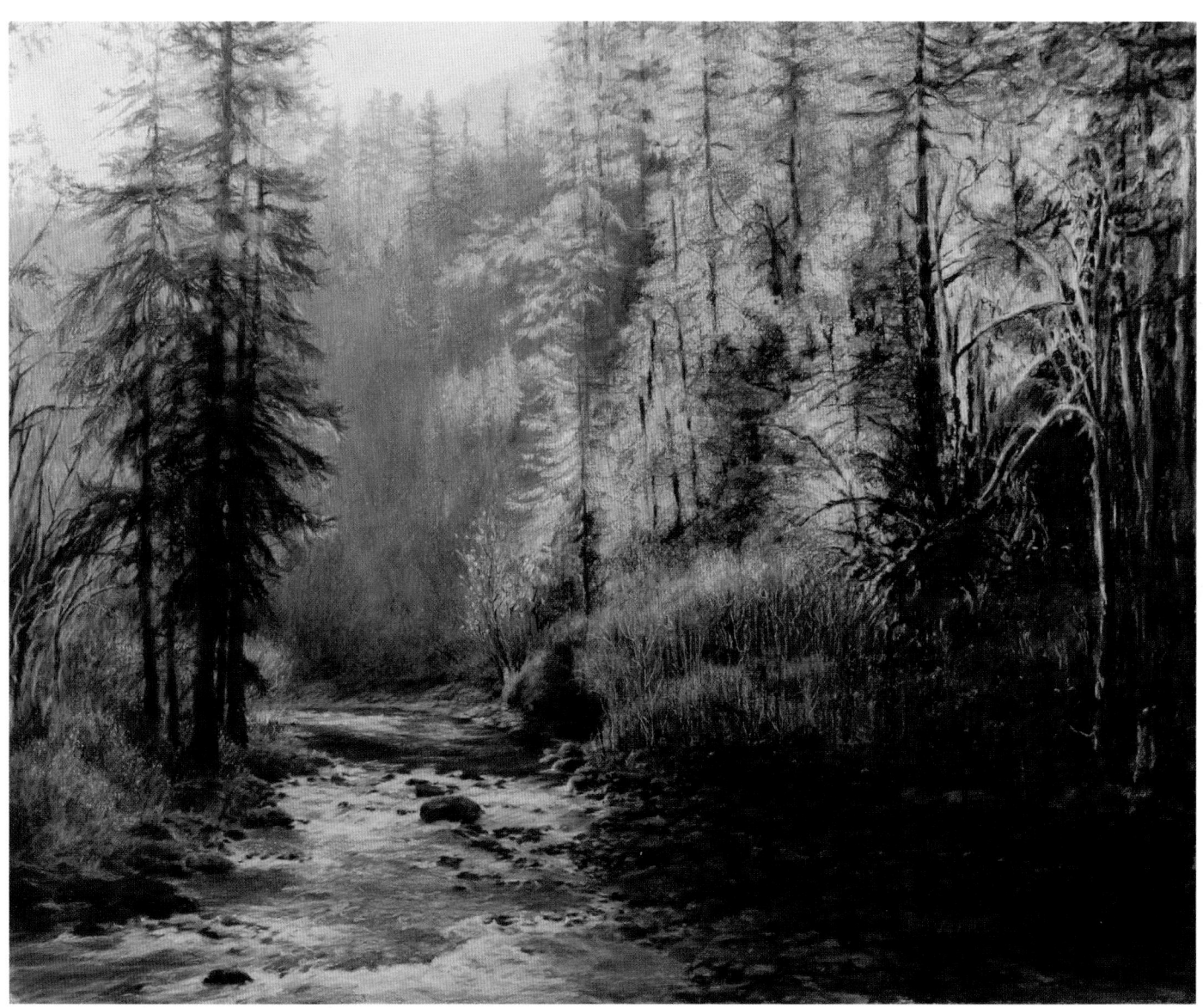

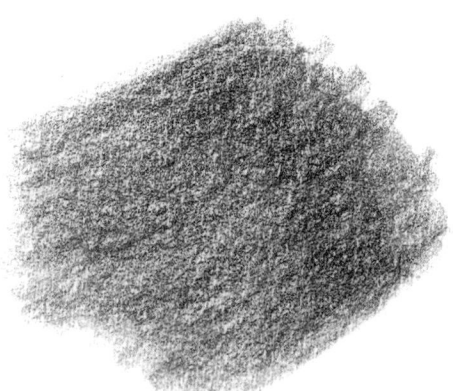

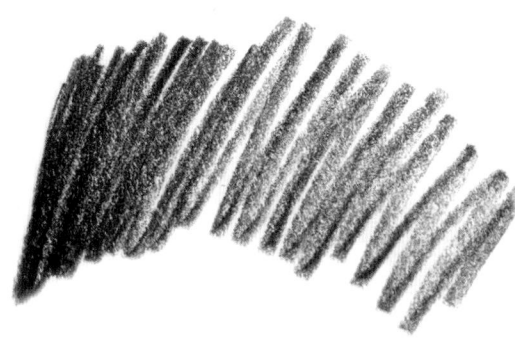

Lightweight, even shading
Light pressure on the pencil tip enables you to build up shaded colour with no linear bias. You can gradually increase the colour by reworking the same area.

Heavy, directional shading
When you put a lot of pressure on the pencil tip, the shaded area naturally forms a directional emphasis following the path of the pencil. The colour effect is also more intense.

Open shading
A loose movement from the wrist, allowing your whole hand rather than your fingers to guide the pencil, produces an open, scribbled effect comparable to free hatching.

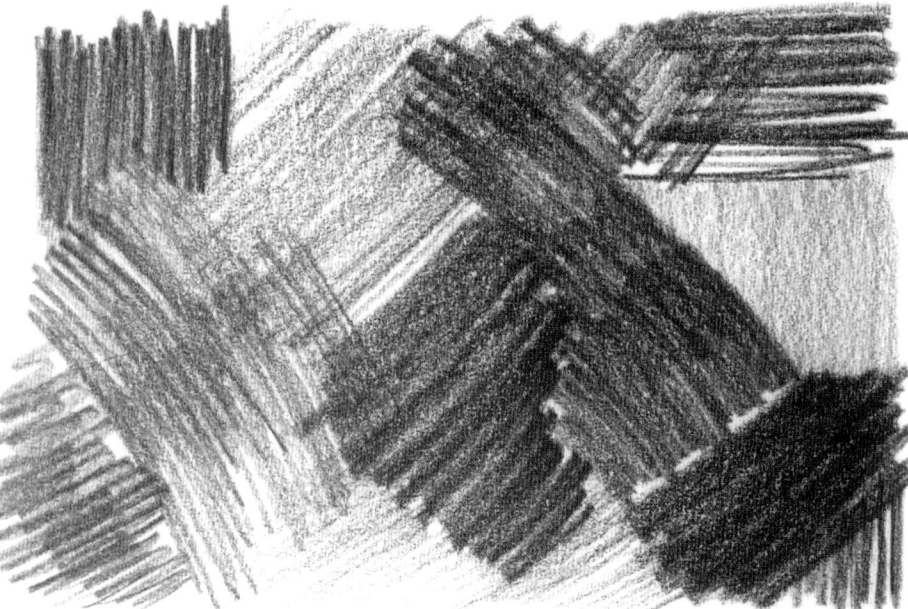

Combining different qualities
When you juxtapose areas of shading of different densities and directional emphasis, the drawing begins to suggest different levels of surface planes, creating space and form.

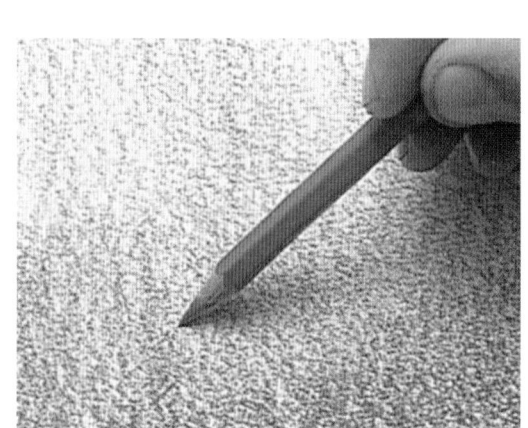

Shaded gradations

Shading is the classic method of
creating smooth gradations of tone
and colour. It also provides different
edge qualities, depending on the
direction of the marks and the
eventual solidity of the shaded area.

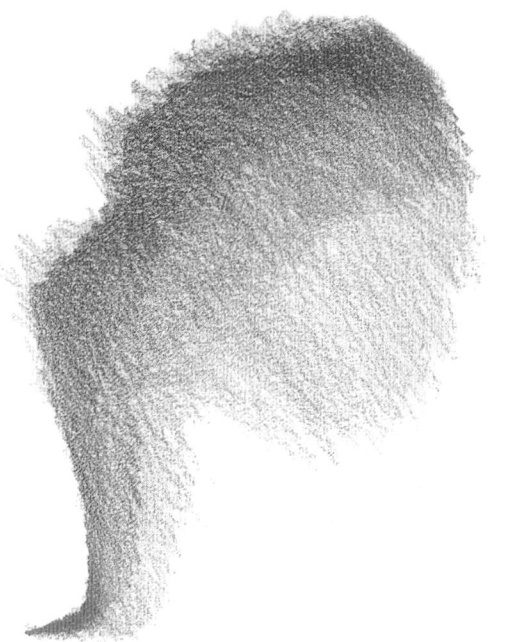

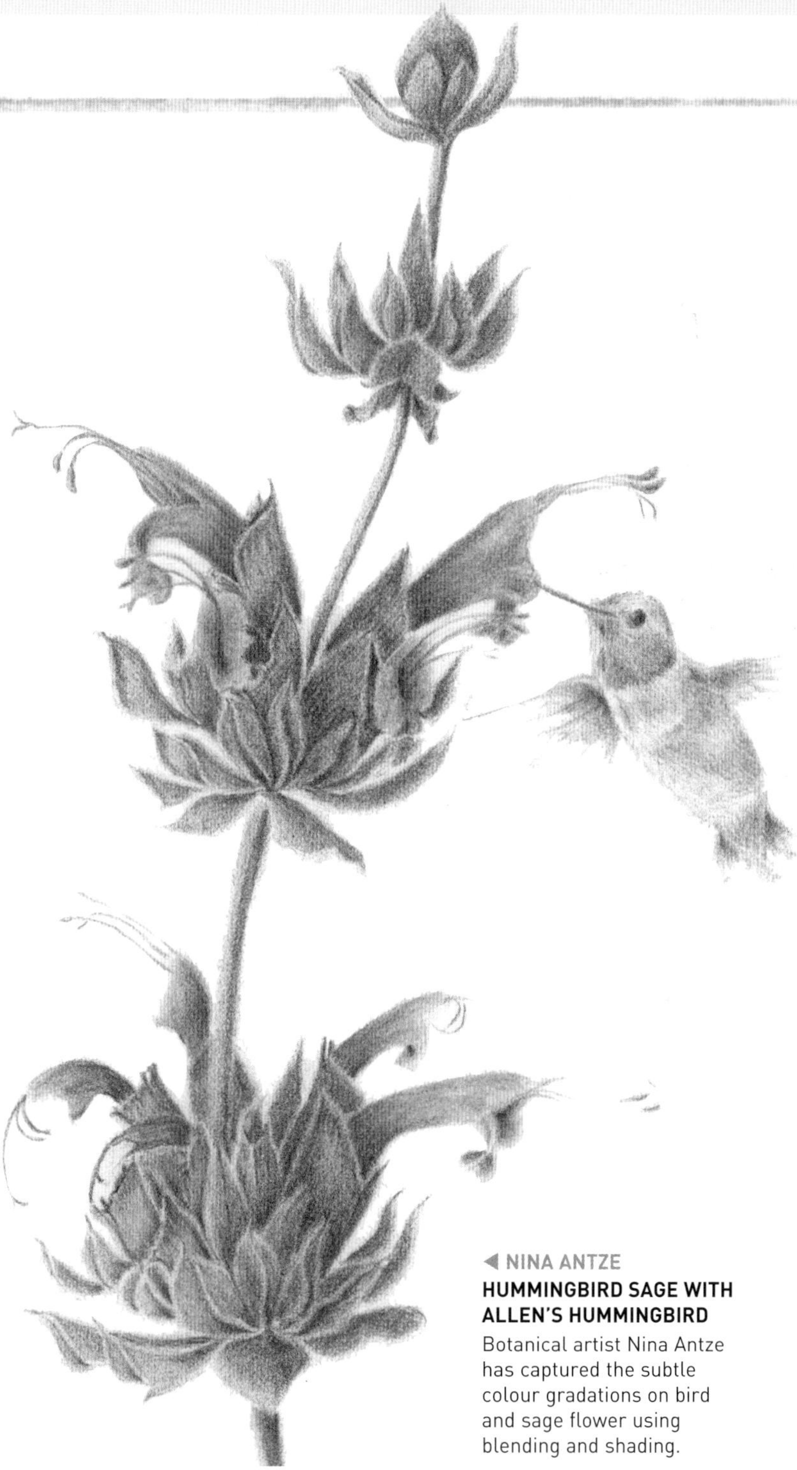

◄ NINA ANTZE

HUMMINGBIRD SAGE WITH ALLEN'S HUMMINGBIRD

Botanical artist Nina Antze
has captured the subtle
colour gradations on bird
and sage flower using
blending and shading.

Blending

There are various different techniques for blending colours effectively. The method you use will depend on whether you want smooth gradations of colour and tone, a layered effect built up by overlaying colours, or an optical mixture created by massing linear pencil strokes to produce overall colour blends, as with hatching or stippling (see pages 28–29 and page 33) .

Using solvents, you can obtain effects closer to the fluid colour blends typical of paint media, while burnishing heightens the effect of graded and overlaid colours (see pages 38–39 and 40–41). Refer to all these techniques to familiarize yourself with their different surface qualities, so you can choose the method best suited to an individual work.

Blending with chalky pencils
1 The texture of chalky pencils allows the colours to be blended by rubbing. Begin by working one colour over another with loose hatching.

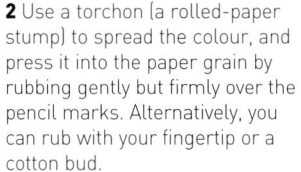

2 Use a torchon (a rolled-paper stump) to spread the colour, and press it into the paper grain by rubbing gently but firmly over the pencil marks. Alternatively, you can rub with your fingertip or a cotton bud.

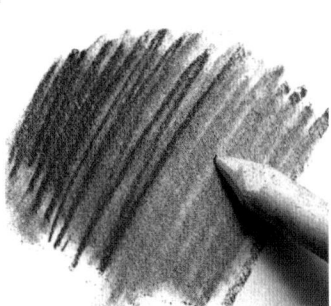

3 In this example, the blended colours still show the direction of the original hatching, creating a soft but active surface effect.

4 To blend flat colour areas, begin by laying down the areas of solid shading. Then, using the torchon, soften the transition from one colour to another where the shaded areas come together.

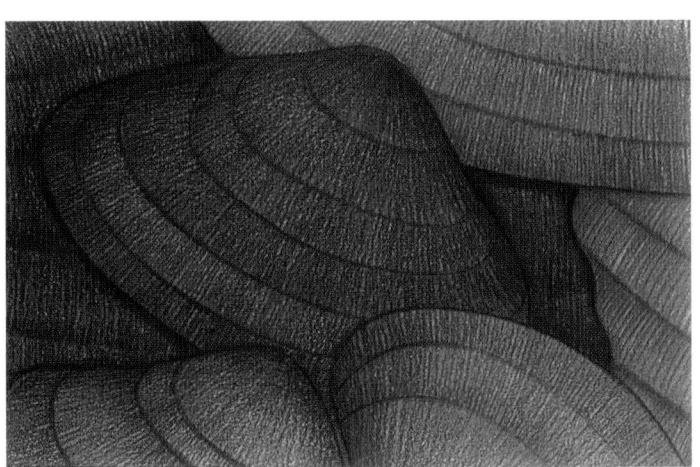

◀ **MATHILDE DUFFY**
SHELL TAPESTRY (DETAIL)
Subtle blends in the range from red through purple to blue have been achieved here by stroking one colour into another with soft shading and hatching. The pencil lines follow the directions of the shell patterns, constructing form and texture at the same time.

Blending with waxy pencils

1 Waxy-textured colour does not spread easily, so you need to blend by working one colour over another. When shading, keep the pencil strokes even and work them in the same direction in each colour area.

2 By overlaying the colours, you create a third colour that merges the hues of the first two. You can shade lightly, as in this example, or rework the colour layers until you fill the paper grain.

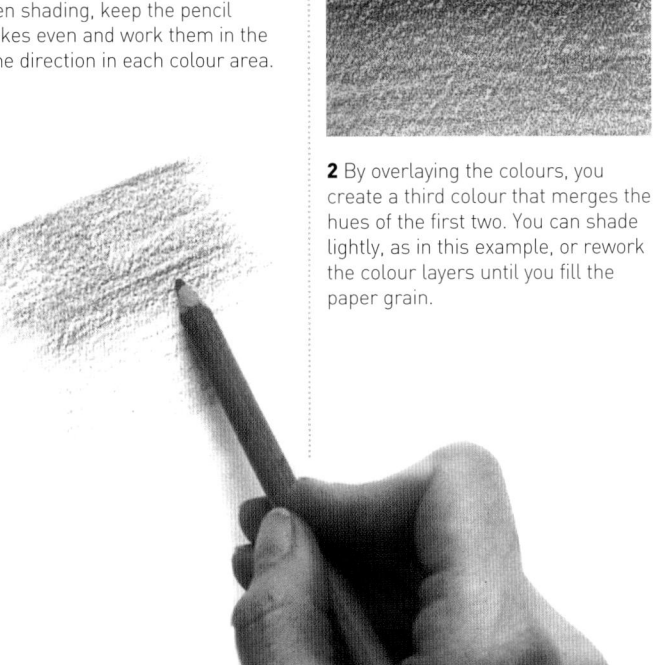

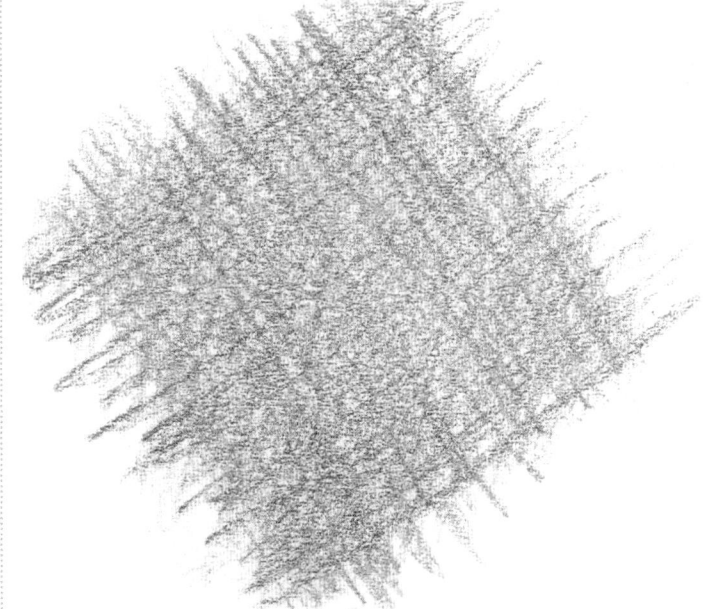

3 An alternative method of blending is to use the technique of crosshatching. Apply a different colour each time you change the direction of the sets of hatched lines.

Hatching

Coloured pencil is naturally a line medium, although there are many ways of building up areas of solid and mixed colour. Hatching and crosshatching are traditional methods of creating effects of continuous tone using linear marks. With a colour medium, they can also be a means of integrating two or more hues and producing colour changes within a given area.

Hatching simply consists of roughly parallel lines, which may be spaced closely or widely, and with even or irregular spacing. In monochrome drawing, the black lines and white spaces read from a distance as grey – a dark grey if the lines are thick and closely spaced, a pale tone if the hatching is finer and more open. The effect is similar with coloured lines, the overall effect being an interaction between the lines and the paper colour showing through.

Crosshatching is an extension of hatching in which sets of lines are hatched one over another in different directions, producing a meshlike or "basketwork" texture. Again, an area of dense crosshatching can read as a continuous tone or colour. However, both techniques bring an additional dimension to the drawing. The direction of the lines can be manipulated to describe form and volume; the textures of hatching and crosshatching produce a more lively surface effect than solid blocks of tone or colour, while still constructing coherent shapes and masses.

The effects of these techniques vary according to the character of the lines you draw, their spacing and direction, and the interaction of hues and tones. With practice, you will discover how these elements can be applied to describing specific aspects of form and space, local colour and qualities of light and shadow in a composition.

Hatching
The technique of hatching can be clean and systematic, or free and variable. The lines can be of relatively equal weight and spacing (far right), or may vary from thick to thin, with gradually increased or decreased spacing (right).

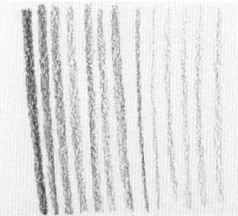 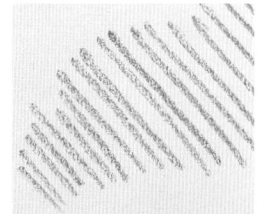

Crosshatching
The denser texture of crosshatching gives the artist more options for developing tone and colour. The same colour crosshatched creates an integrated network of lines (far right) which can be straight, curved or directional. Using different colours (right) adds tonal and colour interest.

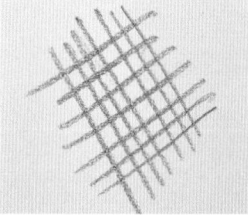 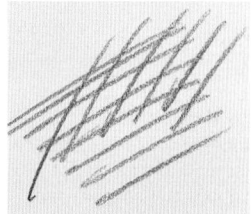

Free hatching
The lines of hatching do not have to be distinct and separate. Here the second layer of colour is hatched over the first with a free scribbling motion.

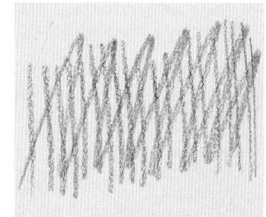

Varying the texture
Different qualities of tone and texture are developed by varying line weight and spacing, and by combining colours. Lines that are converging rather than parallel (top right) suggest space.

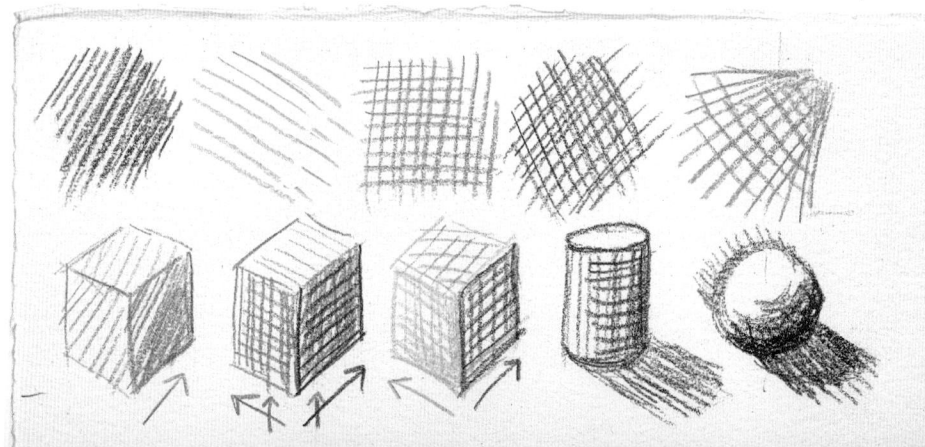

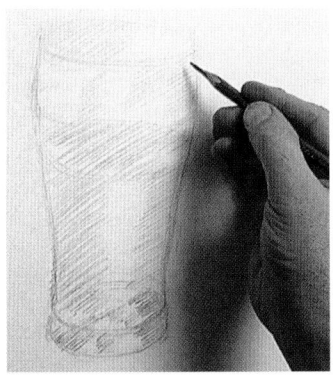 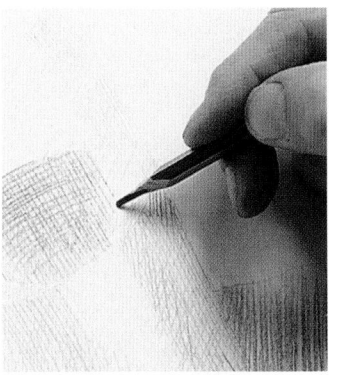 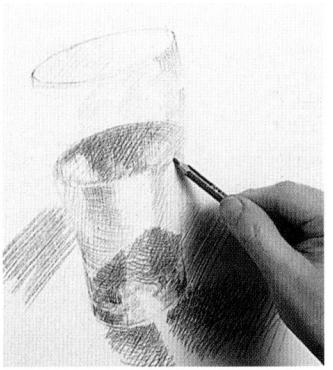 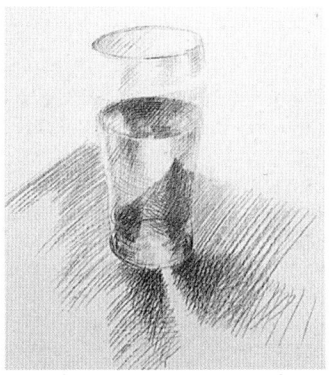

Constructing form

1 To model a form with hatching and crosshatching you need to begin with a clear impression of the shapes and tones in your subject. This drawing starts with a pencil outline and lightly hatched indication of light and shade.

2 The mid- and dark tones are developed with black and blue pencils. When you are working on fine hatching, the pencil needs to be kept quite sharp to maintain an even line quality.

3 With the introduction of a lighter blue and the gradual build-up of dark crosshatched areas, the drawing takes on the impression of three-dimensional form.

4 The tonal structure is continually intensified, keeping to the basic monochromatic palette. The different densities of the hatching and crosshatching divide the overall shapes into distinct areas of light and shadow, describing the glass, the flat table-top and the effects of transmitted and reflected light.

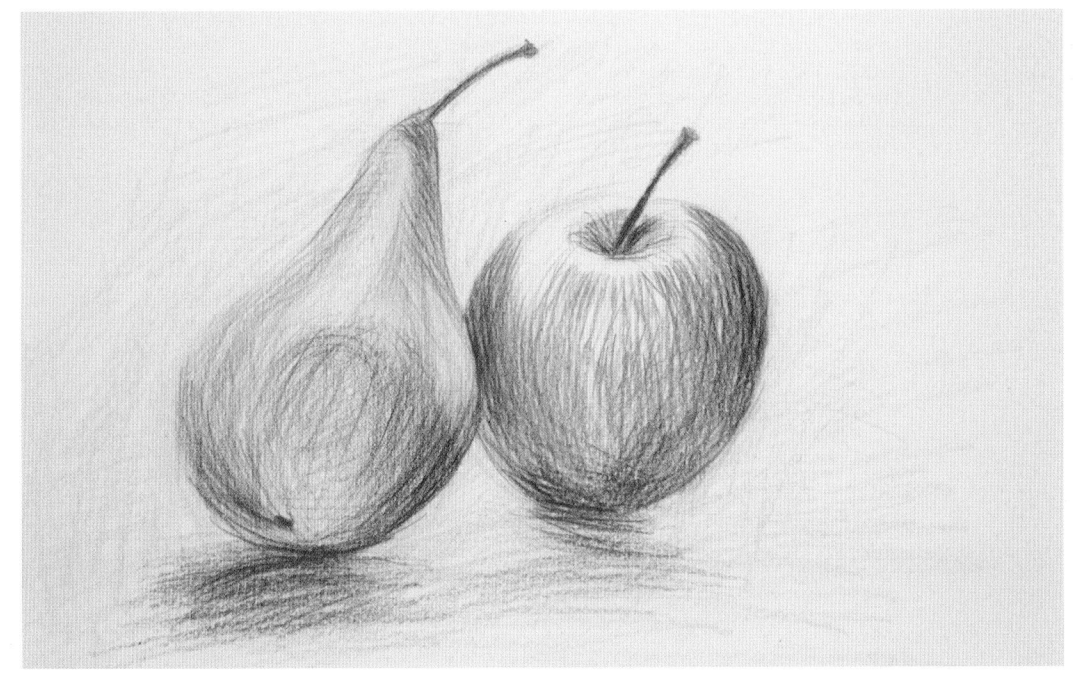

◀ JANE STROTHER
APPLE AND PEAR
Worrying about the precise direction and spacing of hatching and crosshatching can sacrifice the sense of life and energy in a drawing, so free yourself with some quick studies such as the apple and pear shown here. The pencils have been allowed to move easily following the form of the fruit, and the directional marks extend into the background.

Blocking In

The term "blocking in" refers to the early stages of establishing a composition in any medium. In coloured pencil work, depending on the complexity of the image and the drawing style, it may involve sketching the main outlines and laying in blocks of tone and colour to indicate form and volume using, for instance, light shading or hatching.

Generally, it is advisable to get a feel for the whole composition before working any single area in detail. This enables you to check that different elements of the image are in correct scale and proportion, and that the whole image area fits on the paper. However, because coloured pencil work often involves delicate surface textures and a gradual build-up of detail, you must take great care not to overload the surface in the early stages, or make deeply impressed marks in the paper that will show through subsequent colour layers.

The key is to keep the treatment light and open until you are satisfied with the overall effect, then you can start to develop the detail of form and colour more distinctly.

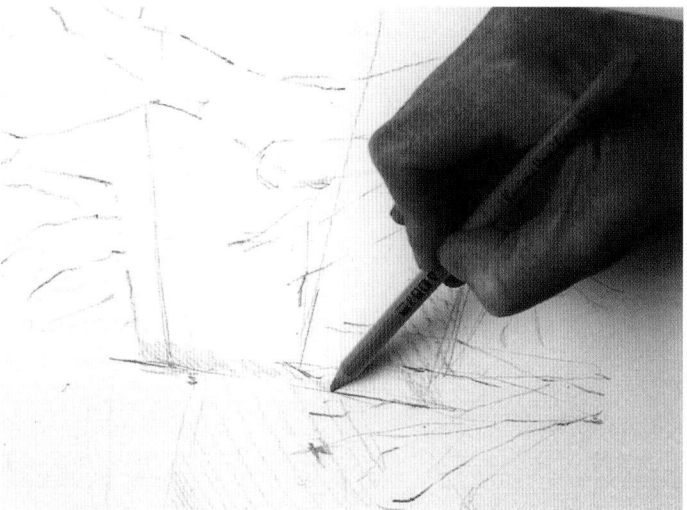

1 The first stage of this piece is the use of lightweight contour drawing to form a basic framework for the composition. The general shapes and patterns of the garden fence and trees are drawn in line.

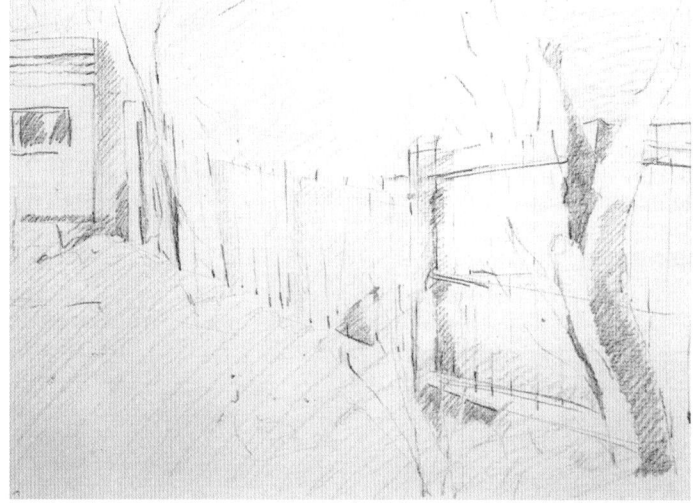

2 As the view takes shape, the main lines are given more emphasis and some soft shading is applied to indicate three-dimensional form. Only two browns and two greens have been used to identify different elements of the garden area.

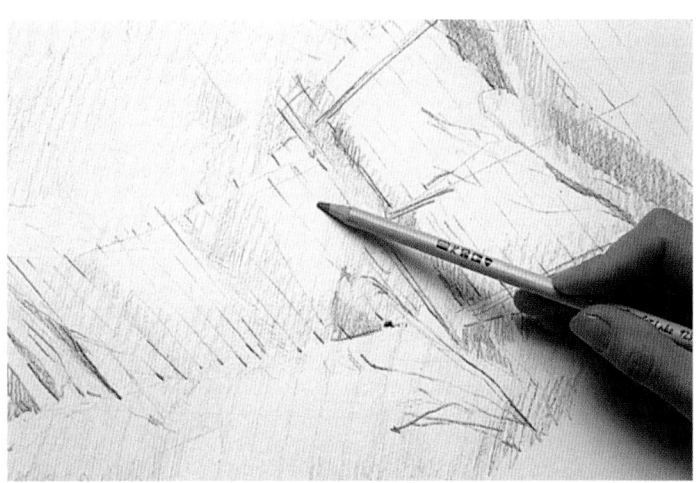

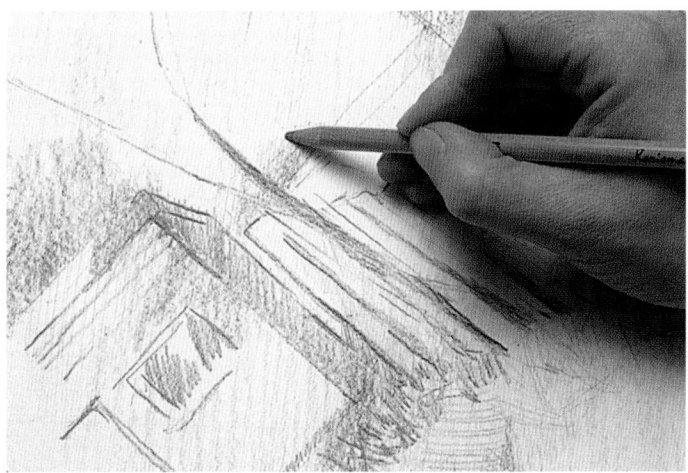

3 The overall impression of shape and colour is developed with hatching and shading in the same colour range, keeping the pencil marks light and open.

4 Gradually, the weight of the shaded areas is built up to give solidity to particular shapes. Additional linear marks are applied to sketch further detail of the trees, shed and fence.

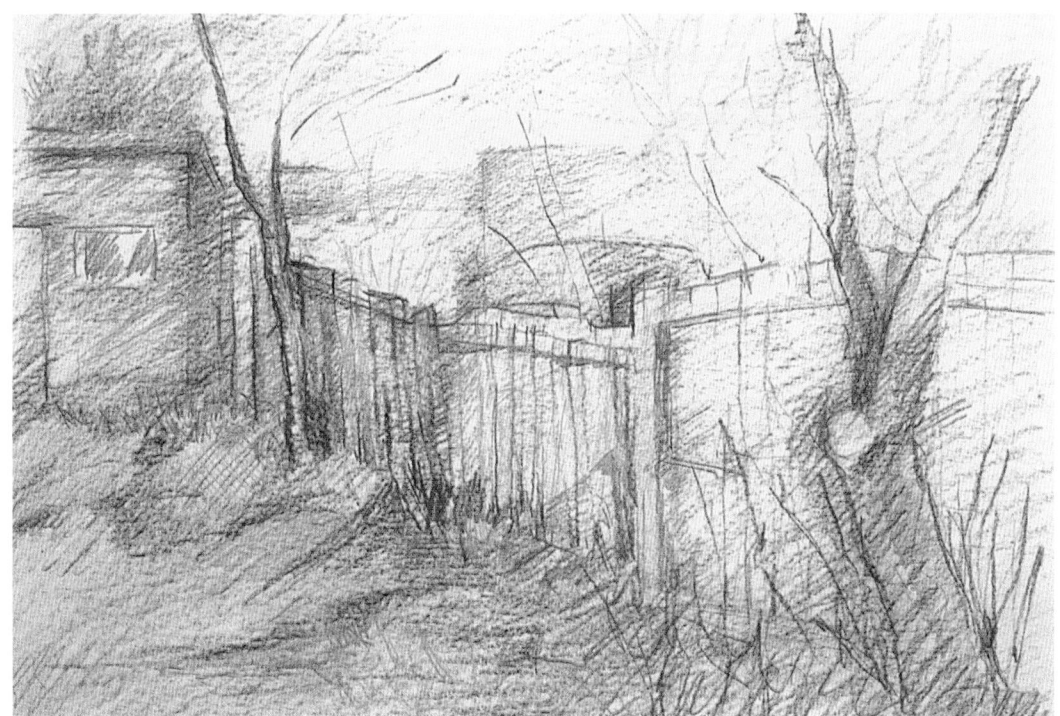

5 The process continues in the same way, introducing more colours but keeping the texture of the drawing open and workable. It is important when blocking in not to apply shading and hatching too heavily, otherwise you close down your options for making changes and developing detail.

Filling In

Certain types of colour drawing will require you to fill a hard-edged shape quite precisely with solidly shaded colour. Controlling the pencil to follow an intricate outline while maintaining consistent pressure and direction in the shading is not easy, but it is a skill that comes with practice.

The method you use to colour a filled shape depends on the edge quality you wish to achieve and the complexity of the colour effects within the shape. If you have to turn the pencil – or the paper – to gain access to various parts of the contour, bear in mind that a change of direction in heavy shading can show up. To obtain a smooth finish, apply the shading lightly so that the directional strokes are barely perceptible, and build up the colour in fine overlays.

A mask or stencil (see also masking, pages 64–65) is a useful device. You can shade up to or over the edge of the masked shape, so that the direction of the strokes remains consistent. If you like the effect of a hard outline, you can use the technique of impressing to give a clearly visible contour, either in the same colour that you are using for the shape or in a contrasting hue or tone.

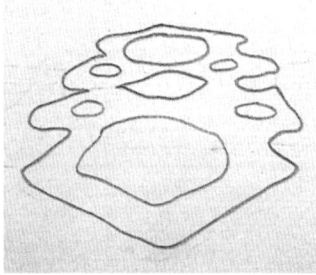

Working to an outline
1 Trace your drawing down lightly on the paper to form a faint guideline. To create a clean, hard-edged shape, draw the outline with the colour you intend using to fill it.

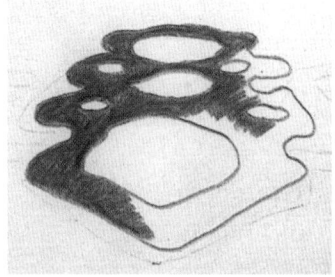

2 Apply solid shading within the shape, working carefully towards the outline. To fill small curves and angles, you can work the shading in different directions, but keep it dense and even to obtain a flat colour area.

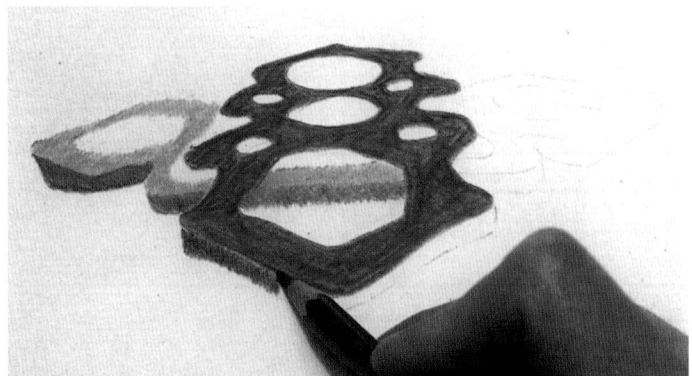

Free shading
Here shapes are freely shaded to provide a soft edge. You may find it easiest to control the colour area by angling the shading towards the contour lines, with strokes of even weight and length.

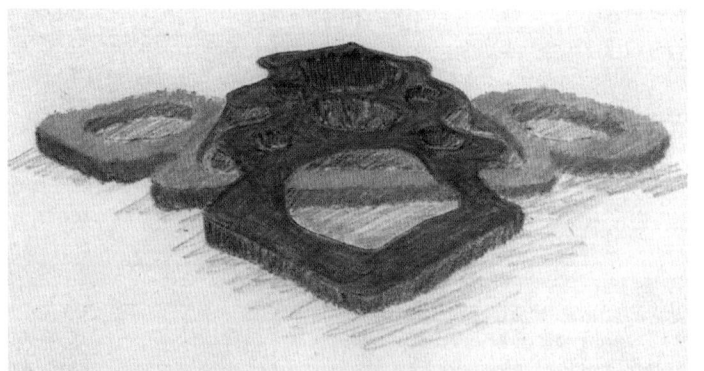

Edge qualities
In the completed vignette, the varied edge qualities give interest to the drawing. The lighter green has been shaded over the brown to bring the colours together. Some loose colour work has been applied on top with moistened watercolour pencils in red and purple, and the ground shadow is loosely shaded in grey to bleed off into the white paper.

Stippling

This is a traditional technique for building up tonal and colour values, and provides an alternative to linear methods such as shading and hatching. Stippling consists of a mass of fine dots, closely spaced. Variations in the size and spacing of the dots create modulations of tone and hue. With coloured pencil, you can integrate several different colours to produce an optical mixture, and you can achieve very subtle gradations by controlling the proportion of one colour to another in any area of the colour mass.

Stippling is time consuming, especially when you use this technique alone to cover large areas of the paper, but it allows great control over the modelling of forms, and the finished effect can be startlingly super-real. Alternatively, you can stipple over blocks of flat or shaded colour to enhance effects of three-dimensional form or develop surface texture.

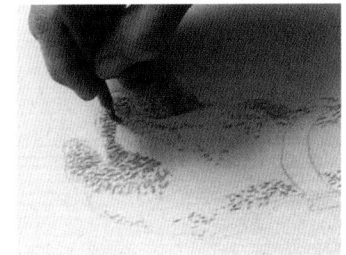

1 The size of the stippled dots and the variations of colour need to be related to forms and tones in the subject. You may find it easiest to begin with a light outline drawing.

2 The pressure on the pencil that you need to apply a strong colour effect means that some dots are rounded while others are flicked into small dashes. Try to keep the scale of the marks fairly even. Select colours that create tonal variation, and build up the marks systematically.

3 The aim of stippling is to model form in the same way as you do with shading, but using active individual marks. This creates free edge qualities but gradually a sense of solid form emerges.

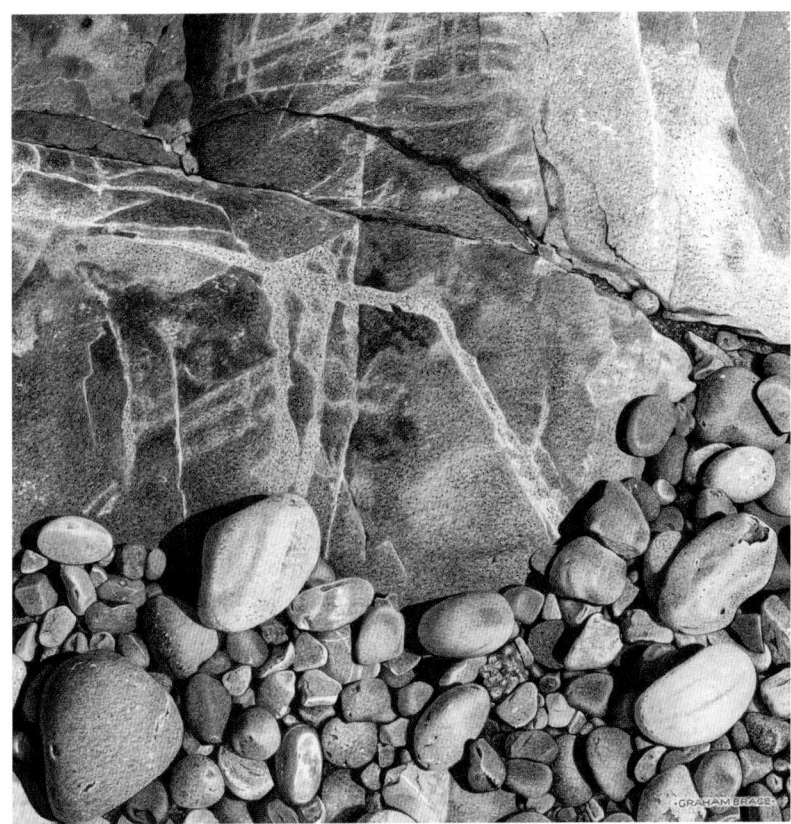

▲GRAHAM BRACE
ROCK FACE, DRUIDSTONE
An "underpainting" is created with soft pastels, which are blended and worked into the support using fingertips. Once this is completed and "fixed", detail and subtle tones are added over the areas of pastel using coloured pencils. In this example, several of the rocks and pebbles have been subtly stippled using sharp coloured pencils and a fine pointed black drawing pen to achieve an impression of texture.

Gradation

Gradation from one hue or tone to another should be smooth and consistent. If you are filling a broad area of sky in a landscape drawing, for example, you do not want to see distinct bands of colour but gentle, subtly varied transitions.

There are various different techniques you can use to create gradations, the one you choose depending on the style and textural qualities of your drawing. Carefully graded shading is very effective if you are aiming for a photorealist finish or an atmospheric mood. But you can get very good results using techniques such as hatching or stippling. To create successful gradations, you need to control very carefully the way you mix and overlay hues and tones to achieve an integrated surface.

Tonal gradation

1 A very subtle transition through graded tones of one colour is achieved by shading carefully with the pencil and gradually decreasing the pressure to lighten the tone. It requires careful handling to avoid abrupt changes that would produce the effect of successive colour bands.

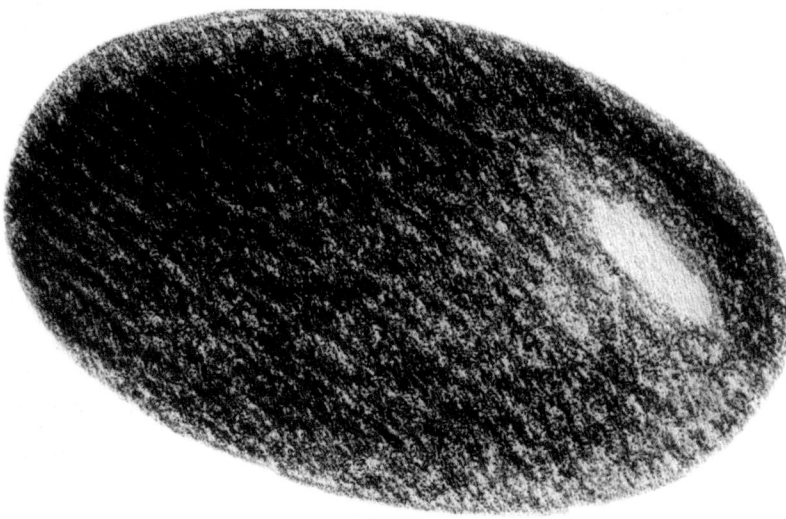

2 Shaded gradation is the classic method of modelling form with pencils. In this example, the overall tone is quite dark, but there is a smaller area of mid-tone surrounding the white highlight.

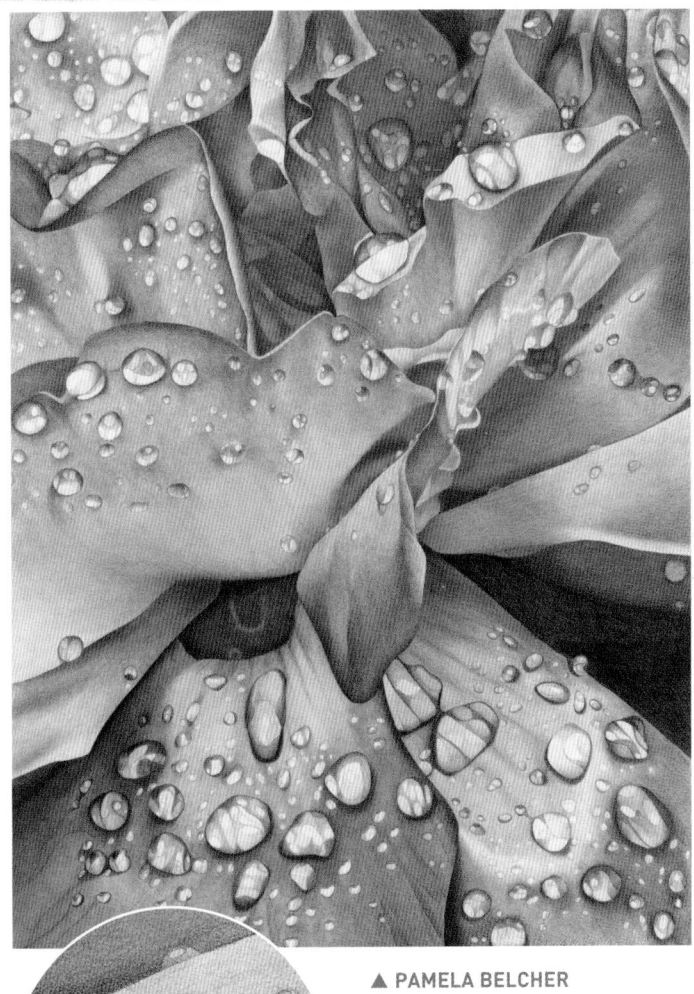

Colour gradation

1 The tonal gradation used in the previous demonstration is transformed into a delicate colour gradation by laying in a lighter turquoise blue over the pale tones of the original mid-blue, shading off on a similar scale of density.

2 A gradation through three colours is expertly controlled to avoid the effect of a hard line at the junction of the colour areas. This technique is only mastered with practice, during which you learn to lighten up the shading by just the right amount, then work in the next colour seamlessly.

▲ PAMELA BELCHER
BEJEWELED
Coloured pencils were laid down first, and smeared with a paper stump (torchon) to create a smooth coverage. Coloured pencils with an oil rather than a wax binder were used. With a gentle touch, it is possible to smear then re-smear the pigment several times over multiple layered applications. Wax-based pencils can be used on top as well. Modelling with graded shades and colours produces a super-realist effect.

Dashes and Dots

Brief marks made rapidly with the point of the pencil by stroking, stabbing and twisting the pencil tip on the paper can be used to build up colour masses or to represent surface texture. This is not the same as the technique known as stippling, which needs a fairly systematic approach if it is to work as an effective modelling method.

Depending on the quality and motion of the pencil point, you can obtain quite a fine, calligraphic effect or an active, aggressive pattern of marks. You can work over flatly shaded colour areas, or build up colour masses by repeatedly reworking the dash and dot patterns with different coloured pencils. This is a lively, informal technique, and by experimenting you will soon find out how it can relate to particular qualities in your drawing.

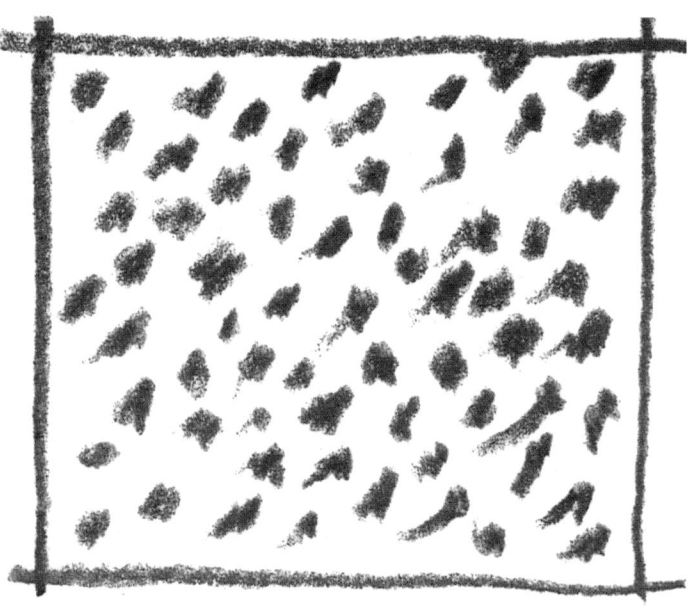

Scribbled dots
Rough-edged, broad dots are created by moving the pencil in a brief scribbling motion, not by stabbing at the paper.

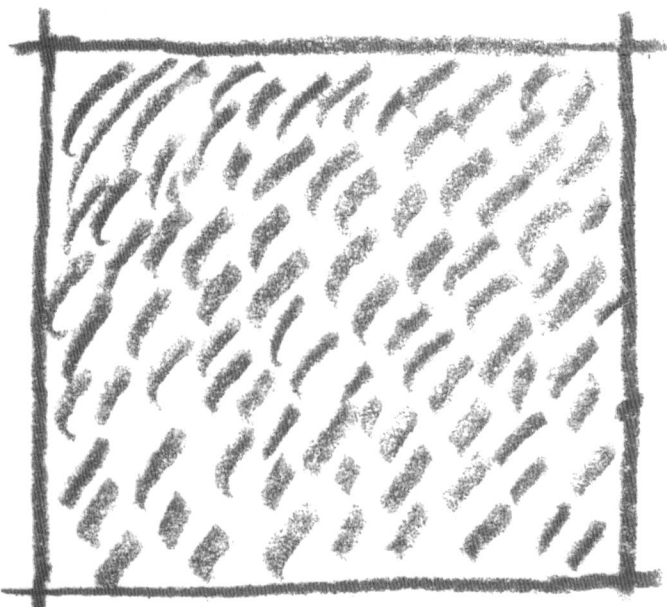

Directional strokes
These loose dashes follow the natural direction of a slanted stroke drawn by a right-handed person. The pencil is used slightly blunted to make a grainy mark.

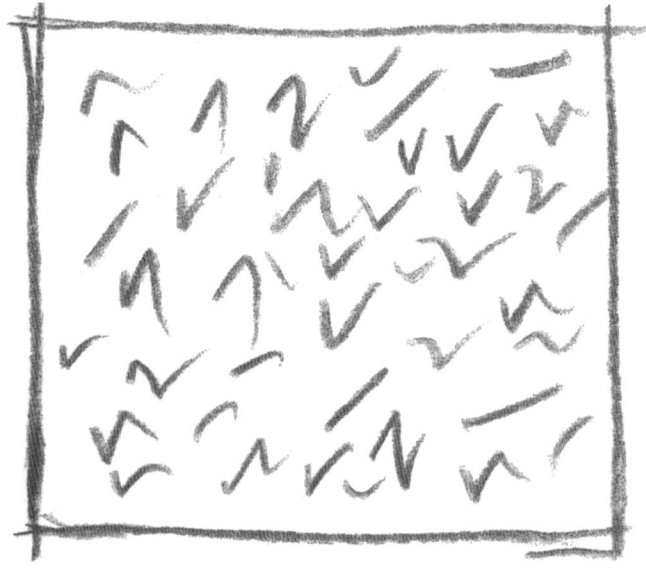

Ticks
Rapid ticks form a loose, open pattern of irregular marks. Some marks are almost straight with a slight hook, while others become active zigzags.

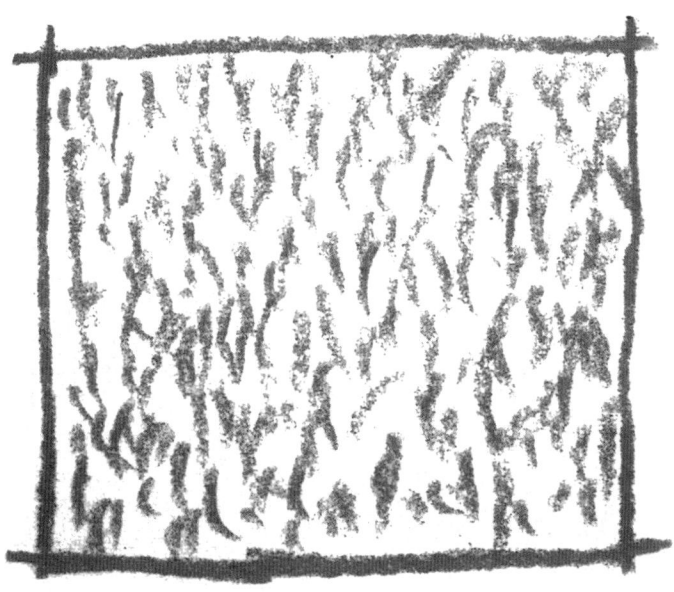

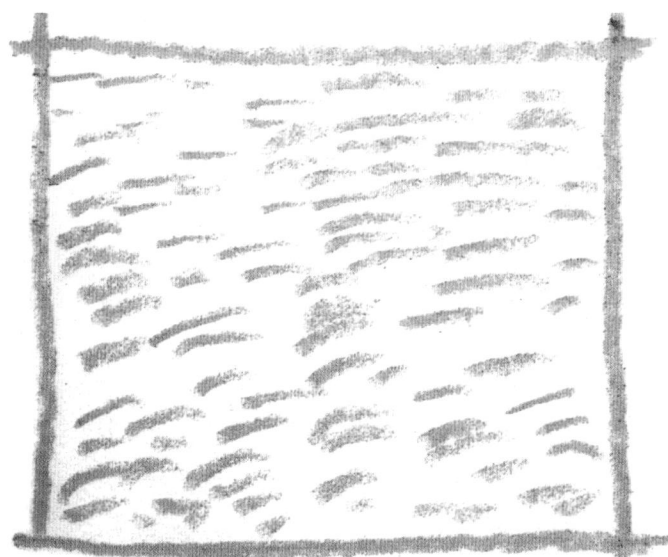

Feathered strokes

Lightweight vertical dashes merge into a soft directional pattern. The blunted pencil tip and gentle pressure create an atmospheric, grainy texture.

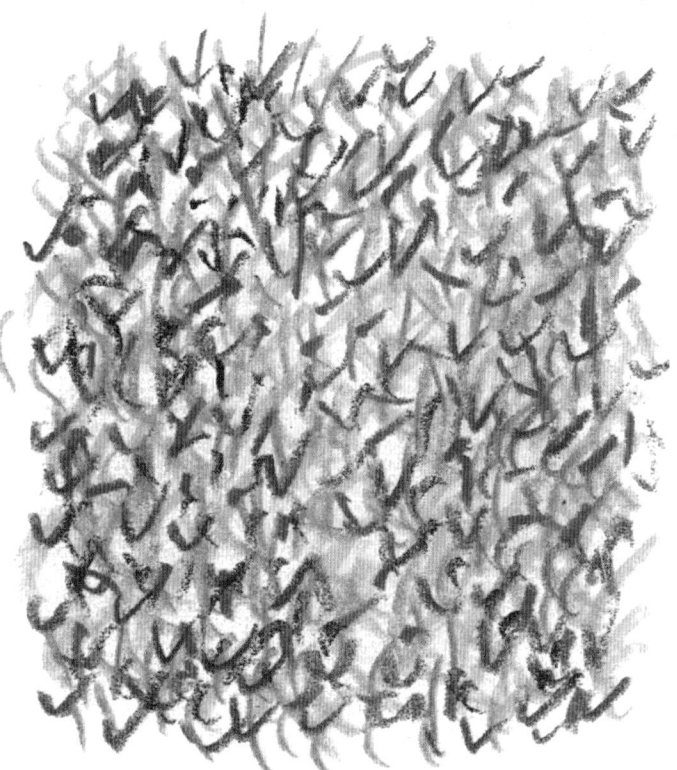

Mixing colours

Yellow, dark pink, burnt sienna and burnt umber are overlaid in open patterns to produce a meshed colour effect. From a distance this reads as a coherent surface. Some kinds of textures and colours are better represented by an active technique than by a smooth blend.

Irregular spacing

While applying these sideways dashes, the spacing and pressure have been varied to suggest an irregular, slightly undulating surface.

Burnishing

The general definition of burnishing is applying friction and pressure to make a surface smooth or shiny. Burnishing with coloured pencils creates a glazed surface effect, compacting the colour and ironing out the grain. It can give the impression of colours being more smoothly blended, and increase the brightness and reflectivity of the surface.

A commonly used method of burnishing is close shading with a white pencil over colours previously laid. You need to be careful to apply firm pressure, which physically compresses the underlying pigment and paper grain. The white overlay unifies colours and tones while also heightening the surface effect.

Alternatively, you can use a pale-toned pencil, a neutral grey or one with a distinct hue of its own such as a light, cold blue or warm pale ochre. This may be better suited to the mood or material of your subject, but remember that the colour you choose will modify underlying hues, and you will lose any pure white highlights unless you leave them unburnished.

Dense, waxy coloured-pencil marks can also be burnished with a torchon (a rolled-paper stump) or a plastic eraser. This avoids the colour changes caused by overlaying a pale tint.

Burnishing can be used to give an overall finish to a whole image or employed selectively to imitate shiny materials such as metal, glass or smooth fabric. It can be the final stage of a coloured pencil drawing, or you can rework the burnished area after spraying it lightly with fixative. The pressure you apply and the layering of colours may cause a "wax bloom" to build up on the surface, coming from deposits of the wax in the pencil lead. This can be gently wiped away with a tissue and the surface fixed to prevent the problem happening again.

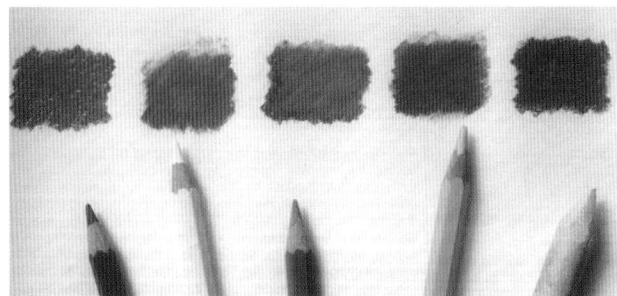

Effects of burnishing
Burnishing with a coloured pencil compresses and polishes the first colour layer. The colour applied in the burnishing naturally affects the original hue. This example shows (left to right) an area of shading in red waxy pencil; the same colour burnished over with white; with blue-grey; and with light yellow; and the plain red burnished with a torchon.

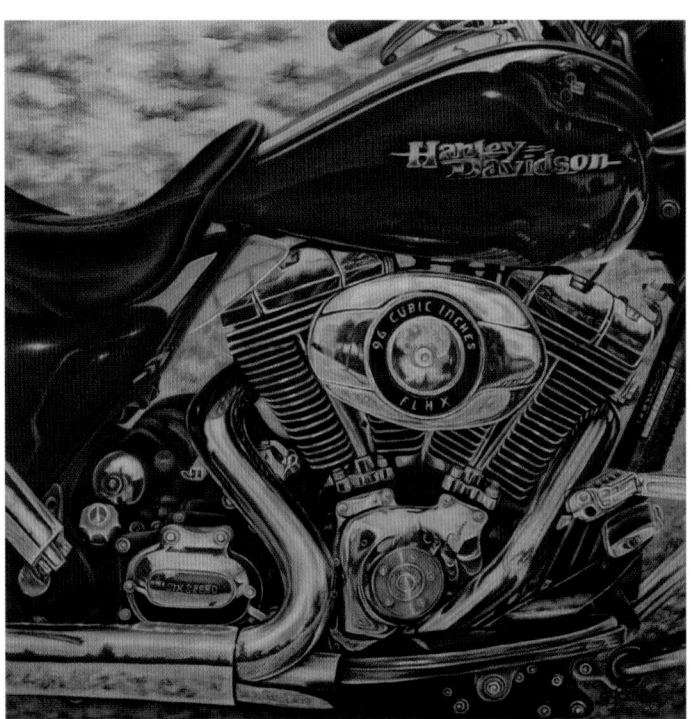

▲ GLORIA CALLAHAN
HARLEY'S DAVIDSON
The artist burnishes with colour, often building up to 20 or more layers of pencil. Burnishing with the local colours of a subject keeps colour clean and does not place a milky surface onto the area (as can happen when you add the blending pencil or use white to burnish with). At the end of the process, a torchon is used to burnish the applied colour.

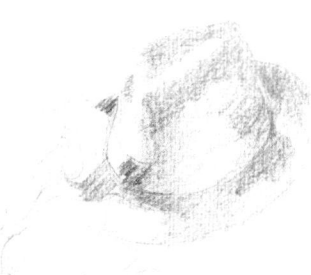

1 The subject chosen has two main coloured shapes, a black hat and a green scarf. Burnishing is used to blend the tones and bring up highlights. First, the outlines are sketched in and the hat is shaded lightly with a chalky black pencil.

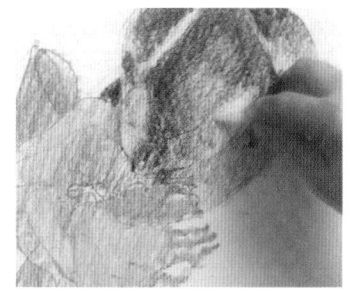

2 By overlaying areas of shading, the shapes of the hat and scarf are modelled in tone. A torchon is used to burnish the colours, blending the tones to create softer gradations.

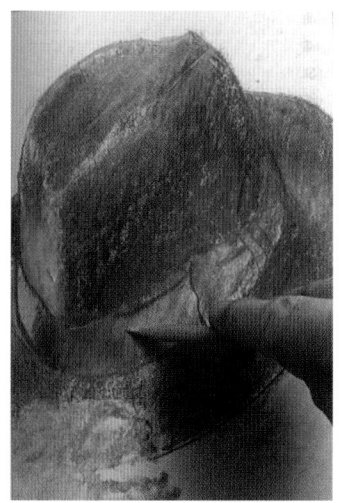

3 The light and shadow on the hat are enhanced by burnishing the highlight areas with a waxy white pencil. This merges the pencil marks, creating solid pale greys.

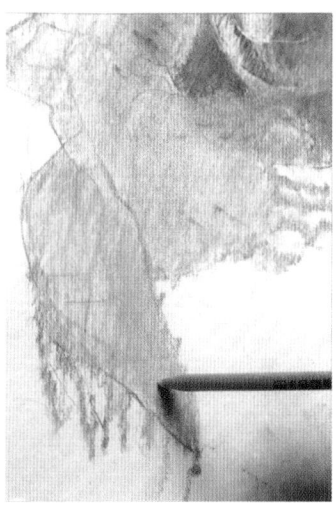

4 The folds of the scarf are modelled by overlaying colour, using a yellow wax pencil over chalky green. You can also see where white has been applied over the green in the same way as on the hat.

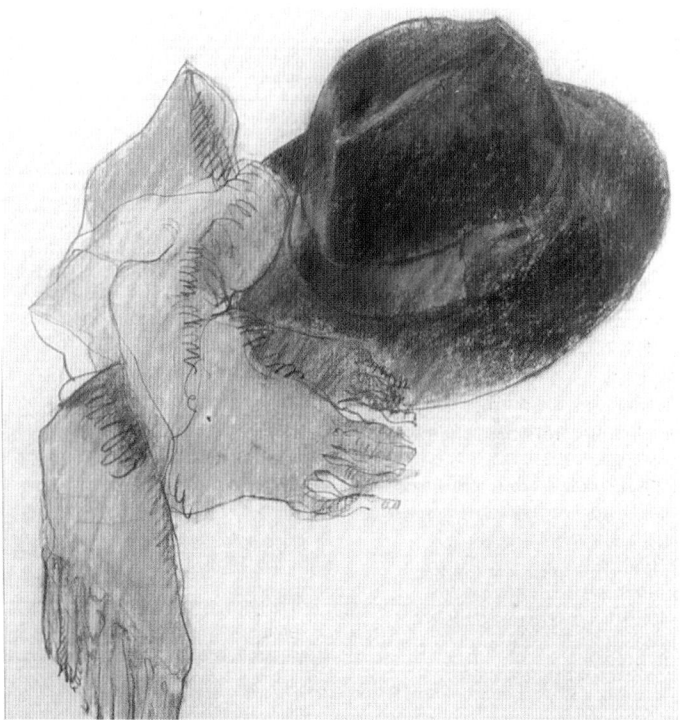

5 In the final stage, loose drawing with a graphite pencil creates texture in the folds and fringe of the scarf. Linear detail can be freely applied over burnished colour, although its surface is quite compact.

Overlaying Colours

The majority of coloured pencil renderings depend upon the effects of overlaying colours. In this way you can achieve richness of hue, tonal density and contrast, and effective three-dimensional modelling of forms and surface textures. Because coloured pencil marks have a degree of translucency, with the colour application reflecting the influence of the paper's grain and surface finish, the process of building up a drawing in layers creates potential for many subtle variations of hue, tone and texture.

There are many different ways of overlaying colours: you can put one layer of shading over another to modify colours and produce interesting mixtures and gradations; you can integrate lines, dashes and dots to develop complex effects of optical mixing; you can enliven areas of flat colour by overlaying a linear pattern or broken texture that subtly meshes with the original hue.

Colour layering provides greater depth and detail in a composition – for instance, you can achieve active colour qualities in highlight areas or dark shadows, which intensify effects of light and atmosphere. In a practical sense, overlaying colours is equivalent to mixing paints in a palette – if you don't have the precise hue that you need, you can create it from a blend of two or more colours.

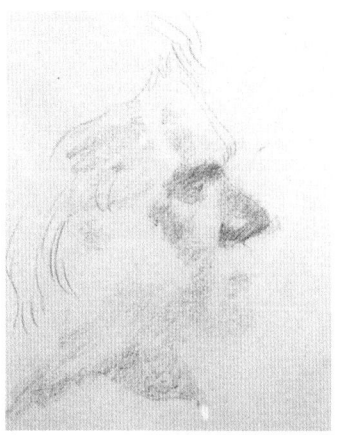

Building up colour shading
1 This portrait drawing begins with the face blocked in lightly with two shades of red-brown.

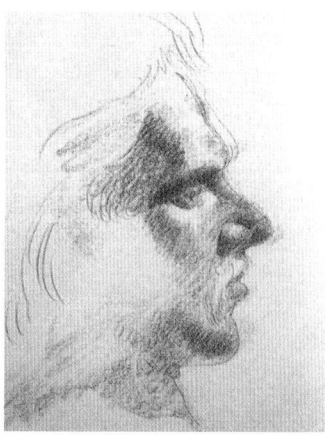

2 To enhance the modelling of the features, a dark brown pencil is used to work over the lighter colour around the eyes, nose and chin.

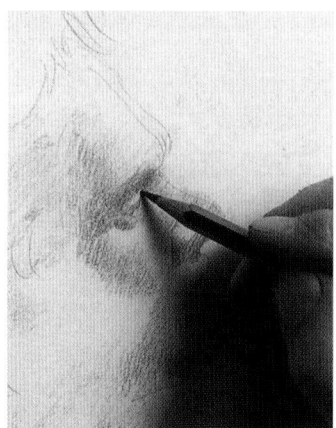

3 Even with this limited palette of colours, the structure of the face is quite clearly defined by the layers of shading.

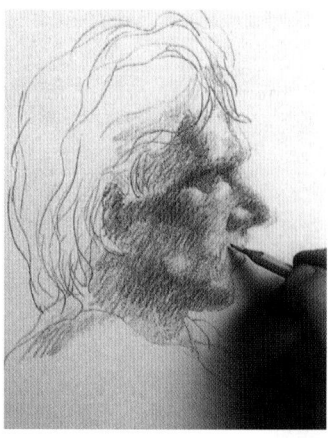

4 Further layers of red-brown build up the contours of the face and increase the contrast of light and shadow. Light yellow is laid over the darker tones around the eyes and mouth to intensify highlighting.

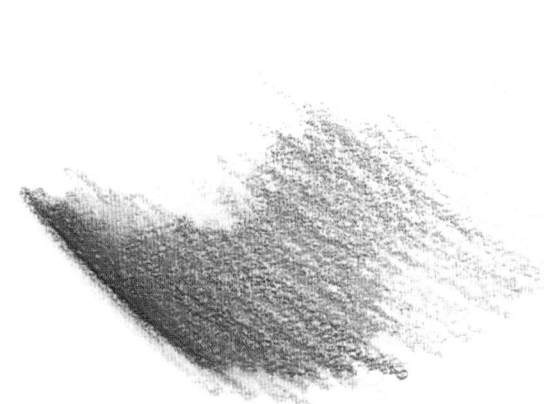

Mixed hues
Overlaid patches of grainy shading produce subtle mixtures and gradations of colour. This sample contains four colours – yellow, yellow ochre, green and grey-blue.

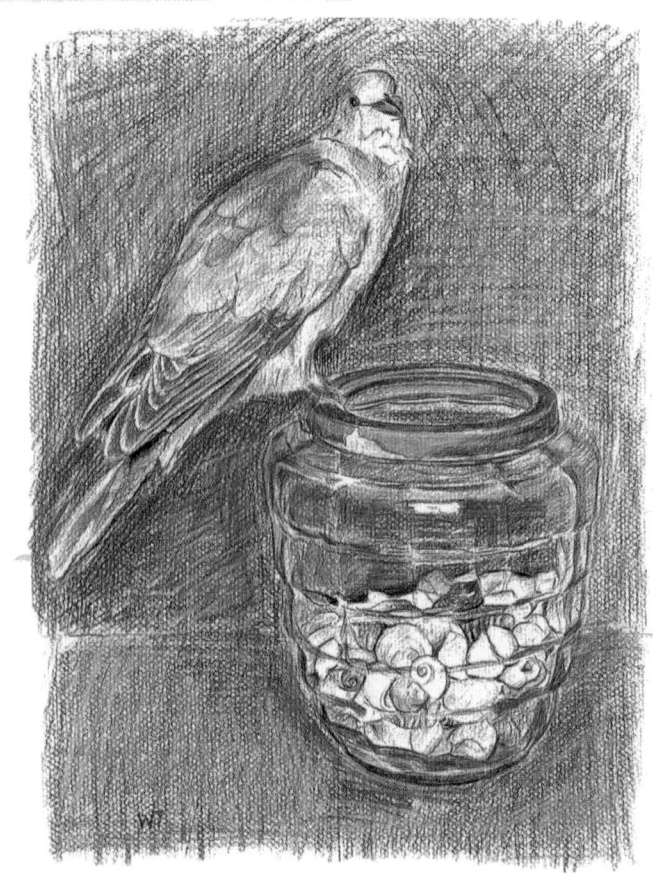

WILL TOPLEY ▶
STILL LIFE WITH BIRD
This interesting drawing shows colour overlays built up with loose hatching and shading. The heavy grain of the paper contributes an open, free quality to the colour mixes, but the layering of colours makes an attractively descriptive image conveying different kinds of textural detail.

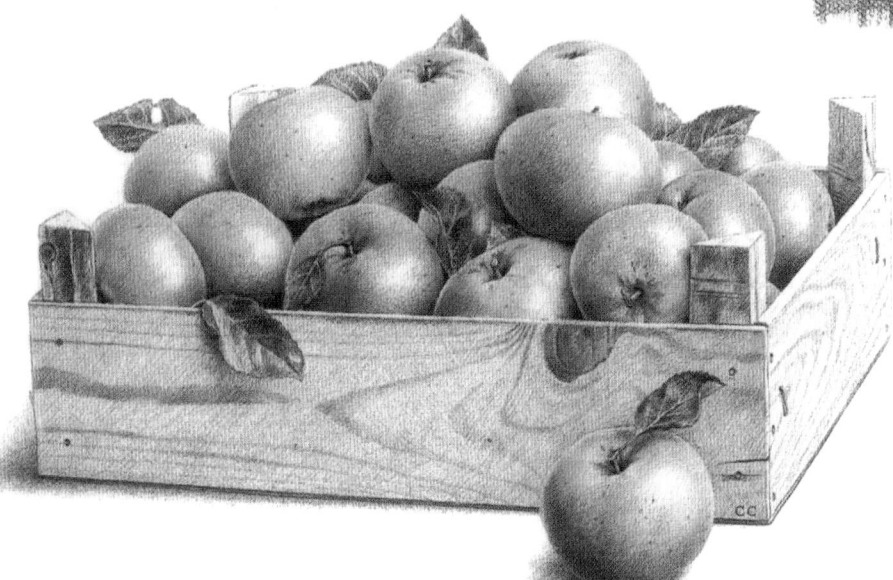

◀ CHRIS CHAPMAN
UNTITLED
Close shading, with the colours tightly knitted together in successive layers, produces a highly realistic style of rendering with subtle treatment of tonal contrasts and colour variations.

Mixing Pencils

The many good-quality brands of coloured pencils now available offer widely varied properties of colour and texture. There are two main advantages to building up a stock of different types of pencils. One is that you can utilize their different qualities of line and massed texture to create interesting variations in the surface qualities of an image. The other is more basic and practical – it is simply that you may find particular colours in one brand that are not available in another.

There is no formal technique governing a combination of pencil types. You need to experiment with the textures of hard or soft pencils, waxy or chalky leads, thin or thick points and pressure variations. The weight, surface texture and colour of your paper is also influential. The effects of mixing different types of pencils may be quite subtle and discreet, but this is appropriate since the scale and detail of coloured pencil work often requires close attention from the viewer.

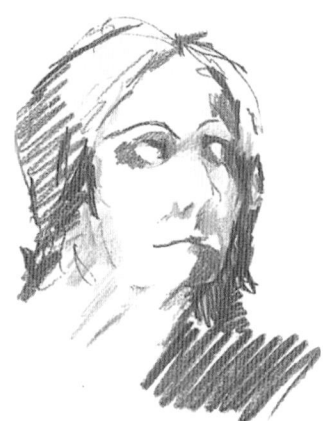

1 The reference for this drawing is a photograph with a soft, shadowy mood. The initial layers are laid in with chalky pencils to create broad, grainy lines and gentle shading.

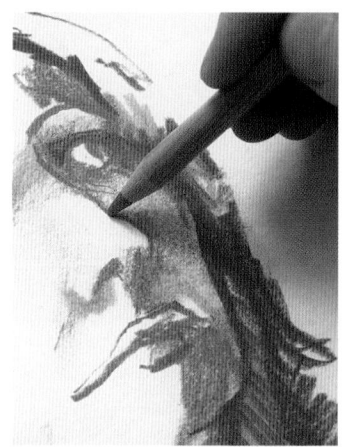

2 The lines and features of the face are sharpened using waxy pencils to create a harder line quality contrasting with the chalky marks.

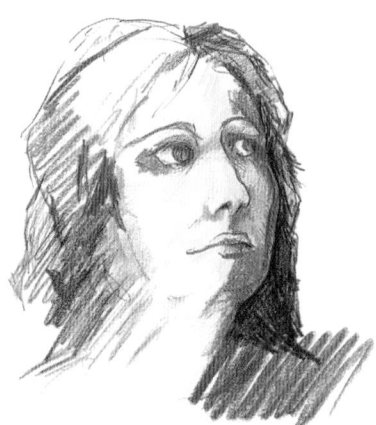

3 Soft-grade waxy pencils are chosen for applying highlighting and shadow to the face and hair. Their texture enables colours to be overlaid cleanly.

4 The linear structure is enhanced with a slightly harder type of moderately waxy pencil, with the same texture used to highlight the face in yellow. The chalk pencils are again applied, to soften the drawing in places.

Types of coloured pencil
Different pencils have different qualities. Shown from left to right: hard watercolour pencil; chalky pencil; hard pencil; waxy pencil.

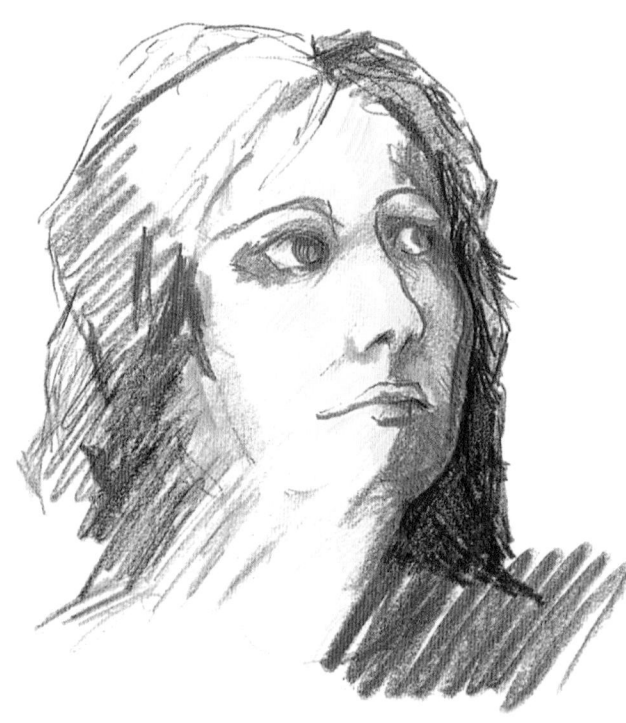

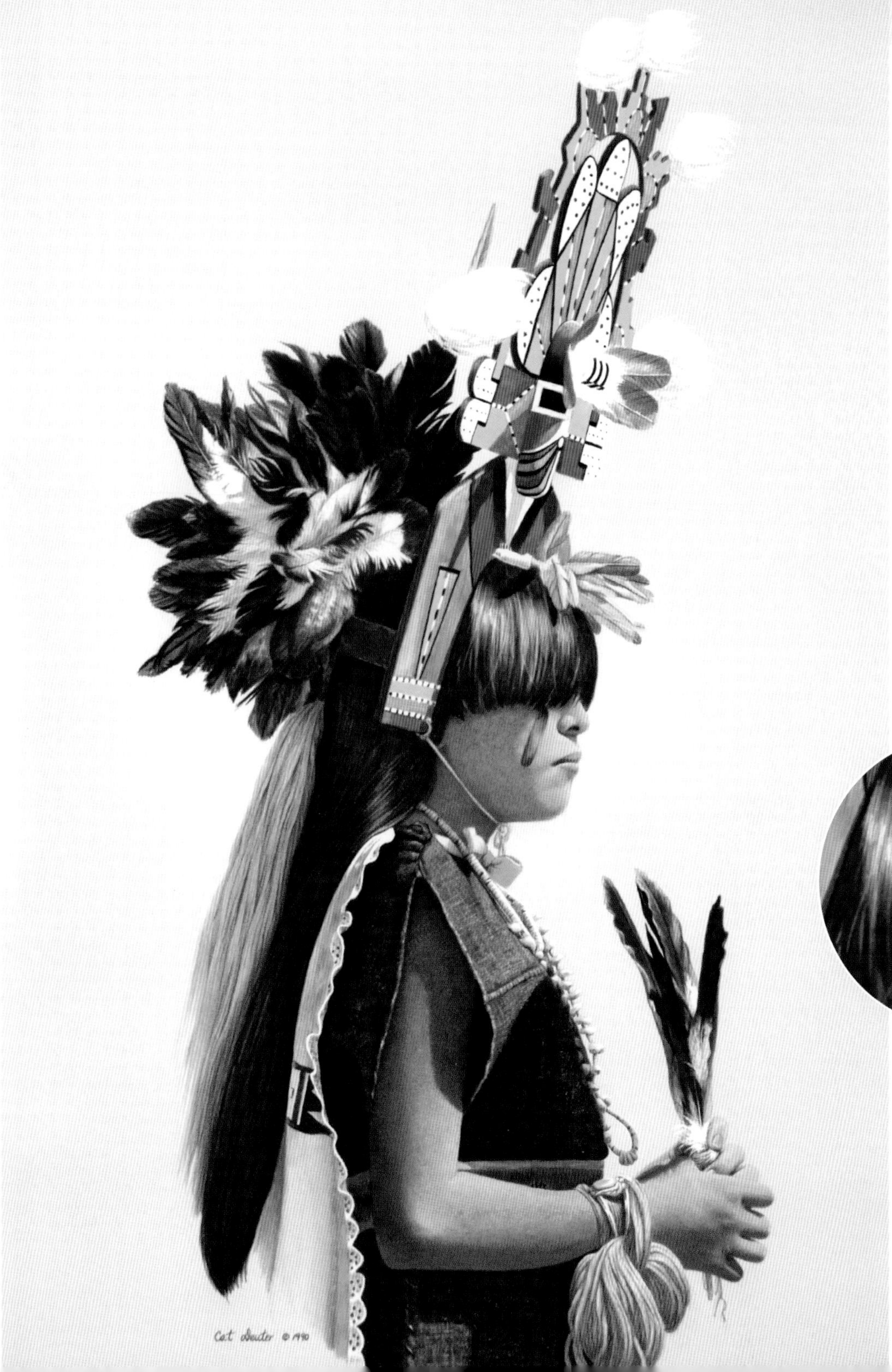

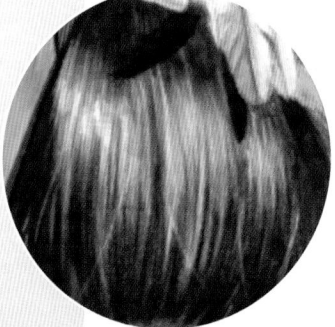

◀ **CAT DEUTER**

WATCHING THE DANCE

Cat Deuter used a combination of coloured pencils and watercolour pencils. She uses water to blend the colours in the model's hair only, otherwise the pencils are used dry. Cat works in layers until the desired density and saturation is reached.

Line Qualities

The quality of line refers not to the gestural energy you give to the pencil strokes, as with linear marks, but to the innate character of an individual line.

Four basic qualities are usually recognized: a sharp, clean line of unvarying width implying firm contour or geometric precision; calligraphic line, tapering and swelling with a directional rhythm to show movement and energy; broken line, appearing variable and hesitant, sometimes actually fractured; and repetitive line – quickly formed, parallel or overlapping strokes eventually tracing a continuous contour.

The linear bias of coloured pencil drawing makes these qualities an important factor in determining the expressive character of an image, especially crucial when exploited in techniques such as contour drawing and hatching (see pages 28–29 and 48–49).

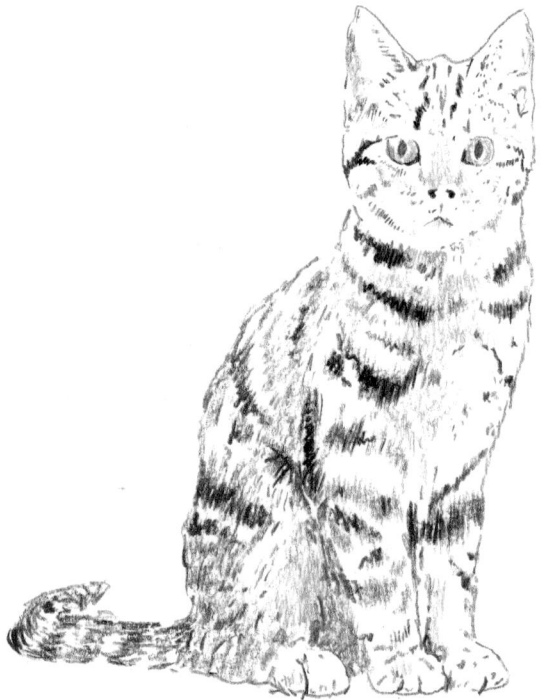

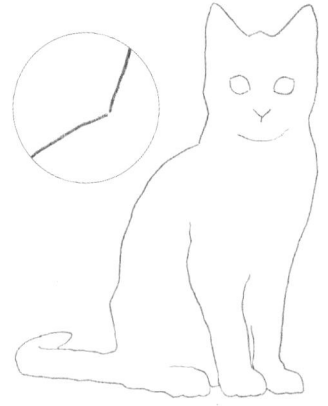

Firm, unvariable line
Because of the "giving" texture of coloured pencil, a line of even weight and density has a sympathetic quality, but provides a strong graphic contour.

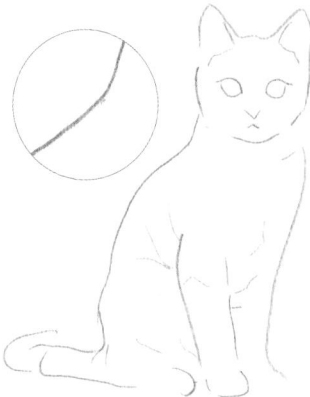

Calligraphic, directional line
Variations in weight and emphasis help to model form in contour drawing.

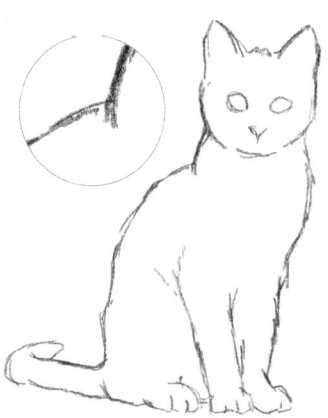

Repetitive line
The retraced contour has the practical advantage of enabling you to modify the shapes you are drawing, and suggests the quality of movement in the subject.

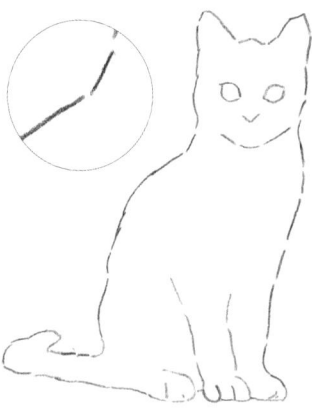

Broken line
A line breaking at different intervals, as you lift the pencil from the page, can be more interesting than an unbroken contour line.

MATTHEW MIDGLEY ▶
CAT

Matthew uses a combination of firm lines and broken lines applied with the point of the pencil and the side of the lead.

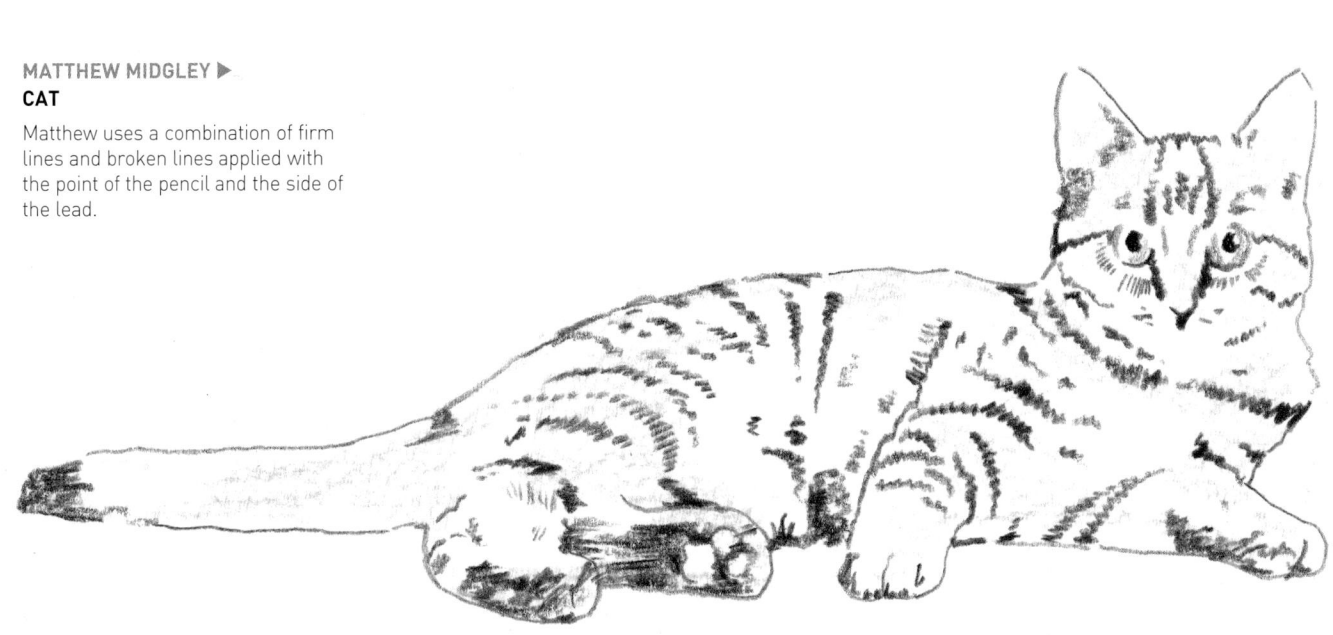

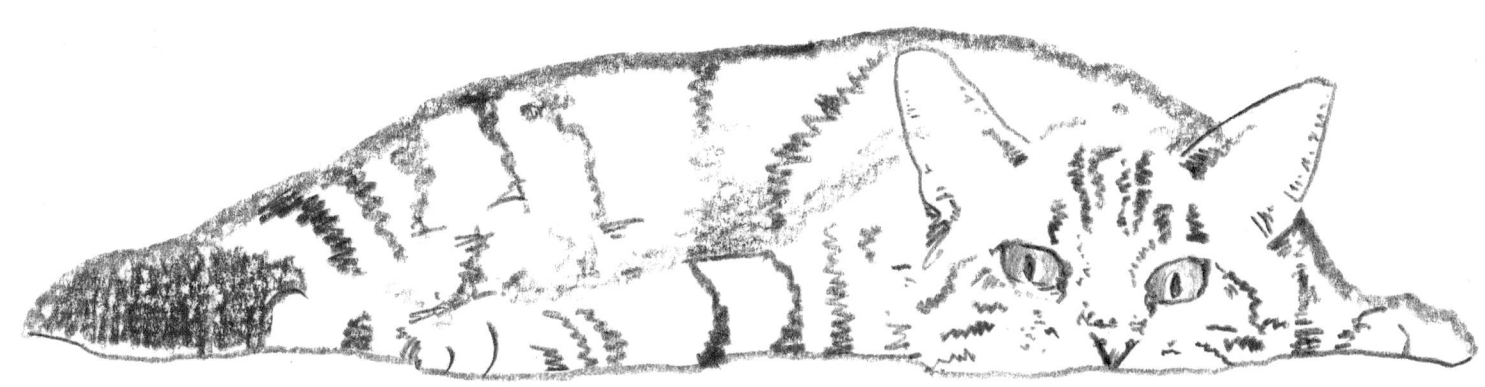

Highlighting

A highlight is the brightest point of reflected light in an image, typically represented in drawing and painting as a flash, spot or patch of pure white. Because of the translucency of coloured pencil leads, it is difficult to obtain a clean effect by applying white highlights as finishing touches, as you can with an opaque medium such as pastel, gouache or oil paint.

There are methods of creating highlights that rely on allowing the white of the paper to show through the colour – leaving the paper bare so that the highlight is a distinct white shape, or erasing the colour to retrieve the paper surface. Erasure only works well if the colour application is light and the paper surface quite resilient. The technique of impressing can be effectively applied to creating fine linear or dot highlights.

If you are working on coloured paper, you can apply bright highlights with a white pencil directly on the paper surface – if the pencil is fairly soft-textured and the paper colour not too intense, you should obtain a clean white. If you do need to impose highlighting over densely worked coloured pencil drawing, you can add opaque colour in the final stage using pastel or paint, being careful to create marks of suitable scale and texture to integrate with the coloured pencil strokes.

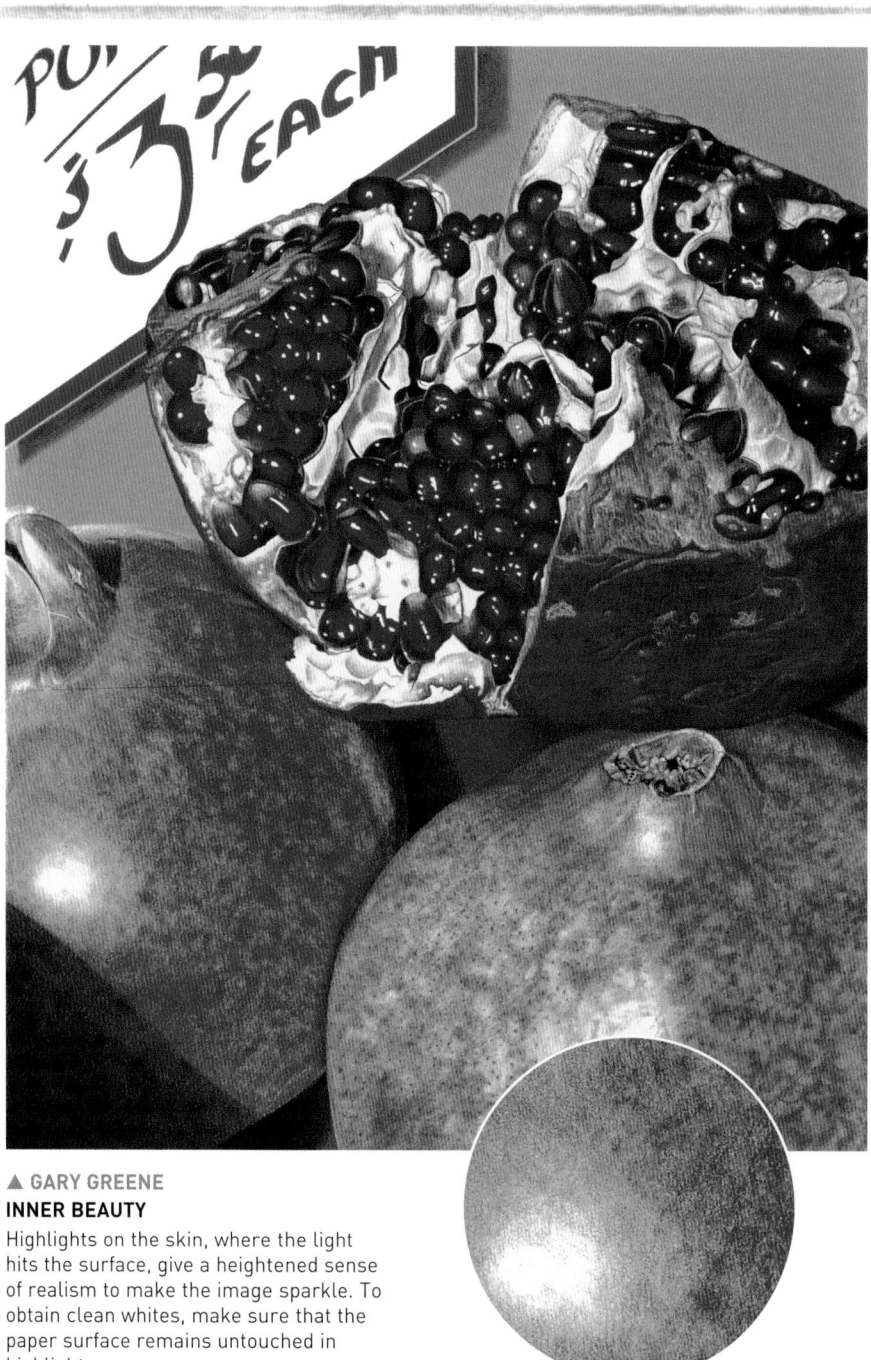

▲ **GARY GREENE**
INNER BEAUTY
Highlights on the skin, where the light hits the surface, give a heightened sense of realism to make the image sparkle. To obtain clean whites, make sure that the paper surface remains untouched in highlight areas.

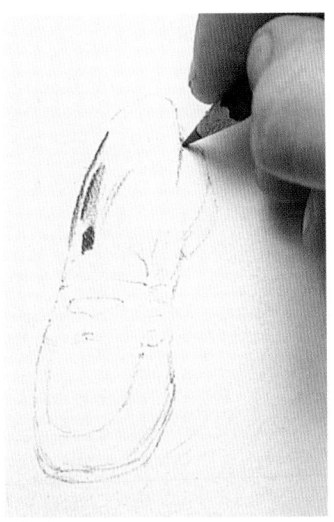

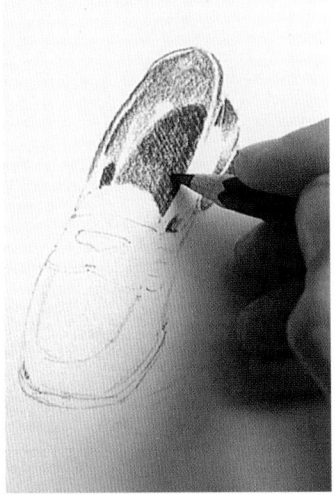

4 The finished drawing gives an effective impression of the shiny leather, by forming an appropriate contrast of the lightest and darkest tones, and leaving soft but clean edges to the highlights.

1 When you are planning to create highlights by leaving the white of the paper bare, you must achieve a clear "map" of your subject before you start shading. Make a light outline drawing that locates the important shapes.

2 Shade in the colour slowly, working up to and around the highlight areas. Take special care when dealing with fine detail, such as the linear highlights on the heel of this shoe.

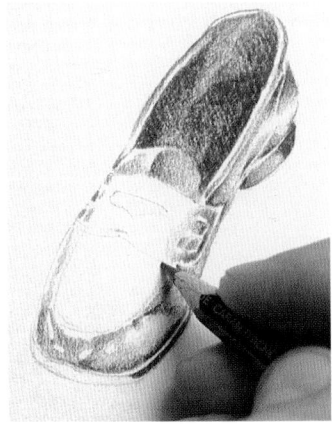

3 Build the tones gradually, keeping the contrast of lights and darks. Try to hold your hand clear of the drawing, to avoid smudging colour into the white areas. When you are working on a broader composition, use a clean sheet of paper to protect the area beneath your hand.

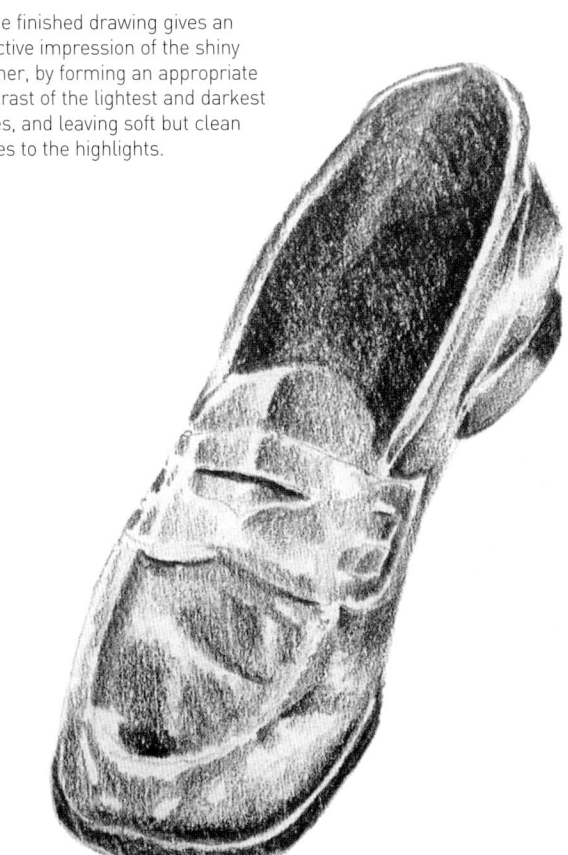

Contour Drawing

This technique takes advantage of the linear capabilities of coloured pencils as a means of investigating three-dimensional form and volume. The planes and curves of solid forms are described in line only, using the outline of the subject and the contours within the overall shape to model the image.

A very economical line drawing can be highly expressive of form – the key is to be sensitive to the line qualities that best describe different elements of the subject. A variable line that swells and tapers, for instance, is more descriptive of curving contours than a line of even weight. Imagine tracing the actual surface of an object with your pencil, so that the pencil point travels easily over the form but with varying pressure relating to surface planes and undulations. The essence of a contour drawing is the same, but you are transferring these impressions to a flat surface.

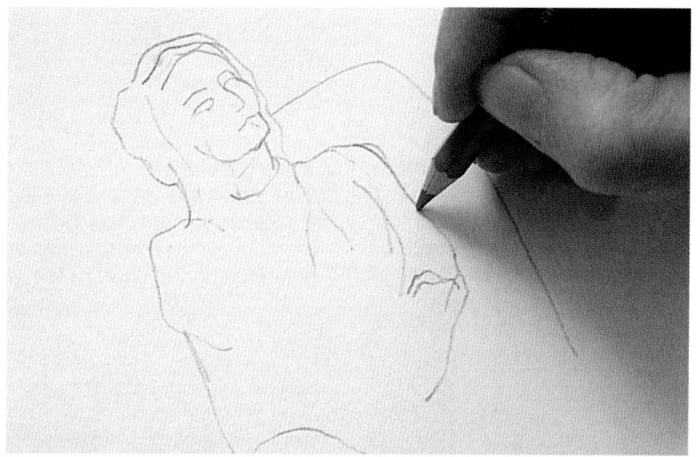

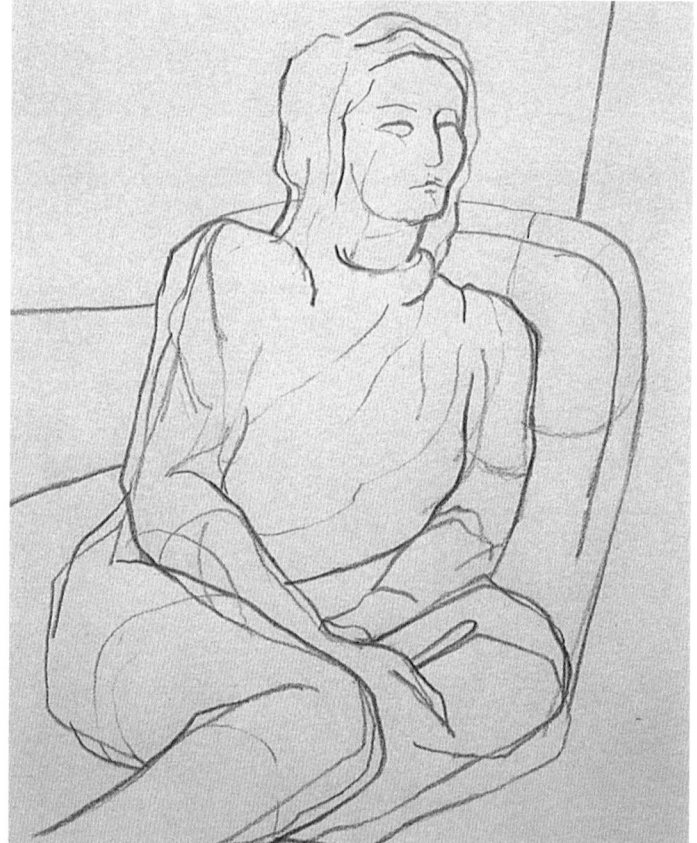

Monochrome drawing
1 In contour drawing, if you are using coloured pencil in the same way that you would draw with graphite pencil, it is best to choose a dark-toned colour. The effect of, say, indigo blue or burnt umber, is softer in mood than black. This drawing begins with the outline and main features of the seated figure.

2 Although contour drawing is a minimal process, using only the linear cues in your subject, you do not have to get it all right first time. As you trace and retrace the contour lines that you see, the "correct" form will emerge, and you can enhance the effect by strengthening the weight of certain lines.

Using local colour

1 With some subjects, you can obtain a good effect by choosing a pencil corresponding to the local colour of the object; that is, the colour that you see under normal light. A rich warm red is chosen to match the skin colour of a red pepper.

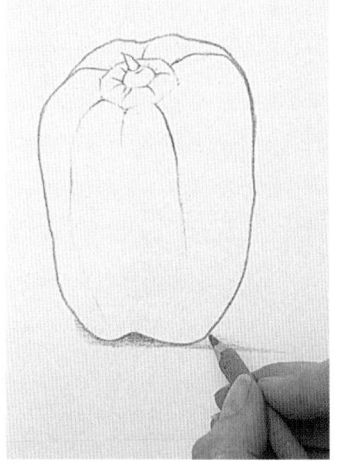

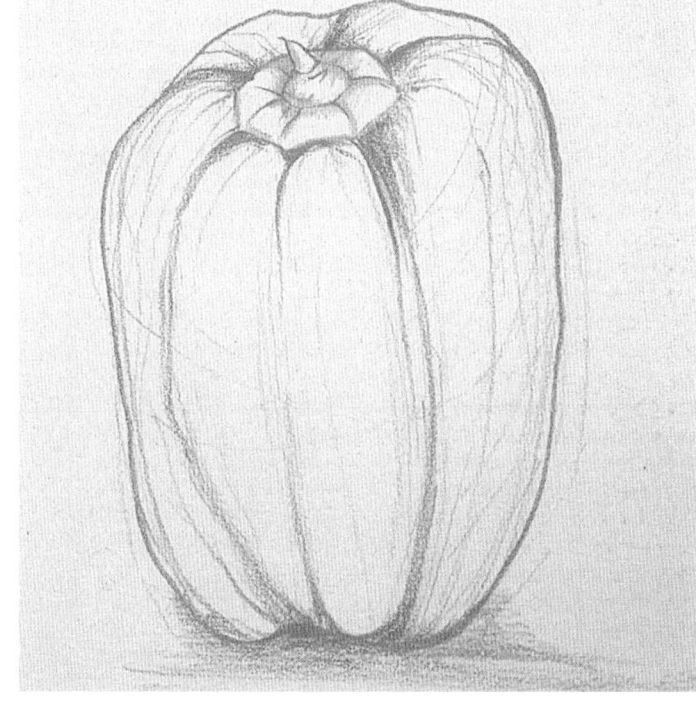

2 The lines of the contour drawing create the overall shape of the pepper and the swelling curves within the outline. For contrast, touches of green are applied within the red outline of the core.

LESLIE TAYLOR ▶

UNTITLED

This drawing shows an interesting combination of contour drawing and subtle shading. Although the shading contributes a sense of volume through surface modelling, the viewer's "reading" of the image depends strongly on the linear framework created by the contour lines.

Sketching

Coloured pencils are an excellent medium for sketching – clean, lightweight, easily portable and very versatile. You can work rapidly in line only to describe individual shapes and forms (see contour drawing pages 48–49) or build up colour masses quickly with loose shading and hatching (see pages 22–25 and 28–29).

When it comes to choosing colours, select at least one pencil in each of the main colours of the spectrum (red, blue, yellow, orange, green and purple) plus the neutrals (black, grey and white). Mixtures of these can be contrived to cover the characteristics of any subject (also remember that you can add written colour notes to sketchbook drawings for fuller interpretation once back in the studio).

If you prefer to carry a more comprehensive range of hues, choose colours suited to your subject – for example, blues, greens and earth colours for landscape; more of the bold, bright hues for a subject such as a fruit market or flower garden; subtle variations of grey, brown and yellow for farm or zoo animals.

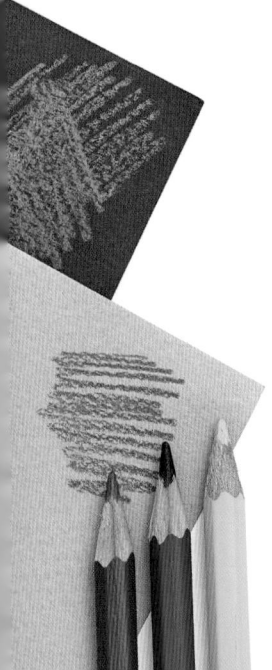

Sketching

Consider using coloured papers for sketching. Pads of tinted papers in subtle mid-tones are available; these can help you to key your range of applied tones and colours more efficiently and may give a more finished look to a quick drawing.

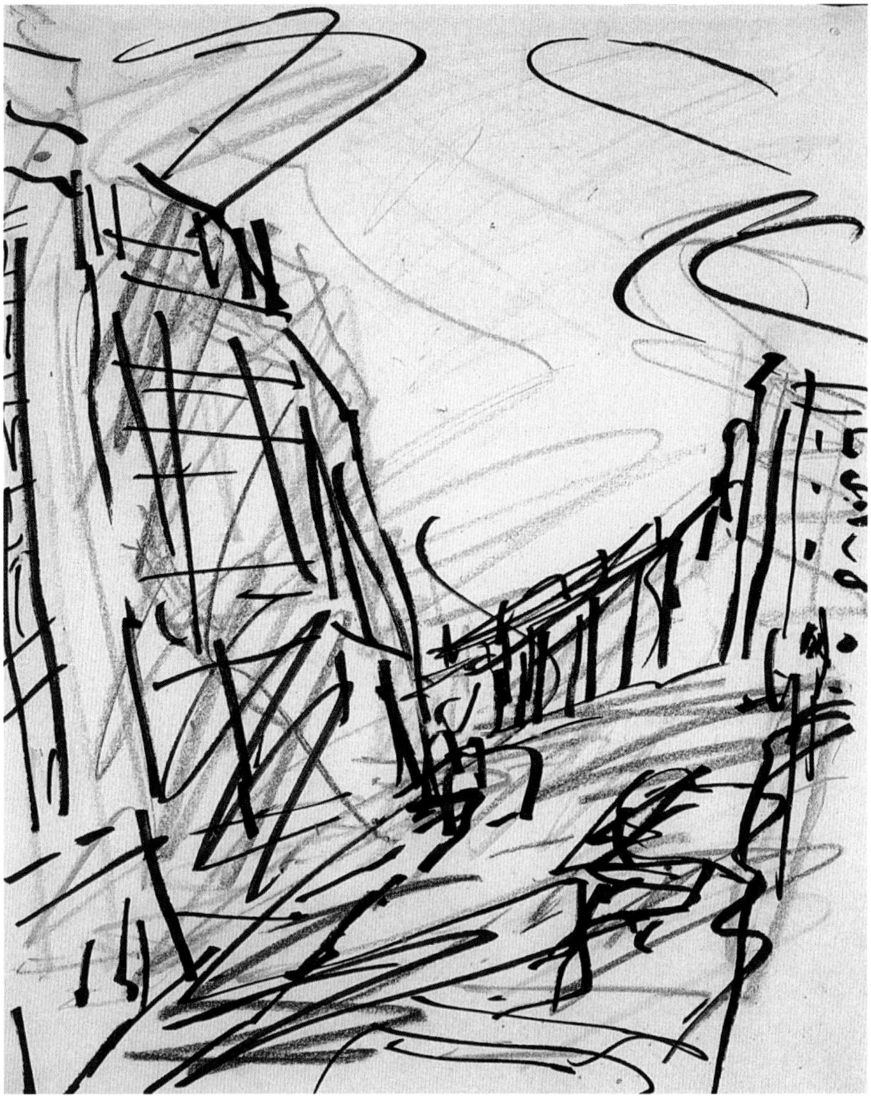

FRANK AUERBACH

WINTER MORNING

The starkness of a winter cityscape is vigorously attacked with ink and pencil, making active use of varied line qualities in both media.

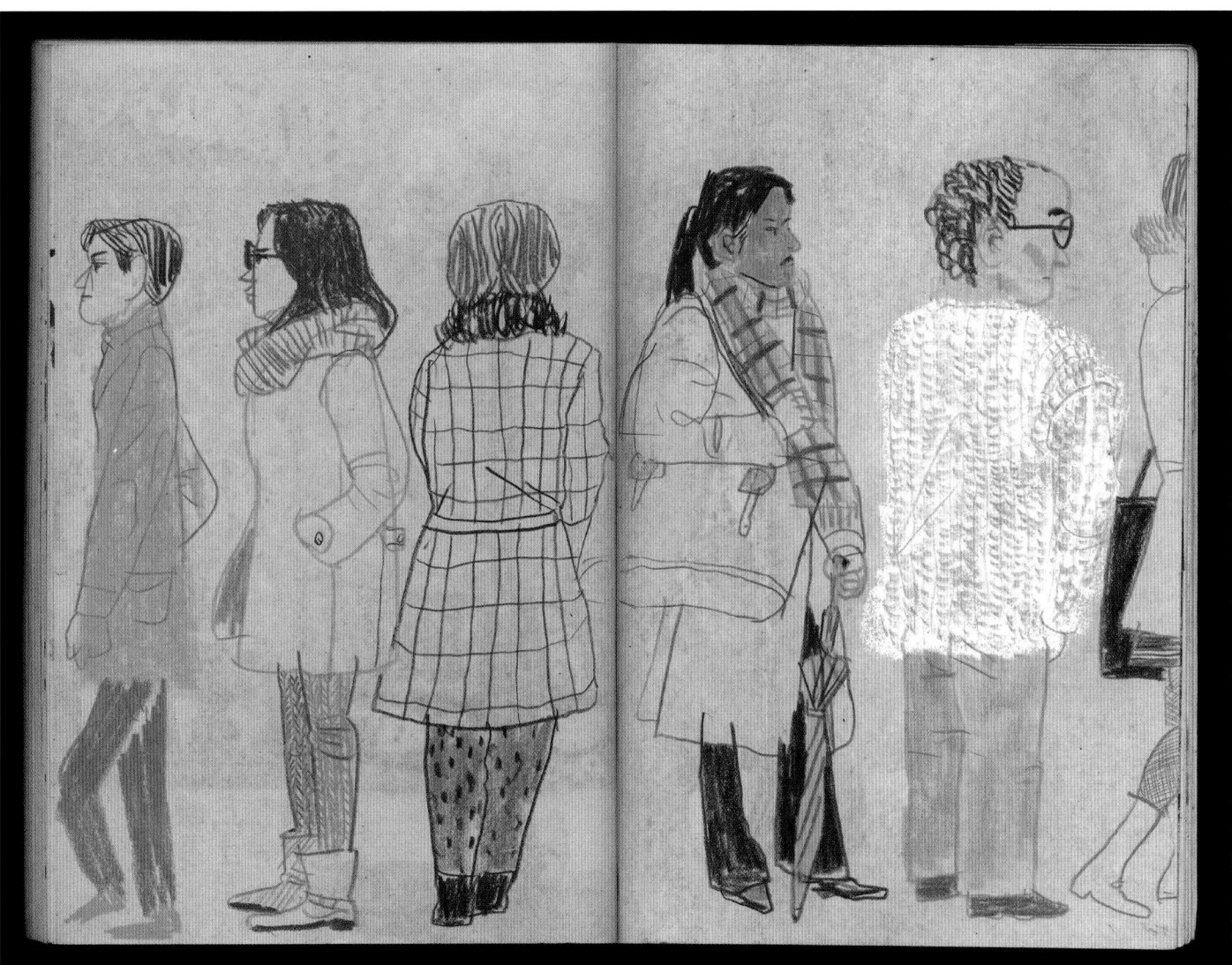

▲TAKEUMA

SKETCHBOOK

The neutral paper allows Takeuma to use really bright colours without them seeming garish. The sketch looks richer than it would on white.

Eraser Techniques

Using an eraser to make corrections is a limited process in coloured pencil drawing. Only lightweight strokes can be eradicated completely; a dense application typically leaves a colour "stain" on the paper even after quite vigorous rubbing with an eraser, and heavy linear marks will also leave an impression in the paper surface that may show through subsequent reworkings.

The efficiency of erasures also depends on the type of eraser and the texture of the coloured pencils you are using. A plastic eraser used on waxy coloured pencil marks may spread the colour rather than lift it – you can use this effect positively as a means of blending colours or burnishing the surface (see pages 26–27 and 38–39).

An eraser may retrieve the surface sufficiently to allow you to rework the area to modify tones and hues. Where you have a thick build-up of waxy colour, use the flat edge of a scalpel blade to scrape away the excess before using the eraser. If you have made a serious error in one part of the drawing at a late stage, it may be possible to insert a patch correction (see pages 80–81).

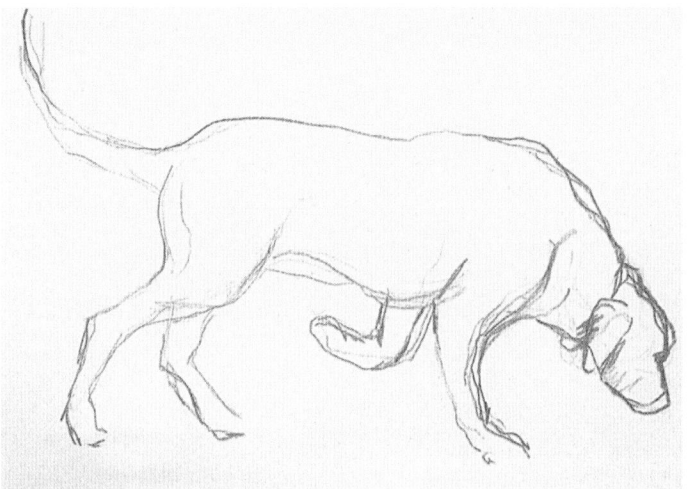

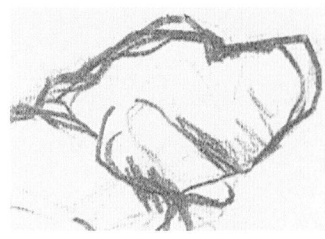

1 Eraser techniques can be used both for correction and as a positive drawing element. The outline of the dog is drawn on smooth paper. The detail (above) shows where corrections have been made to the head.

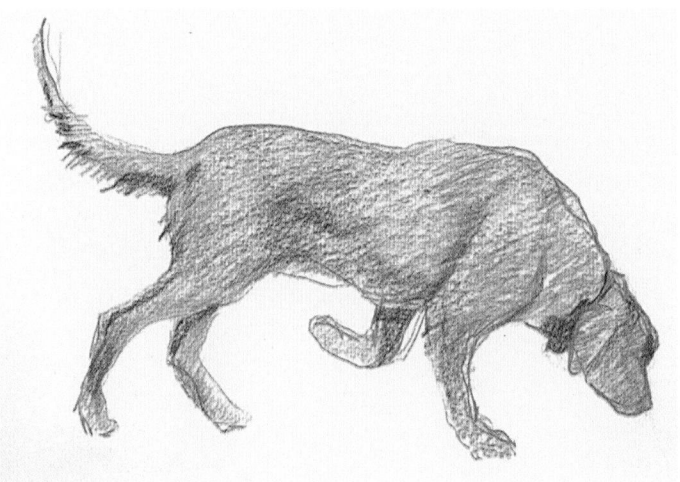

2 The shape of the animal is roughly modelled overall, using light warm brown and dark umber to shade in the basic tones and colours.

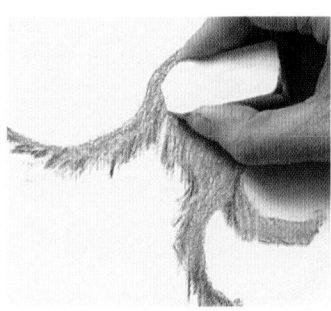

3 A plastic eraser is used at the contours of the animal's tail and underside to drag the colour outwards, making light, feathered marks corresponding to the texture of the longer fur.

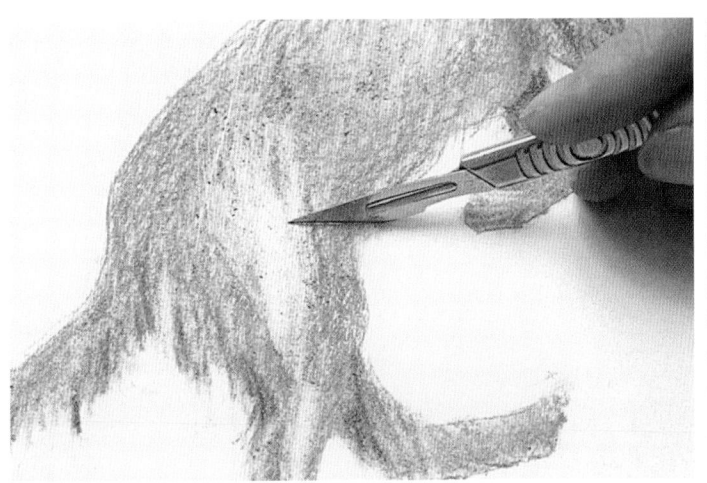

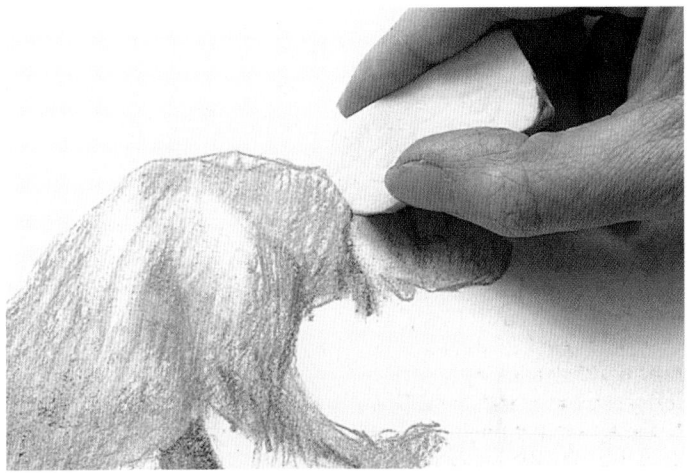

4 To brighten the highlight areas on the flanks and shoulders, the colour is scraped back with a scalpel blade. This works best on smooth-surfaced paper, and you must keep the edge of the blade flat to avoid gouging the surface.

5 The plastic eraser is used again, this time for cleaning up the drawing and burnishing the highlight areas where the colour has already been scraped back.

6 Compare the finished image to step 2: the work with eraser and blade has enhanced the impression of form and texture as well as allowing amendment of incorrect shapes and over-heavy colour. A little more loose pencil work has also been applied to roughen up the furry texture.

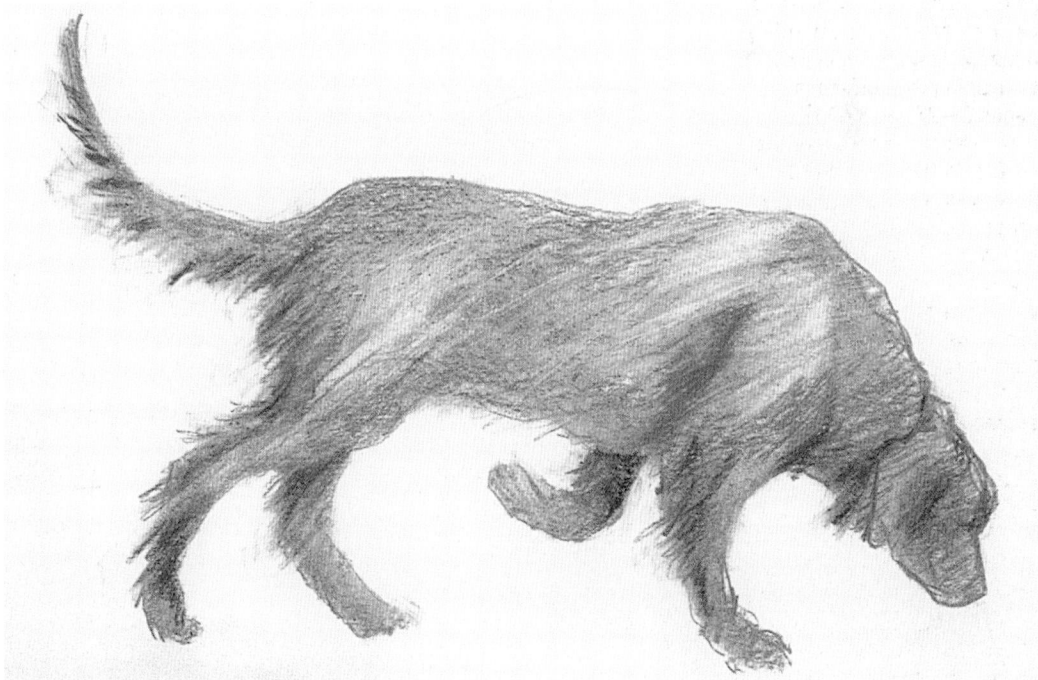

Solvents

The marks made with some types of coloured pencil can be spread and blended with solvents – water, turpentine or the spirit-based medium in a colourless marker blender. Only pencils formulated to be water-soluble will react with water. Spirit solvents may dissolve the colours of pencils intended to be used dry – this has to be a matter of experiment, as it depends on the proportions of pigment and binding materials in the pencil lead, and effects are not wholly predictable.

There are two methods which enable you to take advantage of the more fluid textures produced by solvent techniques. You can either dip the tip of the pencil into the solvent, so that the colour becomes softened, and spreads as you lay it down; or you can shade or hatch with the dry pencil tip, then work into the colour area with solvent using a brush, torchon or cotton bud – or with a marker blender, which is simply a marker pen that contains colourless solvent. You can combine the effects of wet and dry colour by allowing the dampened marks to dry, then reworking the area with the pencil points.

To avoid distortion that may occur through the paper buckling when it is wetted by the solvent, stretch the paper beforehand, or work on a pre-stretched paper block or illustration board.

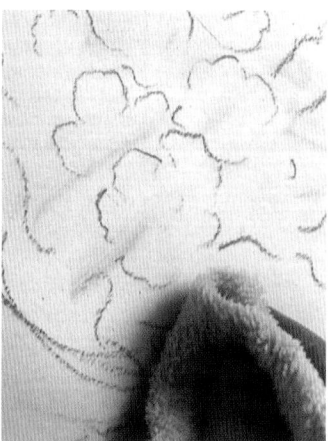

Using spirit solvent

1 The shapes of the flowers are rapidly sketched with a soft waxy pencil line. A rag dampened with white spirit is used to spread the colour delicately, indicating the areas of darkest tone.

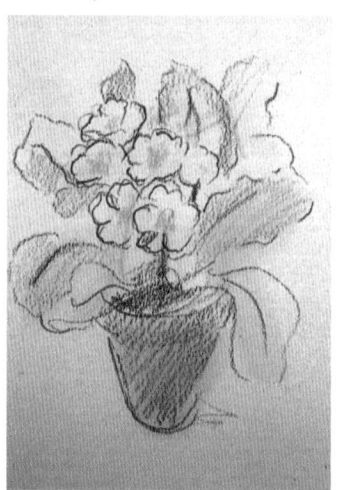

2 The line drawing is strengthened and some broad colour areas blocked in with light shading. Notice the heavy grain of the watercolour paper – when applying spirit solvent, you need to use good-quality paper to avoid buckling or tearing.

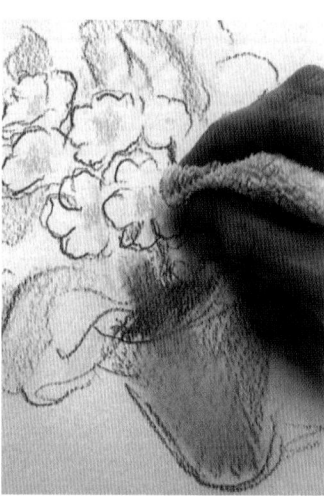

3 A second stage of rubbing with white spirit softens the colour and spreads it into the paper grain. The pencil marks are just moistened, not flooded with the solvent.

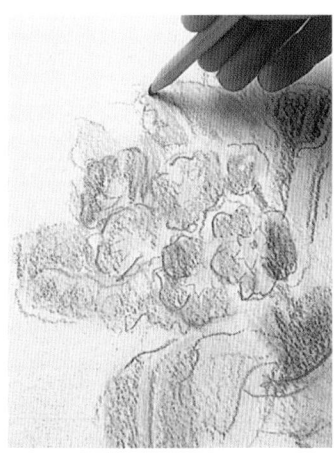

4 To develop the intensity of colour, pencils are used again to shade in the solid shapes. The moisture from the underlayers makes the pencil marks smoother and stronger.

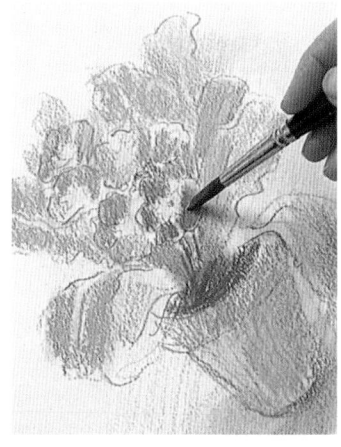

5 Applying solvent with a brush makes the colour dissolve and spread more like paint. It is possible to do this selectively, to build up a contrast of different textures.

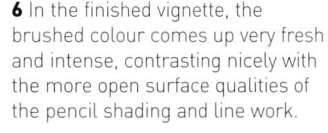

6 In the finished vignette, the brushed colour comes up very fresh and intense, contrasting nicely with the more open surface qualities of the pencil shading and line work.

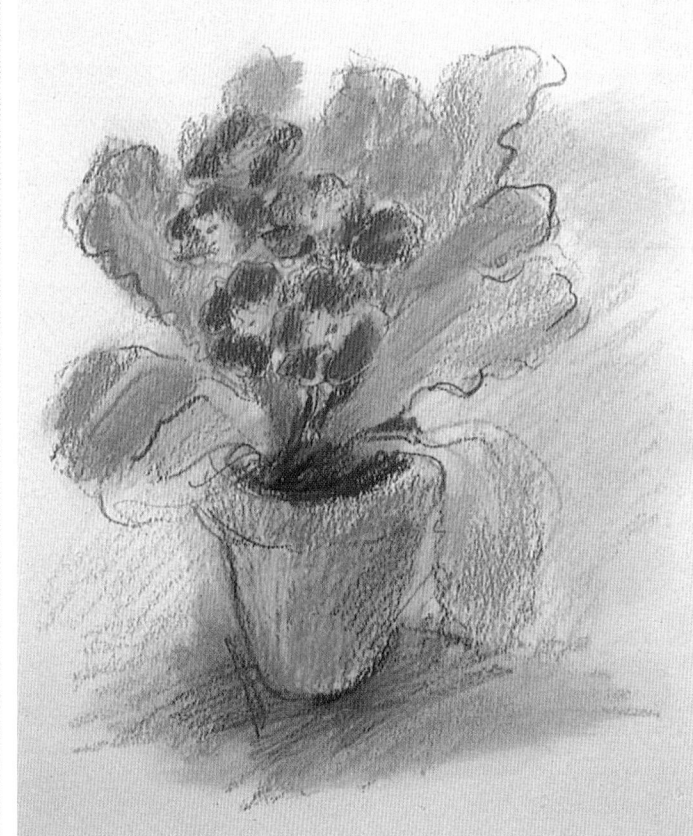

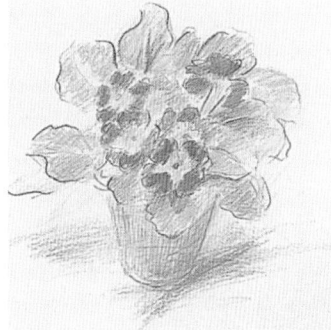

Using water-soluble pencils
This example is worked in much the same way, except that water-soluble pencils have been used for the drawing with clean water as the solvent. The techniques of rubbing and brushing the colour apply equally to this medium.

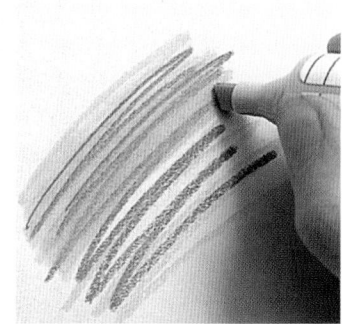

Using a marker blender
The blender is exactly the same tool as a broad-tipped marker, but the fluid content is colourless. To blend pencil colours, rub the tip of the marker firmly over the pencil marks.

Impressing

The basic principle of impressing is that of making a mark that actually indents or grooves the surface of the paper. You can then work over it with gentle pencil shading which glides across the impressed mark, so that it remains visible through the colour overlay. For a clean effect, the impressed line should be pushed well down below the paper surface, so place a newspaper beneath the drawing paper to allow some "give" when you apply the pressure.

The impression can be colourless, made with a hard pointed instrument that marks the paper firmly but is not sharp enough to tear it. A blunted stylus or the wooden end of a paintbrush could be used, for instance (and artists have been known to improvise using keys, their own fingernails or any suitable hard object). This means that the impression shows itself as the paper colour (white or tinted) after you have shaded over it.

Alternatively, you can make the same sort of "blind" impression by working on tracing paper laid over the drawing paper, using a stylus, hard pencil or ballpoint pen to apply heavy pressure. The process of constructing a complex image in this way is demonstrated under white line (see pages 58–59).

If you want the impressed marks to appear in colour, you can either form them with the sharpened lead of a coloured pencil or you can put down an initial area of solid colour and make a blind impression on it as described above, before overlaying a second colour.

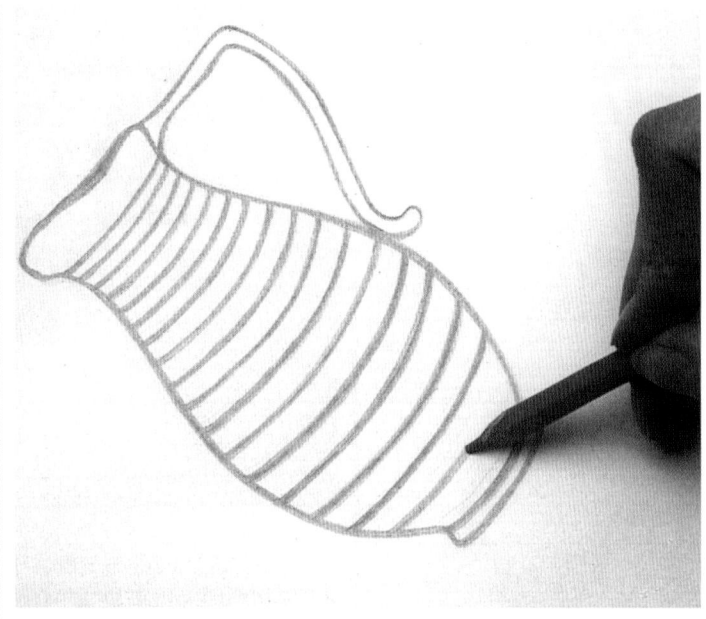

Impressed coloured line

1 Make a drawing of your subject with firm, even contour lines, pressing the tip of the pencil hard into the paper.

Layers of newspaper placed underneath help to create the necessary "give" in the paper surface.

2 Shade lightly over the drawing, allowing the pencil tip to skip over the impressed lines. You will see that the original lines read clearly through the overlaid colour. You can use more than one colour for both the outline drawing and the shading, to form a more complex image.

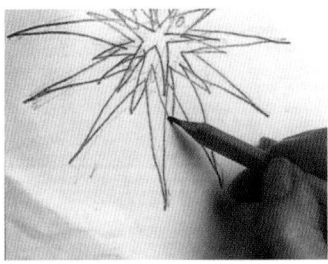

Blind impressing

1 Make your initial drawing on tracing or thin layout paper. Place a clean sheet of drawing paper on newspaper and lay the tracing over it. Retrace the outlines very firmly with a sharp pencil point or with a ballpoint pen.

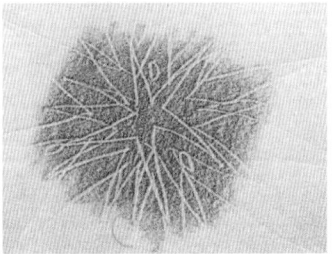

2 Lift the tracing paper from one corner to check that the line is distinctly impressed on the drawing paper. Be careful to keep one edge of the tracing in place, so it goes back in precisely the same position.

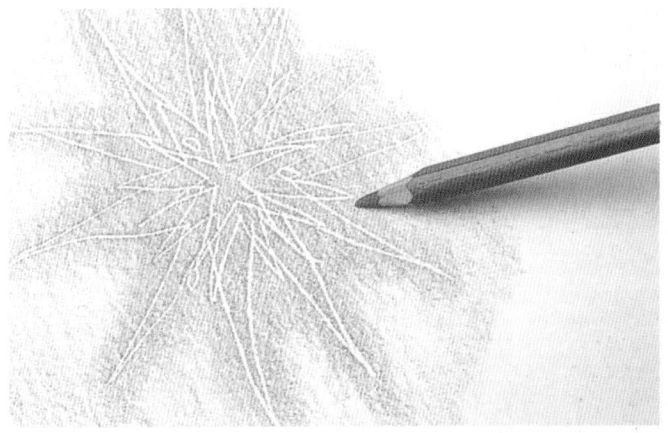

3 When the impressing is complete, remove the tracing and put the paper on a drawing board or other suitable work surface. Shade colour over the impressed lines, using a light but even motion. You can blend or overlay colours in different areas of the drawing. Be careful not to apply so much pressure that the pencil tip is pushed into the white lines.

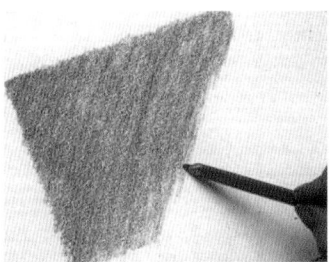

Blind impressing over colour

1 The basic method used here is exactly the same as blind impressing, but you work onto colour instead of on white paper. First, create an area of even shading in one colour.

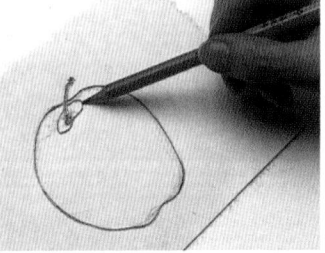

2 Use a trace drawing, as before, as the guideline for your impressing. Make sure you locate the image in the right position over the shaded colour.

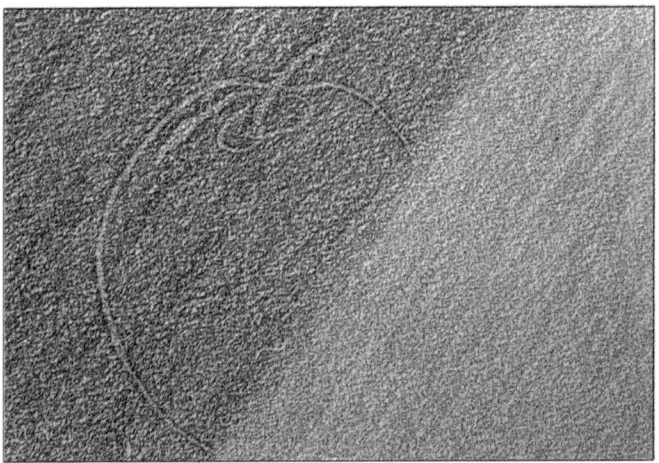

3 Shade over the impression with a second colour, so that the first colour appears as line only. The overlay creates a subtle effect, but to read the line clearly, you need to choose colours with a good degree of contrast.

White Line

This technique is a formal way of using impressing to create specific decorative effects in a drawing. You construct a detailed line drawing on tracing paper, then place it on your drawing paper and work over the lines firmly with a sharp pencil, stylus or ballpoint pen to impress them deeply into the paper. You can then build up the image in colour by shading over it with the required range of coloured pencils.

The method is an excellent way of reproducing particular patterns and textures, such as fine lace in a curtain or tablecloth, or a delicate tracery of leaf veins; or it can be employed to form a "negative" outline drawing, describing forms and volumes that can be filled with applied colours. The impression in the paper surface gives a kind of relief effect to the positive shapes.

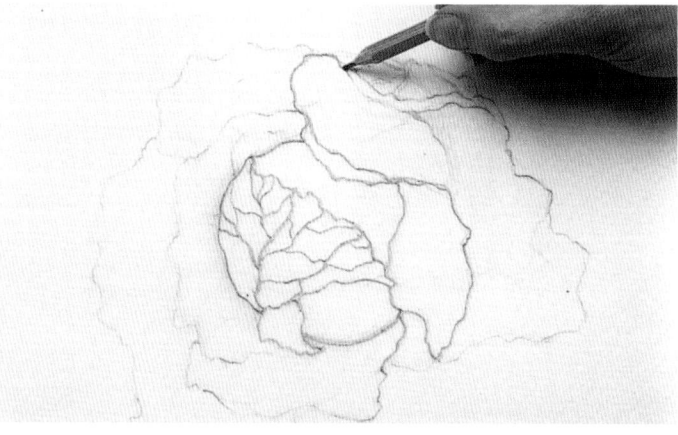

1 Make your initial line drawing in graphite pencil so you can easily make corrections until you have a satisfactory image. Use thin tracing or layout paper.

This drawing shows the contours of the frilled cabbage leaves and the lacy pattern of the veins.

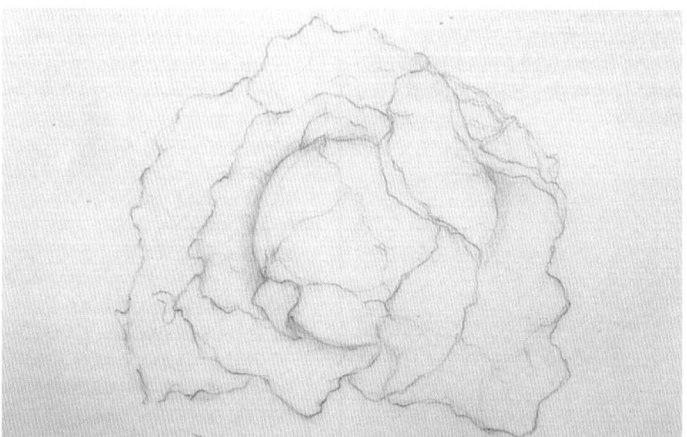

2 Position the keyline drawing over your drawing paper. Go over the outlines again with a pencil, ballpoint pen or scriber, pressing hard to push the lines into the paper. A layer of newspaper underneath helps to provide a "giving" surface.

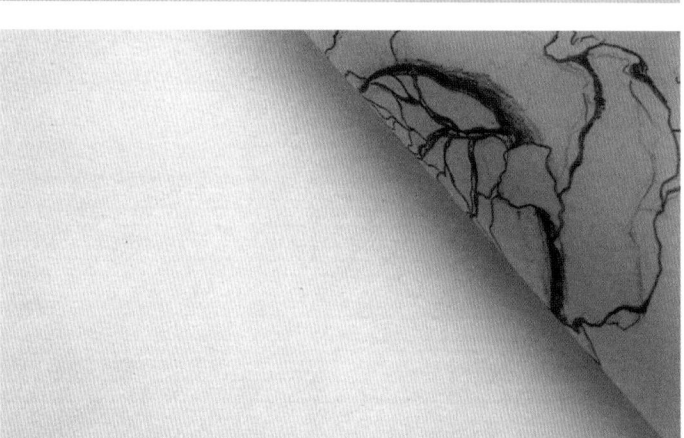

3 Turn back the top sheet to check whether the impression shows clearly on the drawing paper. Keep the keyline drawing accurately in place and retrace lines where necessary.

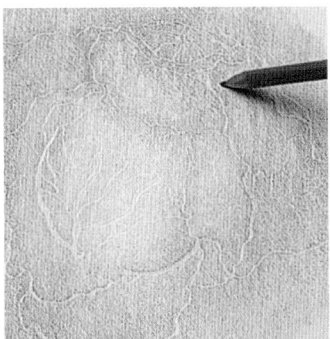

4 When the impressing is complete, remove the top sheet and start to work in colour on the drawing paper. Shade lightly over the impressed lines to allow the image to appear.

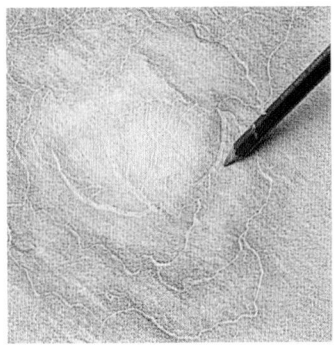

5 Gradually work over specific areas of the drawing with different colours, developing the variations of colour and tone within the outlined shapes. Keep the layers of shading light, to avoid filling the white lines.

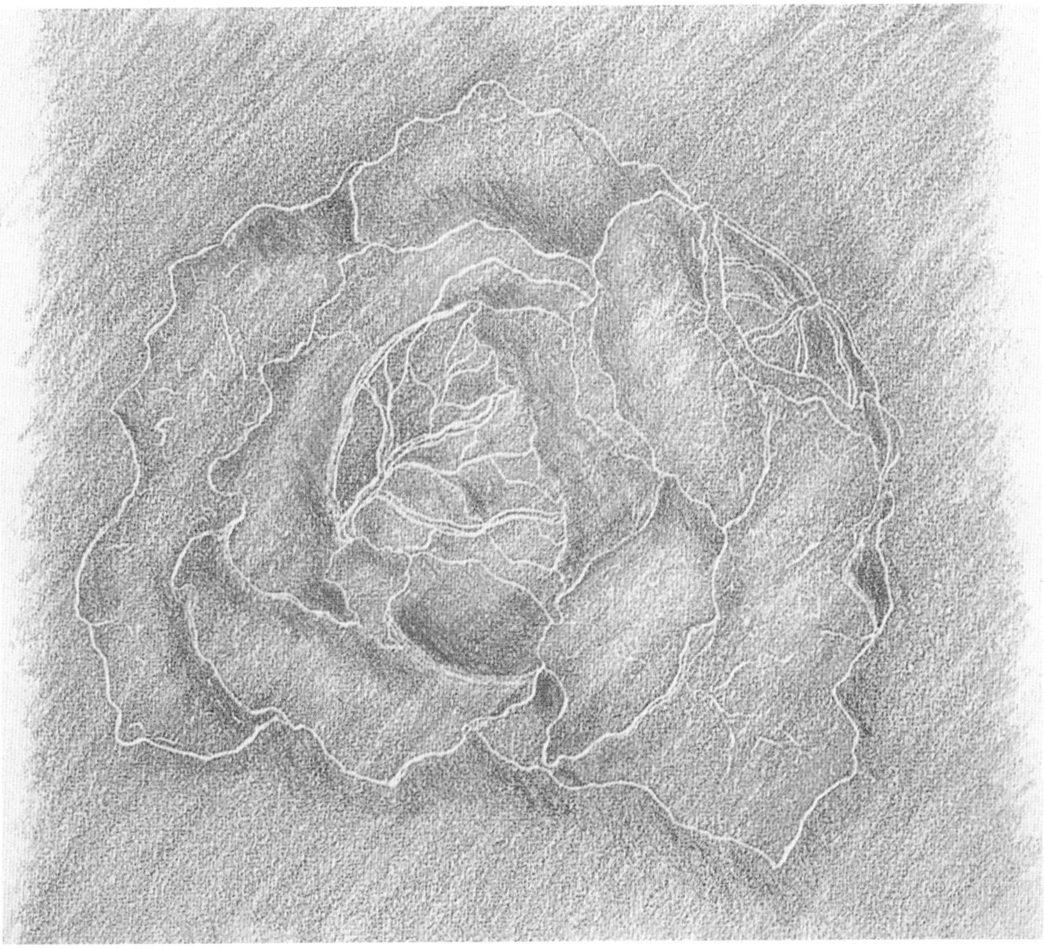

6 The completed drawing shows the structure and texture of the subject, with the folds of the cabbage leaves defined by dark shading. You can plan your drawing to include as much or as little detail as you wish.

Sgraffito

The technique of sgraffito involves scratching into a layer of colour to reveal the underlying surface. In effect, it is a "negative" drawing process, as you create linear structures and surface textures by removing colour, rather than by applying it.

To achieve the effect with coloured pencils, you first lay down a solid block of colour by shading heavily with the tip of the pencil (see pages 22–25). You then apply a second layer of a different colour over the top, again built up solidly so that it covers the lower layer uniformly. The sgraffito drawing can then be made with a stylus, or with the point or edge of a craft-knife blade.

An alternative method is to shade pencil colour over a thick ground previously applied to the paper. An emulsion primer or gesso base can be applied to paper or cardboard as the ground for the sgraffito. (As this dampens paper and may cause it to buckle, it is advisable to stretch it first.) This technique can be used in a similar way to scraperboard, to etch an image through a dark colour, or you can apply a tinted ground and overlay a contrasting colour.

1 Build up the pencil colours quite thickly and freely, using dense shading – the technique works best with soft, waxy pencils on fairly smooth-textured paper. Follow the general lines of your subject and the variations of colour and shading.

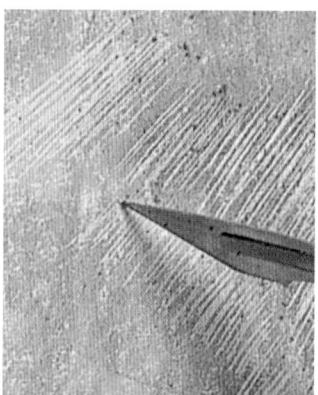

2 Start "drawing" into the colour with a sharp blade. Scratch the colour gently, taking care not to dig the blade into the paper surface. Faint lines are scratched back here to suggest the texture of the leek.

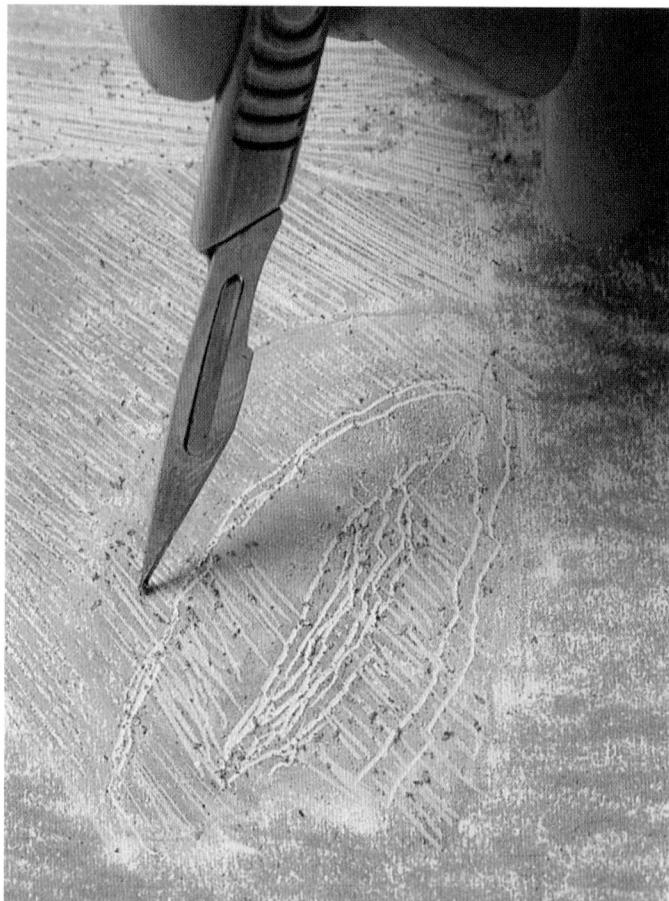

3 To emphasize contour lines and structural elements in the drawing, angle the blade to lift a thicker line of colour, revealing more white. You may find it easiest to turn the paper when tracing an irregular contour, rather than to manipulate the blade around awkward curves.

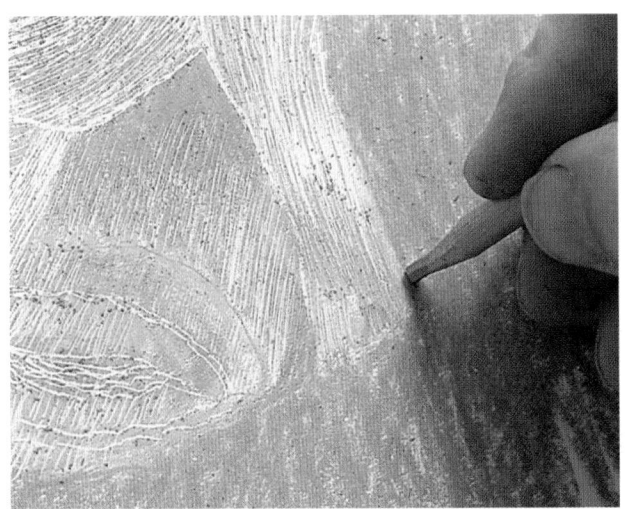

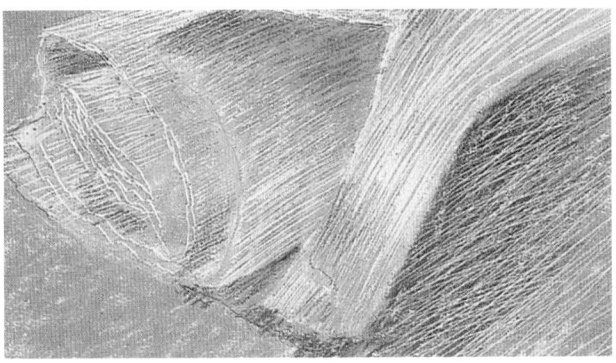

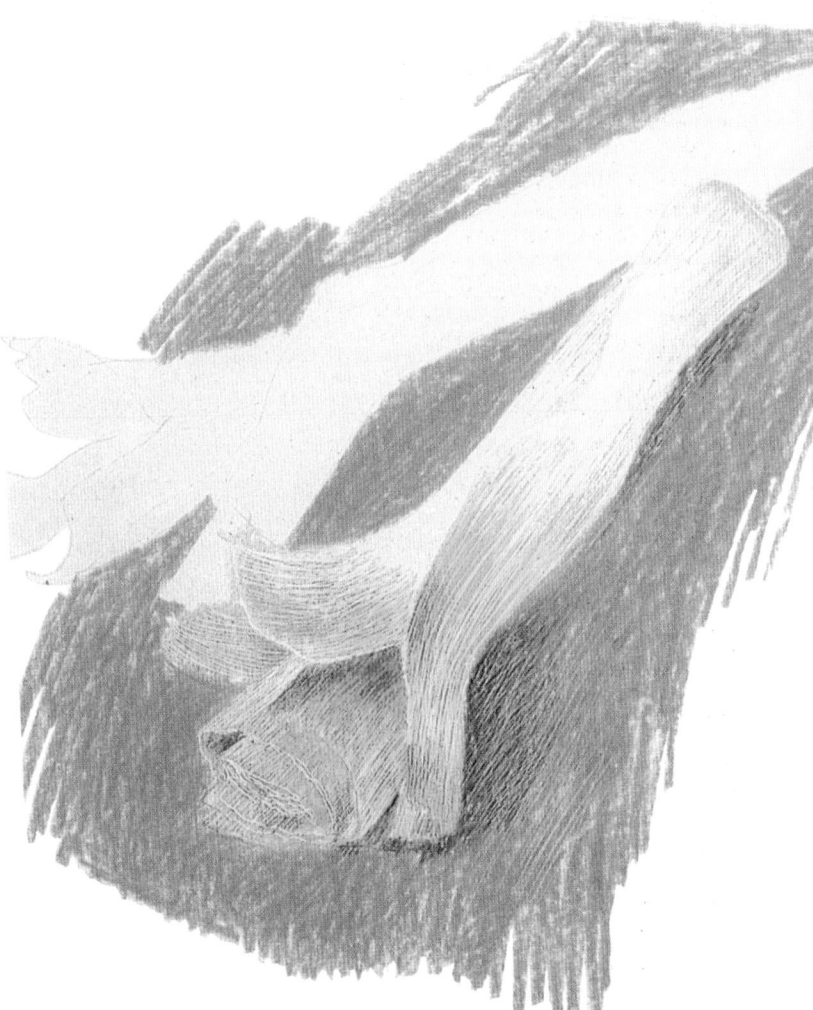

4 As the sgraffito drawing progresses, parts of the image are reworked with coloured pencils to give depth to the shadows and intensify the colours. You can also correct errors this way.

5 The technique is best suited to a subject that has a distinctive linear framework or texture. In this example, the sgraffito has been used to model both the rolled layers of the leek and the veiny leaf texture.

Frottage

This technique consists of shading with a pencil on a piece of paper laid over a textured surface; an impression of the underlying texture comes through. Because coloured pencil leads are quite fine and responsive, you can obtain detailed effects from all kinds of material – wood, brick or stone; engraved or embossed metal, glass or plastic, or fabrics with a coarse, woven mesh.

The frottage can create an abstract pattern to enliven colour areas, or it can be used to simulate the actual material. An even texture such as that of hessian, for instance, forms an effect similar to dense crosshatching; you can build up its complexity by shifting the paper slightly and reworking with a second colour. Wood grain reproduces very effectively – if the subject of your drawing includes a wooden floor or table, you can take an impression of wood texture in a dark tone, then work into the grain pattern with a range of colours to create a very naturalistic effect.

The rubbing can be made directly on the relevant area of your drawing or it can be inserted as a collaged element.

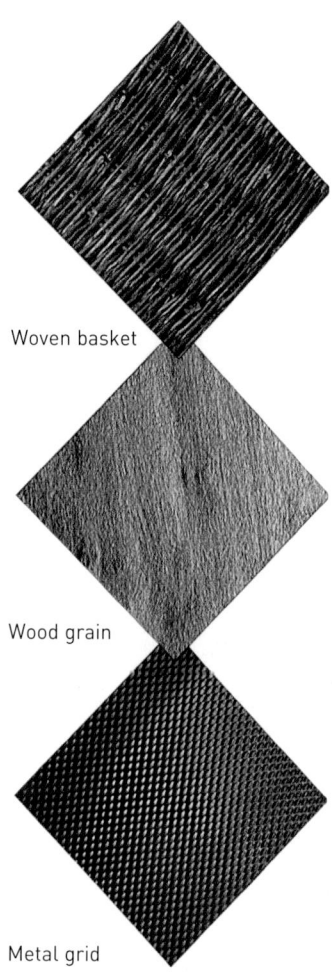

Woven basket

Wood grain

Metal grid

Materials for frottage
It is possible to obtain detailed effects from all kinds of materials.

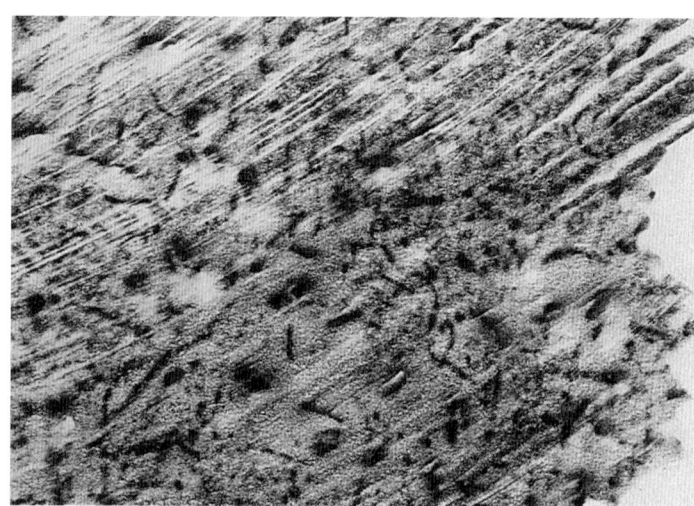

Textured wallcovering
This rubbing from a section of wood-chip wallpaper found in an ordinary domestic interior produces a broken, irregular texture that could be used to simulate natural weathered stone or rough concrete.

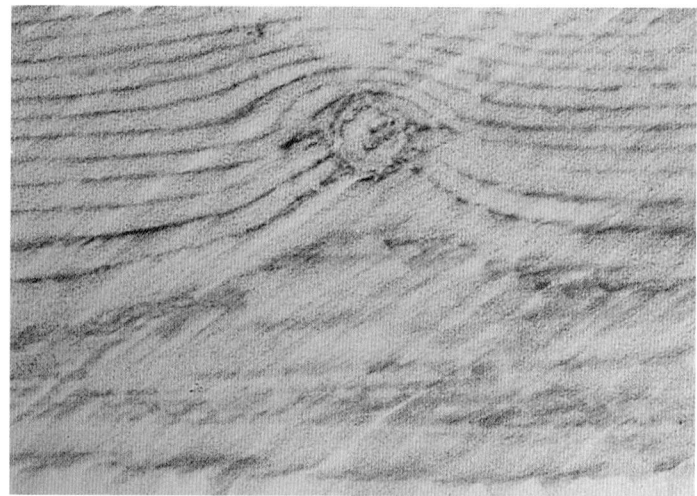

Wood grain
Some types of finished wood, as used for shelving and furniture, for example, are too smooth to provide good surfaces for rubbing. This example comes from an old wooden plank broken off from a garden fence. The knot and grain come up very clearly.

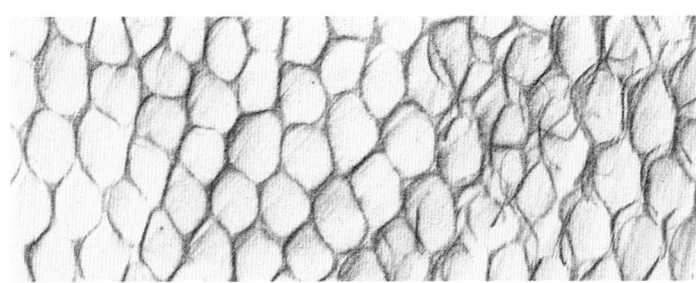

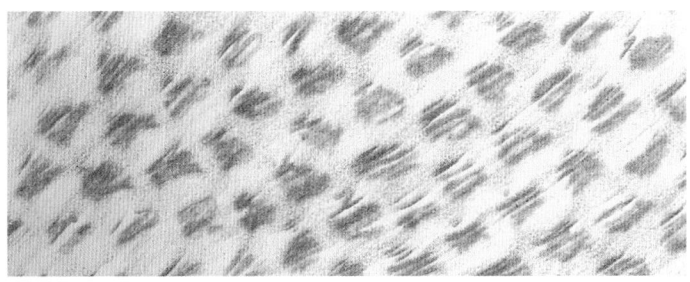

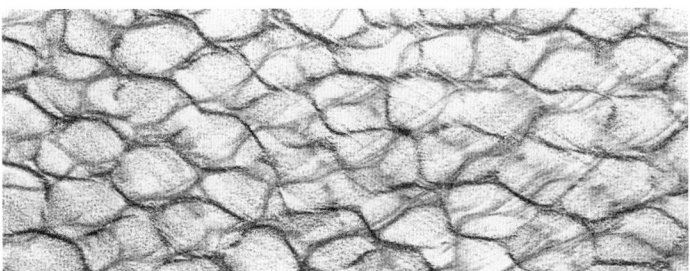

Textured glass

Window glass with a lumpy, "pebble" texture produces an interestingly graphic network of colour (above). On the other side of the glass, the swellings and hollows are reversed and the frottage forms a kind of leopard-spot pattern (above right). Two colours overlaid, using the front of the glass to give the texture, create a fluid, rippling pattern of interwoven lines (left) that could form a pictorial equivalent for the surface of flowing water.

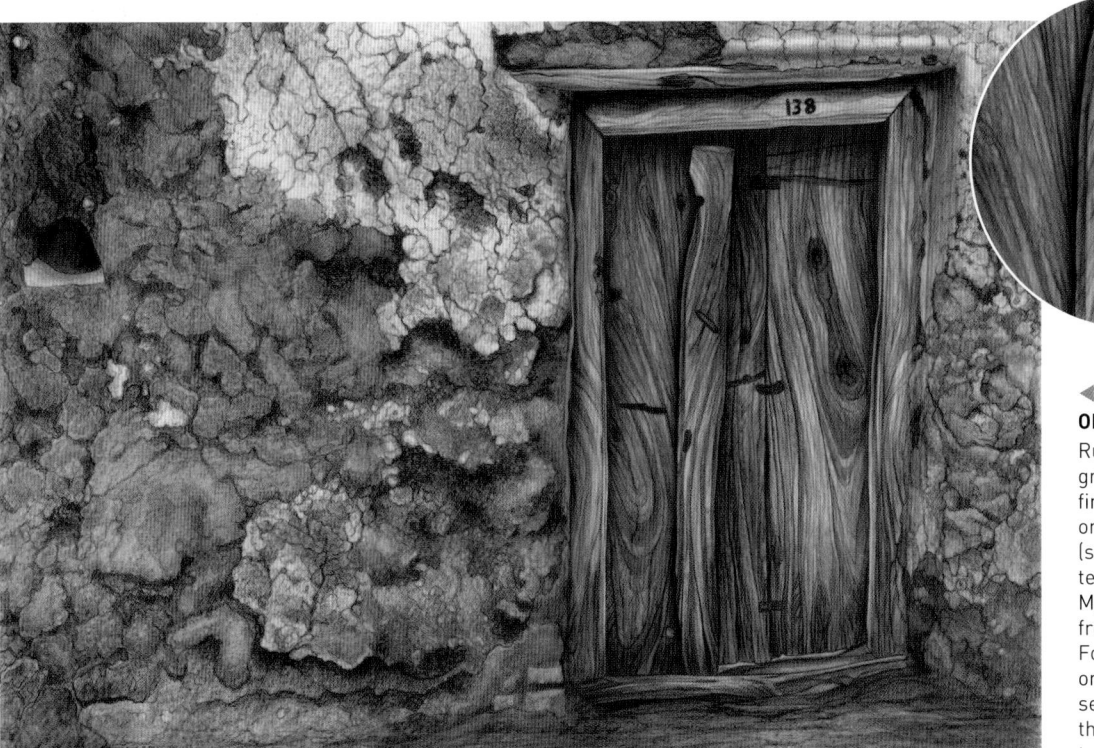

◄ **PAMELA BELCHER**
ONE THREE EIGHT

Rubbings from several different grits of sandpaper and a sheet of finely dotted glass were applied on both sides of the drafting film (see pages 82–83) to create the texture of the house exterior. Myriad fine lines drawn on the front side defines more texture. For the door, pigment was applied on both sides by stroking in several different directions with the side of the pencil without trying to make an even, solid tone.

Masking

A mask is anything that protects the surface of your drawing and prevents colour from being applied to a specific area. The simplest form of mask is a piece of paper laid on your drawing paper; the pencil can travel up to or over the edge of the paper, and when you lift the mask, the colour area has a clean, straight edge. You can obtain hard edges using cut paper; torn paper makes a softer edge quality. You can also use thin card, or pre-cut plastic templates such as stencils and French curves.

If it is important to mask off a specific shape or outline, which may be irregular or intricate, you can use a low-tack transparent masking film which adheres to the paper while you work but lifts cleanly afterwards without tearing the surface. You lay a sheet of masking film over the whole image area and cut out the required shape with a fine scalpel blade. Carefully handled, the blade does not mark the paper beneath. Low-tack masking tapes can also be used to outline shapes; they are available in a range of widths, and the narrower ones are very flexible for masking curves.

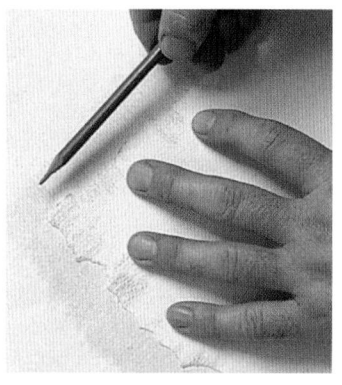
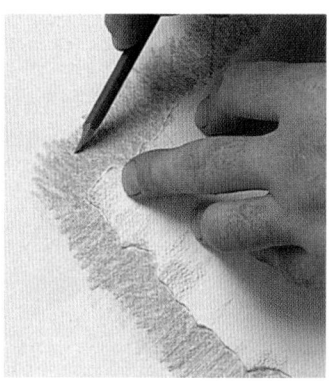

Loose masking
1 Place the paper mask on the drawing paper and hold it down firmly. Begin by shading lightly over the edges of the mask.

2 Build up the shaded colour to the required density, keeping the direction of the pencil marks consistent at each side of the mask.

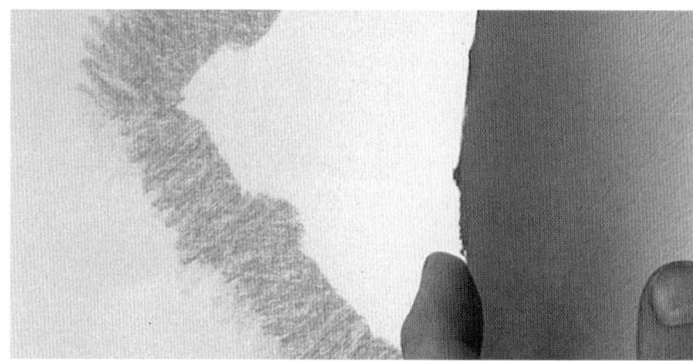

3 Lift the top corner of the mask to check that you have a clean edge quality and the right intensity of colour. Keep the lower edge of the mask in place, so you can just drop it back if you need to rework the colour area.

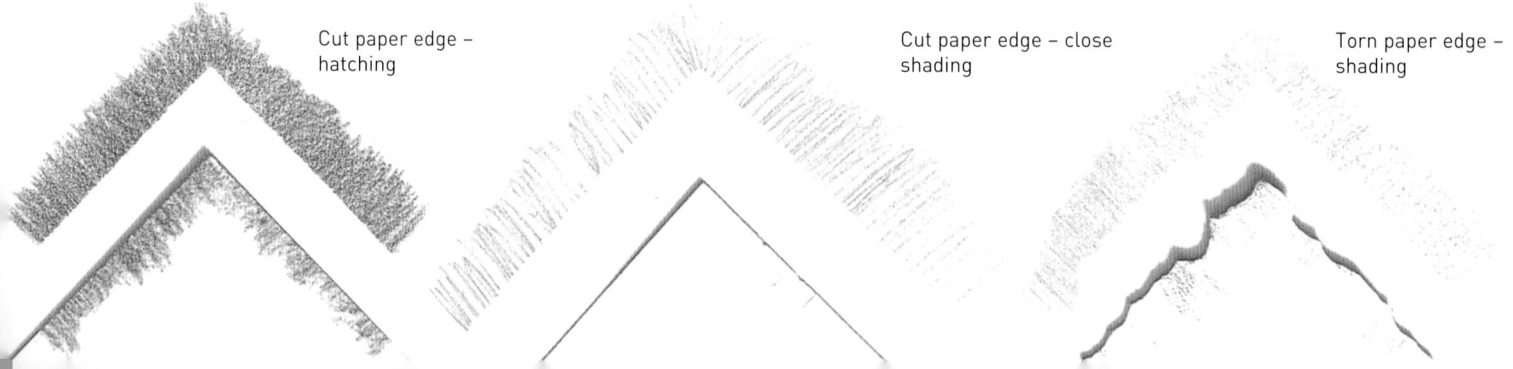

Cut paper edge – hatching

Cut paper edge – close shading

Torn paper edge – shading

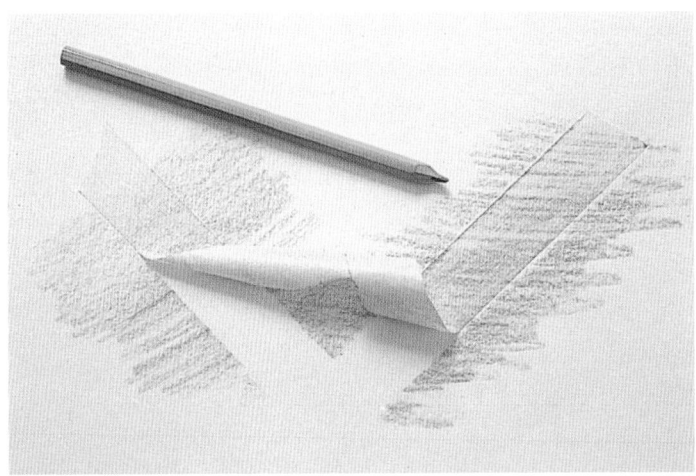

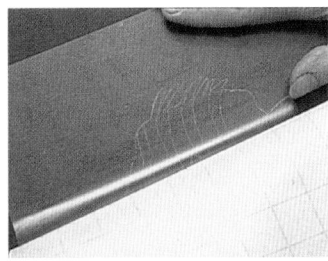

Using masking film

1 Trace down the outline of your drawing on paper. Detach the top edge of the masking film from its backing sheet and smooth it down on the paper, covering the image area with a border of film all around. Gradually pull back the rest of the backing sheet, smoothing the film across the paper as you go.

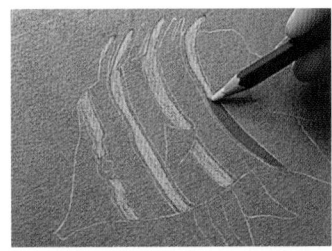

2 Identify the first shapes you are going to colour and cut round them with a sharp scalpel blade. Lift one corner of the cut film and peel back the shape. Repeat as necessary.

Apply the coloured pencil to each shape, filling it with colour up to and over the masked edges.

Using masking tape

1 Lay down the masking tape evenly but do not rub too firmly, or you may have trouble lifting it without damaging the paper surface. Shade colour over the edges of the tape, as with the paper masks. An advantage of masking tape is that you can work over both sides of the tape at once if required. When complete, peel back the tape carefully.

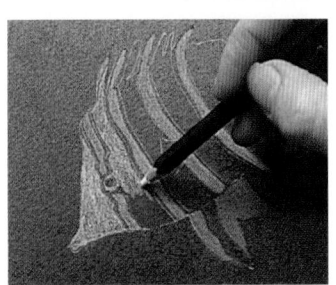

3 When you have completed all the areas in one colour, move on to the next. Cut and lift the mask sections in sequence, then shade in the colour.

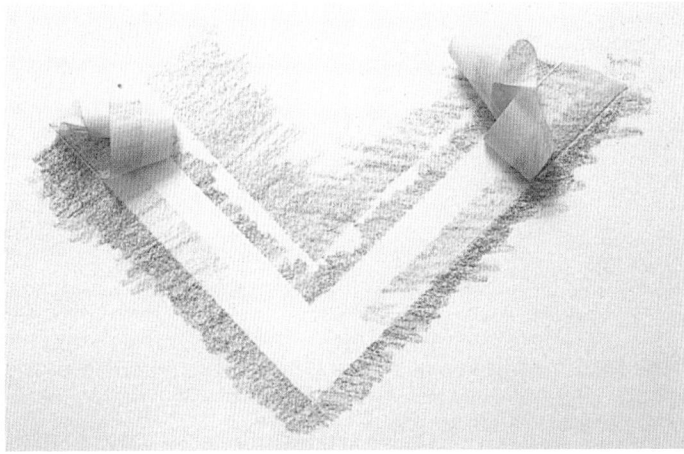

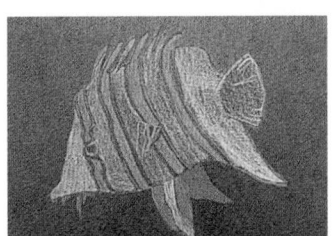

4 At this stage the colouring is complete, and the uncut masking film is still on the paper, causing the black background to look greyed. The next stage is to remove the remaining masking film completely.

2 If you are overlaying colours, you can use the same mask or a fresh piece of tape to cover the paper while you lay in the second colour.

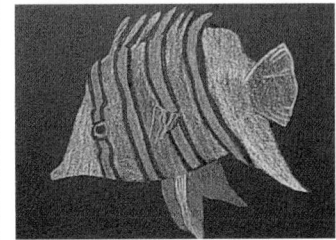

5 Compare the finished effect to step 4. With the mask removed, the edges of the coloured areas stand out sharply against the blacks, making each shape clean and distinct.

Graphite Pencil

Graphite pencils and coloured pencils are natural partners, since they are drawing tools of exactly the same shape which are handled in the same ways. Every artist finds different values in exploiting mixed-media techniques for particular purposes. A technical advantage of incorporating graphite with coloured pencils is the range in quality of graphite leads – you can obtain varied characteristics from the fine silvery greys of H and HB pencils to the increasingly strong, intense blacks of the softer B series. Because graphite is a slightly greasy substance, and more gritty than coloured pencil leads, it gives a different kind of line quality, and the dark tones are not the same as those produced by coloured pencils containing black pigments.

You can either mix the two kinds of pencils freely or use the graphite to create a monochrome drawing which you then "glaze" over with colour by shading in coloured pencil. Both media are highly responsive to delicate and vigorous handling, and are easily applied to a wide variety of paper types.

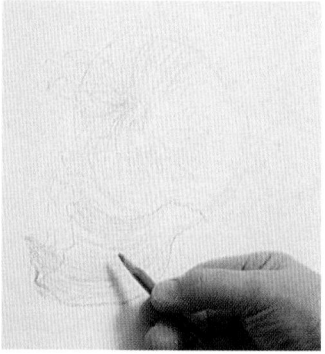

1 When producing a drawing which integrates the graphite and coloured pencil textures, begin working with the graphite to set the linear framework and dark tones.

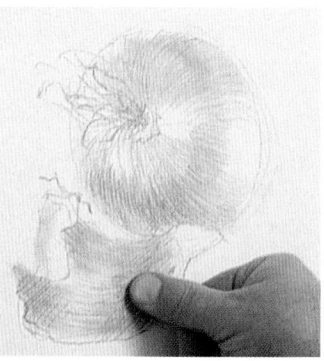

2 Soft graphite spreads easily when rubbed with the fingers. In this example, the shadow areas are softened by rubbing.

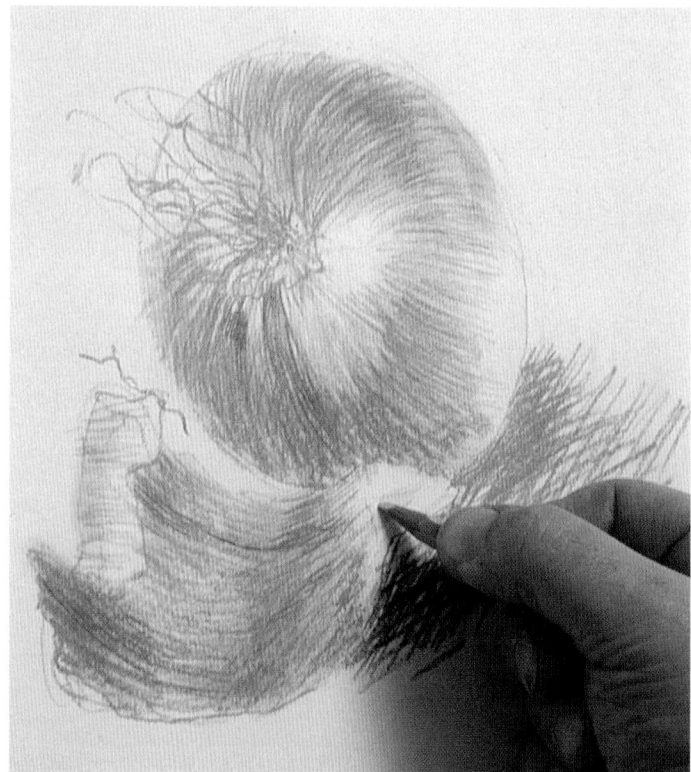

3 The basic range of colours on the onion is introduced with light shading and hatching in yellow, yellow ochre and burnt sienna.

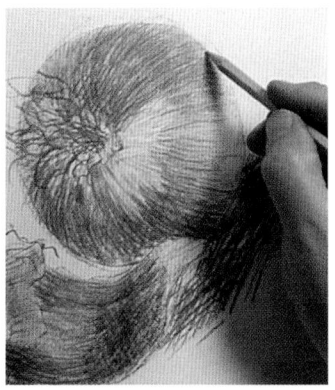 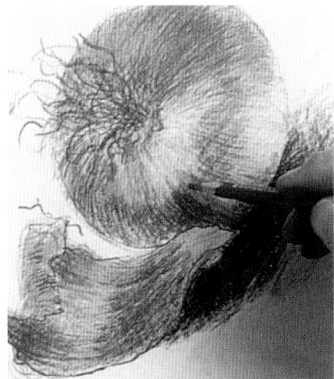

4 As the drawing progresses, further colours are applied to obtain the subtler hues and shadow colours. The textures of the graphite and coloured pencils are allowed to mix freely.

5 The colour is built up gradually to develop solid form. The graphite pencil is used again to sharpen some of the line detail in the drawing, enhancing the veined effect of the onion skin. Notice that the cast shadow has been strengthened with dark brown and grey shading.

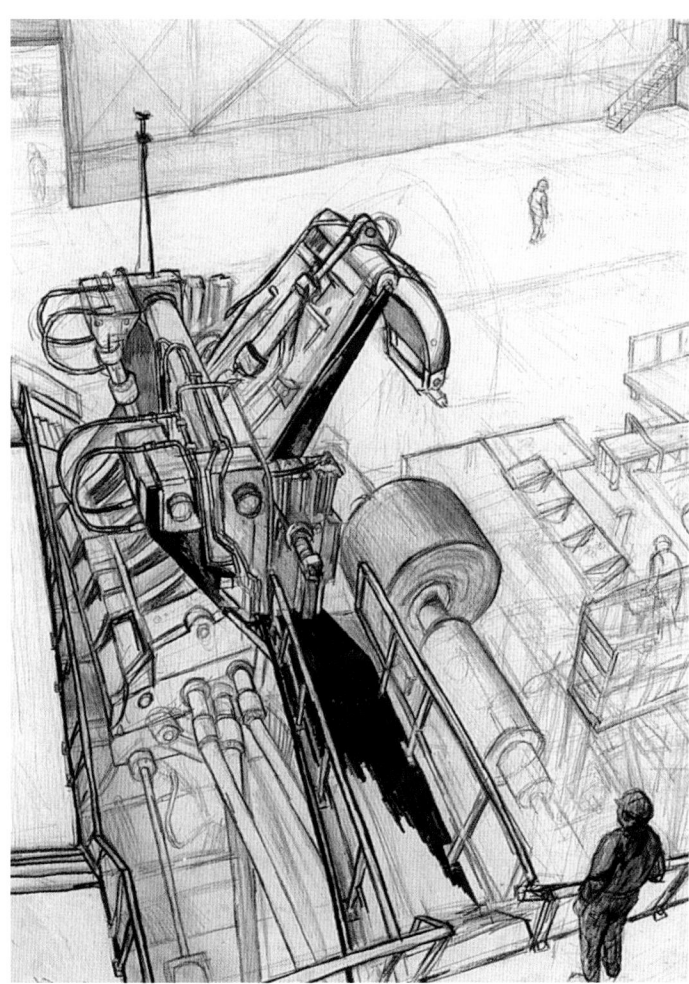

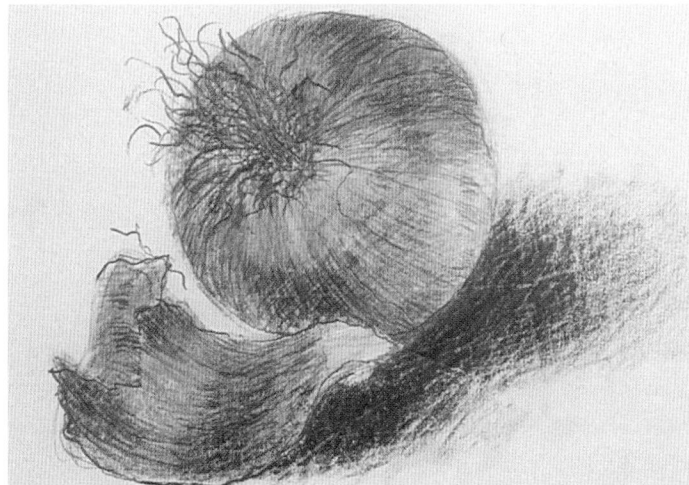

6 In the finished drawing, the graphite lines and shading describe the basic shapes, texture and dark shadow, while the coloured pencils contribute local colour and highlighting.

▲ **PHILIP STANTON**
BRITISH STEEL

In this drawing the artist has used graphite pencil to sketch out the complex framework of the composition and establish the relationship of forms. The tones and linear detail have been strengthened with black pencil, and colours have been introduced where appropriate. When a subject presents a difficult perspective or elaborate structure, as in this example, using graphite pencil enablesthe artist to draw freely, and erase and correct before they apply colour. The graphite lines further contribute lively calligraphic styling and textural contrasts.

Ink and Pencil

Black ink line has a fluidity and clarity that marries well with the bright colours and soft textures of coloured pencil. It provides a clean, graphic framework that supports the colour work. You can combine the different line qualities of the media and integrate them using tonal techniques such as hatching, shading and stippling.

Like coloured pencils, pens and inks provide a wide range of visual properties, from the fine, uniform line of technical pens and rapid, flowing action of fibre-tip pens to the sensitive variability of dip pens with pointed or squared nibs. Black drawing inks are dense and velvety, while writing inks often have subtle blue or sepia tints. You can also combine coloured pencils with the extensive palette provided by coloured drawing inks in similar ways.

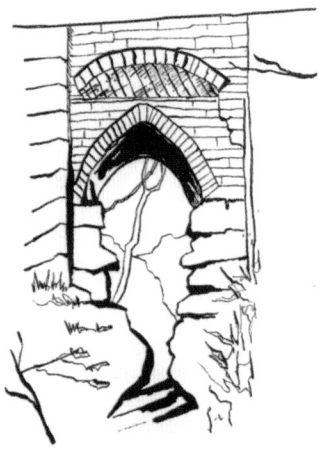

1 A simple outline drawing of the view is constructed using black waterproof ink and a dip pen with two different types of nibs. The intention is to create a strong graphic framework for the image, and then to add colour and texture with the pencils.

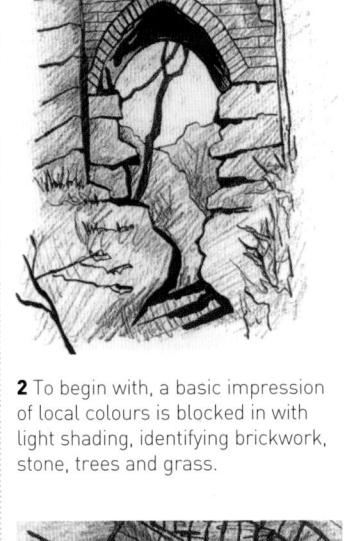

2 To begin with, a basic impression of local colours is blocked in with light shading, identifying brickwork, stone, trees and grass.

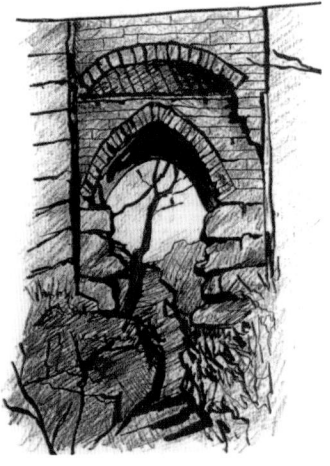

3 Each area is given more textural interest by overlaying hatching, shading and linear marks and gradually increasing the range of colours used.

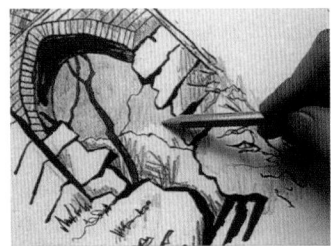

4 The waxy texture of the pencils has softened the blacks where colour has been freely worked into the drawing. More drawing is done with pen and ink to sharpen and strengthen the linear textures.

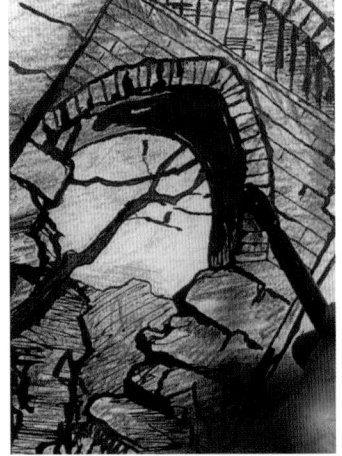

5 With the increasing density of both media, the drawing has a more cohesive effect, with a livelier interplay between the black line and pencil colour. None of the detail is "realistic" (see right), but the drawing has a descriptive character.

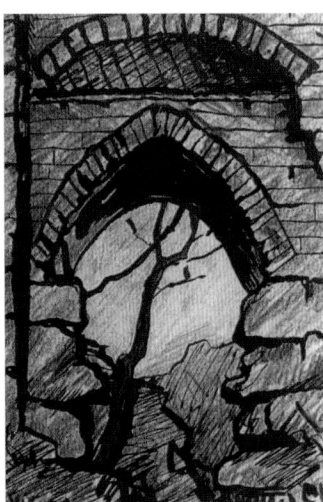

Line and Wash

Traditionally a technique associated with pen and ink drawing, line and wash is a method of adding tone and colour to an image with a strong linear framework. The lines create the structure of the composition; modelling and colour detail are then introduced with washes of diluted ink or watercolour.

Lines made with ink or graphite pencil are typically black or very dark in colour, standing out quite strongly against the fluid, paler areas of wash. If you use coloured pencils for the line element, they contribute a new dimension in which you can use colour to enhance the impressions of space and form created in the initial drawing, or to emphasize a mood. You can flood the washes into and over the coloured pencil lines, and when they have dried you can use the pencils again to rework basic structures and develop the detail. Remember that working over colour washes will somewhat modify the intensity of the pencil hues.

A very direct way of exploiting this technique is to use water-soluble pencils, used dry for drawing, then brushed over with clean water. In this way the texture of the line and wash elements are more closely integrated.

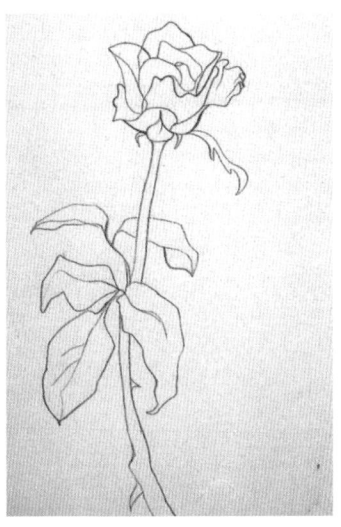

Using water-soluble pencils
1 Make an outline drawing of your subject with firm lines and strong colours. The line needs to be quite heavy, as you will be using the pencil pigment to create the wash.

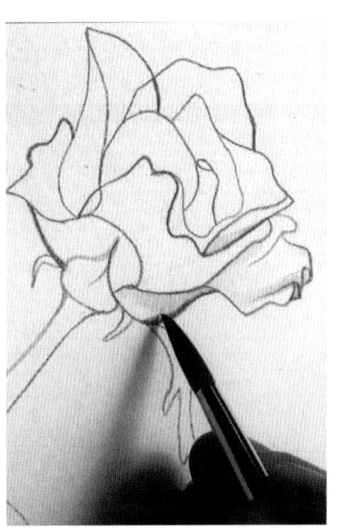

2 Moisten a fine sable or synthetic, soft-haired brush with clean water. Brush just inside the pencilled line, picking up and spreading the colour into the shape.

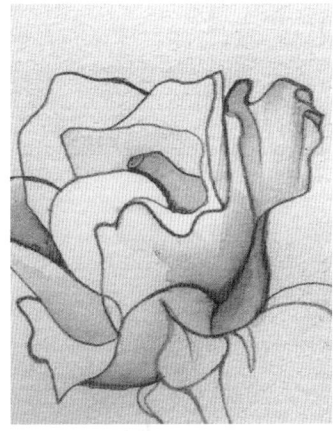

3 Continue in the same way, gradually shading and blending the colours to produce a range of hue and tone. If you do not have enough intensity in one area, go over the pencil line again and dissolve more of its colour with the brush tip.

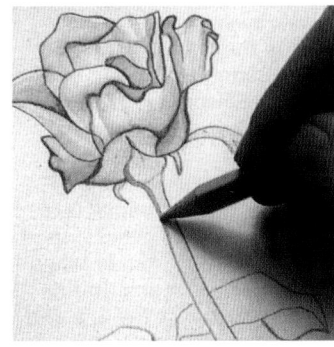

4 At each stage of the drawing you can choose whether to strengthen the line work or deepen the washed colour. Be careful when working in water-soluble pencil over a wash, because the moisture softens the pencil tip and spreads the line.

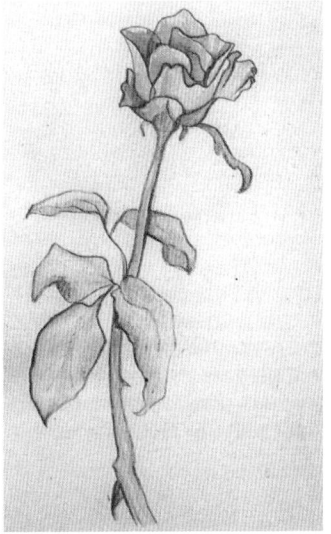

5 This approach to line and wash drawing produces a delicate colour effect, as the washed colour is relatively lightweight. To produce a denser, more graphic image, use paint washes.

Pastel and Pencil

Like coloured pencils, pastels can be manipulated to exploit their linear qualities or to produce colour masses and complex surface textures, so a combination of the two media is generally sympathetic. Another thing that these media have in common is that there are different types of both, caused by variations in the composition of the binder that holds the pigment, and qualities also vary between different brands.

There is no specific recipe for mixed-media work; individual artists develop personalized methods that produce effects suited to their style and subject matter.

The different types of pastels are soft pastels, hard pastels, oil pastels, water-soluble pastels and pastel pencils. All combine readily with coloured pencils and contribute varying qualities of colour and texture. The greasy texture of oil pastel is more resistant to coloured pencil than the dry, powdery finish of soft and hard pastels, but you will find that effects differ according to the properties of the particular brands you are using, the pressure you apply and the density of the colour build-up.

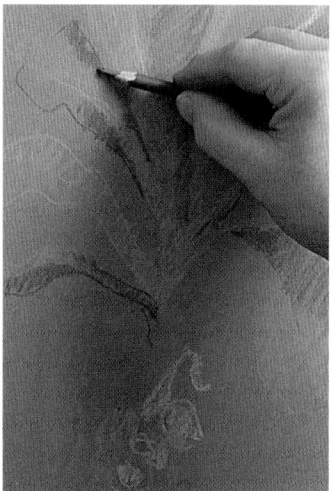

1 The drawing is loosely blocked in with soft pastels and pastel pencils to create grainy blocks of colour establishing the general shapes of the plant's leaves and stem.

2 Waxy pencil is used to define the contours of the leaves and develop a sharper, more distinct image.

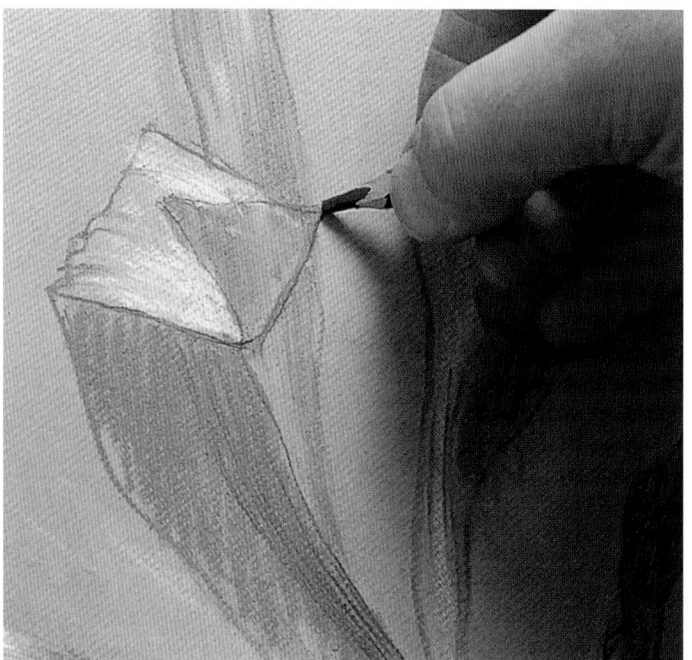

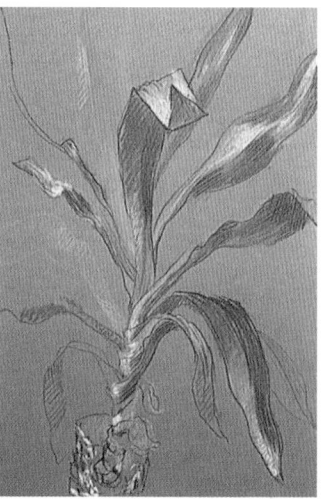

3 Details of the textural qualities of the leaves and stems are enhanced with line work and shading, laid in with waxy and chalky pencils.

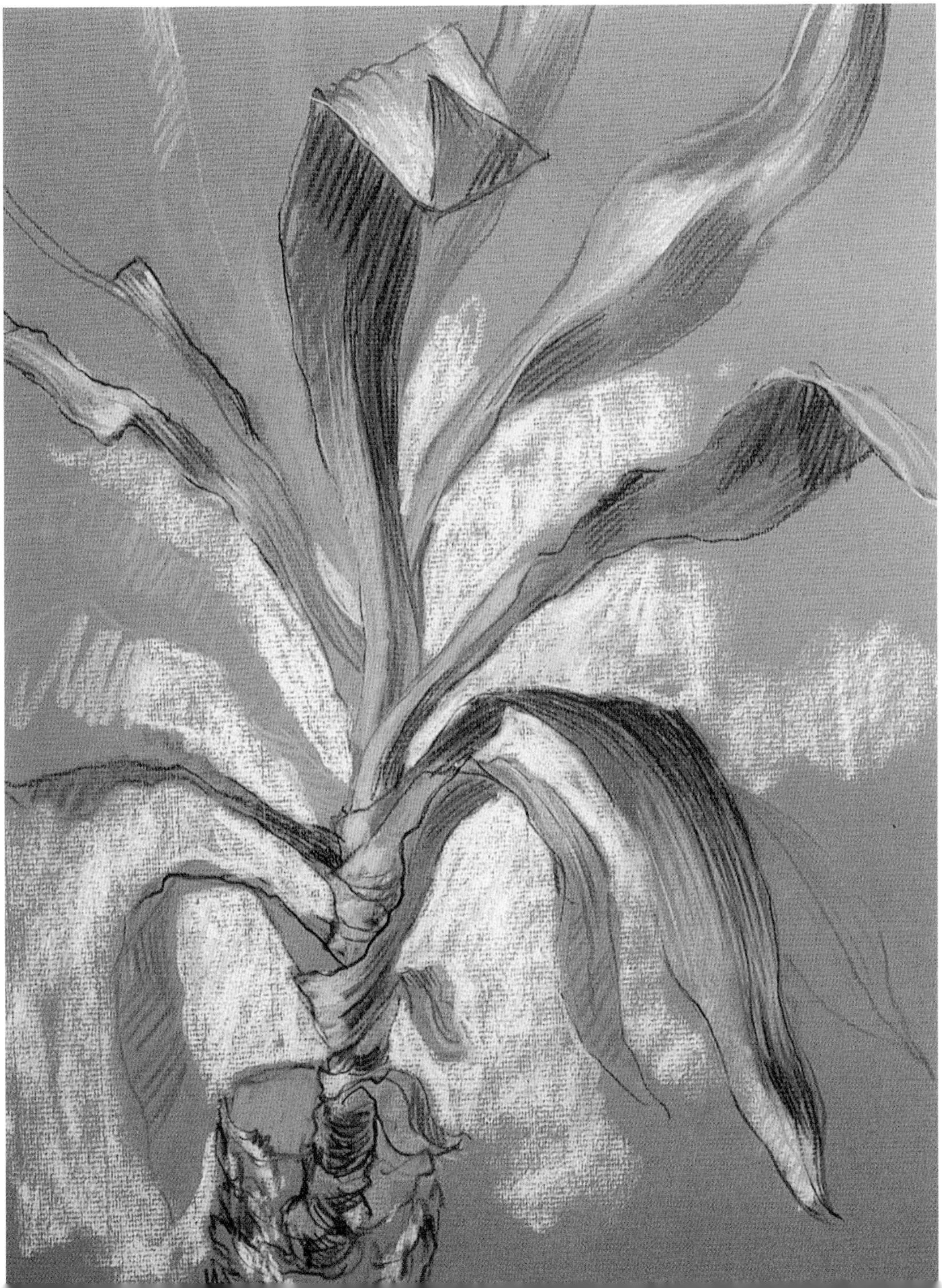

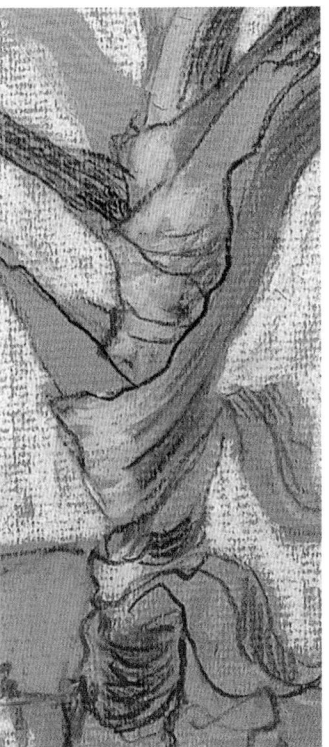

4 With the structure of the plant more clearly defined by the pencil work, soft pastel is again used to introduce highlight areas and block in a pale background. The contrast of hard line and grainy colour (see detail above) gives richness and depth to the rendering.

Watercolour and Pencil

Watercolour is a translucent paint medium that combines well with the clear hues of coloured pencils. The two media can be loosely integrated in free, impressionistic images or used in a more formal way to create finely structured colour drawings.

The clean, crisp line qualities that you can achieve with coloured pencils form a striking visual contrast with fluid brushstrokes and washes laid in with watercolour. An interesting effect comes from applying water-soluble pencils while the paint layers are still damp; the moisture softens the pencil tip, encouraging broad, brilliantly coloured marks. Be careful when working into watercolour with non-soluble pencil types, however, as the pencil point is likely to tear the wetted paper surface. If you wish to apply detailed line work, wait for the watercolour washes to dry completely.

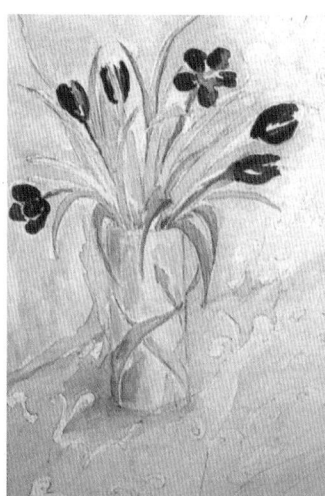

1 You can begin by blocking in direct in watercolour, or you can start with a coloured pencil outline and paint into it. Here a faint outline has been drawn to establish the composition and the basic colours are freely washed in.

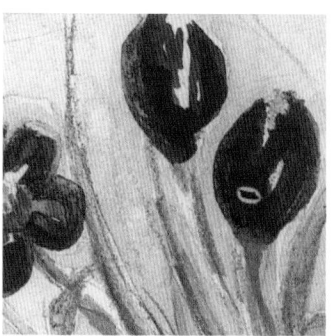

2 Successive washes are overlaid to build up the paint colours, with the linear forms of the stems and leaves strengthened with light shading in waxy coloured pencils.

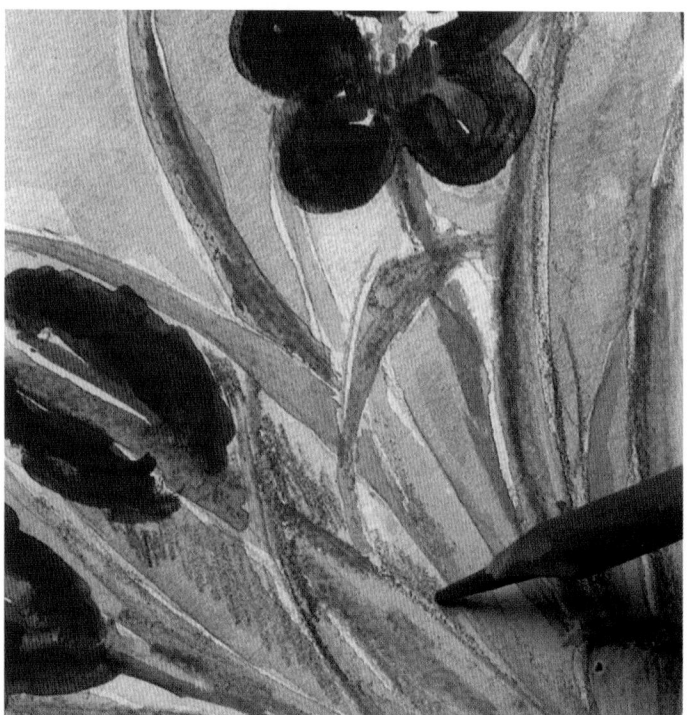

3 Some shading is put in behind the flowers to develop the relationship of shapes against the background. At each stage the technique is quite free, leaving the surface open and workable.

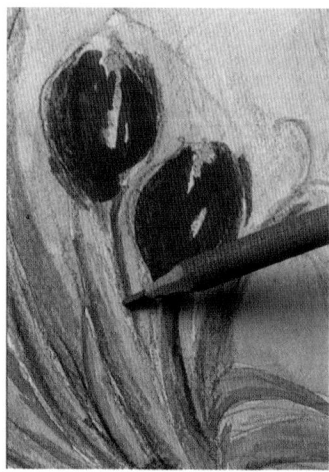

4 The process continues, working back and forth between different shapes to enhance the definition. Avoid drawing over painted areas that are still wet, as the pencil tip could either slide, or tear the paper surface. Allow washes to dry partially before drawing on the colour.

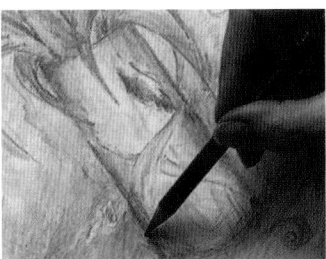

5 Where the initial washes have suggested shadow areas, the pencil shading is built up more strongly to heighten the intensity of colour and tone.

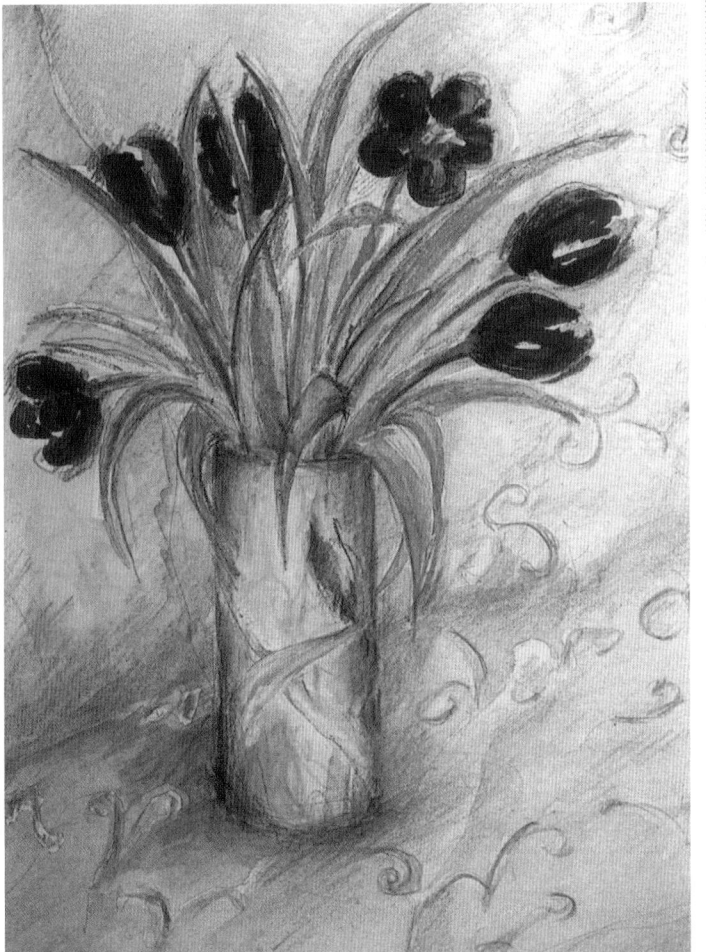

6 The combination of pencil and watercolour allows you to develop a free interpretation. The paint provides the overall impression and the pencil marks emphasize structure and linear detail.

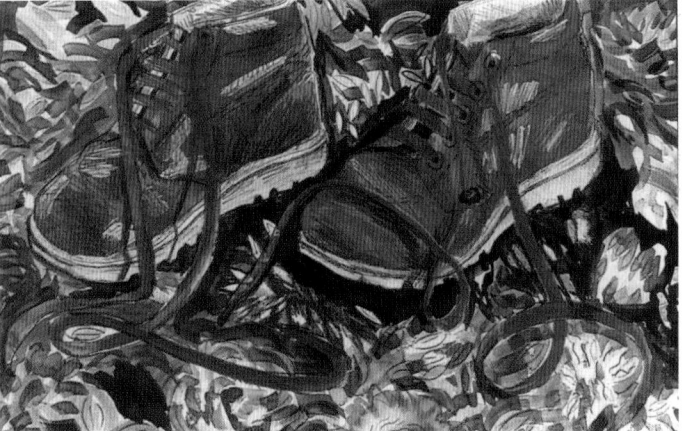

▲ **SARA HAYWARD**
BOOTS
This drawing shows a very vigorous, confident approach to the combined media. The watercolour is built up in layered washes to develop strong hues and the pencils are used to overlay pattern and texture.

Collage

Drawing on a collaged surface extends the principle of working on coloured papers, allowing you to use different colours and textures of paper within a single image. It applies most effectively to subjects which contain distinctive forms and hard-edged shapes – it is a particularly appropriate technique for still life, architectural views and interiors, and also works well for informal portraits.

You can use papers varying from lightweight tissues to coloured cartridge and pastel papers. Tear or cut the papers into the required shapes, assemble them on the base paper and stick them down. You can then work into the image with coloured pencils to develop linear structure and textural detail.

To avoid tearing, especially of fine papers, allow the adhesive to dry before you start to draw. Remember, too, that the thickness of a torn or cut edge will disrupt the path of your pencil slightly, so be careful when working on drawn details that cross between different areas of the collage.

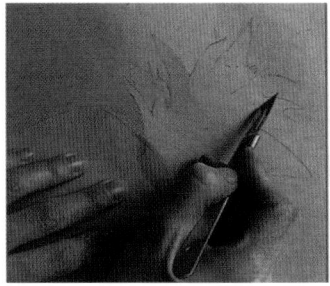

1 The main shapes in the still life are cut out of coloured papers corresponding to the basic colour of each fruit. A brief outline is sketched before cutting, and the first cut shape is used to determine the scale of adjacent shapes, as here with the leafy tuft of the pineapple.

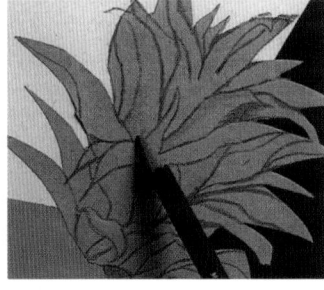

4 Allow your adhesive to dry before drawing over collage — if the paper layers are damp, the pencil point may tear the surface. The drawing begins with detail of the pineapple leaves, using line to define the intricate shapes and introducing tonal shading and colour variations.

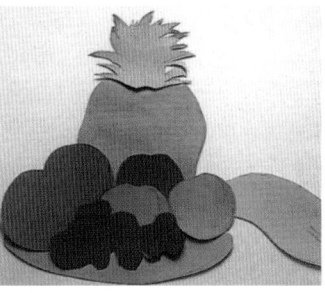

2 When all the main elements are cut out, the pieces are assembled roughly on the backing paper, to get the composition right and check the relationship of shapes.

3 To make a dramatic image, the artist decides to use strong, solid colours to form a simple background. These geometric blocks are cut and pasted down, then the fruits are stuck on one by one to complete the still life. If you use a spray or rubber adhesive, you can lift and reposition the shapes when necessary.

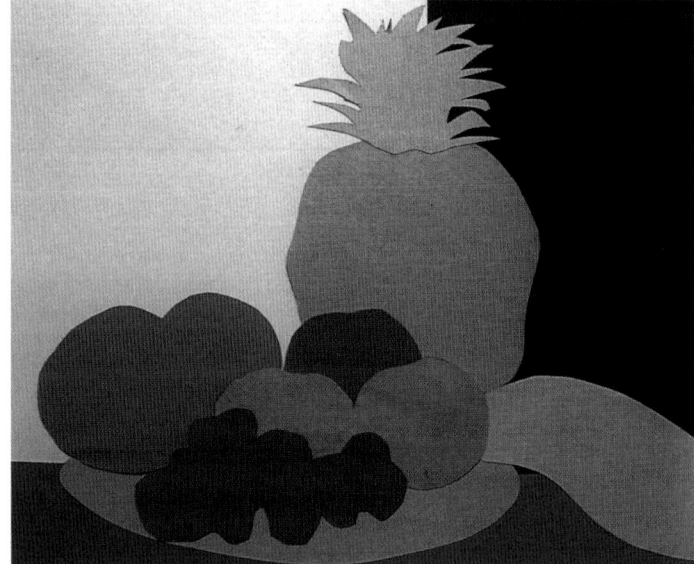

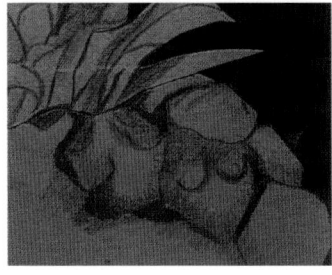

5 The faceted texture of the pineapple skin is treated in the same way, using line work and shading to develop form and texture. Notice that you can apply coloured pencil over the background if you wish, to refine the contour of the original collaged shape.

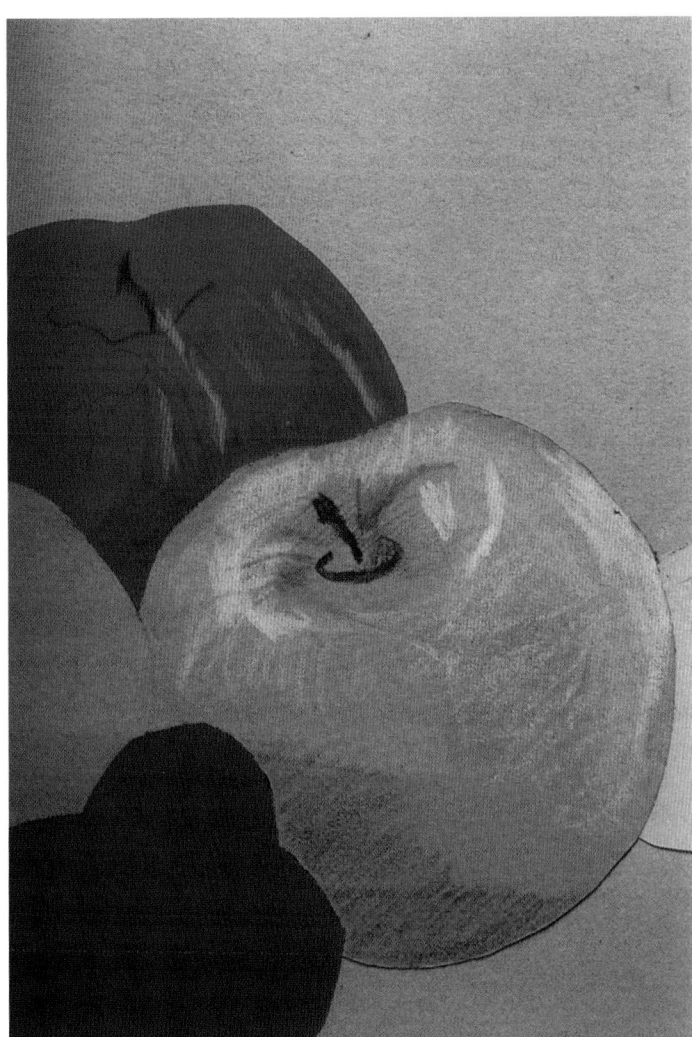

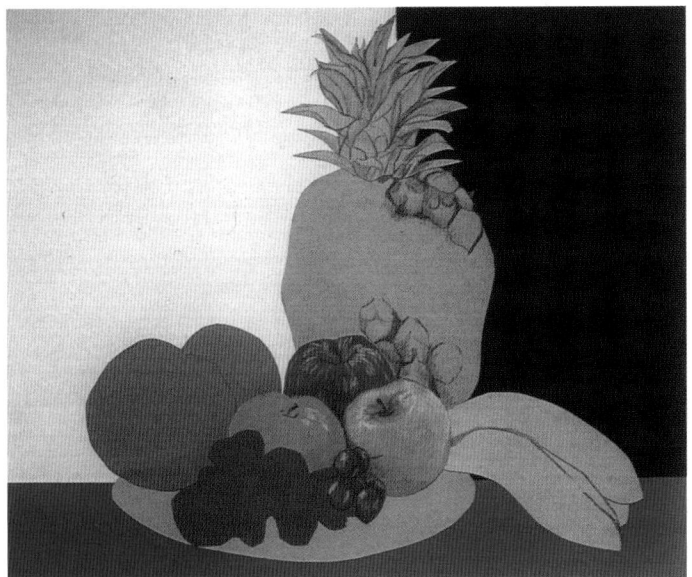

8 The process will continue until all of the fruits are drawn in detail, then any problems with the balance of colour and tone can be corrected with final touches to the coloured pencil drawing.

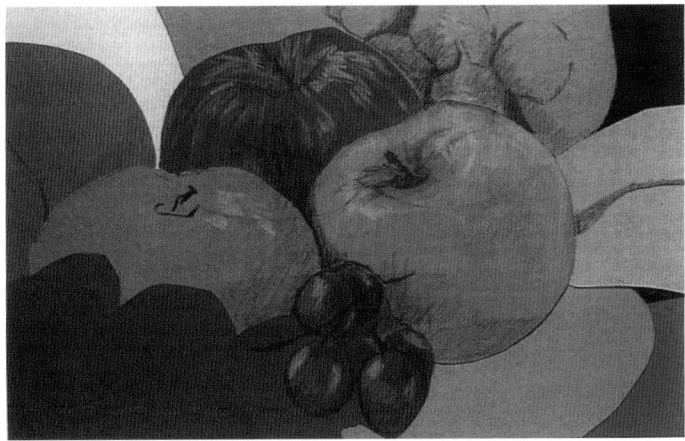

6 The paper colour for the green apple is a good match for its skin colour. Lightweight shading in dark green, white and yellow is applied to model the rounded forms and bring up highlights. The red apple has more complex colour variations, which are stroked in with rapid lines.

7 The drawing mainly adheres to the outlines of the collaged pieces, but contours and shadow areas drawn with dark pencil colours are used to redefine shapes when required.

In the grapes, this technique is used more extensively to create the smaller shapes of the individual fruits and stems within the overall colour area.

Tracing

With some types of coloured pencil drawing, it is important to have a clear, accurate guideline. Extensive corrections and erasures can spoil the paper surface before you begin the colour work, so to avoid this you may wish to produce a working drawing which can then be transferred cleanly to the final drawing paper with no alterations. Similarly, you may wish to trace off the outlines from a photograph as the basis of your composition.

You can do this by the conventional tracing method, drawing around the outlines on tracing paper, scribbling over the back with a graphite pencil or soft pastel, then going over the outlines again to trace the image down on the drawing paper. Alternatively, you can use transfer papers, available in a range of colours. These are thin paper sheets coated on one side with a fine, even layer of "crayon-type" colour. You simply slip the transfer paper, coloured side down, between the tracing and the drawing paper, then go over the outlines again with light pressure using the point of a graphite or coloured pencil. With either method, be careful not to press too hard when retracing the outlines, or you may leave an impressed line on the paper which cannot be eradicated. (See also squaring up or down, page 78.)

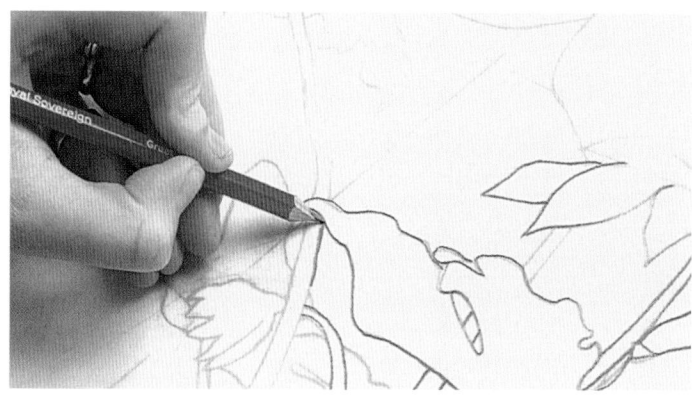

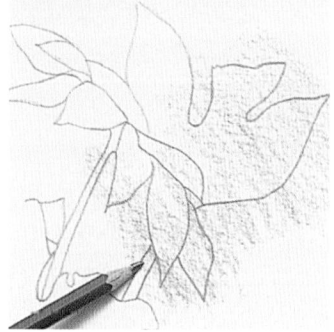

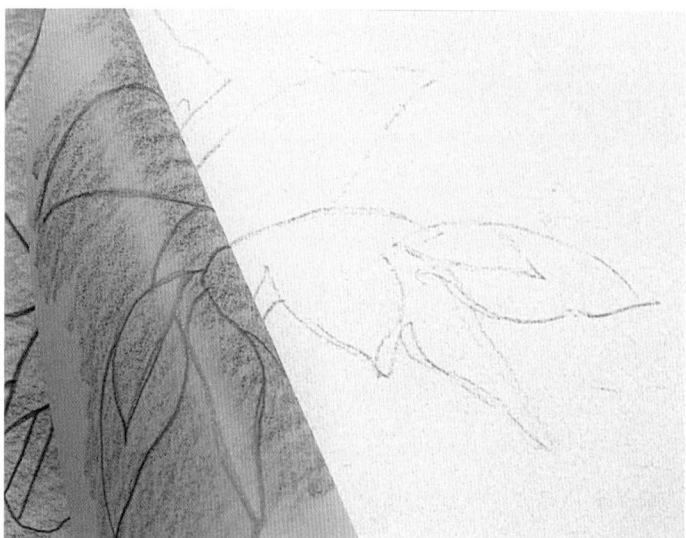

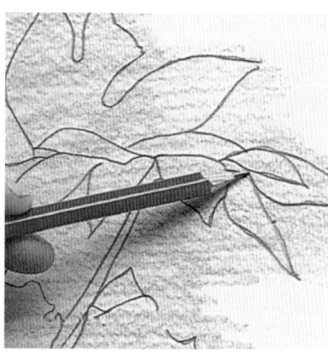

Tracing method
1 Place the tracing paper over your original drawing and follow the main outlines with a firm pencil line.

2 Turn the tracing over and scribble on the back with the pencil, making sure all the lines of the drawing are backed with shaded tone.

3 Place the tracing on a clean sheet of drawing paper and go over all the lines with the pencil point. Don't press too hard, or you will make a permanent impression on the drawing paper.

4 Keep the tracing anchored at one corner so you can lift it to check the quality of the traced line, and return it to the right position. Do not remove it completely until you are sure all the required lines show distinctly.

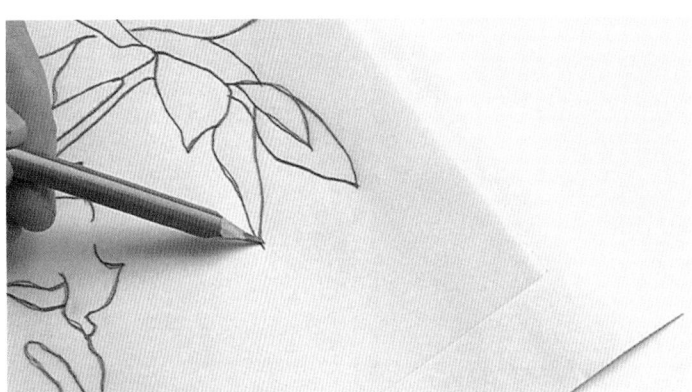

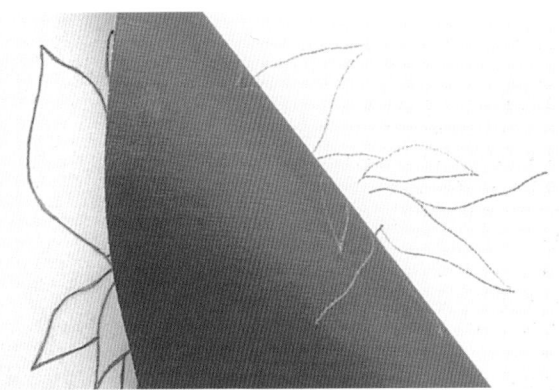

Using transfer paper

1 Make the initial tracing by the conventional method. Place the tracing over the drawing paper, with the transfer paper slipped between the two layers, colour side down. Retrace the image.

2 Lift one corner to check that a complete guideline is being transferred. The powdery line is easily covered as you build up the coloured pencil work.

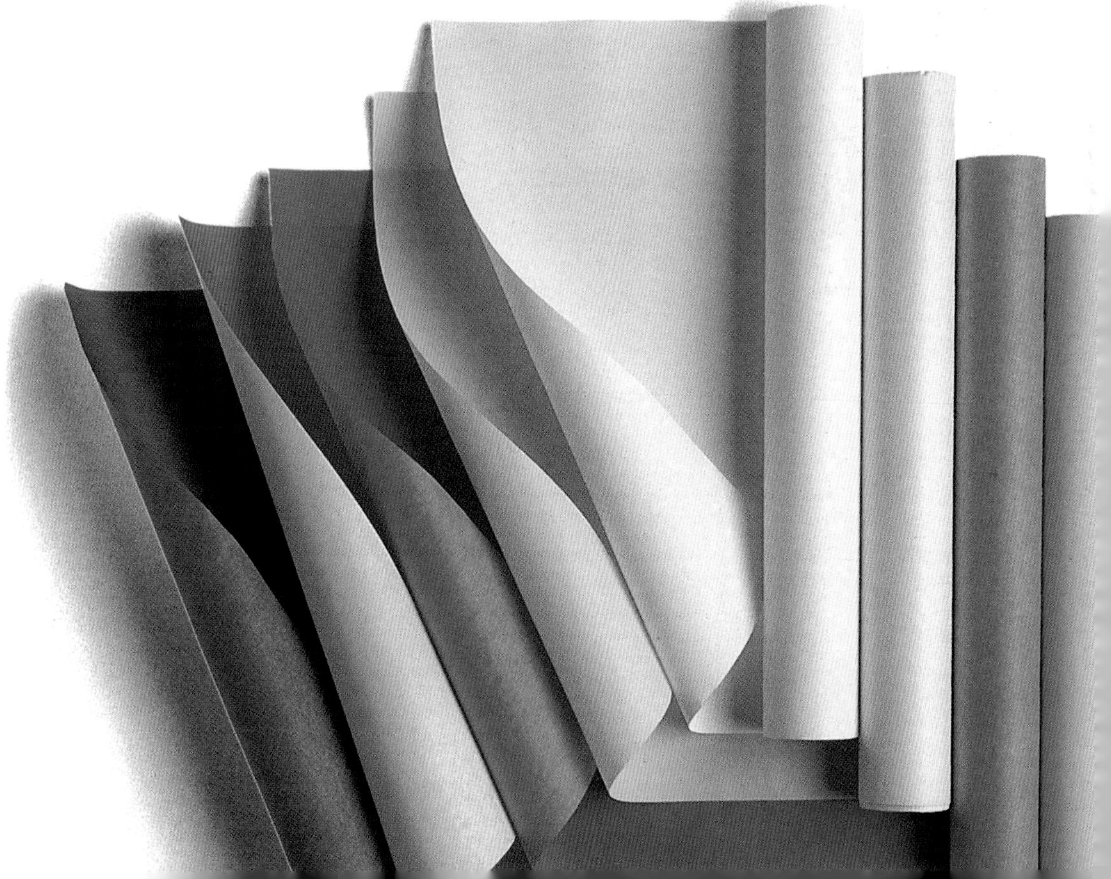

Transfer papers

These come in a range of different colours, so you can choose a bold hue or a lighter tone appropriate to the style and subject of your drawing.

Squaring Up or Down

Many artists work from photographs, not only for the convenience of being able to tackle outdoor subjects without having to work on location, but also because the limitations of photography – the way the camera reads an image selectively – can create dramatic and unusual compositions containing special qualities of light, colour and surface texture.

When using either reference photographs or sketches you may need to enlarge the image, and it can be difficult to scale up accurately working freehand. The method of squaring up or down on a grid helps you to locate the various elements of the composition.

First draw a pencil grid over the original image and then mark up a similar grid on your drawing paper but with each square proportionately larger or smaller – for instance, one and half or twice the size of the original to enlarge, or half the size to reduce. Now work across the grid square by square, copying the main lines and shapes within each section, and taking careful note of where each element in the photograph intersects a line on the grid. This simple method provides an outline drawing in proportion to the original, but because it is not strictly mechanical, you do have scope to adjust elements of the composition if you wish.

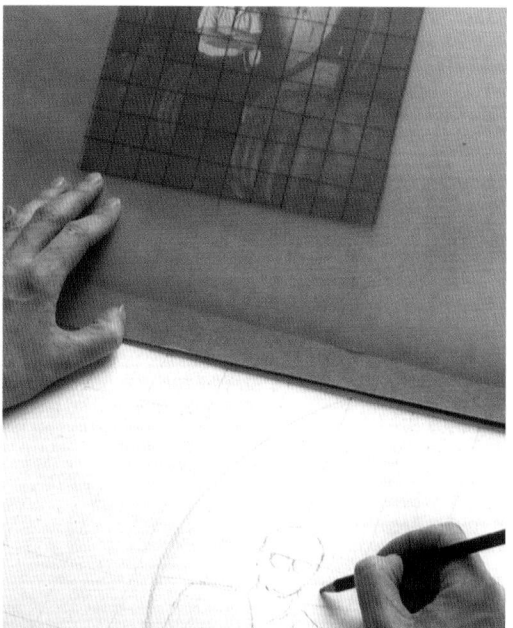

1 You can mark a grid for squaring up on the original photograph or drawing, or on a sheet of tracing paper overlaid on the image, as shown here. Draw the grid with suitably sized squares, according to the degree of detail in the picture.

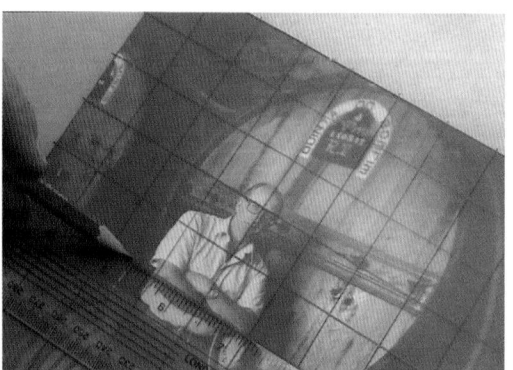
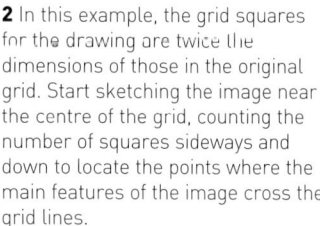

2 In this example, the grid squares for the drawing are twice the dimensions of those in the original grid. Start sketching the image near the centre of the grid, counting the number of squares sideways and down to locate the points where the main features of the image cross the grid lines.

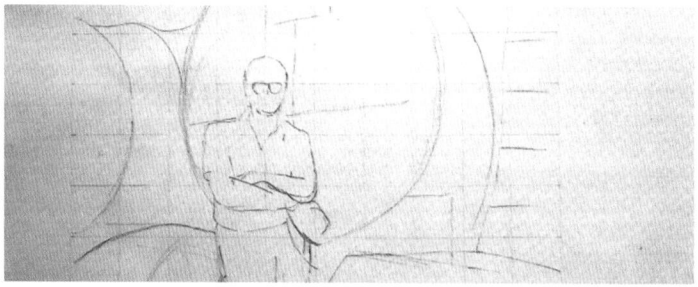

3 Even if you work systematically through the grid, you may misjudge some of the proportions and create "false" lines. But you can easily correct such errors by rechecking the position of particular features of the drawing in different squares.

Fixing

Fixing is by no means essential, although useful in some types of coloured pencil work, but in general, the finish of a coloured pencil drawing is not fragile, nor is it prone to smudging under normal handling. However, where you have a heavy build-up of soft-textured coloured pencil, you may wish to apply a light spray of fixative as a finishing coat to protect the surface.

Fixative can also be applied at intermediate stages of the drawing. This sometimes makes it possible to go on working a surface that has become slightly resistant.

Spray fixatives, available in CFC-free aerosol cans, are colourless in themselves, but they can affect the colours you have laid down, sometimes darkening their tones or dulling their brilliance. You can carry out a simple test by shading blocks of colour and then masking off one half while spraying fixative on the other. When it has dried, you can see whether the fixed half of each colour block differs from the original hue and tone.

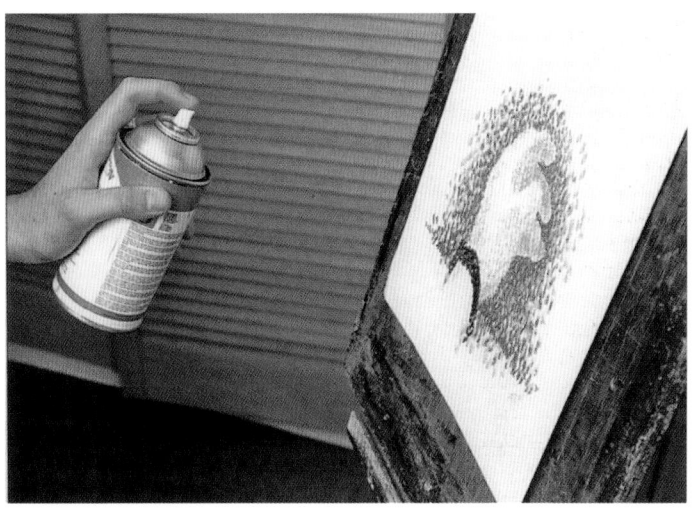

Applying fixative
Hold the can of fixative about 30cm (12in) away from the surface and spray lightly but evenly to cover the whole of the drawing. If you are using chalky pencils that deposit very loose colour, you can apply a second coat, but be careful not to saturate the surface.

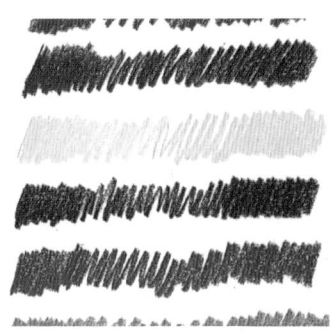

Colour testing
1 Select the colours that you intend to use in a drawing and make blocks of shading with each one on white paper. You can use this method to test your whole range of pencils.

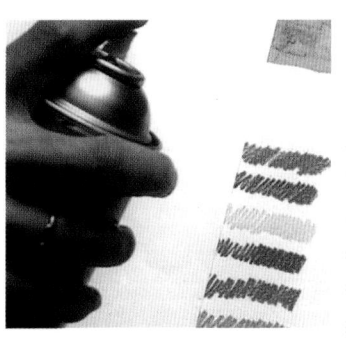

2 Place the colour chart flat on your work surface and cover half of it with a clean piece of paper. Apply fixative as described above.

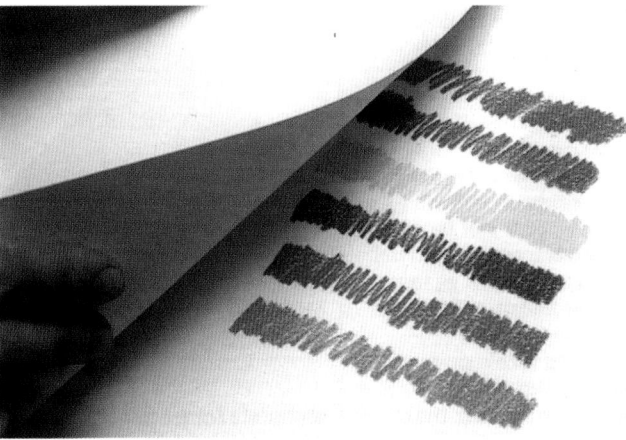

3 Pull back the covering sheet and compare the sprayed and unsprayed halves of the colour blocks to see if the fixative has affected the hue or tone. In this example, there is no appreciable difference.

Patch Correction

It can be very frustrating when you have put a lot of work into a coloured pencil drawing to find that one area simply does not work, and attempts to correct it make the effect worse rather than better. Repeated overworking may make the surface slippery and resistant, while heavy erasure can ruin the paper.

If one part of the drawing has gone completely wrong, you do not have to abandon the whole thing. You can make a patch correction that sits flush with the rest of the drawing. You create the patch by cutting through a piece of clean paper at the same time as you cut out the error, so it is exactly the right shape. You then insert it in the drawing, secure it with adhesive tape on the wrong side, and rework that section of the image.

Although this type of correction can be almost invisible, the fine seam around the new patch may snag the pencil tip, picking up a heavier colour application that could draw attention to the outline. The technique works best, therefore, in a drawing that is composed of distinctive shapes. However, by working very carefully towards the edges of the patch you should be able to integrate the redrawn section quite effectively.

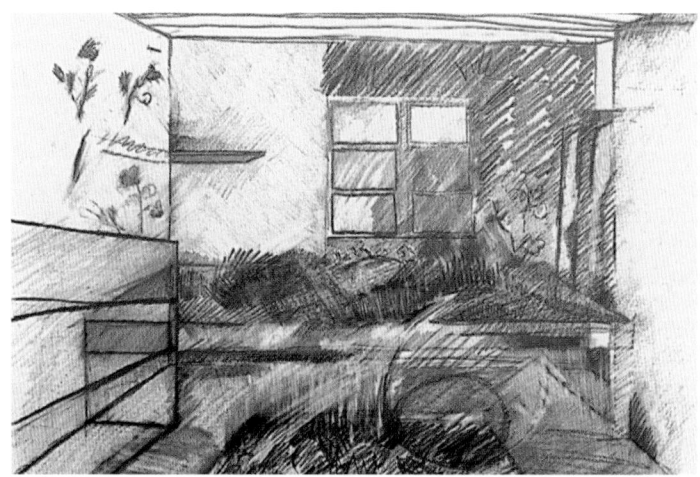

1 In this drawing there is a round shape in the foreground that relates to an element of the composition subsequently deleted. Because the pencil lines are hard, the shape cannot be covered by overlaying colour.

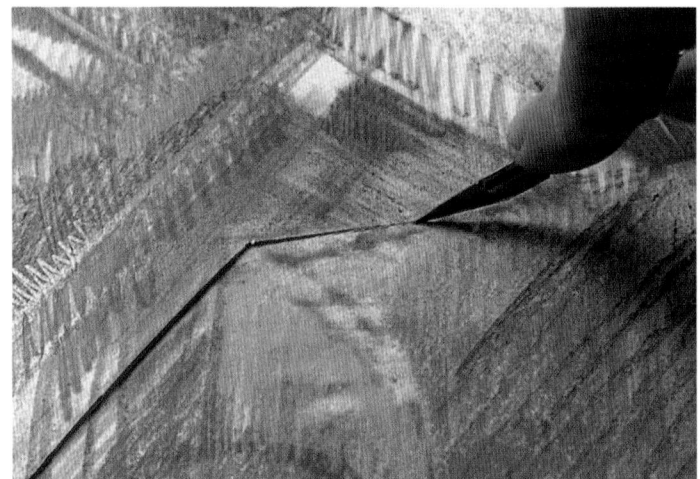

2 The area containing the round shape is cut out following, as far as possible, hard edges already established in the drawing. A clean sheet of paper has been laid underneath, and the cut is made through both layers.

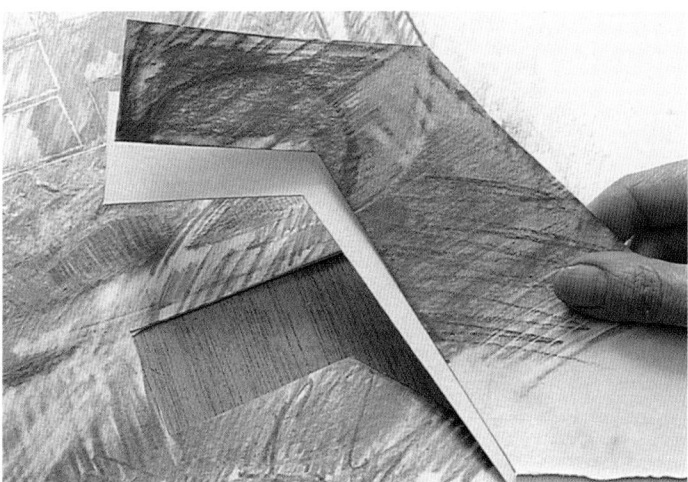

3 Both pieces are lifted out after cutting. Working through both layers ensures that the clean patch is cut to exactly the same shape as the piece being removed.

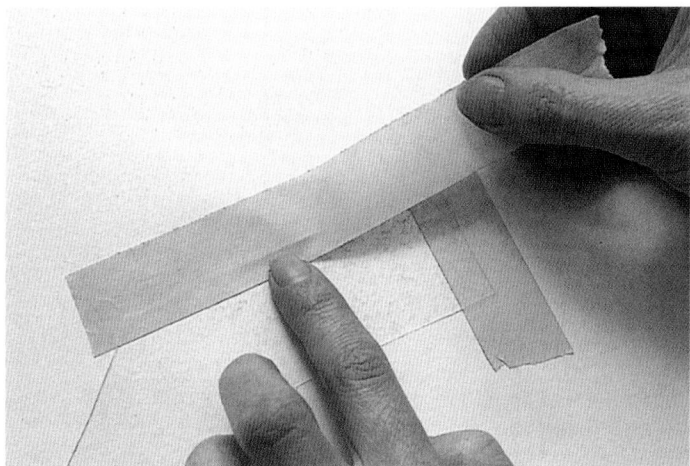

4 The clean patch is inserted in the "hole" in the drawing to check the fit.

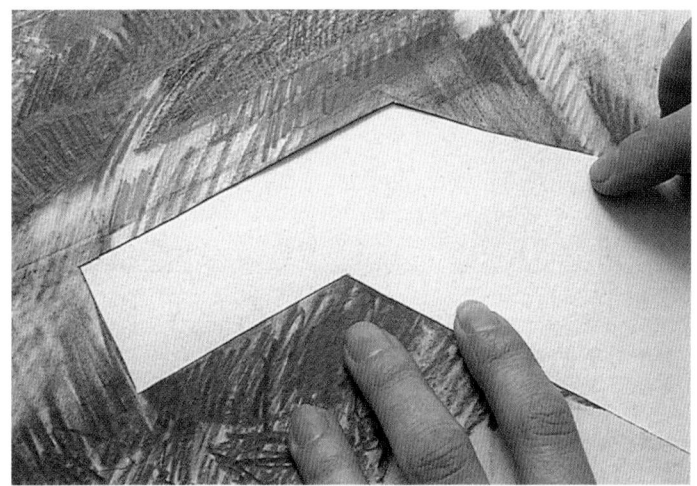

5 Once firmly in place, the drawing is turned over and the patch is secured with masking tape along all the cut edges. From the front of the drawing, the patch fits neatly, with no overlap on the edges that would form an awkward ridge to catch the pencil tip.

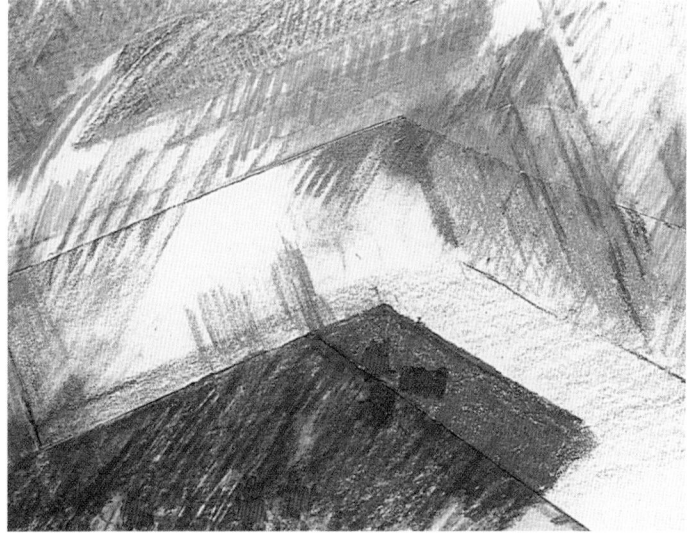

6 As the coloured pencil drawing is gradually reworked, with pencil strokes crossing the patched section in different directions, the edges of the patch become less noticeable and the new section can be fully integrated.

Transparent Supports

The use of a transparent drawing surface, such as drafting film or high-quality tracing paper, has been widely adopted by illustrators and has become a standard practice in coloured pencil drawing. The special characteristic of this method is that you can apply colour to both front and back of the transparent support, which increases the potential range and subtlety of colour mixing.

Drafting film is a polyester sheet material, highly translucent, although it typically has a slight blue or grey cast which has a minimal influence on the applied colours. It is a very tough and stable medium, but comparatively expensive. You need a type that has a matt surface texture on both sides. If you prefer to use tracing paper, choose a type that is weighty and firm-textured; cheap, thin tracing paper becomes distorted by the pressure of the pencil and may easily tear.

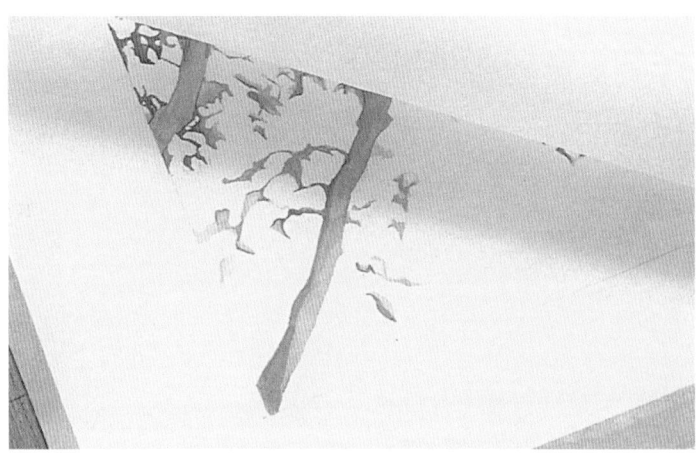

1 This example is drawn on a strong, smooth-grained tracing paper. The coloured pencil drawing will be an interpretation of a monochrome watercolour study. The tracing paper is first taped down over the original.

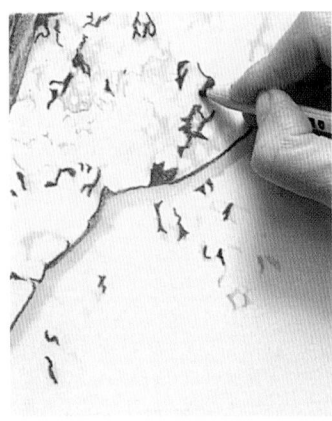

2 The darkest tones in the subject are drawn with a burnt umber pencil. The drawing below is used as a guide, but it is not necessary to copy every detail precisely, as the pencil drawing should have its own character.

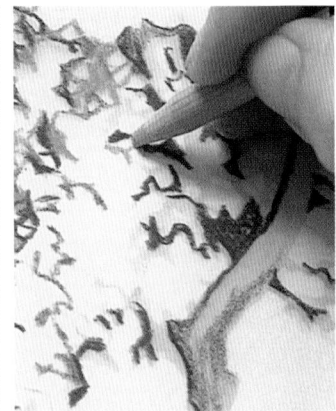

3 The decorative shapes of the tree trunks and leaves are developed using olive green and burnt sienna as well as burnt umber. This produces an effect similar to the original monochrome, but with livelier colour interaction.

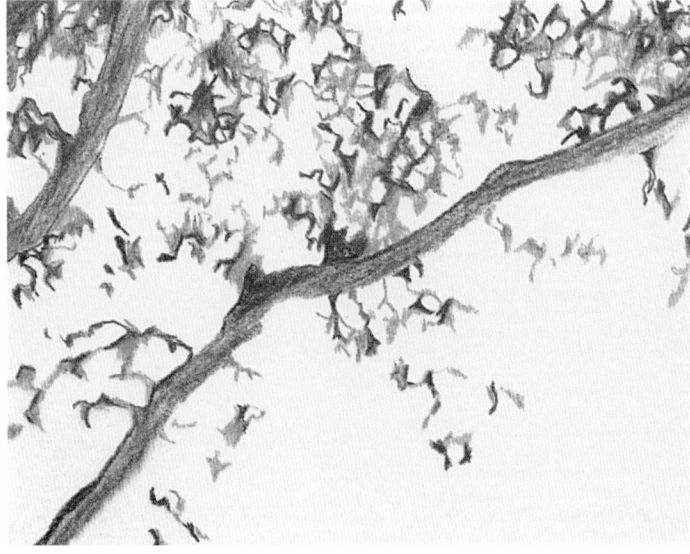

4 This completes the first stage of drawing on the front of the tracing paper. The basic structure of the tree branches is fully established.

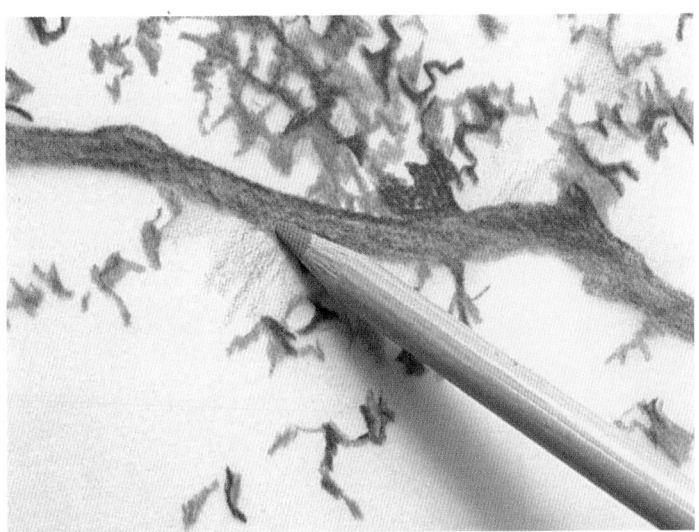

5 The lights and colours in the sky background are laid down on the back of the tracing paper. This enables the artist to work freely, without having to shade around the outlines of existing shapes.

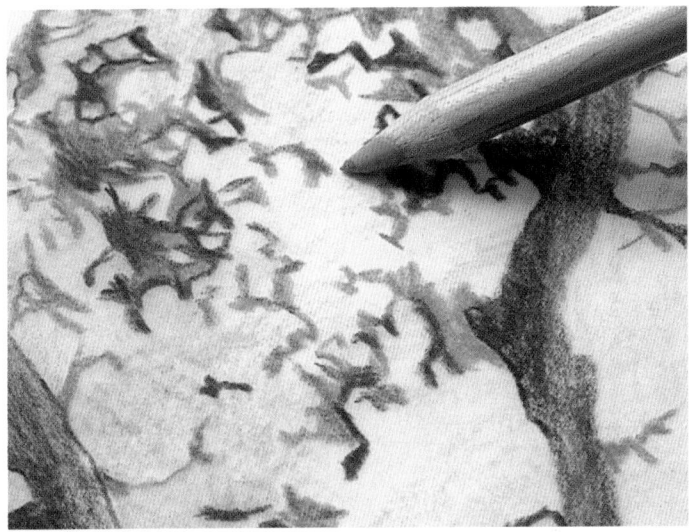

6 Gradually the shading on the back of the paper is built up to cover the whole image area with delicate colours.

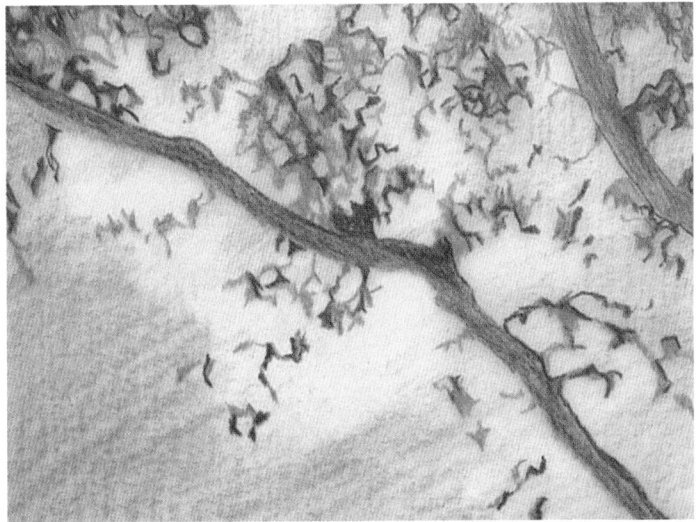

7 The drawing is turned over, and some additional sky colour is applied to the front of the paper, strengthening the tones and hues and helping to merge the light tones.

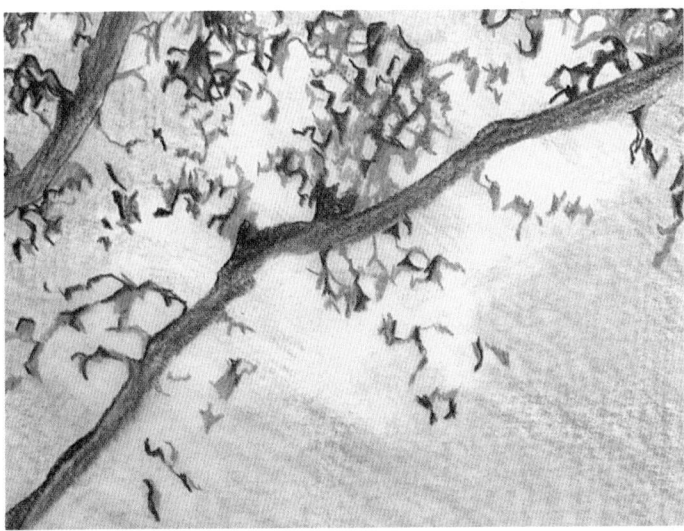

8 The process of separating the different colour ranges, so that pale tints on the back of the paper can be broadly blocked in without picking up colour from the darker tones, creates a good effect of bright light behind the trees.

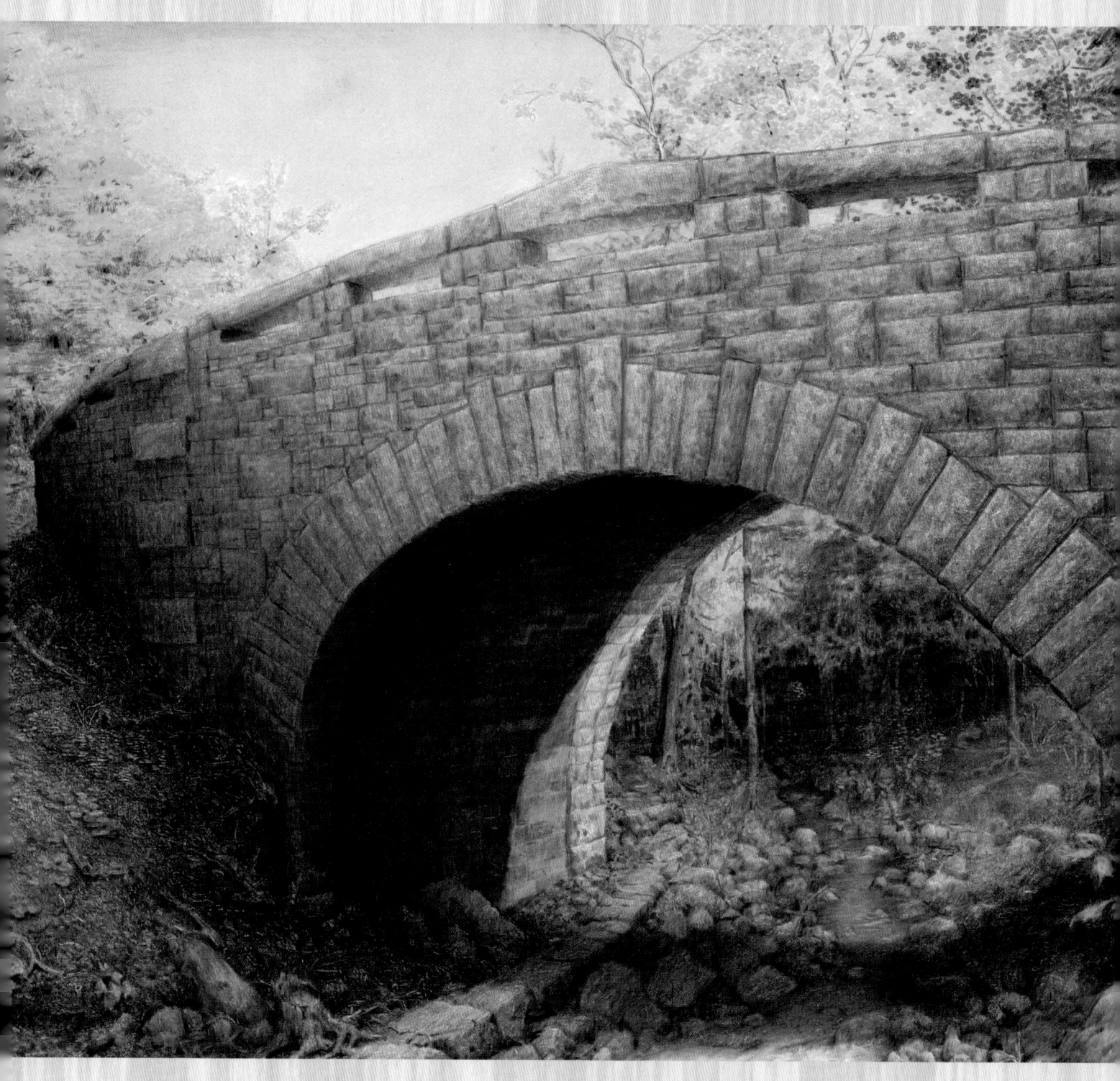

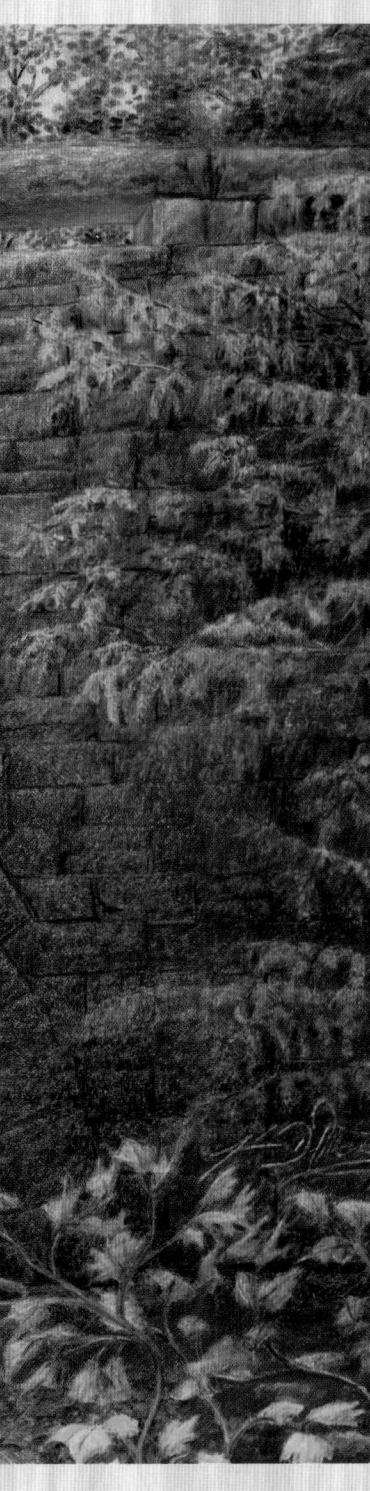

Themes

■■■■■■■■■■■■■■■■■■■■■■■■■■■■■■■■

At one time, coloured pencils were treated as secondary tools, useful for sketching and making preparatory drawings for paintings, but not considered suitable for highly finished works. One thing that has radically changed the status of coloured pencils is the increasing range of high-quality brands available, with improved handling properties and colour qualities.

Coloured pencils are particularly valuable for illustration work, being versatile, quick and clean to use and capable of producing bright, detailed images that reproduce well. The result of this has been a remarkable exploitation of coloured pencil techniques and the imagery deriving from them that continues to develop in new ways.

The gallery of drawings assembled in this second section demonstrates how the technical expertise of individual artists is applied to a surprising variety of subjects, some among the classic themes of art, others closely associated with the specifics of this medium. Text and captions give cross-references where appropriate to the techniques previously demonstrated, to enable you to relate the working method to the end result.

JOHN DELMASTRO
BRIDGE AT AMPHITHEATRE

Landscape and Townscape

Interpreting large-scale subjects with a medium that is essentially fine and linear is a particular technical challenge. If you intend producing a detailed colour study of a landscape view, this can take a great deal of time as you build up the individual marks and colour areas into a tightly constructed, cohesive image.

For this reason coloured pencils are more frequently used to make sketches and working drawings that will be interpreted in another medium, such as watercolour or oil paint. Such preliminary studies have an interesting character in their own right, and provide a good practice ground for exercising the versatility of your techniques. However, you can also see from examples in this section that the labour of producing a highly finished work in coloured pencil is often well worth it, resulting in a vibrant, active style of imagery.

Sketching in coloured pencils

Very few artists actually complete a landscape or townscape image in front of the subject due to the inconveniences of working outdoors. The habit of sketching outdoors to produce a body of reference work that can be reinterpreted in the studio is a long-established working method. Coloured pencils are an ideal medium, being clean and easily portable. All you need is a useful selection of colours and a sketchpad of good-quality cartridge or watercolour paper.

In addition to the subtle greens and ochres that you immediately identify, remember to include some brilliant, strong hues to capture light effects – you will often find it necessary to create bold contrasts and enhanced colour interactions. Consider bright yellows and pinks, and cold, pale blues as well as rich hues such as red and purple to counterpoint the earth colours and foliage greens.

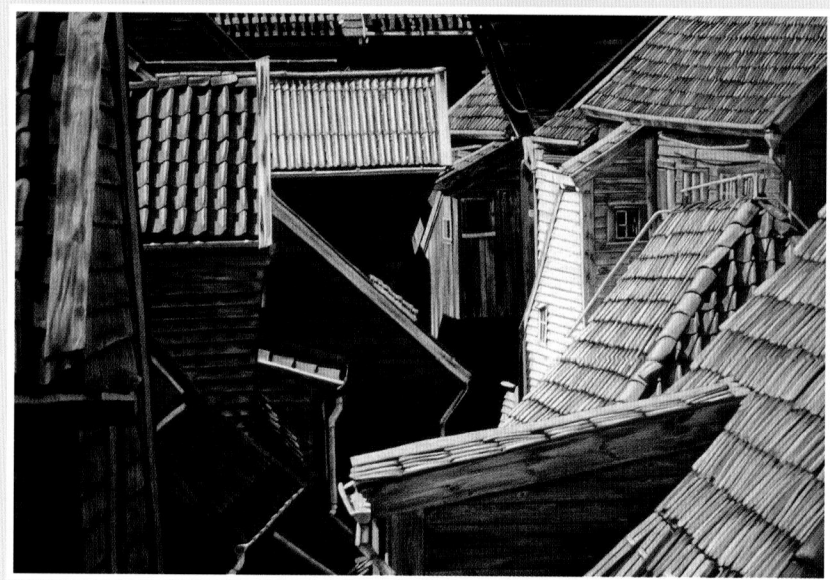

▲ PAMELA BELCHER
BEHIND BRYGGEN
Some images are perfect to be executed on black paper, and this was one. Deep and consistent dark tones are often hard to achieve with coloured pencil. With black paper, you need to reverse the process, laying in the lights and leaving the dark areas alone; a mental adjustment is needed at first. Drawing on a black or coloured ground also speeds up the drawing process in that one of the major tones is already present.
• COLOURED PAPERS

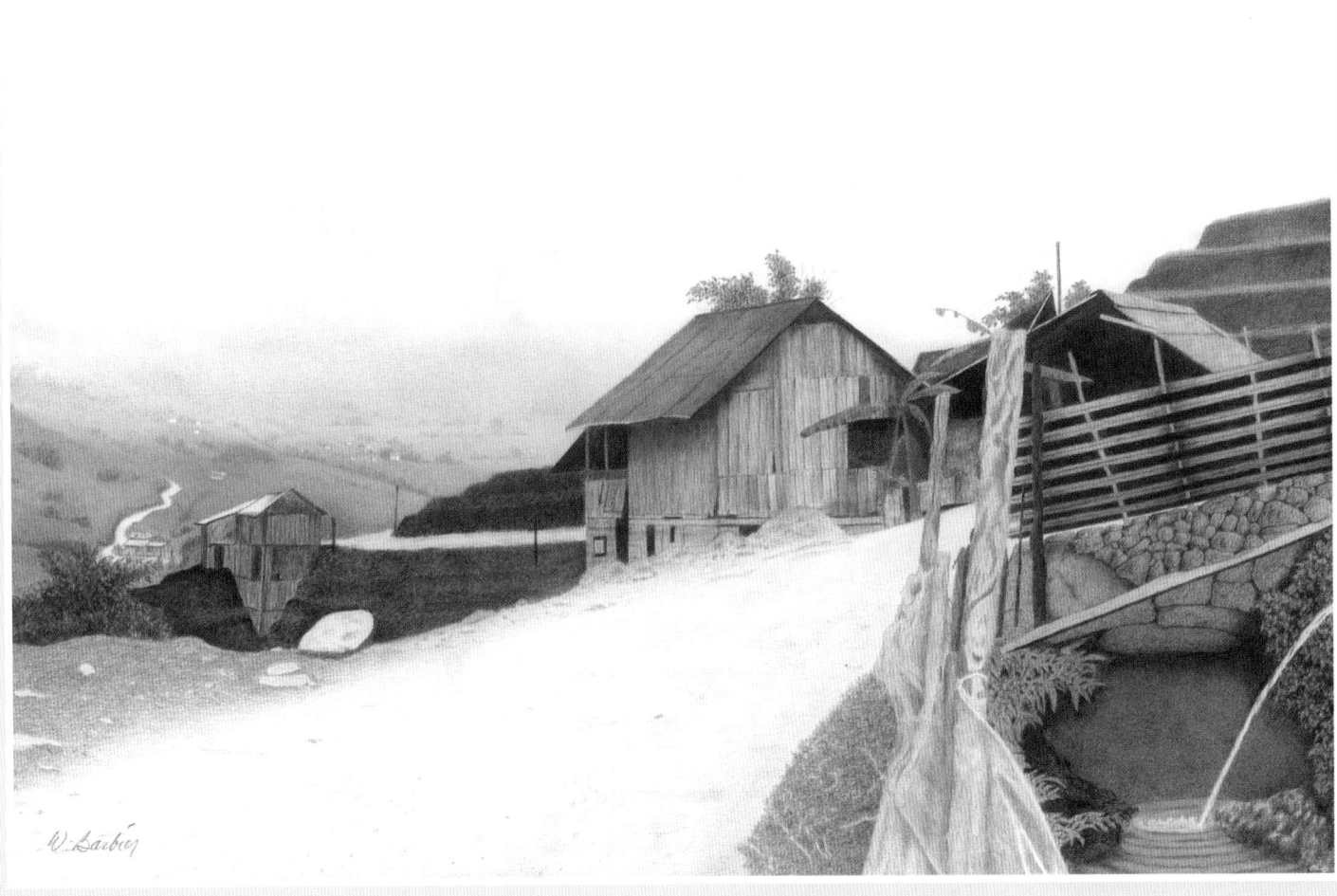

▲ **WILFRID BARBIER**

04

Coloured pencils are the artist's favoured medium and enable him to capture landscapes and city streets in a "realistic figurative style". The image here encapsulates the artist's style and illustrates the impressive final results achievable when using coloured pencils.

• BLENDING

• SHADING

Space and Distance

The pictorial space of a landscape is defined by your viewpoint, your position as spectator setting the level of the horizon line. The proportion of sky to land is significant in creating space, and the elements of landscape need to be carefully orchestrated to define spatial recession towards the horizon.

A relatively small area of the paper may represent a vast area of land and you must achieve an accurate sense of scale, assessing the relationships of interlocking shapes and the way colours and textures are layered within the compressed space. Because coloured pencils are linear, careful judgement of the scale and direction of the marks you make is crucial to a convincing impression of space and distance.

Framing of the image is an important factor. A horizontal format in itself helps to express the breadth of landscape and is more commonly used than a picture format with vertical emphasis. The overall shape of the image also affects the sense of space – the picture area need not be strictly rectangular – as does the extent of the view that you choose to include.

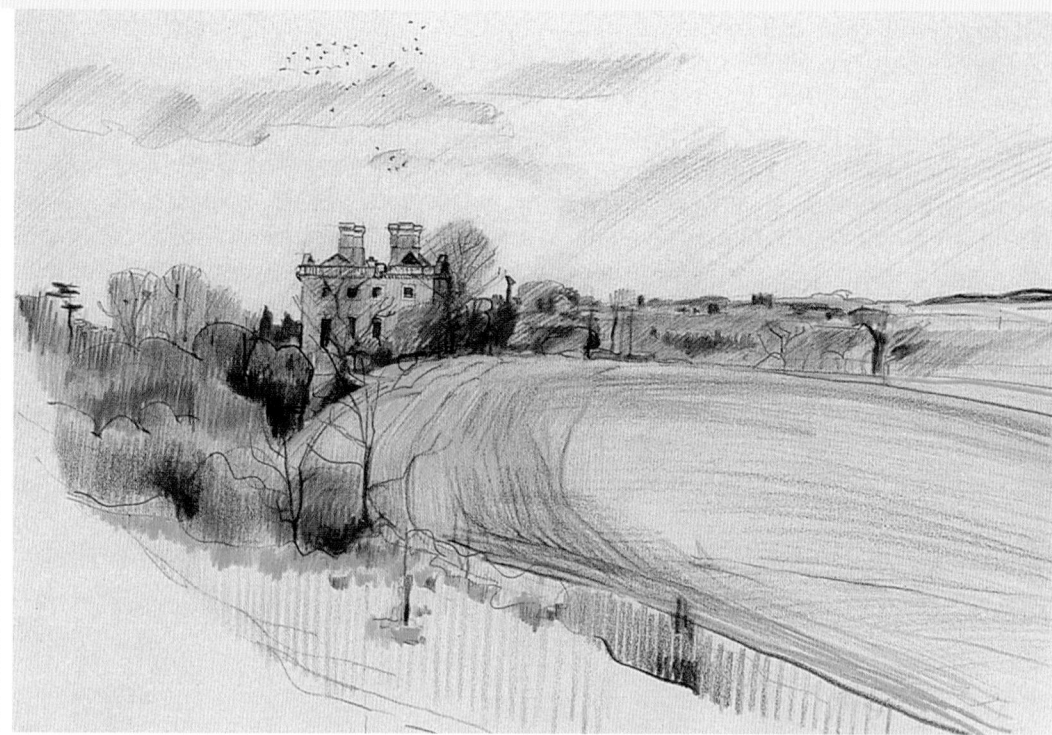

▲ JOHN TOWNEND
COPPING HALL
The sweeping space of the landscape is achieved by locating the focal point of the building on the horizon line and emphasizing the curve in the foreground. Layers of loose shading create a rich impression of autumnal colours.
• OVERLAYING COLOURS

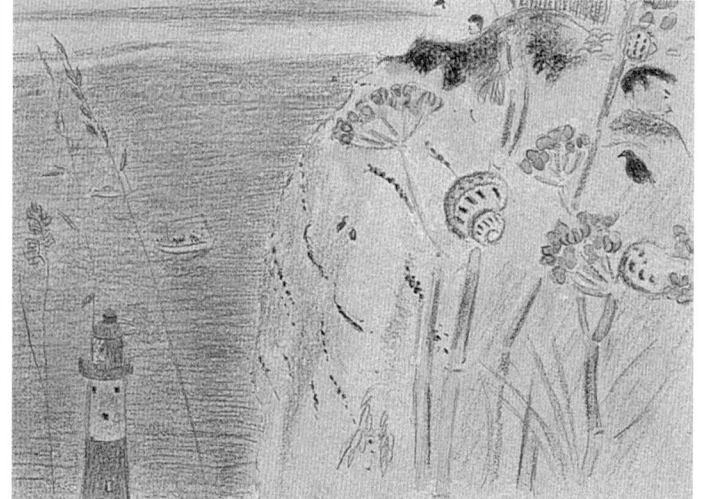

▲ JEFFREY CAMP
CLIFFTOP
Simplified shapes and gentle colours produce a charming effect. The grainy pencil marks are wetted and spread in brief touches. The odd sense of floating above the scene is created by the absence of a true ground level in the perspective.
• SOLVENTS

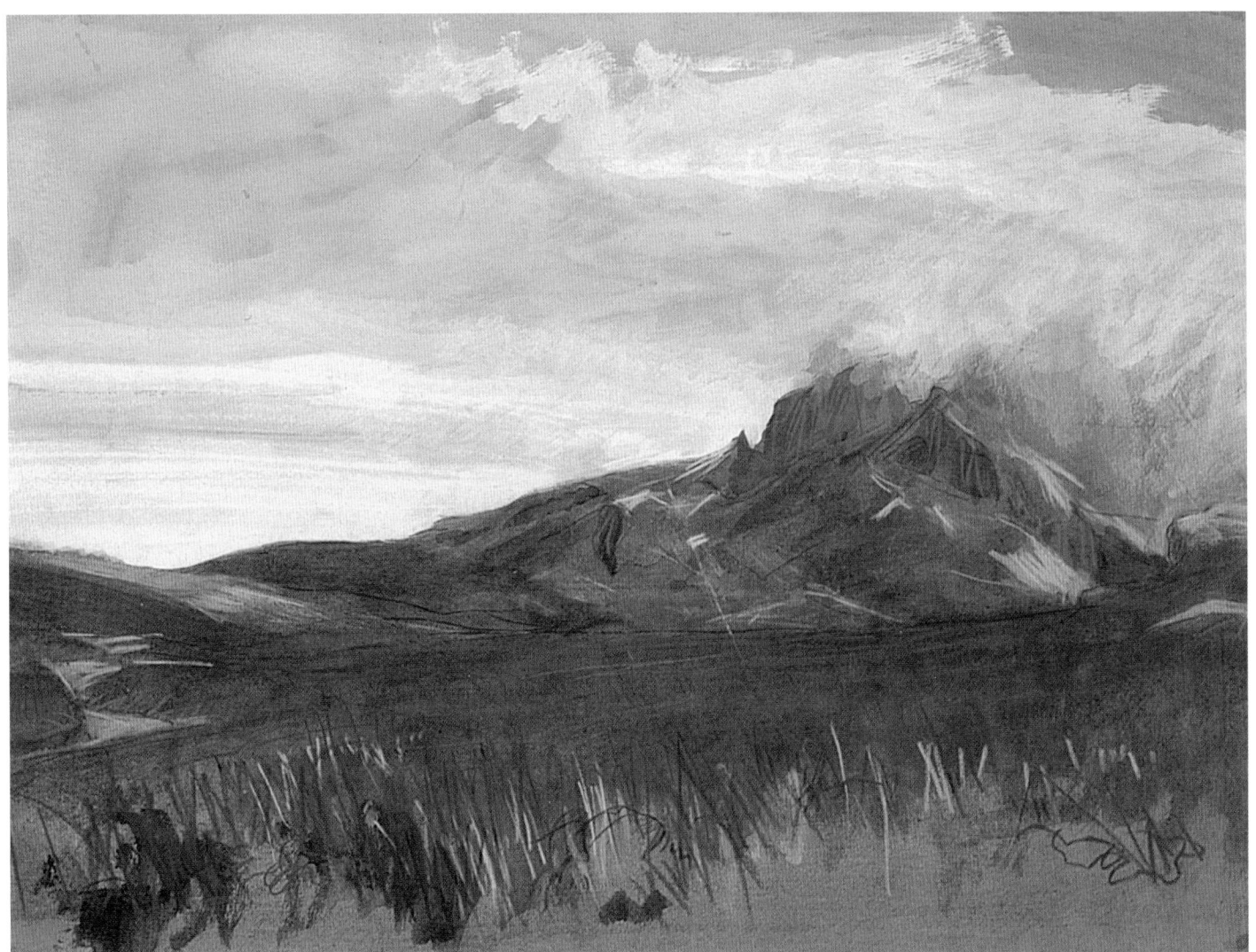

▲ MARK HUDSON
MOUNTAIN LANDSCAPE
Light washes of paint form the ground of the landscape and are complemented by the soft quality of the pencil drawing. Rough shading and hatching contribute to the atmospherics of the sky, while slashing and trailing lines in the foreground suggest the textures of grass and stony ground. The colours chosen are natural hues, reflecting the subject, and create a harmonious mood.

• LINEAR MARKS

• WATERCOLOUR AND PENCIL

Colour Studies

The subtle variations of colour in a landscape are a challenge to the artist working in coloured pencils. Rather than trying to match the individual colours that you see in nature, you need to develop the skills of analyzing colour relationships and finding satisfactory equivalents by manipulating the qualities of hue, tone and intensity in your pencil colours. Important factors to consider include the extent of one colour against another, whether mixed colour effects are best achieved by interweaving or juxtaposing the pencil marks, and the selection of hues and tones that interact to create the right nuances.

Qualities of light and shade should be achieved with vibrant mixes to keep the picture surface alive; using the neutrals – black and white – to strengthen tonal contrasts can deaden the image. Dark shadows can be shot through with red-brown, indigo or purple; highlight areas can be intensified with touches of bright pink or yellow.

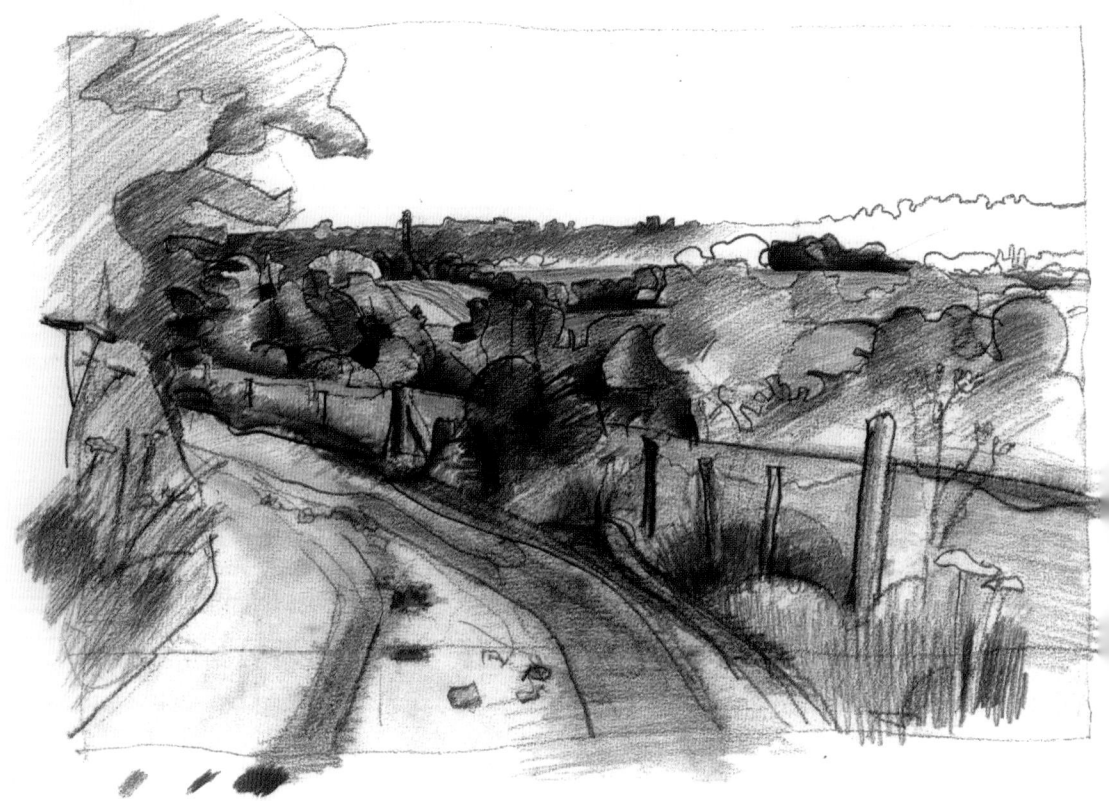

▲ JOHN TOWNSEND
A VIEW NEAR BIGGIN HILL
The style used here is bold and free. A strong sense of rhythm and movement is achieved through heavy outlines defining individual forms, together with multi-directional hatching and crosshatching, especially noticeable in the foreground.
• HATCHING

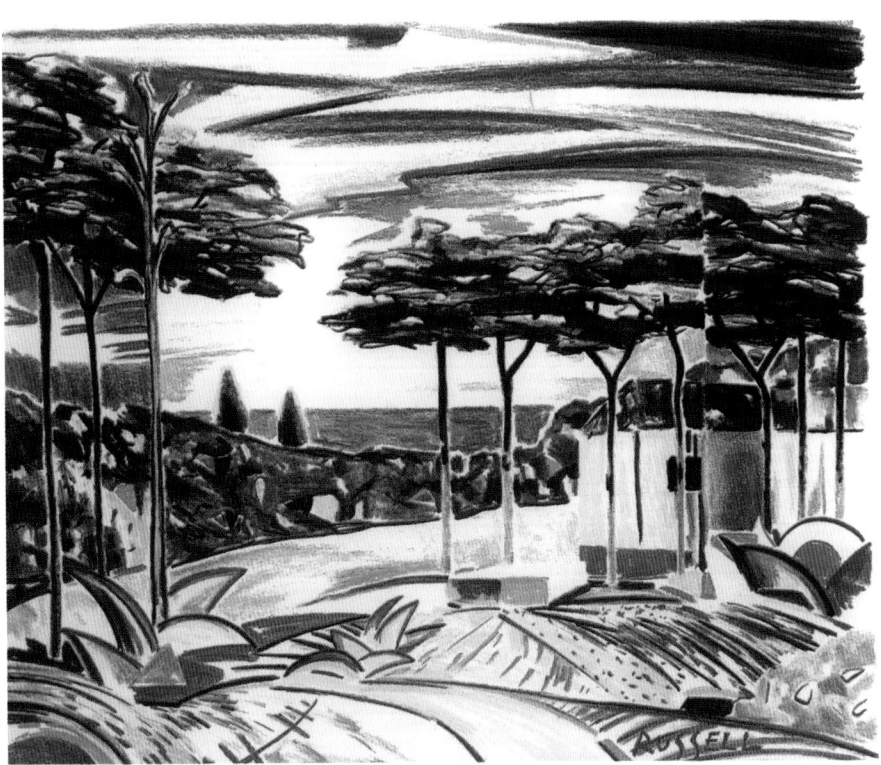

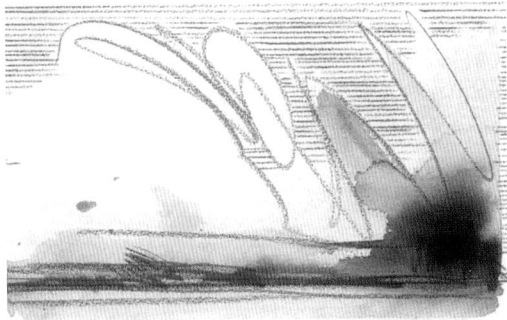

◄ **STEVE RUSSELL**
CALA HONDA, SPANISH LANDSCAPE
Soft-leaded waxy pencils are combined with chalky
pastel pencils to provide the bright colour scheme
of this sunlit view. The shapes are simplified to
emphasize the rhythms and patterns of the landscape.
Using broadly shaded patches of bold colour gives an
attractively exotic impression, enlivened by formal
pattern elements in the foreground.
• LINEAR MARKS
• MIXING PENCILS

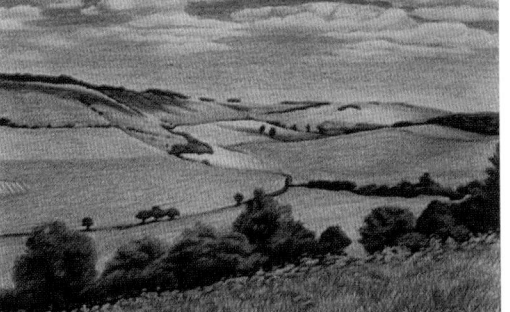

◄ **JO DENNIS**
ENGLISH COUNTRYSIDE
The gentle contours of the land are
framed to create a classic pastoral
scene, described in naturalistic
colours. Solid shading is varied in
density to bring colours up more
intensely in the foreground than
in the distant parts of the view.
Emphatic line drawing is overlaid
to enhance the detail.
• LINE QUALITIES
• OVERLAYING COLOURS
• SHADING

▲ **DAVID HOLMES**
LANDSCAPE
In an abstract interpretation, mere hints of colour
can be selected and emphasized to provide a dramatic
contrast. The boldness of the red-blue opposition
matches the vigour of the gestural mark-making in
broad-leaded, waxy pencils and watercolour.
• HATCHING
• LINEAR MARKS
• WATERCOLOUR AND PENCIL

Shapes and Textures

Landscape is composed of shapes within shapes, from the broad levels of the land to dominant features such as rocks and trees to the delicate details of foliage and flowers. Form and texture in a landscape image are developed out of concentration on the relative scale and complexity of these different elements.

However detailed your drawing, it is inevitably an approximation of what you actually see – no one draws every leaf or every blade of grass, and even the major forms acquire some modification as you translate them into a two-dimensional representation. The choices made in selecting particular aspects of the subject and working out ways of interpreting them technically are the ingredients of an artist's personal style.

This selective process means that it is important to find those things that most effectively describe the character of the subject and convey your special interest in it, whether they are generalized forms or specific textures. Because coloured pencils allow you to work up an image slowly, you can make continuous adjustments and focus quite precisely on the elements of the landscape that you wish to bring out.

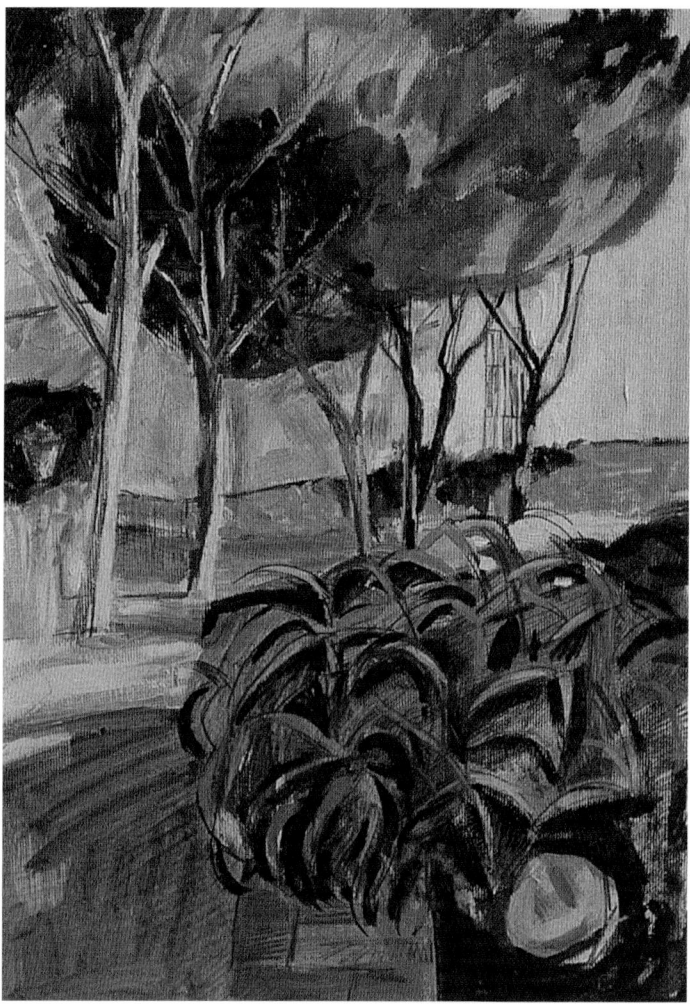

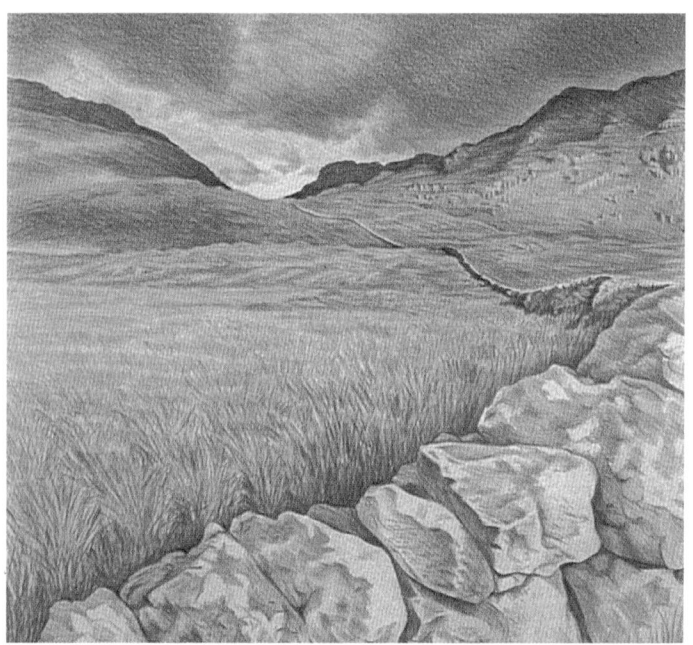

◀ JO DENNIS
STONE WALL
The wall forms a curving line, leading the viewer right through the space of the picture and effectively cutting the composition into two parts. The focus on the large stones in the foreground startlingly enhances the perspective. These interlocked shapes contain an interesting pattern of smaller shapes within.
• GRADATION

▲ HELENA GREENE
TREE-LINED ROAD
Loosely brushed acrylic paint on a canvas-board ground is the main medium for blocking in the shapes and textures of the foliage and tree trunks. Coloured pencil drawing is added to sharpen the edge qualities and enhance the lights and shadows, redefining the play of natural forms.
• DRAWING INTO PAINT

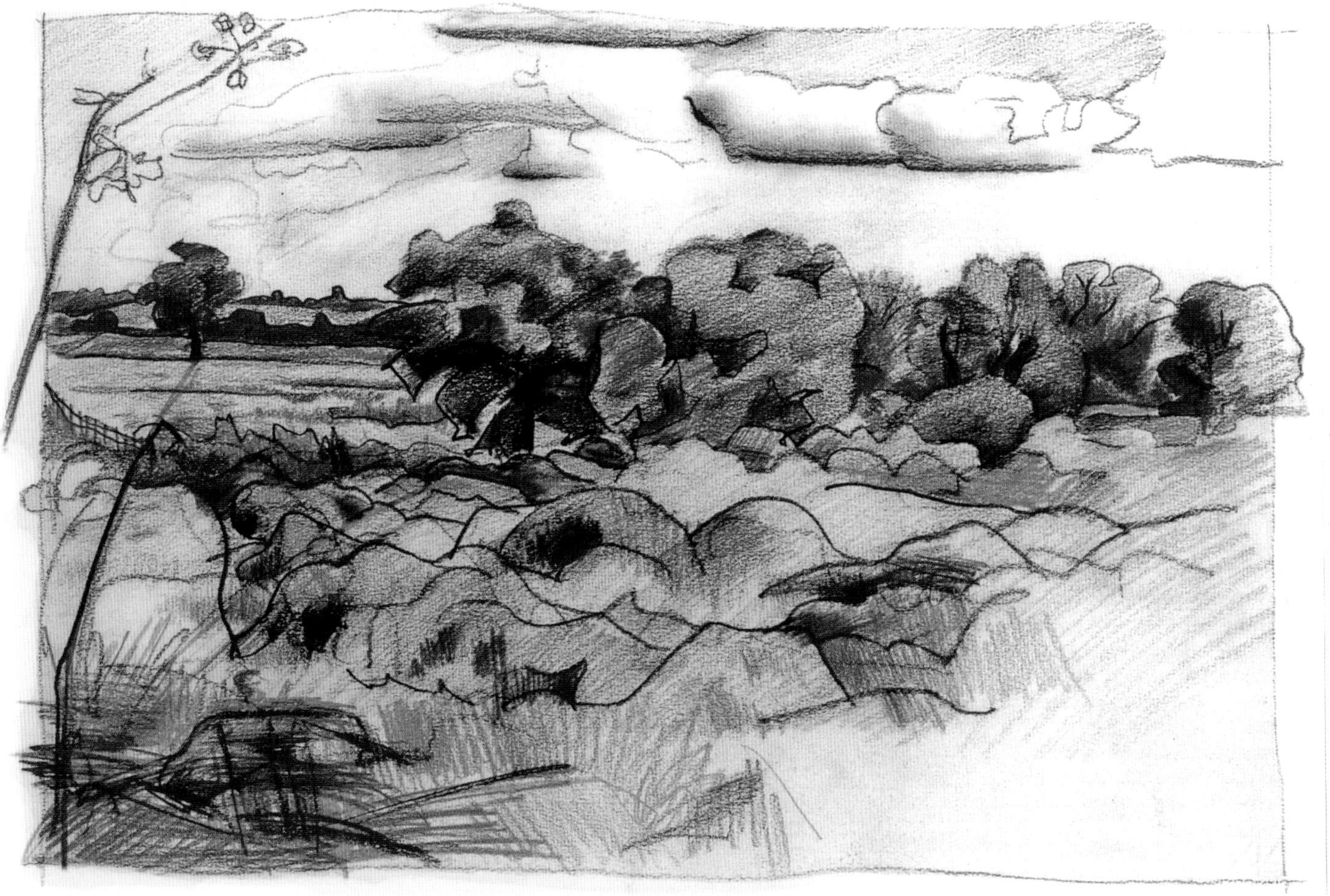

▲ JOHN TOWNEND
HAYMAKING
Each different element of the
landscape is interpreted as
contributing to an overall
schematic rhythm, with individual
forms defined by bold contour
lines. The texture of the free
shading is varied, as well as the
colours, to help differentiate the
hayfield from the trees flanking
the far side.
• CONTOUR DRAWING
• HATCHING
• SHADING

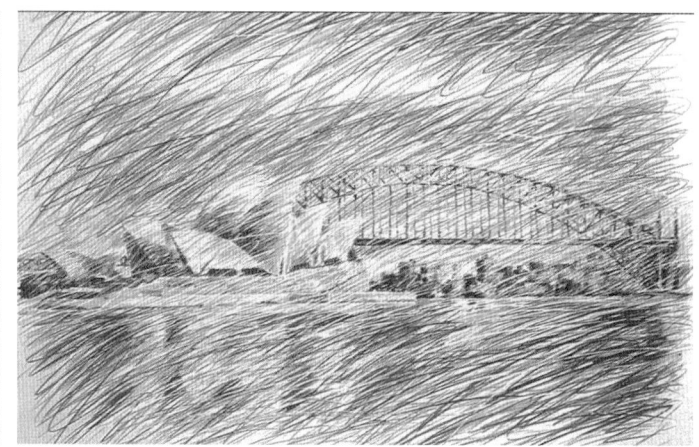

◀ CARL MELEGARI
SYDNEY HARBOUR BRIDGE
Although he has used an active,
all-over texture of vigorous line
drawing, the artist has contrived
the colours in a way that allows
distinctive forms to emerge from
the busy surface. The texture of
the image itself is as important
as the structures it portrays.
• LINEAR MARKS

Light and Atmosphere

If you are working in coloured pencils only, qualities of light and atmospheric impressions can be difficult to handle. Whereas with paint or pastel you can rely on overworking with pale tints to retrieve the lights and modify blends and colour mixes, with coloured pencils your means of adjusting the high-key tones are restricted if you have laid in colours too heavily or broadly. You need to have an organized sense of the composition from the start, especially if you rely on using the white of the paper to make the highlights.

Degrees of tonal contrast sometimes have to be exaggerated to achieve a vibrant impression of light effects. Coloured pencil drawing allows you plenty of time to build up contrasts; if you find the drawing looks flat, don't be afraid to attempt radical measures, introducing a darker colour or more vivid hue.

You may wish to work very quickly and spontaneously to develop the mood of a landscape deriving from the quality of light or particular weather conditions. Mixed-media approaches are frequently successful for landscape work.

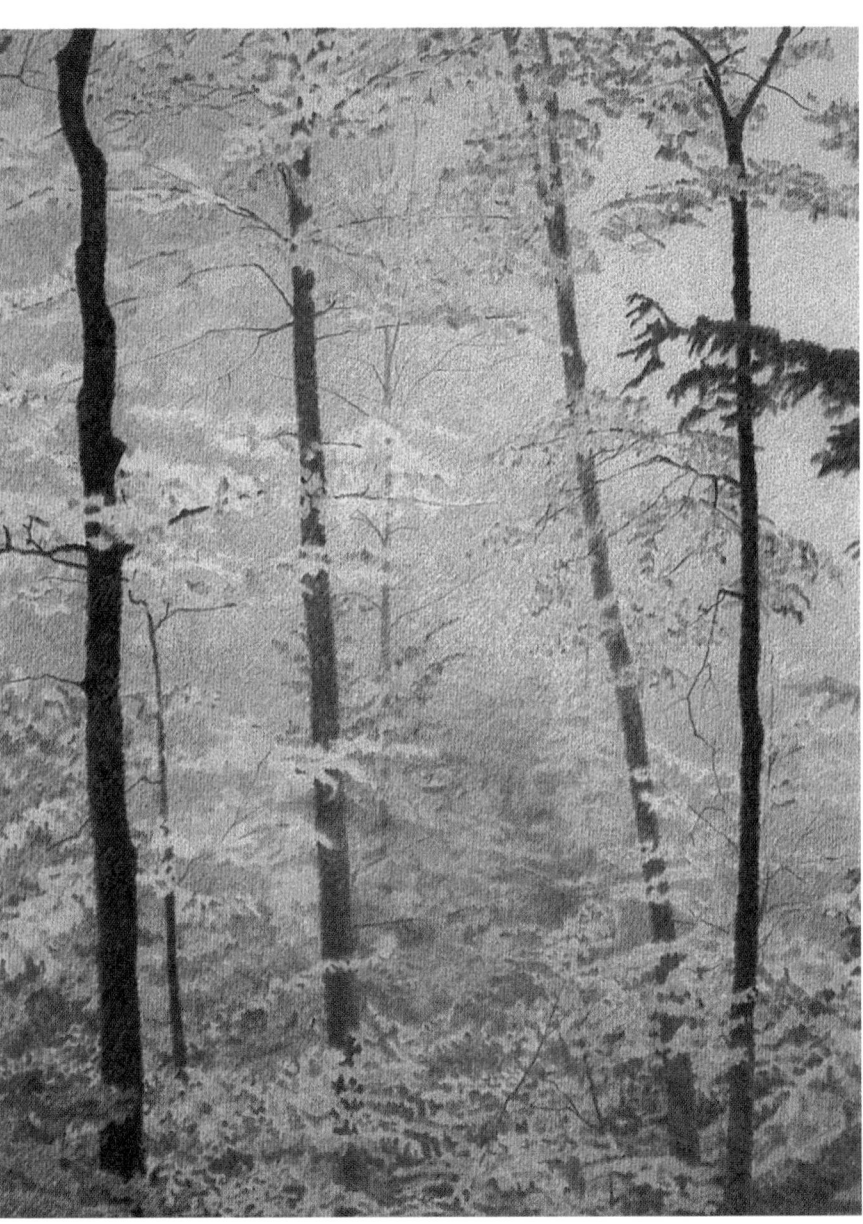

MIKE PEASE ▶
FOREST LIGHT
The effect of strong light is created with tonal contrast. There is a misty, fragile quality to the rendering – due to the muted background colours and smaller, more intricate shapes – that describes the atmosphere.
• GRADATION
• SHADING

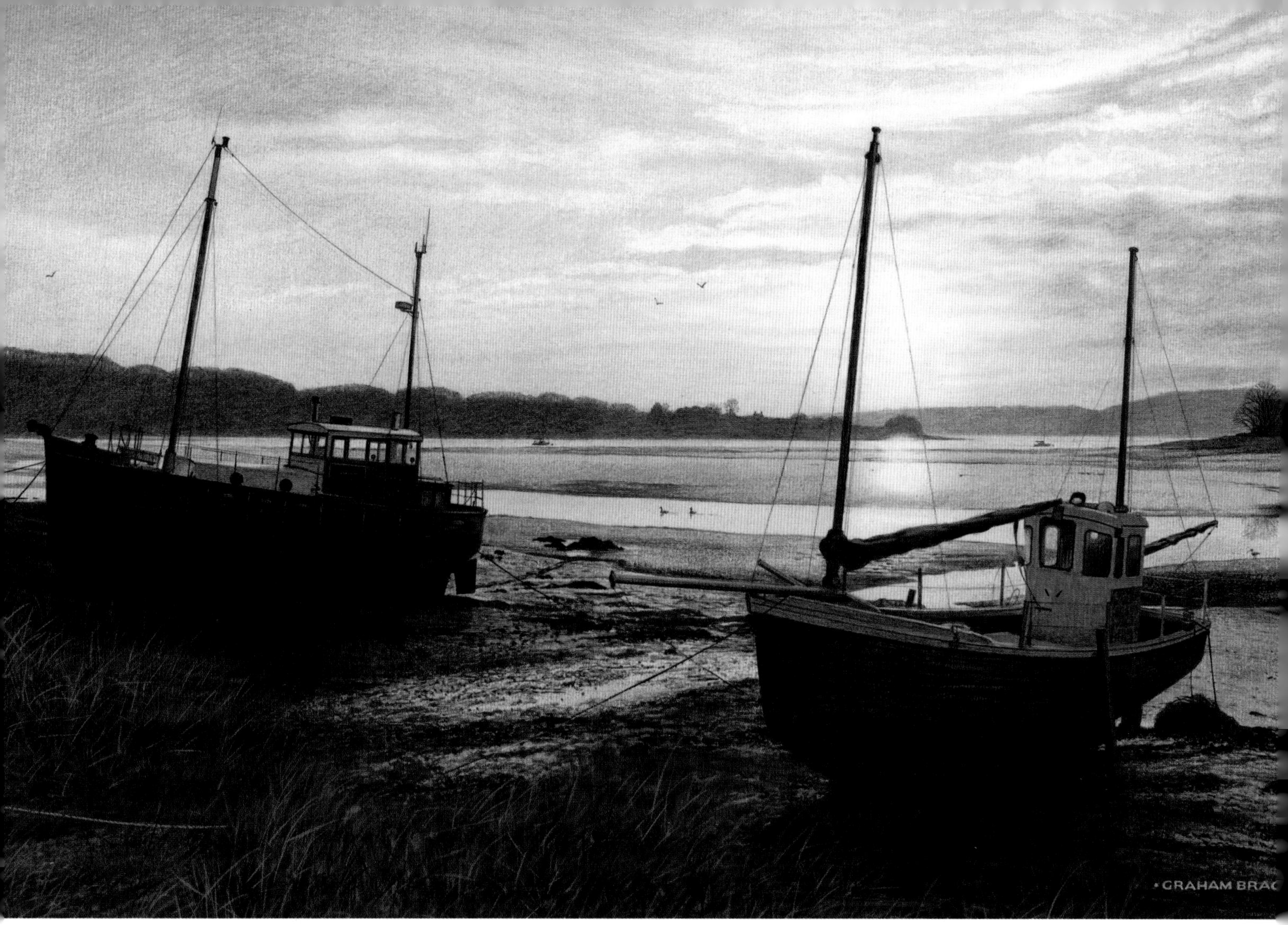

▲ GRAHAM BRACE
CLEDDAU SUNRISE WITH TWO BOATS
A combination of media were used to create this photoreal seascape in Pembrokeshire, Wales. The artist tends to begin by laying large foundation colours in soft pastel onto the board and blending these with his fingers. Coloured pencils come into their own for the finer details. Finally, gouache is employed to highlight certain elements in the piece.
• PASTEL AND PENCIL
• ERASER TECHNIQUES

DAVID HOLMES ▶
CORNFIELD
A dramatic image can be achieved by reducing a subject to its bare essentials. The artist here has chosen the basic abstract qualities of the scene – broad shapes, directional lines, tonal contrast – to form the composition. These underlying elements are present even in the most representational imagery.
• LINE AND WASH
• LINEAR MARKS

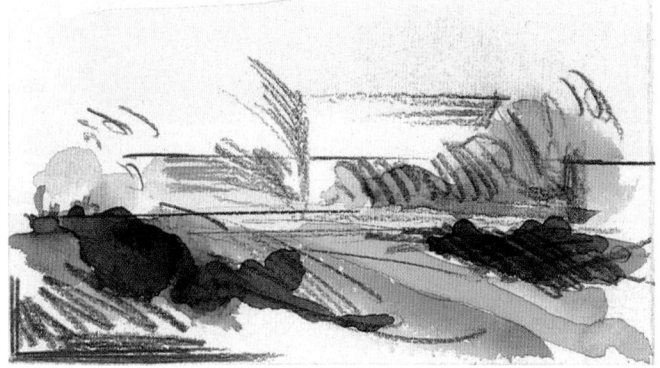

Buildings

The shape and structure of an individual building may evoke a particular sense of place, or it may draw associations with a personal "narrative" relating to its own function and a suggestion of the lifestyle of people living or working there. You can use the colours and textures of pencil marks to convey mood in a drawing, and you can use them to create basic structures.

In terms of formal composition, a building is an arrangement of broad planes and volumes intercut with more detailed frameworks, such as windows and doors, roof coverings and architectural ornament. You need not always try to include all the information that you see. Use a selective eye to search out those details that are both descriptive and decorative.

The geometry and perspective of the view need not be strictly accurate, unless the real space of the building is your primary interest. Often a slightly quirky or exaggerated angle of view adds to the impression of how a well-ordered architectural structure acquires a distinctive character through its age and style, and the way it reflects its surroundings.

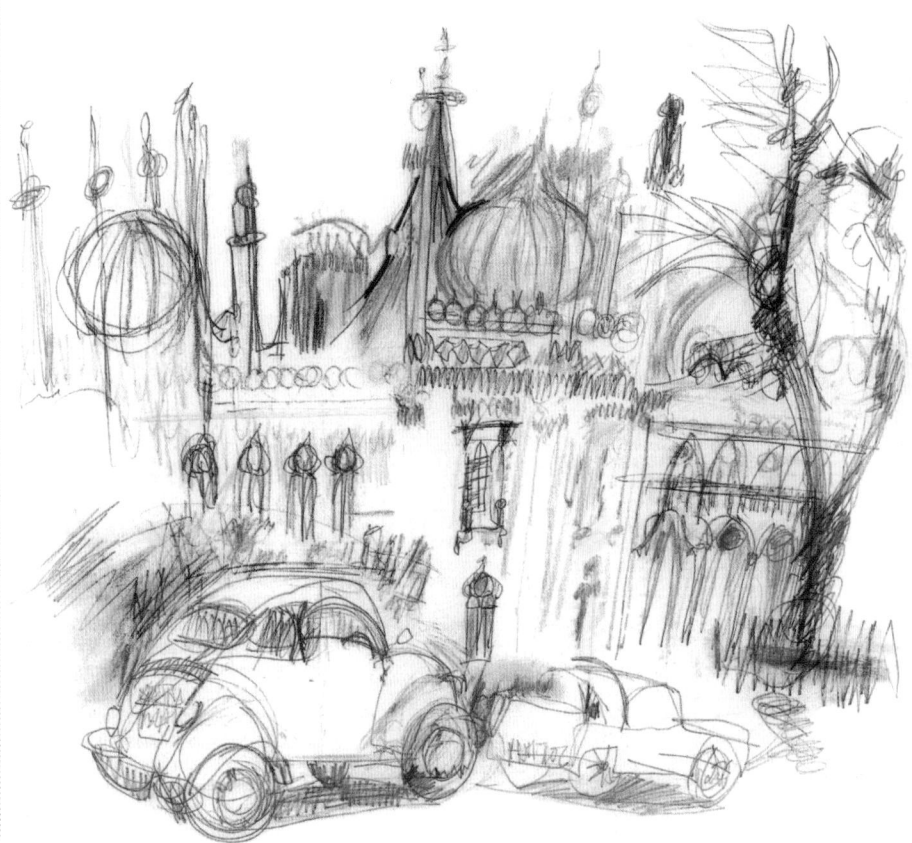

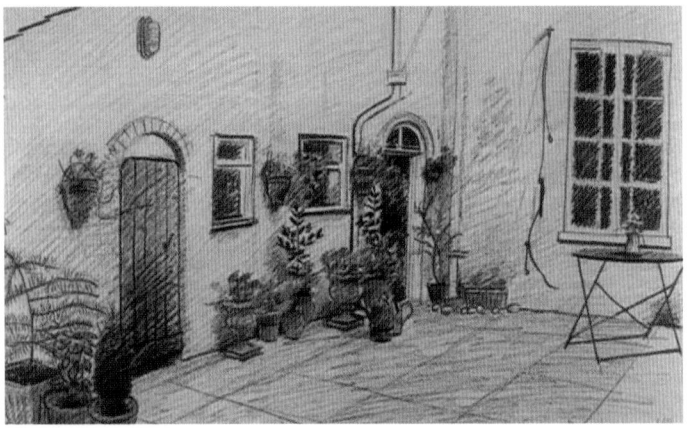

◄ **SARA HAYWARD**
COURTYARD
Loose shading puts a pale glaze of yellow over the courtyard walls, giving the whole drawing a warm, sunny tone. The structures of the building are economically described with line and the actively scribbled and hatched colour overlays.
• LINEAR MARKS

▲ **JEAN ANN O'NEILL**
BANGKOK
This drawing looks for decorative qualities, but builds them solidly with free shading and distinctly drawn shapes.
• FILLING IN
• SHADING

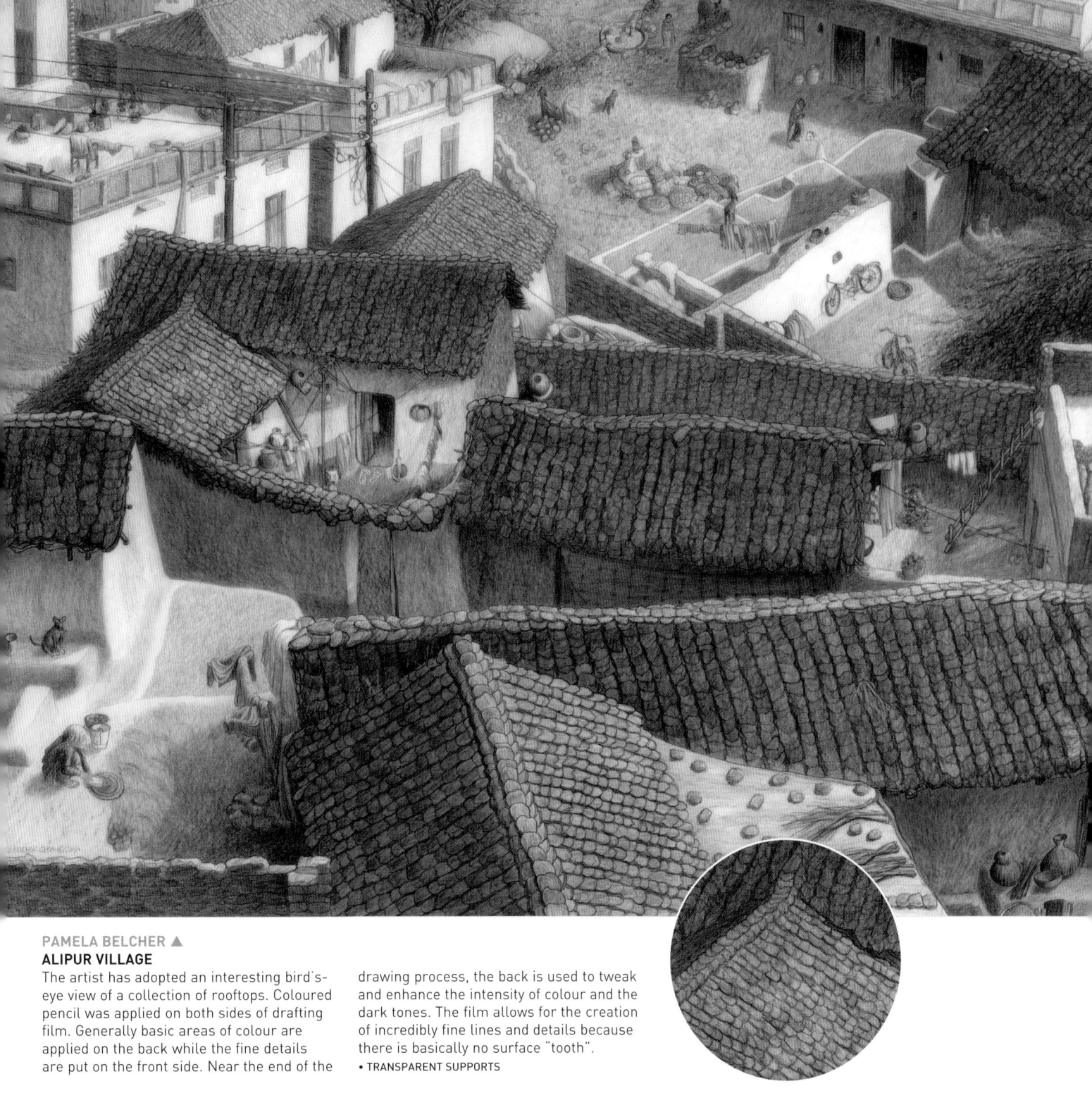

PAMELA BELCHER ▲
ALIPUR VILLAGE
The artist has adopted an interesting bird's-eye view of a collection of rooftops. Coloured pencil was applied on both sides of drafting film. Generally basic areas of colour are applied on the back while the fine details are put on the front side. Near the end of the drawing process, the back is used to tweak and enhance the intensity of colour and the dark tones. The film allows for the creation of incredibly fine lines and details because there is basically no surface "tooth".

• TRANSPARENT SUPPORTS

Facades

Concentrating on the facade of a building is like drawing its portrait. The three-dimensional depth and interior space become irrelevant; you focus on the details of the architecture that give the essence of the building's style and make it recognizable and memorable. You have to work out which details contribute to a true likeness of the building as you see it.

Since a direct, frontal viewpoint eliminates many elements of perspective, it simplifies your task in terms of identifying basic structures – but because there is no surrounding detail to distract the eye, the elements of the facade that you wish to portray need to be well chosen and accurately rendered. The accuracy lies not in reproducing shape and proportion correctly as if from an architect's blueprint, but in defining the relationships of shape, form, colour and texture – the ways they interact and how each element functions within the whole. As can be seen from the examples here, this can be dealt with as an apparently detailed, naturalistic image or as a "portrait sketch" homing in on the bare essentials.

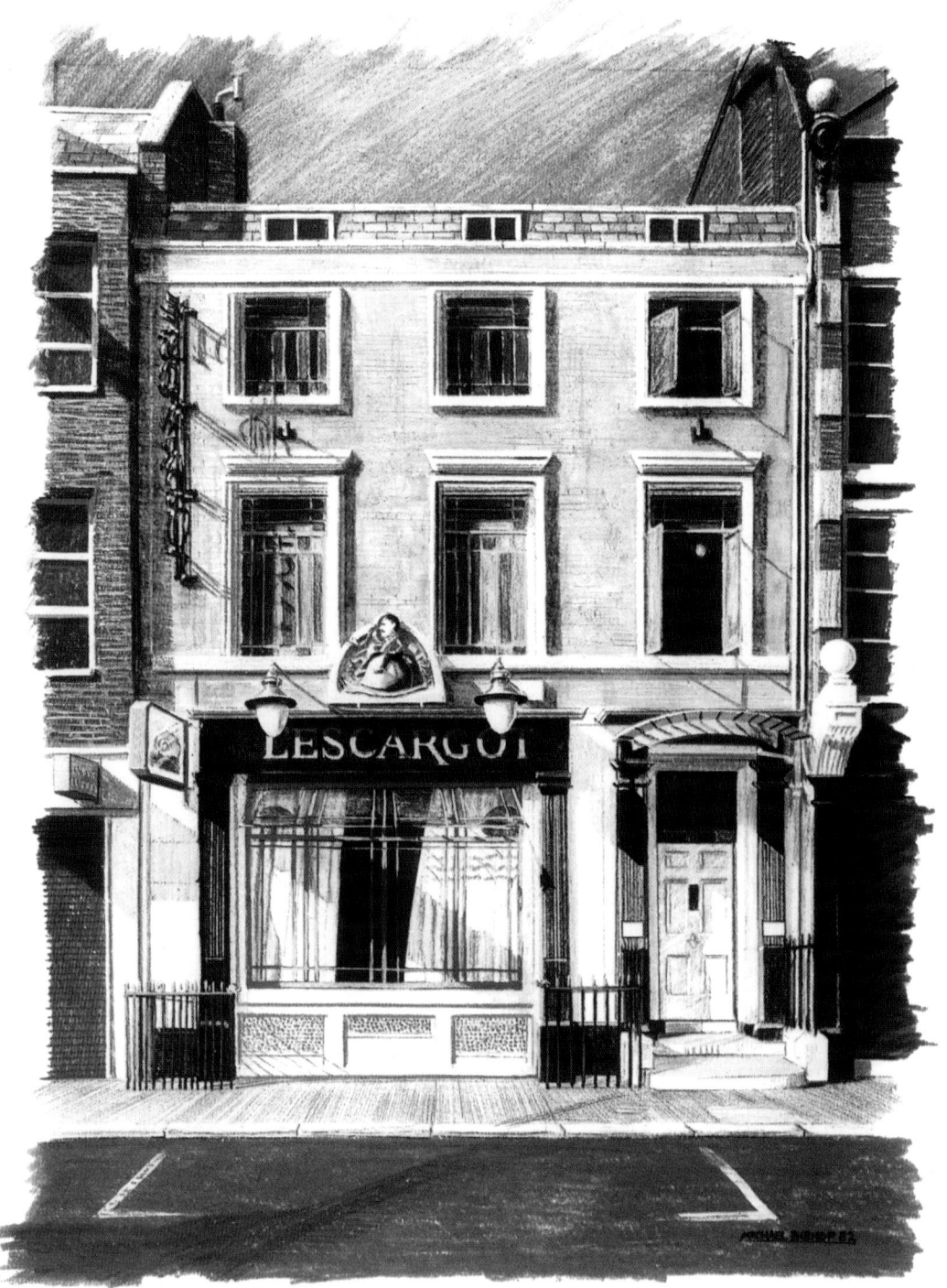

◀ MICHAEL BISHOP
L'ESCARGOT

Many clever touches contribute to the detailed impression of this imposing facade. For example, in the brickwork, a few faint lines serve to convey the overall texture and the cast shadows on the flat surfaces emphasize the detail of the architecture. The quality of the pencil marks is varied to suggest different textures and the organization of colour strongly underlines the structural framework.

• DASHES AND DOTS
• LINEAR MARKS
• SHADING

RAY EVANS ▶
NAVAL COLLEGE, LENINGRAD

A complex architectural structure is described in line, with soft washes of colour forming coherent surface planes within the framework. This treatment makes the most of the soft textures that can be achieved with water-soluble pencils.

• LINE AND WASH
• SOLVENTS

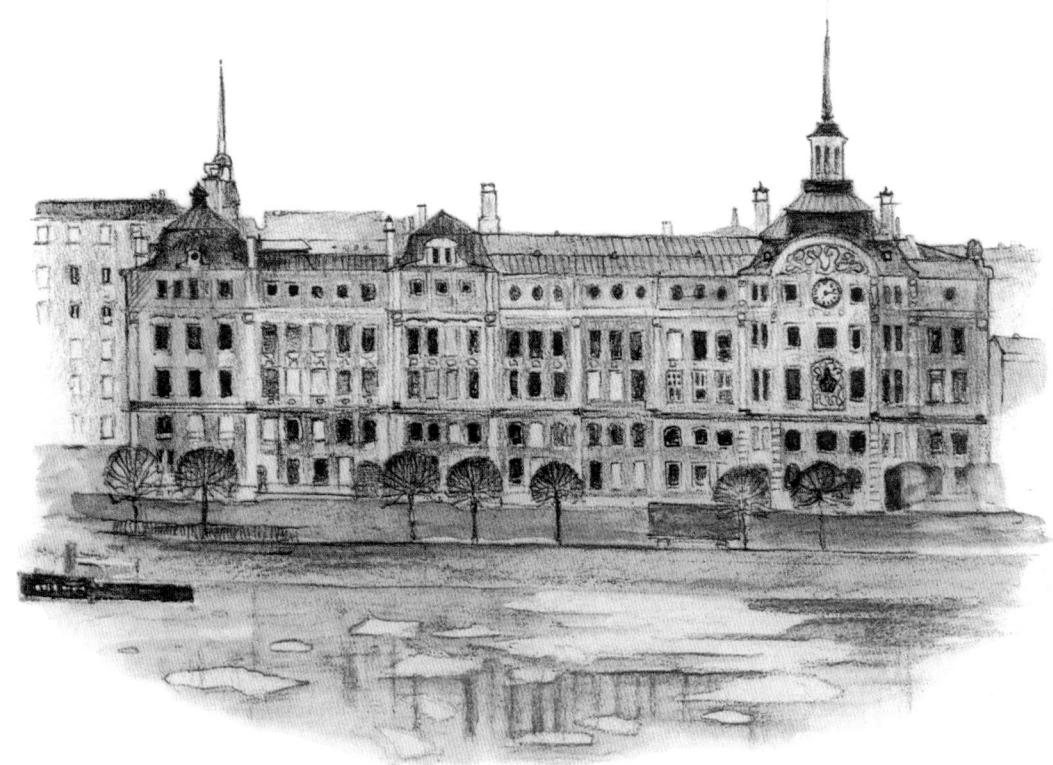

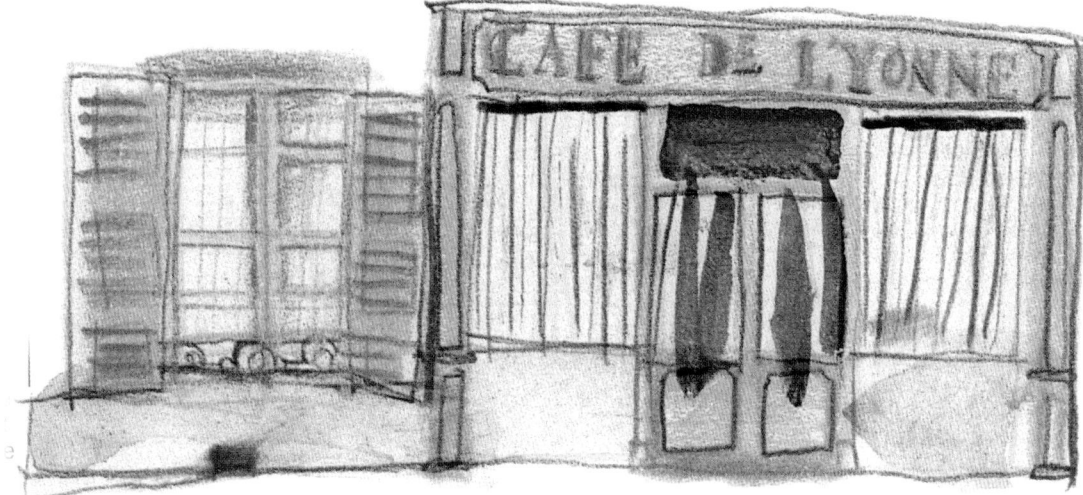

◀ CHLOË CHEESE
CAFÉ DE LYONNE

Focusing on the simple cutout shape of the cafe facade eliminates all distracting detail. The artist's technique and interpretation can therefore be at its most economical, but, at the same time, highly effective in drawing a charming portrait of the continental cafe.

• SKETCHING
• WATERCOLOUR AND PENCIL

Townscapes

The massed structures that form a townscape are inviting to the artist, containing many interesting juxtapositions of shape and form. Both the viewpoint that you take and the degree of detail that you include are important factors in developing the character of the scene.

To record the "layered" architecture of a small, picturesque town, a high-level viewpoint is often favoured; it typically reveals a sense of order in the arrangement of streets and buildings that you do not appreciate in the view from ground level. A normal eye level, however, has the advantage of leading the viewer into the townscape and focusing on familiar territory. In this case, the drawing techniques may be employed in a way that expresses something beyond the simple appearances of things.

There is a useful discipline to be gained in choosing a familiar location as the subject of your drawing; it is a challenge to see it with a fresh, objective eye and devise a suitable technical interpretation. But it is often the charm of a foreign place that appeals, such as in towns you visit on holiday.

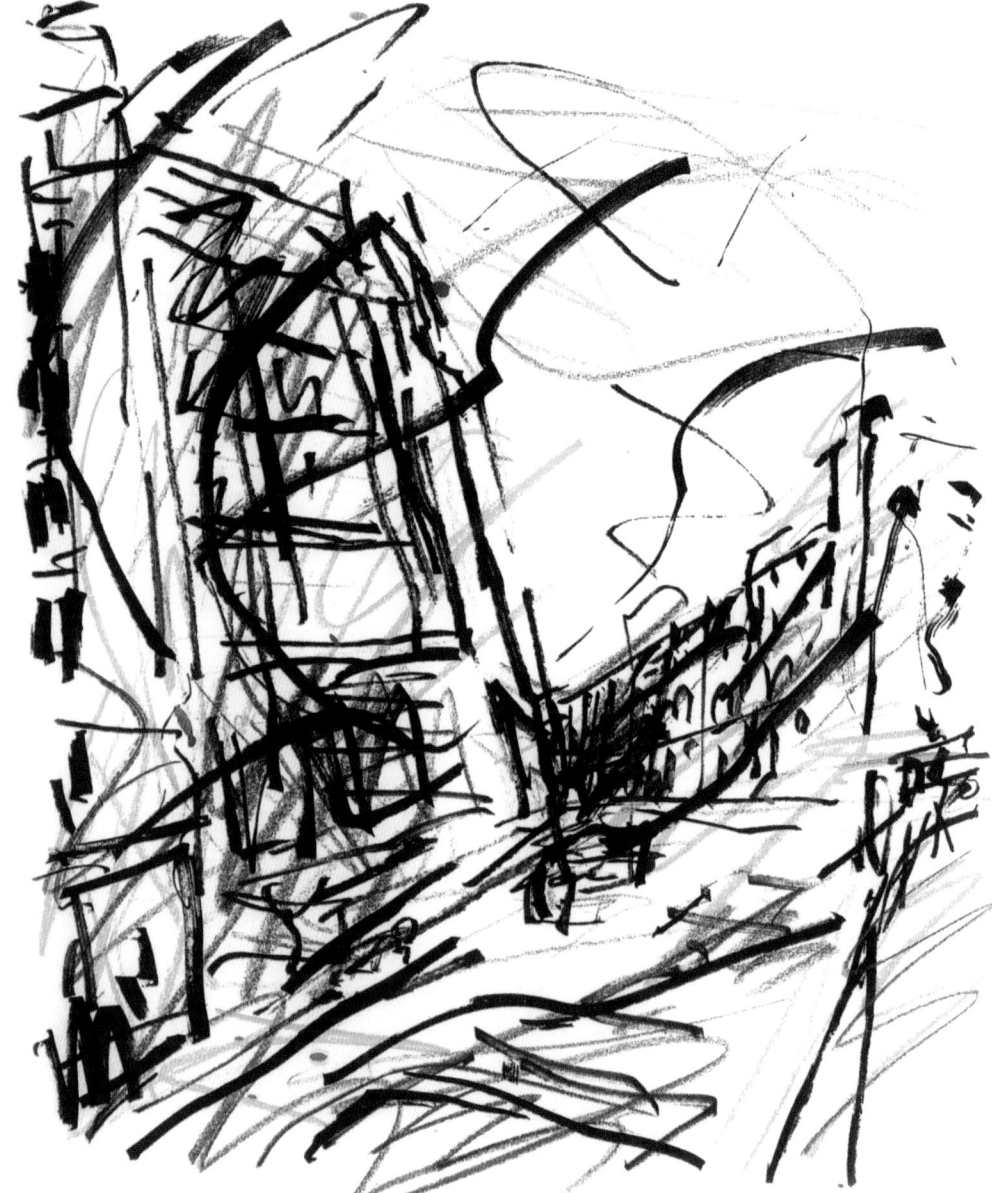

▲ FRANK AUERBACH
STREET
A streetscape can be harsh, busy, even threatening in mood. The vigour and intensity of the marks you make can express an idea or feeling about the place as well as its formal structure. The calligraphic qualities of pen-drawn and coloured pencil lines are combined to strong effect in this abstracted study.
• INK AND PENCIL
• LINE QUALITIES

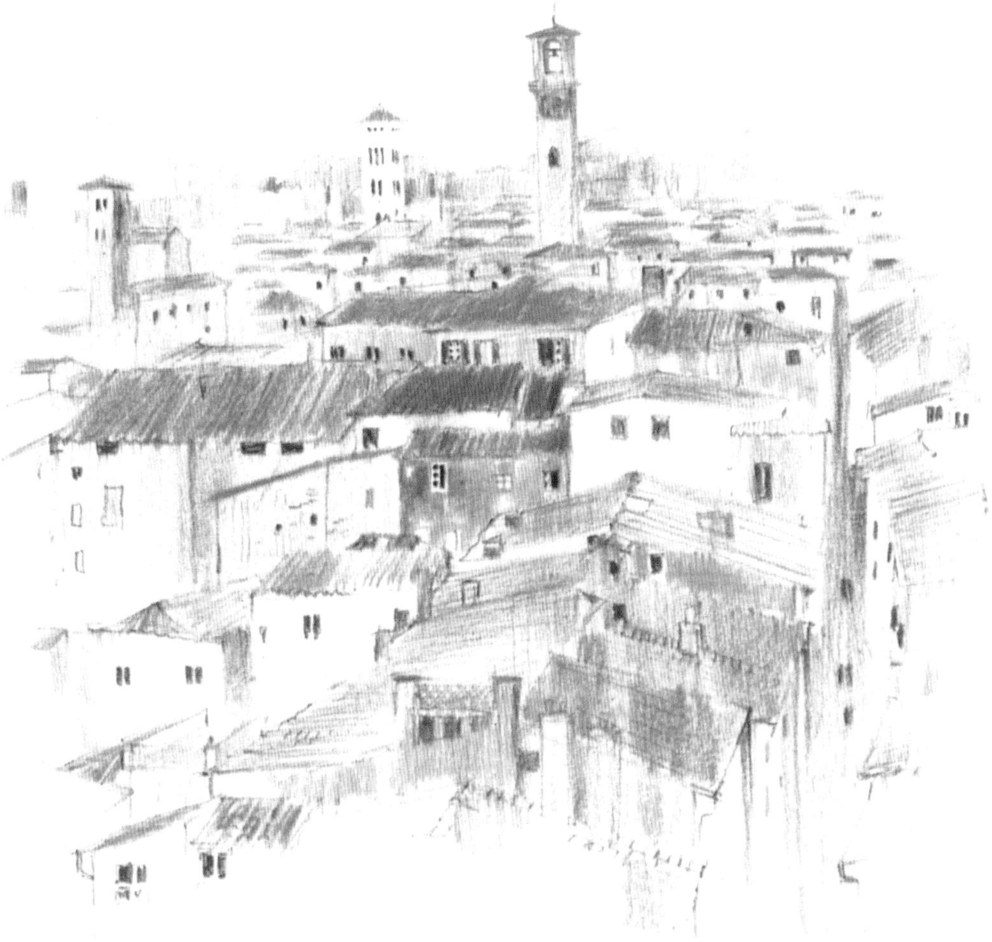

◀ RAY EVANS
LUCCA FROM TORRE GUINIGI

There is enduring visual fascination in the pattern of interlocking planes, the slanted roofs and staring walls that compose a townscape. The high viewpoint here provides an overview of the structural logic. Two different kinds of soft-leaded pencils have been used to build up the colour areas with gentle but emphatic strokes.

- HATCHING
- SHADING
- SKETCHING

LUC VAN DER KROOY ▶
WATERSIDE

The stepped arrangement of the buildings provides a charming framework over which to drape the Mediterranean colours. The detail is minimal and loosely described, but still achieves a sense of character intrinsic to the location. The faintest hints of reflection on the water are sufficient to separate its glassy surface from the opaque textures surrounding it.

- WATERCOLOUR AND PENCIL

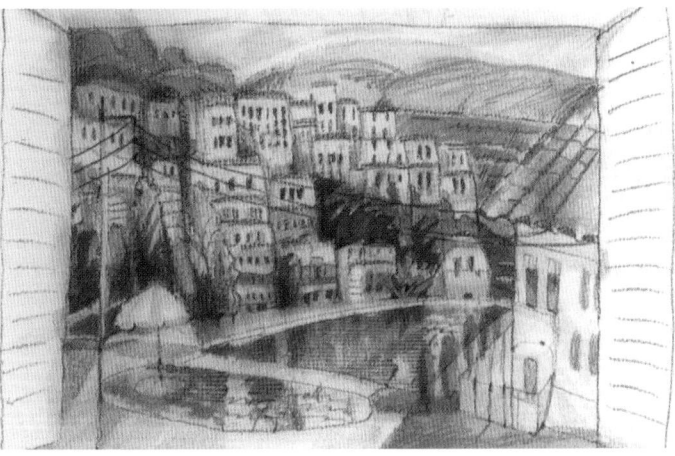

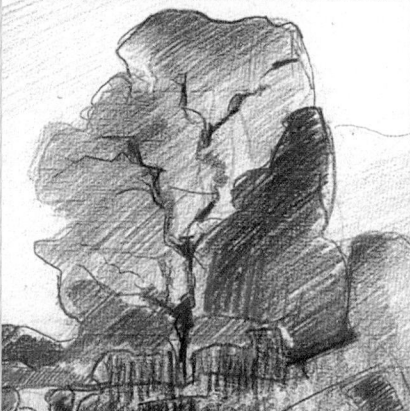

Landscape
Space and light

John Townend

Any landscape view provides a wealth of visual information – space, light, form, texture, colour – so you need to focus clearly on selected features of your subject and ways of interpreting them effectively with coloured pencils, otherwise it is difficult to know how or where to start. Techniques such as shading and hatching enable you to build colour blocks quite rapidly, while the linear qualities of your pencils can be used to develop form and texture within the broader shapes. In this demonstration, John Townend works towards achieving the particular sense of space and light inherent in his subject. The roadway leads into the distance, flanked by the solid shapes of trees, bushes and fences, and the quality of light, reflecting from the damp surface of the road, creates unusual colours and tones in the sky at the central horizon.

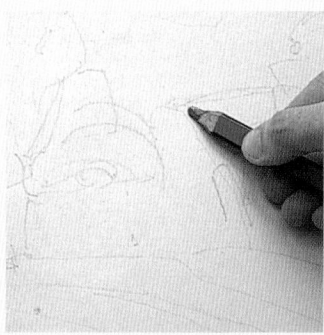

▲ **1** The artist begins by drawing in the main guidelines of the landscape view with a soft pencil. These lines have a sketchy quality, creating the basic forms and rhythms of the composition.

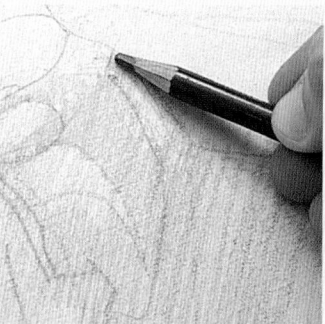

▲ **2** Light shading is used to lay in broad areas of colour. In this initial stage of blocking in, varying intensities of yellow indicate the high tones, overlaid with a mid-toned olive green to give depth.

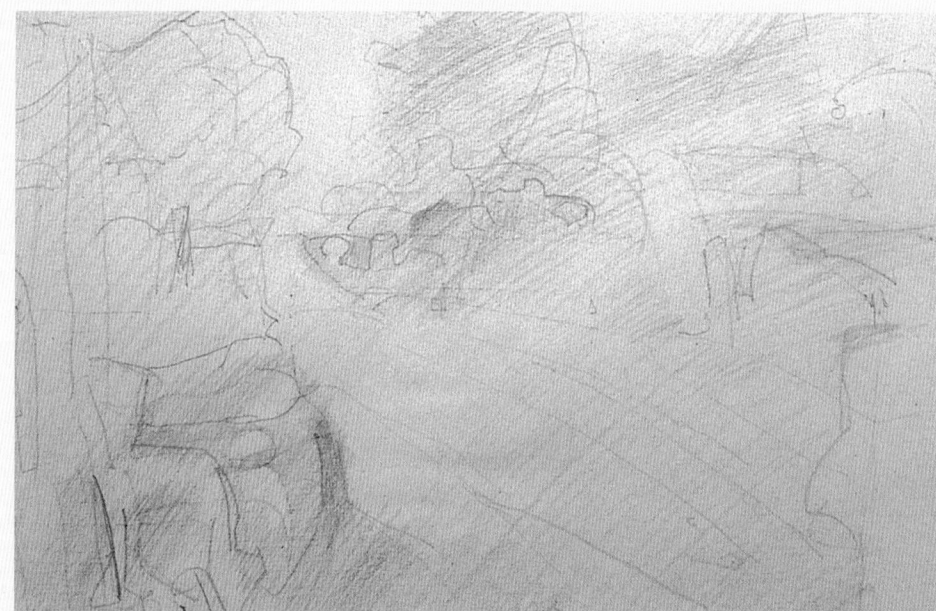

▲ **3** The whole drawing is lightly covered with free, open shading and hatching to "knock back" the luminosity of the white paper and activate the drawing surface.

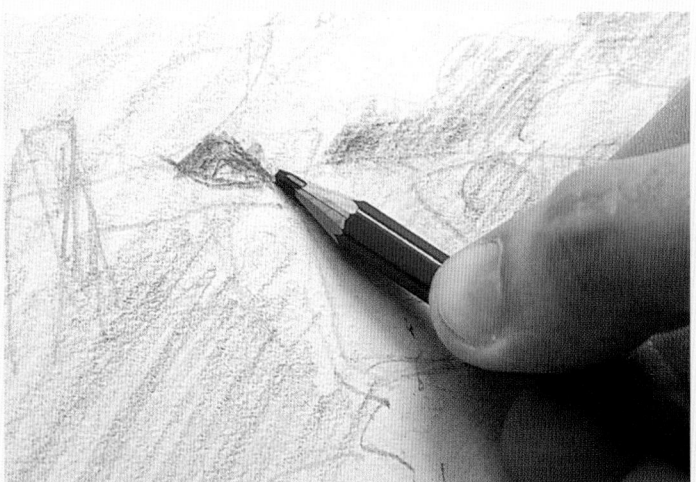

◀ **4** Colour variations are developed gradually by overlaying areas of shading and hatching. The artist begins to pick up some of the smaller and more detailed shapes and work into them.

▼ **5** This step completes the basic stages of blocking in, establishing a definite structure to the composition and suggestions of individual forms and textures.

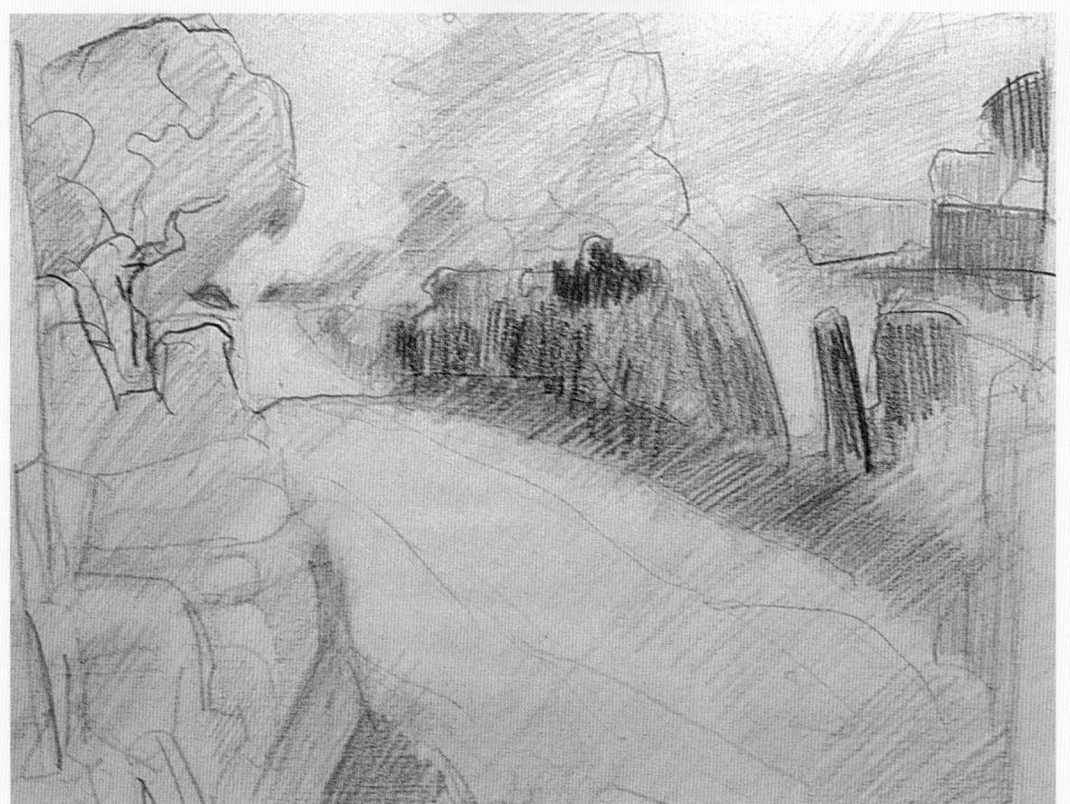

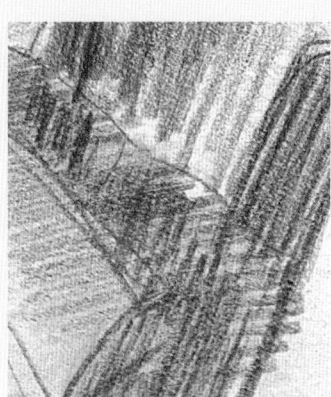

▲ **6** The drawing develops depth and texture through the overlaying of different colours and tones, but, as this detail shows, the pencil marks are still kept loose and open to avoid filling in the paper grain.

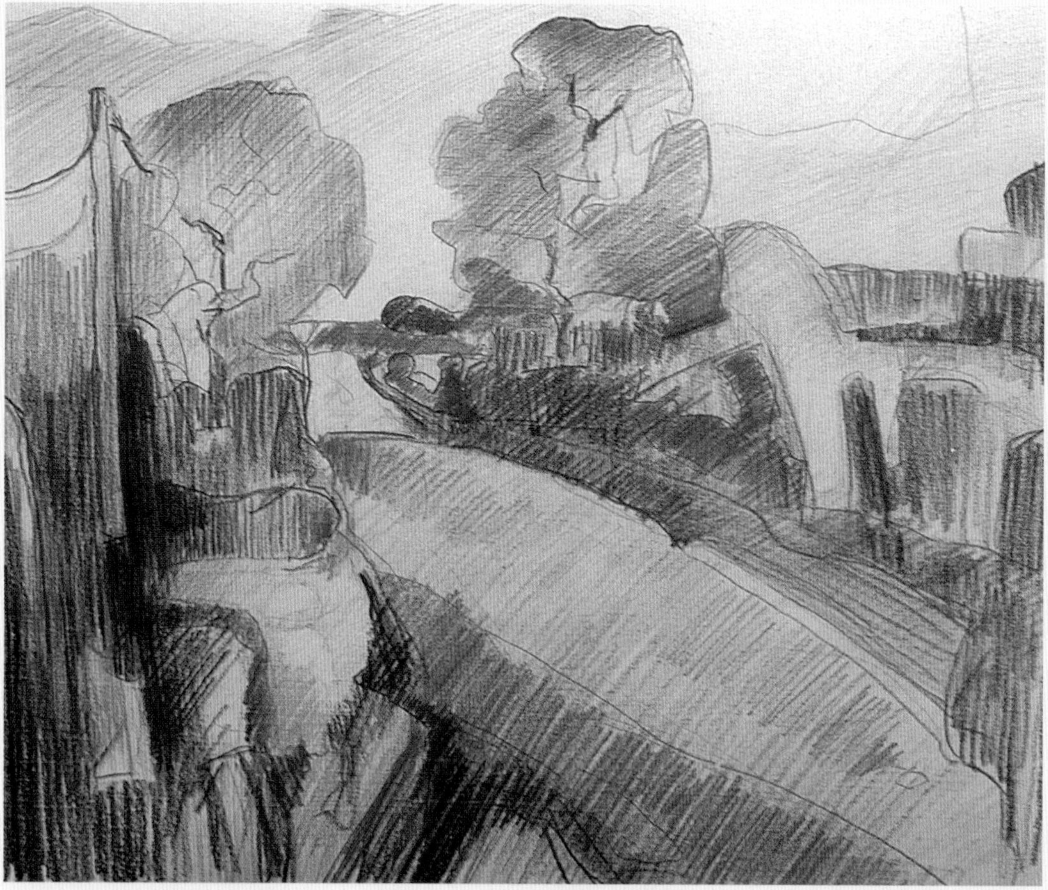

◀ **7** The definition of the overall composition is enhanced by laying in areas of non-naturalistic colour, but the hues and tones are chosen to create a harmonious palette of colours equivalent to the effects seen in the features of the landscape.

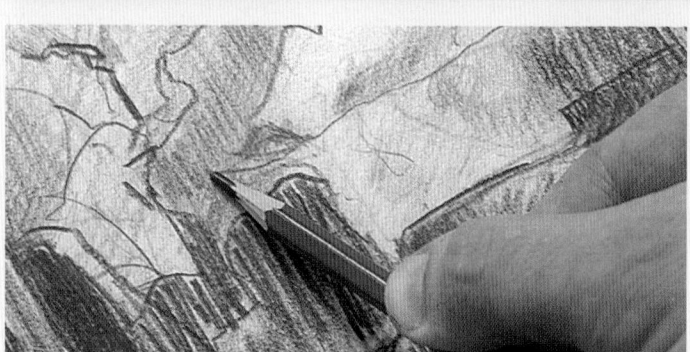

▲ **8** The artist here holds the pencil by the underhand grip (see handling pencils) to give emphasis to the linear marks that create the rhythms and directions of the landscape.

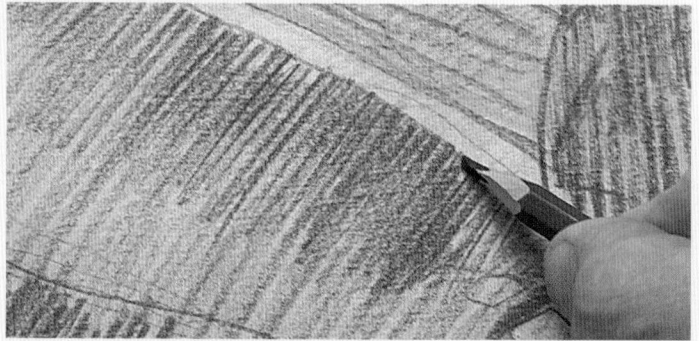

▲ **9** The surface sheen of the wet road needs to be represented by distinctive tonal variations. Colour blending and tonal gradation are built up with overlaid blocks of hatching in strong colours.

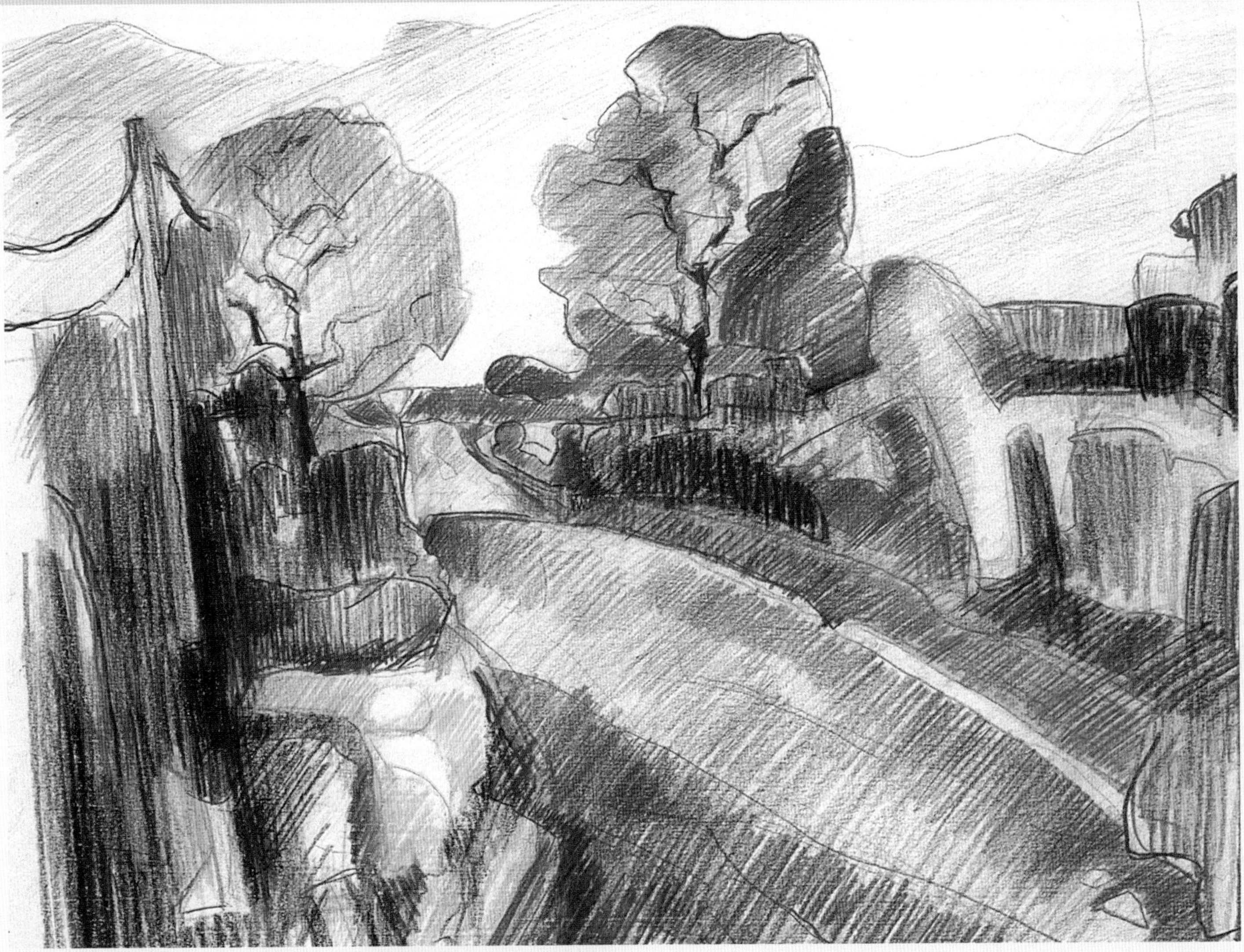

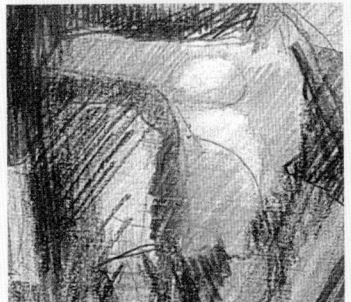
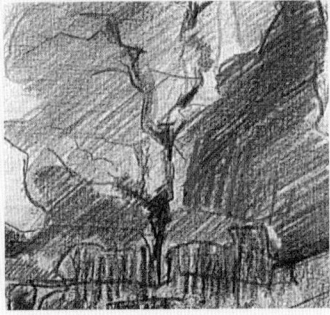

▲ **JOHN TOWNEND**

AUTUMN ROAD

In the final image, the artist has achieved the sense of space and receding forms and surfaces characteristic of this view, while attending to the abstract properties of shape and colour that give the drawing techniques an active presence in forming the image. In the final stages, he has used graphite pencil mixed in with the colours to strengthen the dark tones (far left) and redefine individual structures, such as the tree trunks and branches (left).

Objects

Individual objects make truly exciting images. They are particularly well suited to the scale and detailed textures of coloured pencil drawing. The range of this theme is extensive; many of the objects shown in this part of the book are readily available items, typically part of your day-to-day life. Others can be bought inexpensively and you can start to make a collection of simple but attractive things to include in your drawings.

▼CARL MELEGARI
FRUIT
A scribbled technique is used here to model the forms and bring in subtle gradations of colour. The colours are lively and the rich shadows add to the charm of the piece.
• HATCHING

Selecting your subject and technique

If you are learning to work with coloured pencils and developing your control of technique and colour mixing, studies of objects are a practical way to train your hand and eye. You can set up a single object or a group out of the way of your daily routine, and it can remain there for as long as it takes to complete the drawing, so you can work in stages with frequent interruptions if necessary. You can start with very simple forms and gradually work though to increasingly more complex images and compositions.

If you treat this category of subject matter as a way of learning your craft, there are two different and equally useful forms of approach. You can select one item, or a group of objects, and make several studies, trying out alternative techniques individually and studying particular aspects of the subject one at a time – devoting one study to distinct individual shapes, for example, another to surface effects or an impression of colour and light. Alternatively, you can make one finished drawing incorporating as much detail as possible and combining different techniques to indicate different elements – contour drawing or solid shading to construct the forms, for example, with linear marks overlaid to show pattern and texture. Selective use of techniques such as frottage, impressing and sgraffito can also be employed to obtain textured effects. Then, when you are satisfied that the interpretation is complete, you can change the still-life set-up or select other kinds of objects for a new composition.

While it is useful to set yourself exercises of this kind, do choose objects that particularly interest and attract you, so that you have no trouble keeping your concentration over an extended period of study. Every item has specific qualities that challenge your technical skills – you can find different ways of manipulating your drawing tools to reproduce such effects as the reflective surface of glass, the fineness of lacy or sheer fabrics, the irregular pattern of wood grain, or the soft downy skin of a peach.

In addition to these technical problems, you have also to deal with the representation of three-dimensional form, the dynamics of a group, the spaces around and between the objects and the shapes created by overlapping forms. Using relatively small-scale subjects to investigate these formal elements of composition and technique also provides you with valuable experience for tackling more complex or ambitious themes.

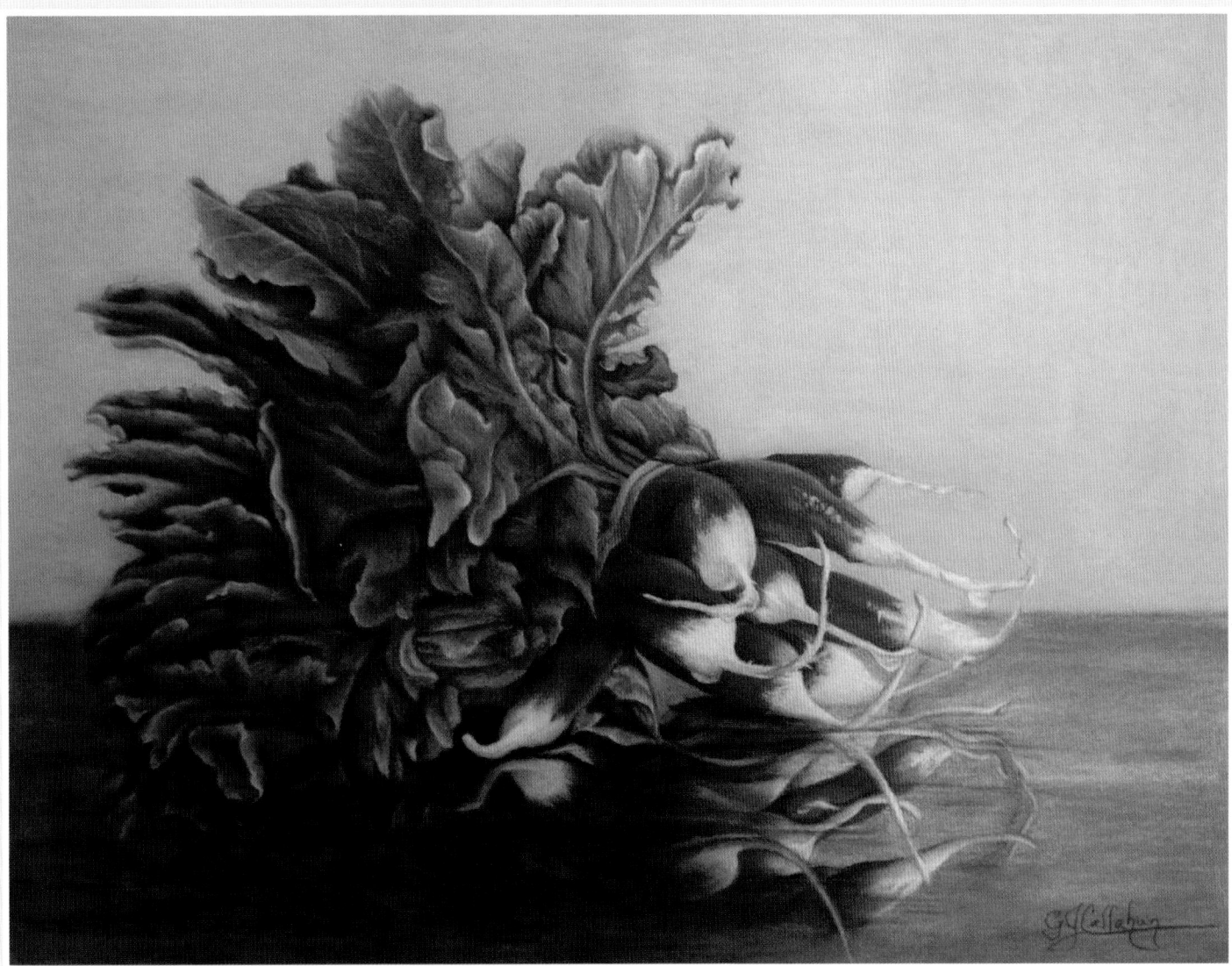

▲ GLORIA CALLAHAN
AT THE ROOT – RADISHES
Inspired by the beauty and colour of nature, the artist combines
pencil and other mediums to give a painterly effect to her work.
This piece, like many of Callahan's, has been painted onto a
board and then fixed in place with up to eight layers of UV
varnish. In doing this, the artist is able to frame her work without
glass, much like an oil painting.
• HIGHLIGHTING
• BURNISHING

Domestic Objects

There is a great deal of material for detailed study in everyday objects found all around your home. Furniture and clothing, which have been chosen originally for the interest and attractiveness of their shapes, patterns and textures, make excellent subjects for coloured pencil drawings. A chair, a rug, a coat hanging up or a pair of shoes sitting on the floor – such apparently simple, familiar items contain a wealth of detail and teach you how to analyse basic shapes and forms, as well as specific surface qualities. Domestic objects are of suitable scale for representation through controlled drawing techniques such as hatching, shading and stippling.

Many smaller items can be found that contribute to colourful still-life groups enabling you to make close-up studies of form and texture. As shown here, simple items from a sewing basket make a fascinating image; other good possibilities are kitchen implements, cosmetics and toiletries, ornaments on a shelf, or the materials and equipment found on a work desk or studio table.

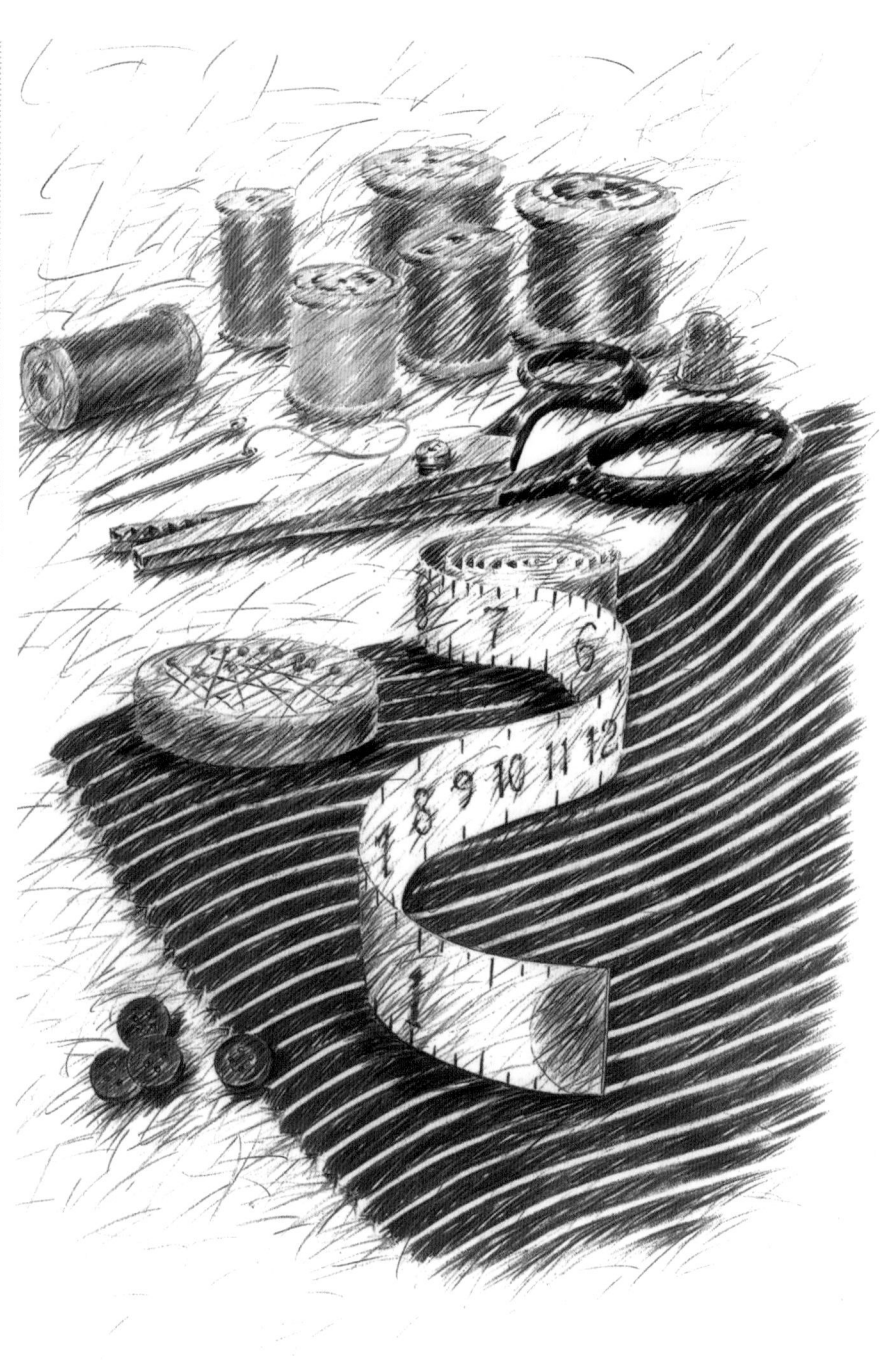

CARL MELGARI ▶
SEWING MATERIALS
The jewel-bright colours of the reels of thread make a vivid contrast to the restrained pattern of the striped fabric. The bright hues are nicely echoed in the reflections on the scissors and pins. The artist's characteristic style of vigorously woven pencil marks is cleverly adapted to the scale of the objects, even encompassing detail as graphic and precise as the numbers on the measuring tape.
* HATCHING
* LINEAR MARKS

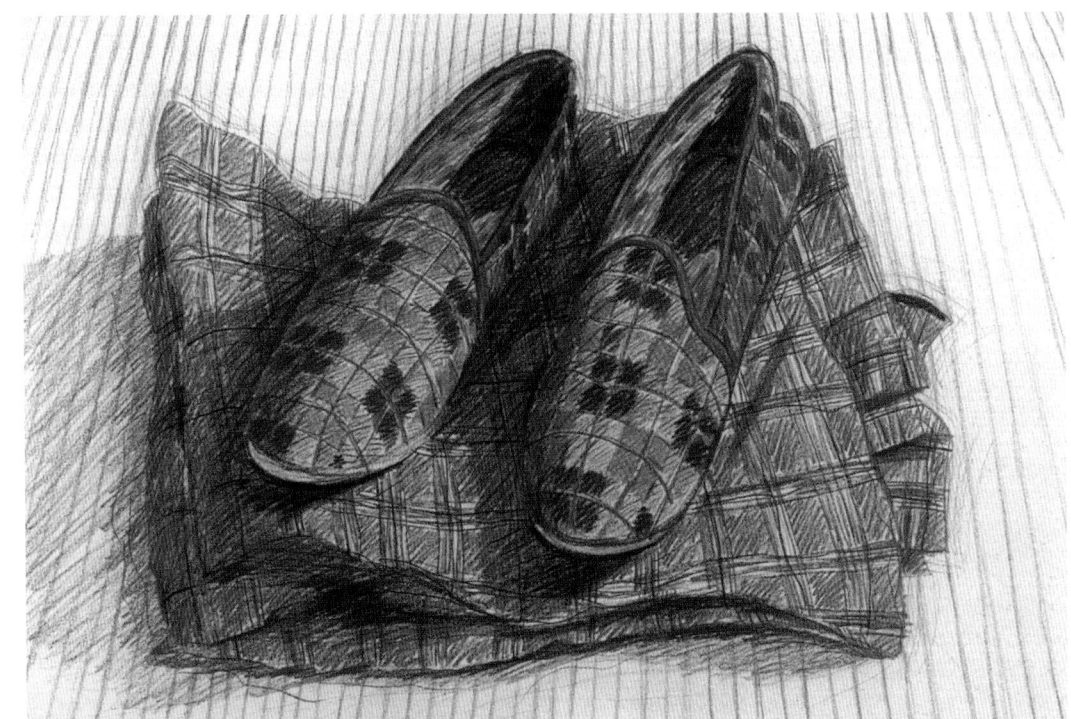

SARA HAYWARD ▶

SLIPPERS

The interplay of line and colour in the patterned fabrics suggests the combination of shading and hatching.

• SHADING
• HATCHING

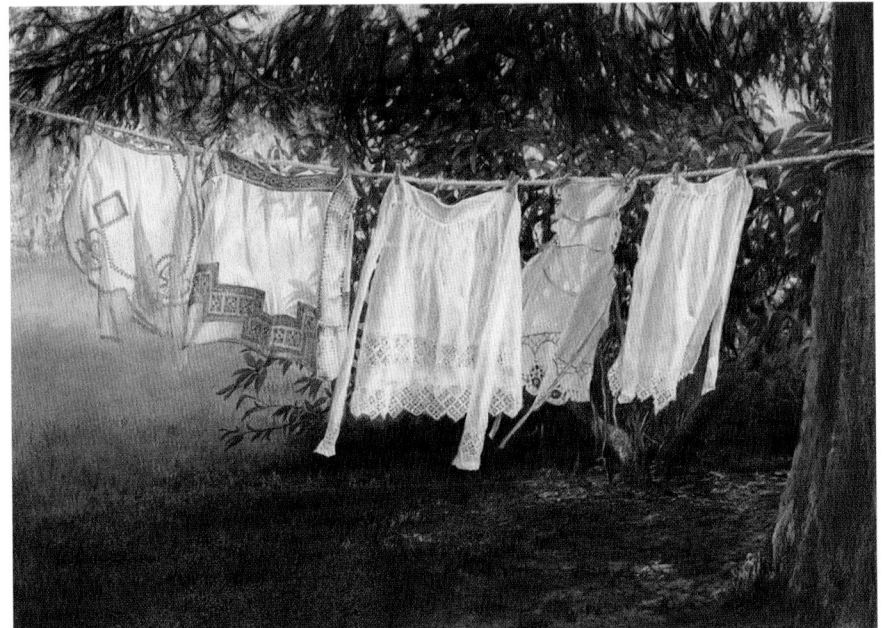

◀PAT AVERILL

JUST HANGING AROUND

Averill has beautifully captured the drape and transparency of the different fabrics in this coloured pencil piece.

• SOLVENTS
• GRADATION
• BURNISHING

Decorative Objects

Many functional objects owe their visual appeal to the colours and patterns applied to them. They are simple forms, made more interesting by the imposition of decorative surface elements – fabric and ceramic items are typical examples.

For the artist, there is a more complex visual challenge underlying the surface colour. A pattern is moulded to the shape of an object, and reflects the contours and volumes of its form. A patterned scarf, for example, is rarely seen as a flat rectangle and when it is draped or folded, the logic of the pattern is broken up, so the relationships of colour and shape within the pattern itself become more complicated. In the same way, patterns on cups, jugs and bowls follow the curves and hollows of the object's shape.

Identifying the ways that the surface elements respond to the underlying form is an interesting problem. An additional factor is the way that light models volume and contour, at the same time modifying surface colour and subtly disrupting the uniformity of an imposed pattern. Thus decorative objects reveal many layers of visual information that you need to take into account in your drawing.

Pattern qualities

Some foodstuffs have interesting pattern qualities relating to their own structure or surface detail – the scales and markings of a fish, for example, or the segmented interiors of certain fruits. In a still-life group, patterns are also created by the repetition of similar shapes. These decorative elements can be brought out and enhanced by coloured pencil drawing, using the technical variety of linear marks, hatching and shading to develop the internal rhythms of the composition.

One way of achieving a particularly bright and busy image is to play off the natural colours and shapes of the chosen foods against the formal, imposed patterns of printed fabrics and decorated dishes. This creates an interesting challenge in how to deal with the interactions of flat patterns and three-dimensional forms. One solution successfully employed in the examples shown here is to use a watercolour underpainting to establish a sense of solid form, over which the coloured pencil drawing develops the surface activity, elaborating the intricate detail of colour and texture.

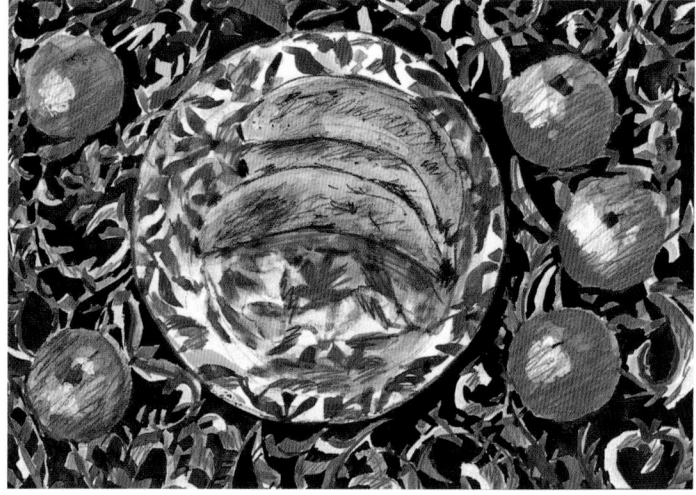

▲ SARA HAYWARD
BANANAS
The very strong black is an important element in bringing up the brilliance of the pure hues, and this has a crisp, solid presence because it is painted in watercolour rather than shaded in pencil. The same applies to the vivid highlights on the oranges, established by a distinct tonal contrast in the watercolour underpainting. Coloured pencil drawing is used to develop the surface interest of the rendering, relating it to texture and pattern rather than form and volume.
• LINEAR MARKS
• WATERCOLOUR AND PENCIL

GRETCHEN EVANS ▶
MARBELOUS
Layers of different colours are applied to the paper until the initial forms are created. The heavily layered effect creates deep saturations of colour and hue. Detail is the artist's forte and the result here is a photorealistic collection of marbles.
• HIGHLIGHTING
• GRADATION

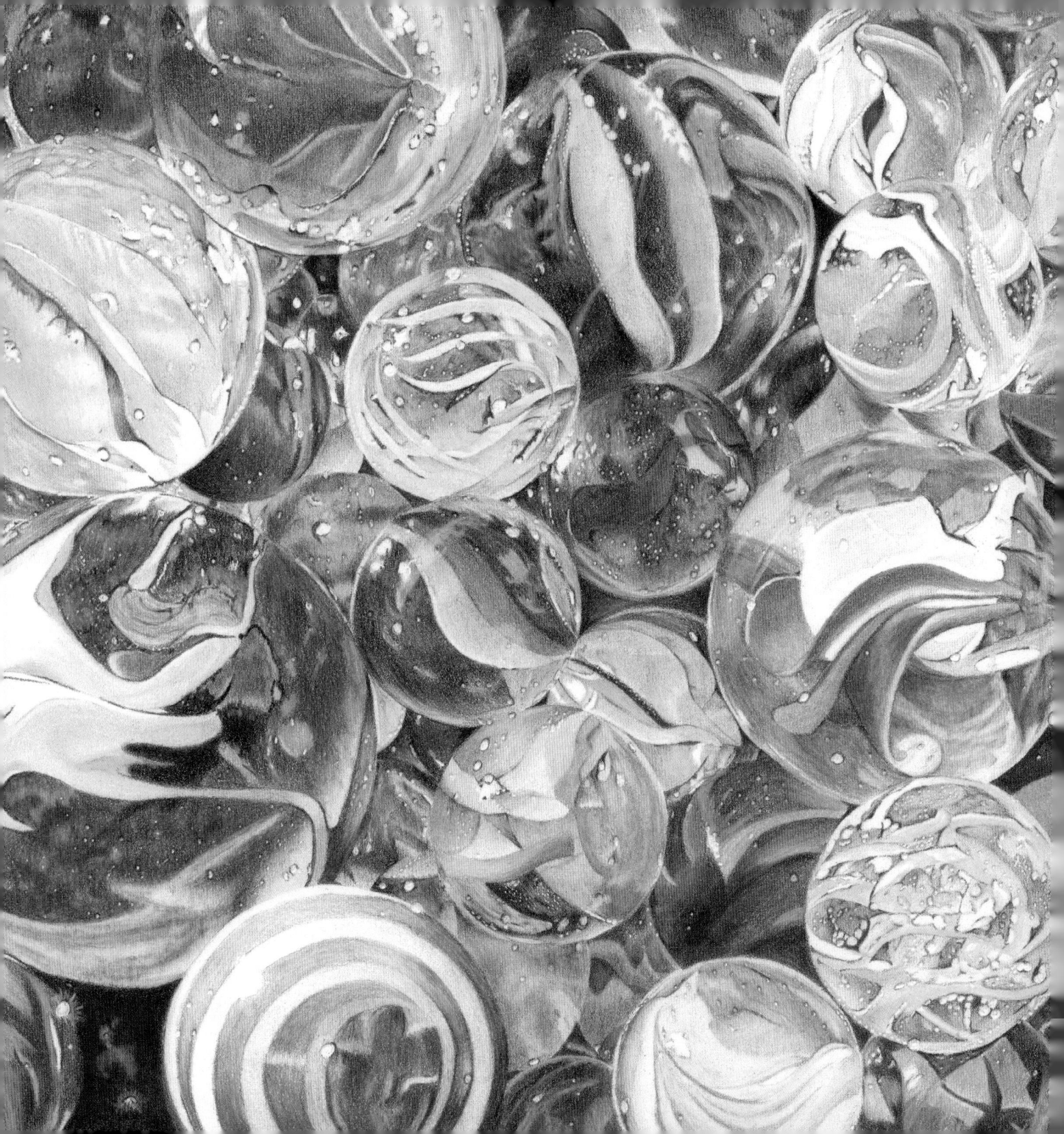

Toys and Ephemera

The variety of coloured pencil drawing found in advertising and magazine illustration has introduced a range of subject matter well outside the traditional focus of fine art themes. Toys, games and chocolate bars, typically designed with wacky shapes and colours intended to give them market appeal, are not the most obvious items for detailed study in a drawing. But they are ordinary and accessible elements of our daily life in the way that more austere still-life subjects have always been, and they make colourful, busy images that are fun to work out technically.

An illustration is put in context in a way that a one-off drawing is not; but as the examples on these pages show, there are similar formal considerations that need to be resolved to create a striking and effective composition. Because the basic shapes and surface colours and textures may be quirky and specific, it is all the more important to analyse them accurately and adapt your drawing techniques effectively to portray individual aspects of the subject.

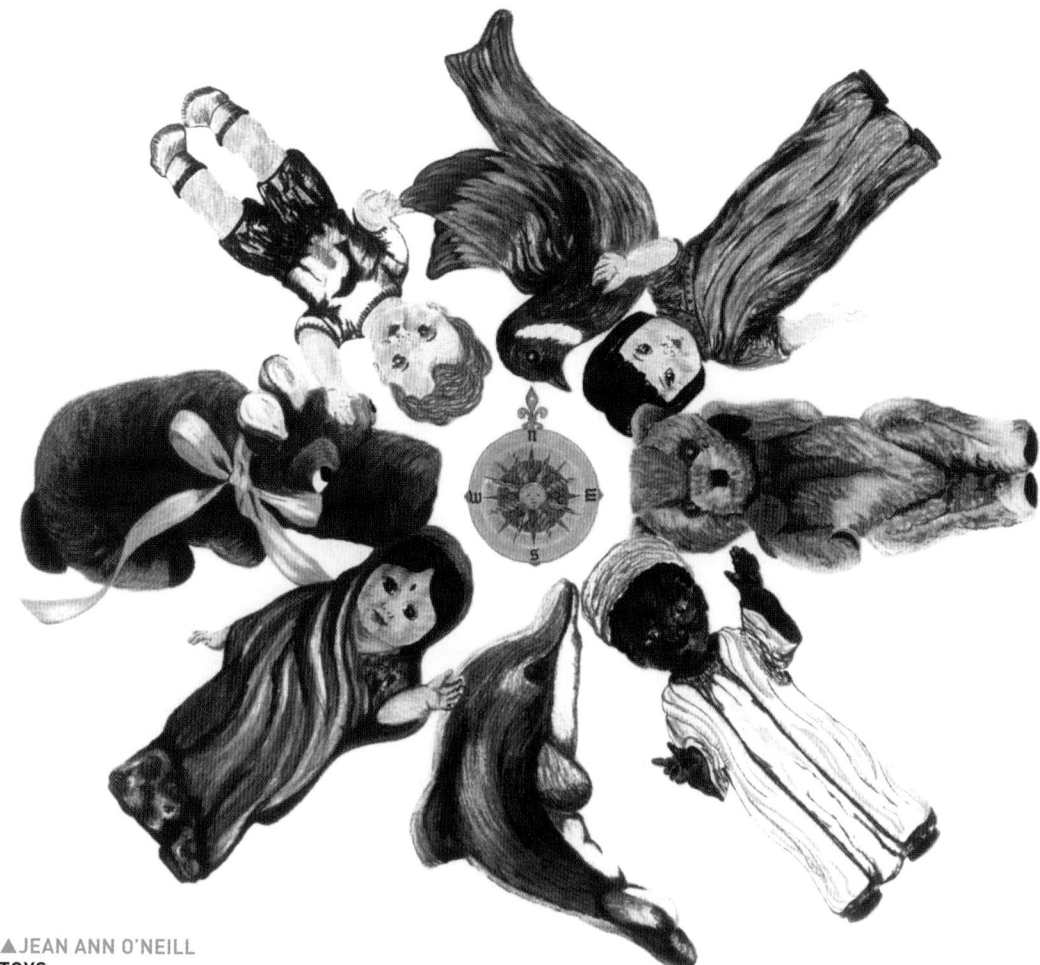

▲JEAN ANN O'NEILL
TOYS
The arrangement of the dolls and animals as a radial group makes an unusual composition. Allowing the shapes to overlap slightly emphasizes the circular rhythm. The technique relies on the real colours and textures suggesting the qualities of pencil marks that best describe each component of the group.
• OVERLAYING COLOURS

◄JEAN ANN O'NEILL
SOFT TOYS
The generalized shapes of the animals are modelled with softly shaded colours, over which various dashes, curves and other kinds of linear marks are imposed to develop their furry textures.
• DASHES AND DOTS
• LINEAR MARKS
• SHADING

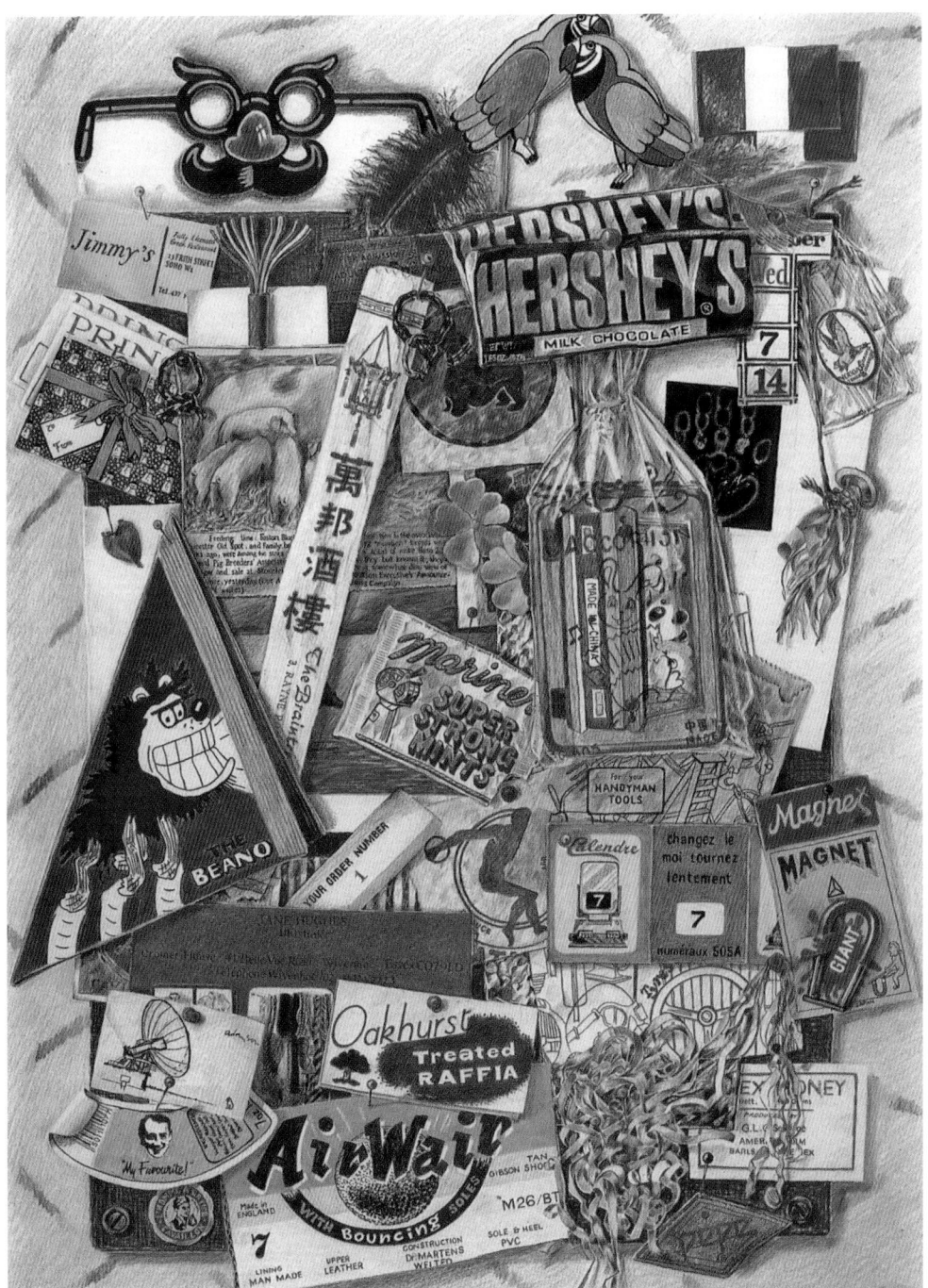

◀JANE HUGHES
CARDS AND WRAPPERS

This self-promotional work includes all manner of ephemeral items, providing a range of bright colours and varied textures that demonstrate the artist's skills in applying her medium. The apparently random selection of objects is arranged to form a strong interplay of shapes and directions. Within this framework, various techniques have been used to build up particular impressions, from the vivid opacity of printed colours to the subtle shadowing and reflection on transparent wrappers. Through careful observation, the artist has achieved an effective rendering of the differences between flat, graphic items and three-dimensional objects.

• BLENDING
• ERASER TECHNIQUES
• FILLING IN

Groups

Grouped objects present you with a number of decisions on how to treat the composition of the group, as well as suitable techniques for interpreting particular forms and surface effects. What angle of view will you take? What are the spaces between the objects, and how much visual interest do they contain? How do you deal with background elements in relation to featured objects? Is your drawing purely a formal still-life study or does it reflect a mood?

If you are dealing with a number of disparate objects – perhaps using a "found" grouping rather than one you have set up yourself – you need to decide whether your techniques will emphasize the differences of form and texture or have the effect of bringing them together visually. With coloured pencil drawing, there is a great deal of scope for blocking in the overall composition in a way that gives it a cohesive structure, then using varied techniques to develop the detail.

Foodstuffs

Foodstuffs have often been important components of traditional still-life groupings. They provide a common theme which unifies a composition, whether the individual items are similar or selected from a varied range. A simple loaf of bread is in itself a fascinating study of specific textures; readily available foods such as fruits, vegetables and fishes all offer great variety of form, colour and surface detail that lends itself to the intimate scale of coloured pencil drawing. Packaged foods introduce an interesting modern variation on traditional still-life themes, mixing bold interactions of shape and form with graphic surface detail.

Setting up a group of objects for a drawing requires thought. A formal arrangement in which each component is clearly visible can look too "posed", but a random grouping may present undesirable combinations of shape and colour. Think about the format of your drawing, how you will handle the colour detail, and the light and shade that brings out characteristic forms.

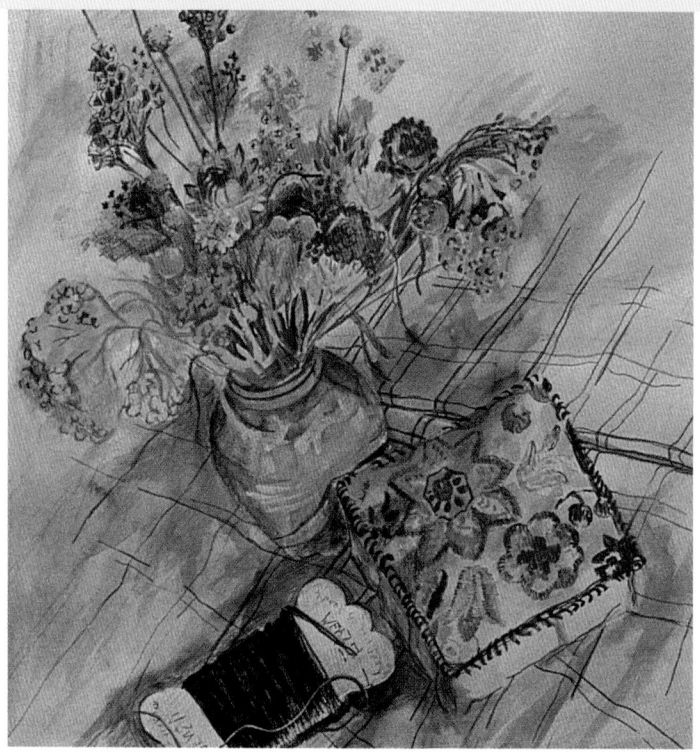

▲ **HELENA GREENE**
STILL LIFE
Free washes of watercolour and lively brush drawing establish basic shapes and forms and a balance of colour and tone. Over the painted ground, coloured pencils add sharpness and detail.
• WATERCOLOUR AND PENCIL

JANE STROTHER ▶
SUMMER PLATE
The attractive sunlit mood of a simple still life is captured with the combination of watercolour and pencil. The slight translucence typical of pencil colours helps to lift the tonal density, but the line work and shading are strong, with a punchy descriptive quality.
• LINEAR MARKS
• WATERCOLOUR AND PENCIL

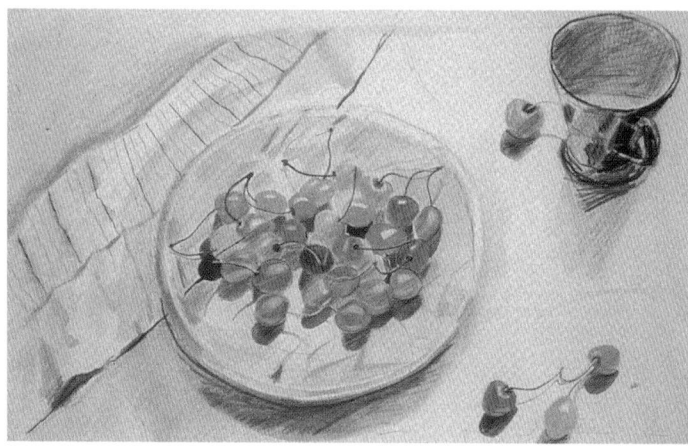

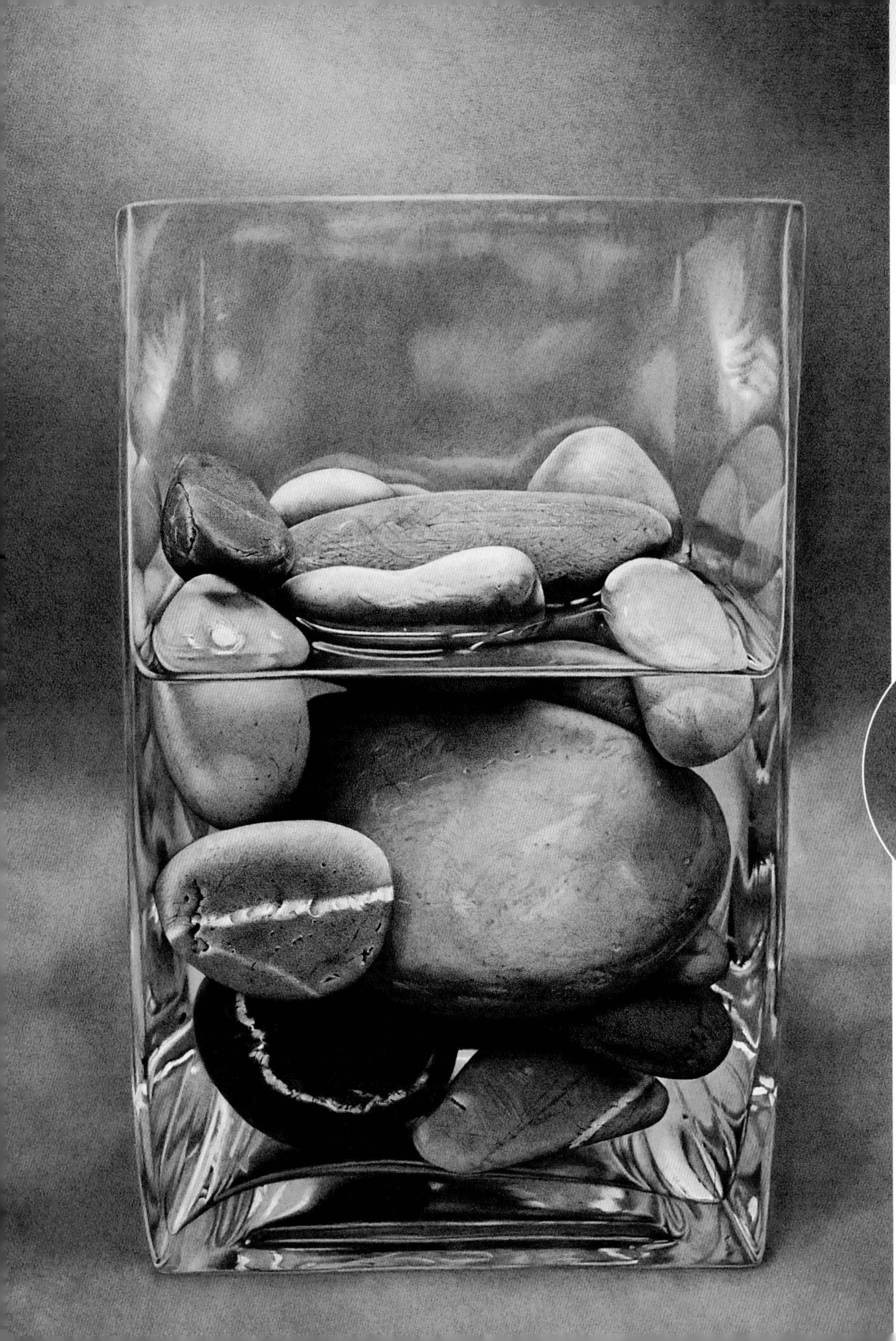

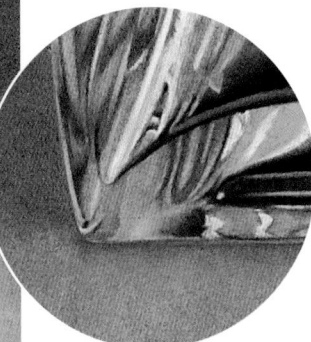

◄ **DEBORAH FRIEDMAN**
COUNTERPOINT IN GREEN
The artist is interested in
exploring ways of looking at
stones as a subject, most notably
being stones placed in clear glass
containers filled with water. The
distortion of glass, light, colour,
shadow and shape are captured
here in the finest detail.

• LINE AND WASH
• MIXING PENCILS

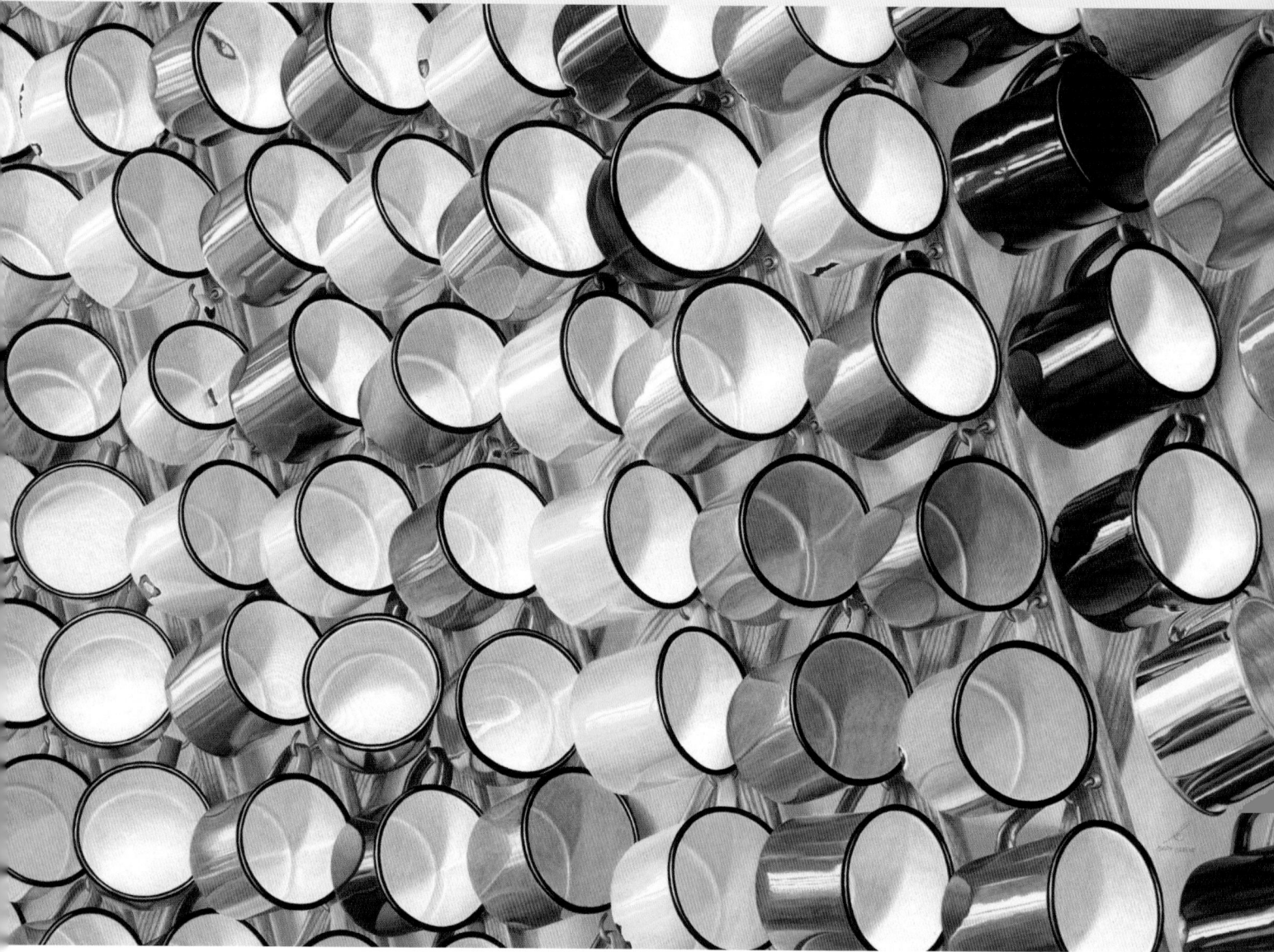

▲ GARY GREENE
CUPS
Layering and burnishing techniques are used to create
this deep and vibrant image. Colours are layered on
top of one another and blended to create a luminous
sheen. Burnishing is used to give the impression of
light striking the cups and to create a realistic piece.
• OVERLAYING COLOURS
• BURNISHING

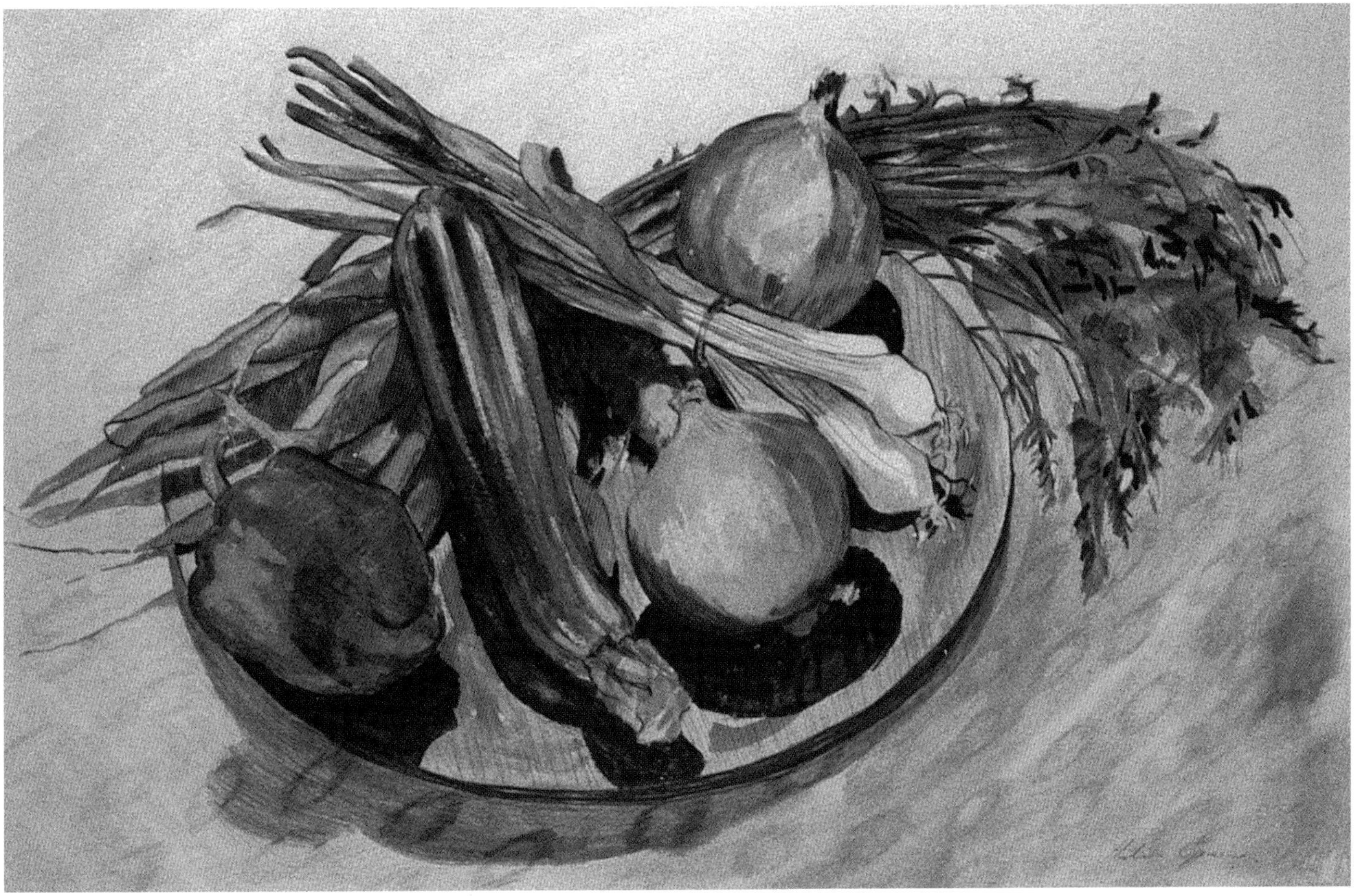

▲ **HELENA GREENE**
VEGETABLES
The painting that forms the basis
of this image is boldly modelled
with colour and tone, but the
individual details of texture, light
and shadow on the vegetables
benefit from discreet touches of
coloured pencil line and shading.
• DRAWING INTO PAINT

RITA D. LUDDEN ▶
SUMMER STILL LIFE
The gradations of colour have been
so subtly contrived in this picture
that it has the smoothness and
delicacy of a watercolour, but it
has been worked completely
in pencils.
• GRADATION
• SHADING

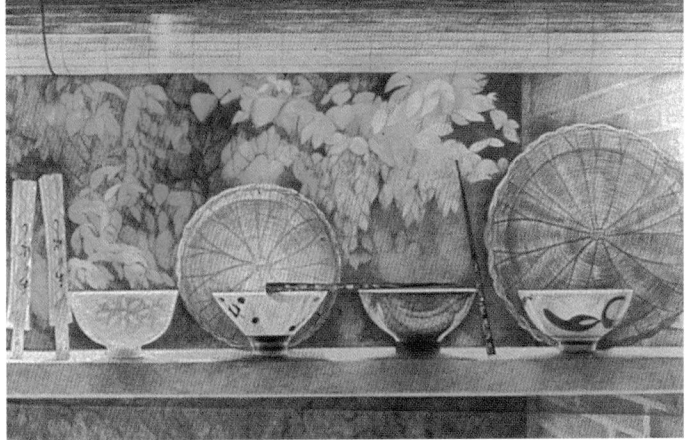

TESS STONE
TEA TABLE
All the objects in this group in reality have cleanly defined shapes and even textures, so the free pencil technique and quirky contours provide an interesting reinterpretation which expresses the artist's own style and energy. The individual colours are mostly low-key and muted, but the particular combination of hues creates a colourful impression.

• CONTOUR DRAWING
• FILLING IN

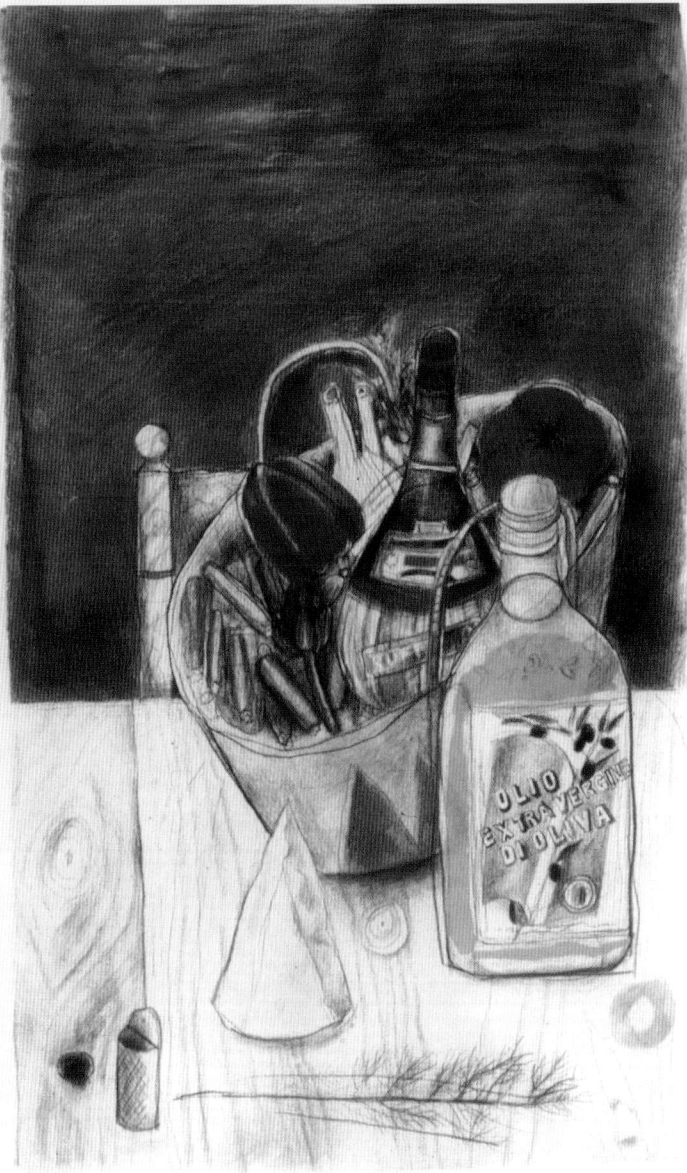

▲CHLOË CHEESE
SHOPPING BAG

Small patches of coloured ink on the red pepper and oil bottle provide a glowing base for the pencil colour, but the overall impression of the drawing and the build-up of detail are mostly dependent on the pencil work. This contrasts open areas of linear pattern with solid colour and subtle shading, to good effect.

- LINE QUALITIES
- OVERLAYING COLOURS

▼JANE HUGHES
STORE CUPBOARD

This drawing represents the kind of found subject that can be overlooked as material for the artist because the components are everyday things. However, this picture shows how the various types of food packaging can create a fascinating composition full of variation, in the same way as more conventional forms of still life. The inclusion of the postcard and photograph tucked into the frame of the left-hand door adds a personal touch.

- LINEAR MARKS
- SHADING
- WATERCOLOUR AND PENCIL

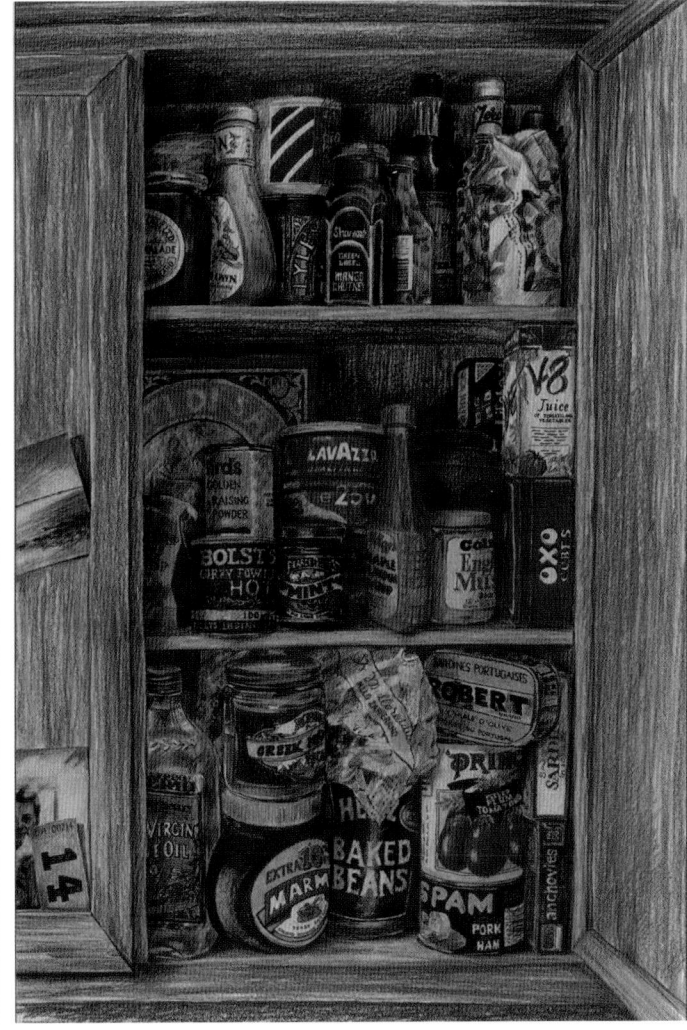

Fruits

All kinds of fruits make ideal subjects for coloured pencil drawing. The shapes are distinct and self-contained, the colours bright and appealing and the variable textures suggest interesting ideas for visual interpretation. Individual items are easily available and mostly inexpensive, and fruits last well if you need to leave a still life in place so that you can complete a drawing over a period of days.

The range of marks you can make with coloured pencils enables you to deal with broad shapes and colour areas and with intricate details of colour and texture. The sense of solid form may be achieved by using the classic technique of close shading, building up the colours in cohesive blocks before surface detail is overlaid, or you can exploit directional linear marks to create an active image area, orchestrating variations of colour and tone to portray the subject descriptively.

These simple, natural forms are excellent vehicles for learning and practising coloured pencil techniques – you can find a great deal to study in just one or two common fruits, such as apples or oranges. To create greater complexity in the image as your confidence builds, you can construct a more ambitious still-life group, perhaps adding fabrics, ceramics or glass items – such as a bowl in which to hold the fruit – to extend the variety of form and texture.

▼ **GLORIA CALLAHAN**
BACKLIT WATERMELON
This still-life study of watermelon slices has been set on varnished hardboard to give the painterly effect of oils rather than coloured pencils. The black background helps to define the individual textures of the melon and adds superb depth to the piece due to its mix of light and shade.
• FIXING
• BLOCKING IN

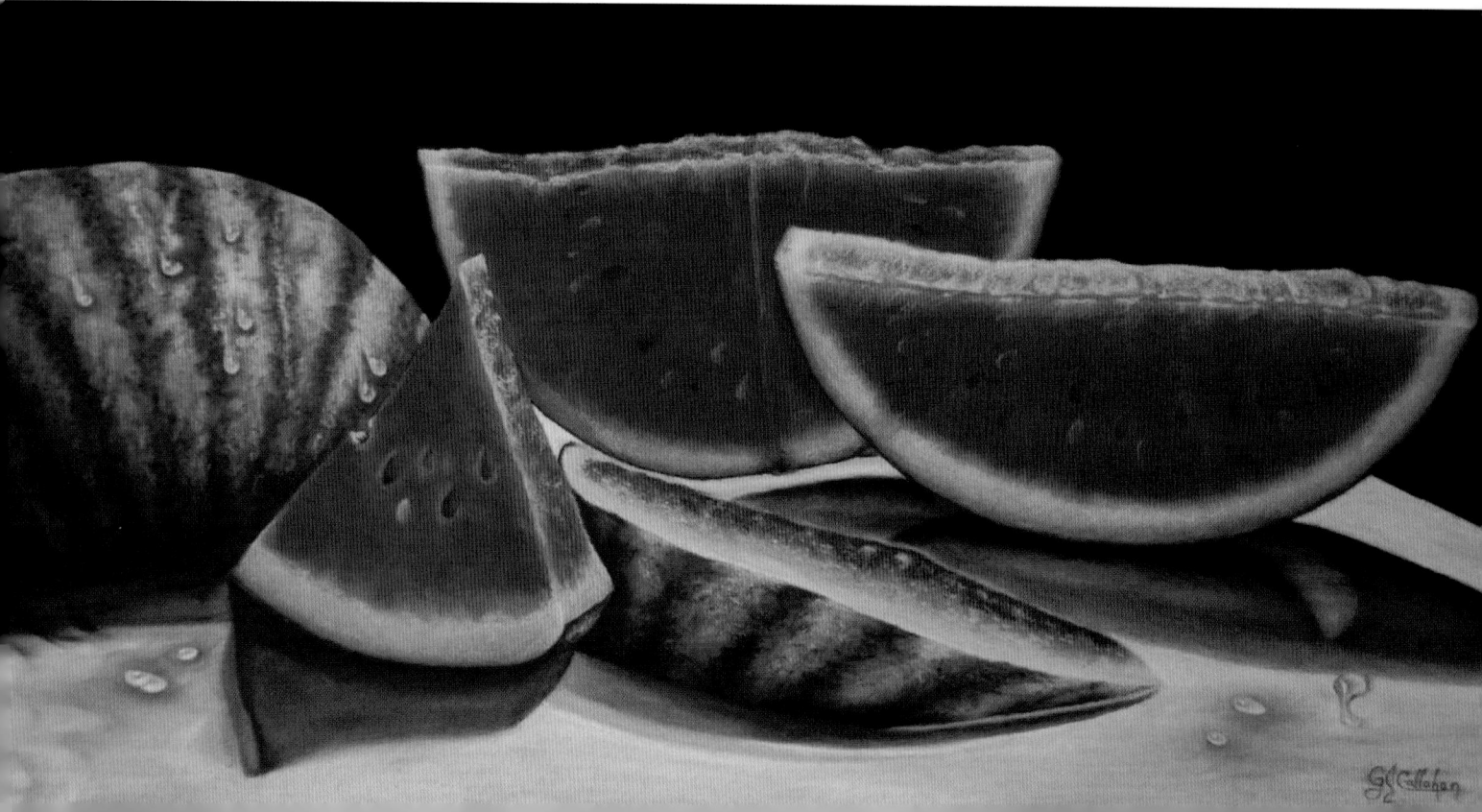

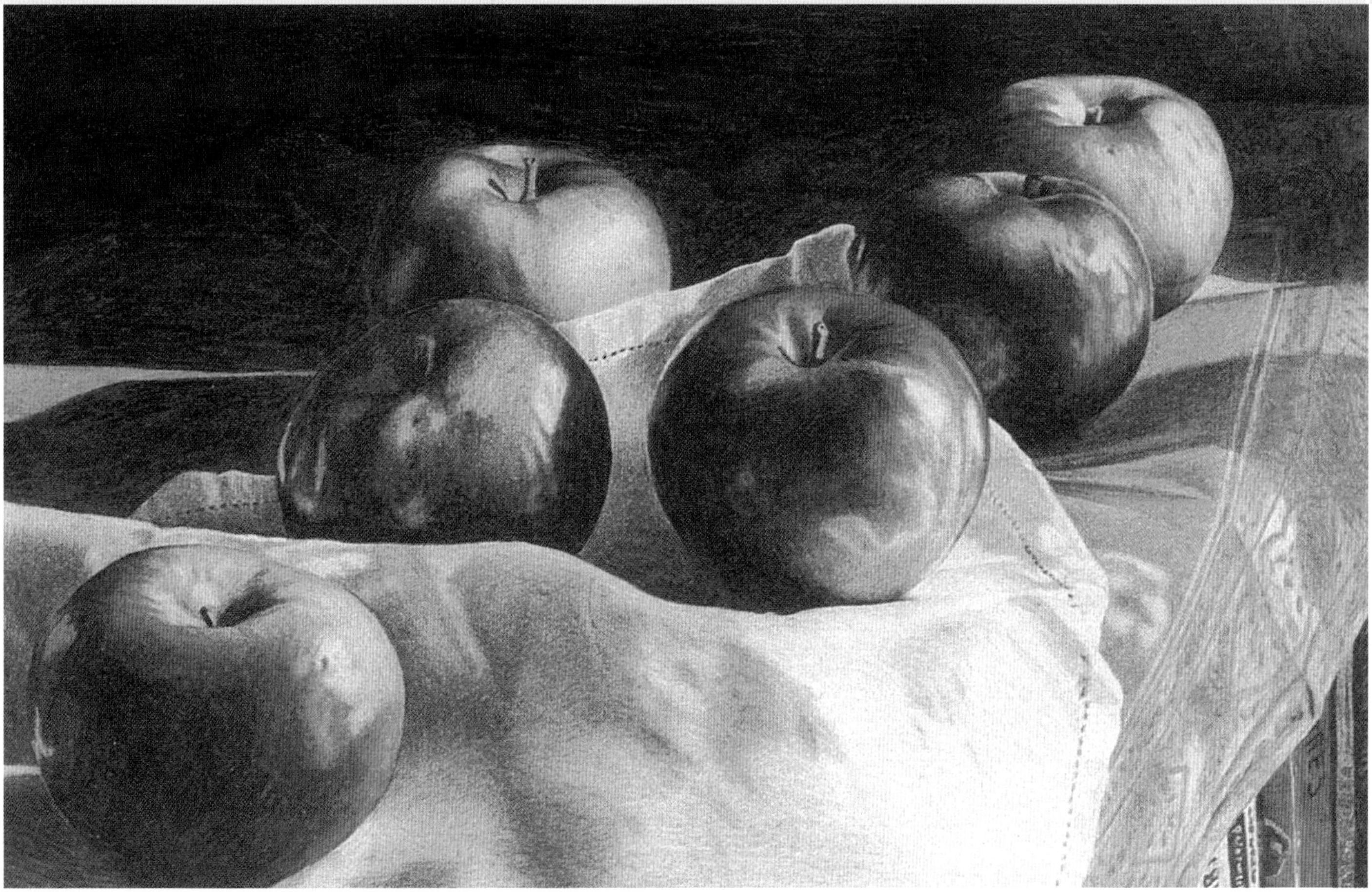

▲ **BARBARA EDIDIN**
VICKI
Part of the effectiveness of this composition lies in confining the still-life aspect to the simple, similar shapes of the apples, rather than selecting very different fruits. The artist concentrates on reproducing their colours and textures very precisely and applies the same sharp vision to the qualities of the fabrics.
• BLENDING
• SHADING

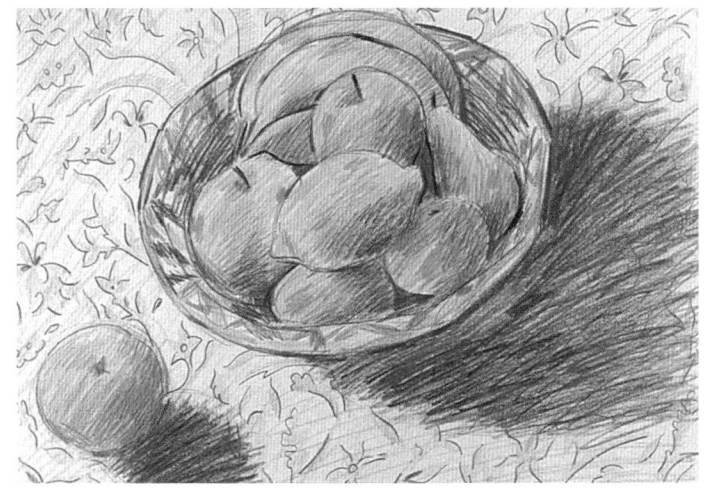

◄ **SARA HAYWARD**
FRUIT BOWL
This unpretentiously attractive subject is interpreted with a vigorous approach to the drawing technique. The combination of hatched and shaded colour creates an open surface texture that allows the colours to sing out clearly. Notice that the heavy shadow areas are also treated colourfully.
• HATCHING
• LINEAR MARKS

Table Settings

One of the pleasures of eating and entertaining is the visual appeal of a table decoratively laid with a variety of foods, dishes and cutlery, bottles and glasses. Not surprisingly, this element features largely in illustrations for magazines and cookery books. But the production of such a drawing can be an end in itself, whereas an illustration is typically an accompaniment to other kinds of information being conveyed. The inspiration of an attractive table setting is something that any artist can exploit.

This is a subject that can be treated quite straightforwardly, as a form of traditional still life, or it can be the starting point for an investigation into particular points of technique, style and composition. The examples shown on these pages include detailed, representational images with a casual naturalness, and also unusual viewpoints and stylized, highly organized compositions.

An important technical factor to be considered here is the scale of your drawing and the ways in which the marks you make will correspond to individual elements of the setting. You may be incorporating quite a large overall area, and at the same time examining quite small, intricate objects. Spend some time planning your approach and relating it to the image area of your drawing – it is worthwhile blocking in the composition carefully, to make sure that you include all the required elements within the drawing's outer frame, and that the arrangement of objects creates a balanced, interesting composition.

▼ **JOHN DAVIS**
BLUE BAR, CANNES
Unusually, the grouping of objects on the table leaves each individual item separate from the next, so the blue tablecloth needs to form a strong background shape and colour. This organization of the objects is partly due to the high viewpoint which, as it is different from our everyday experience of ordinary settings, also creates a distinctive mood.
• OVERLAYING COLOURS

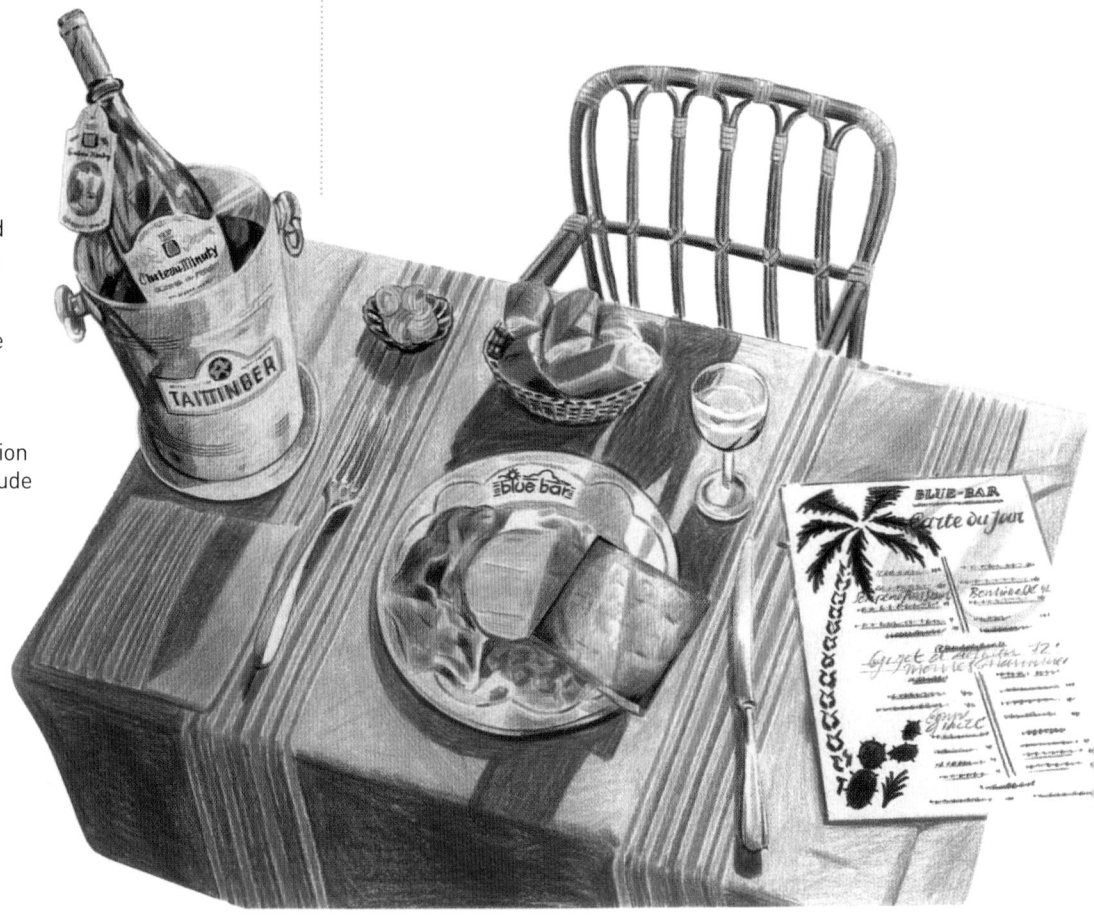

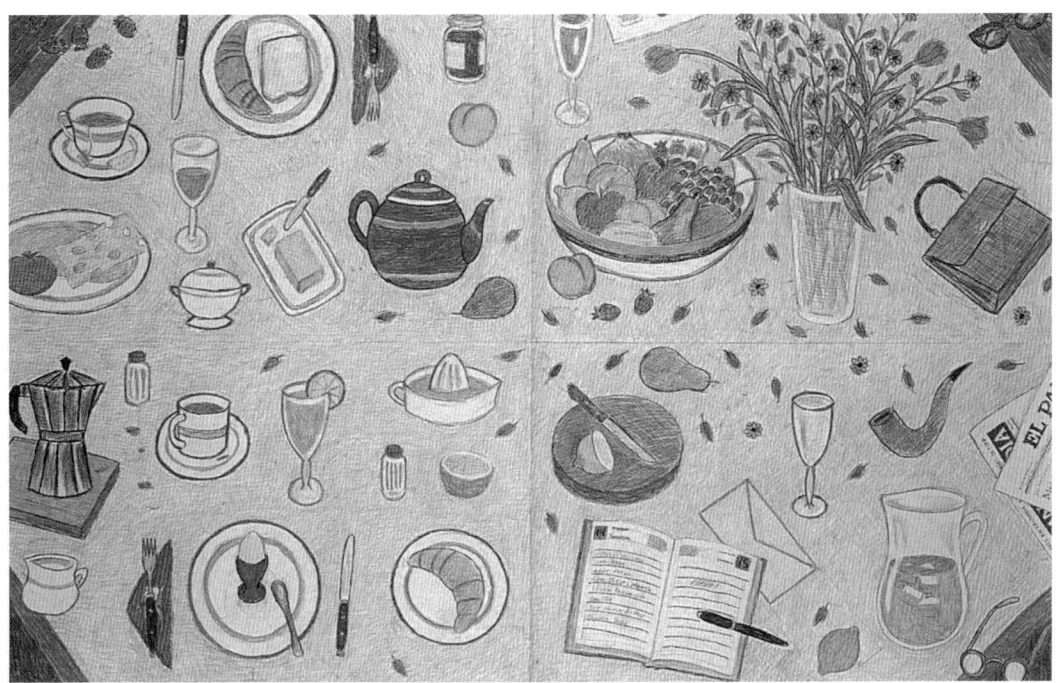

◀ PHILIP STANTON
SUNDAY BREAKFAST
As in the picture opposite, the objects are laid out on the table as separate items, but this time the device represents a deliberately formal styling that gives ordinary, recognizable objects a kind of abstract presence. The impression of even, flat colour adds to the effect, although there is plenty of detail to be discovered.
• HATCHING
• SHADING

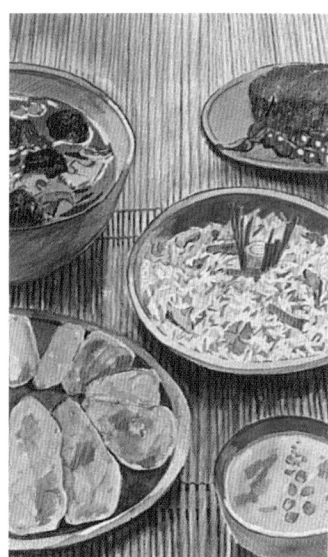

▲ HELENA GREENE
SUMMER LUNCH
Coloured pencil is used here to supplement the detailed work in watercolour, adding mainly linear touches that sharpen the shapes and textures, together with stronger emphasis in the shadows.
• DRAWING INTO PAINT
• HATCHING
• LINE QUALITIES

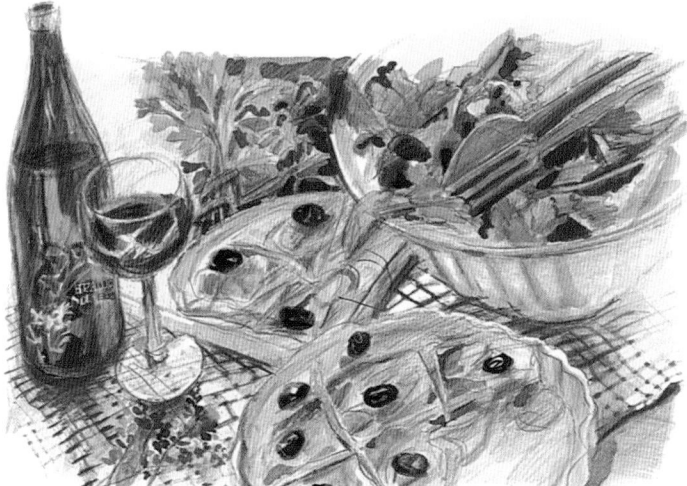

◀ JANE STROTHER
PIZZAS
The ingredients of a simple, tasty meal make a vibrant still life full of colour and texture. The variations of form and surface detail are matched by the varied methods of applying watercolour and pencil. In places the colour is washed in broadly, elsewhere water-soluble pencils have been laid over a damp ground to make thick, rich, linear detail that contrasts with the finer pencil work.
• SOLVENTS
• WATERCOLOUR AND PENCIL

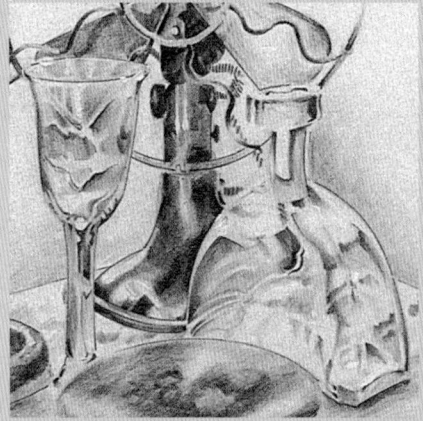

Objects
Form and surface detail

Stuart Robinson

When you choose objects to arrange a still life for colour drawing, think as you do so which techniques will most aptly describe their shapes, textures and patterns and how these will work with each other in the finished picture. In this demonstration sequence, the objects are made of polished and naturally reflective materials – glass, wood and metal. This creates quite a lot of intricate detail in the surface qualities, which is interwoven with the intricacies of form. The way the still life is lit and the movements of your head when you are drawing can also cause the reflected colours and tones to change. This apparent variation helps to increase the richness of your image, but you don't have to record every tiny nuance. Select what seem to you to be the most important elements of form and surface texture. Stuart Robinson uses a tightly controlled shading technique which allows him to develop plenty of descriptive detail and build the density of colour and tone.

◀**1** As the still life is a detailed, quite intricate subject, the artist begins by making a precise outline drawing of light graphite pencil lines.

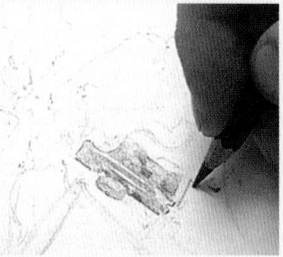

▲**2** Specific areas of the image are chosen for tonal interpretation, enabling the artist to key the high and low tones. The base of the fan is described with controlled shading and gradations in burnt umber.

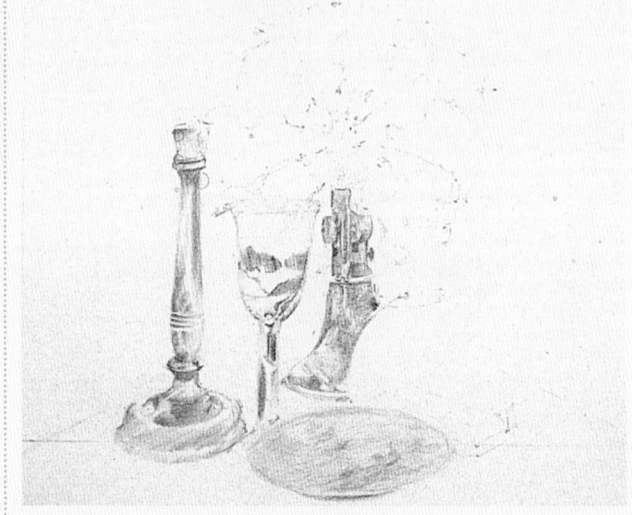

▲**3** A similar technique is used to describe the candlestick, glass and dish, using colours appropriate to the dominant colours of the objects.

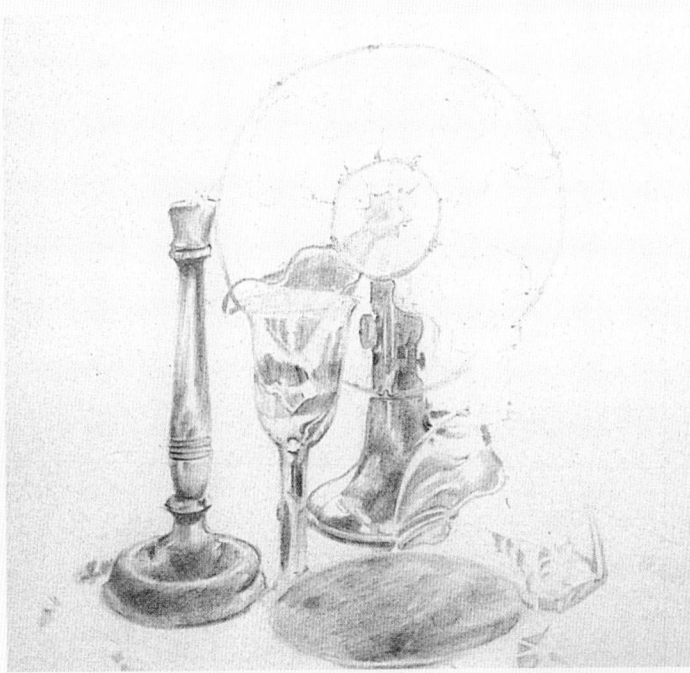

▲ 4 The colour range is gradually made more complex, but the artist continues to work with even shading and overlaying colours, building up mixed hues and tones.

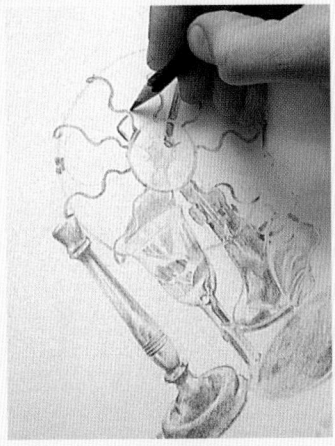

▲ 5 Where the shapes become finer and more intricate, the artist follows the forms carefully, filling in the pencilled outlines quite precisely. Notice how the different layers of the composition are preserved.

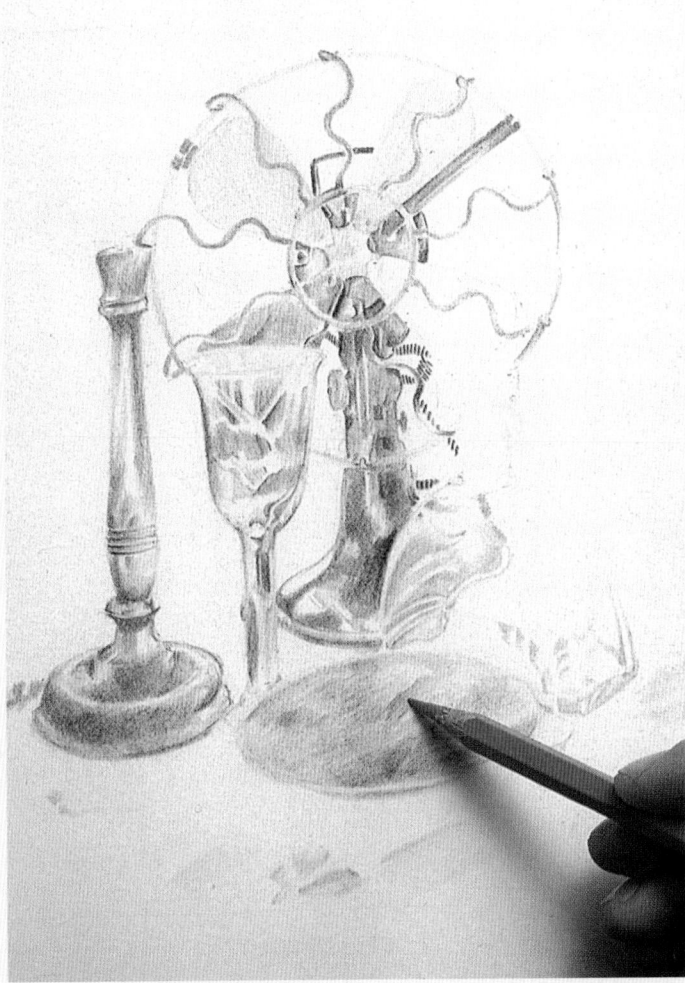

▲ 6 The overall impression of the objects is now well defined, so the artist begins to develop the colour values, introducing stronger hues to enliven the tonal treatment.

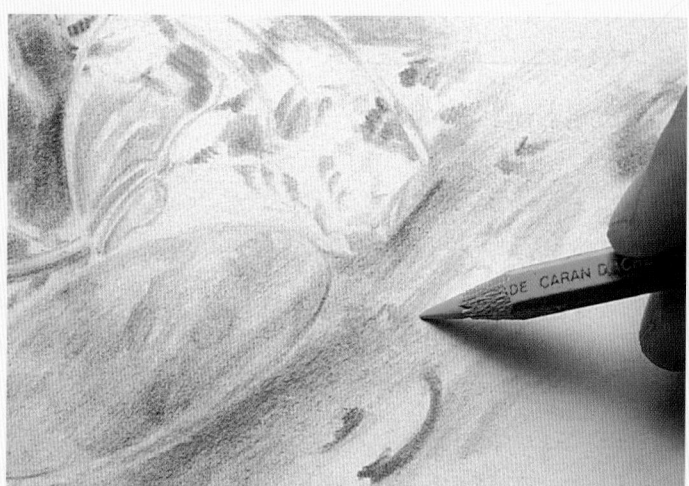

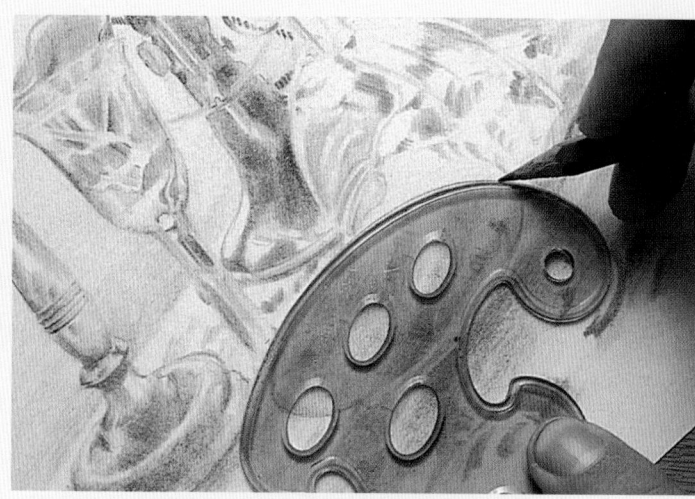

▲**7** Colours are gently blended and overlaid using a range of bright hues chosen to match the pattern of the fabric on which the still life is arranged.

▲**9** To sharpen the outlines of the objects, they are redrawn using a plastic stencil to guide the graphite pencil around the curves.

▶**8** To obtain the shiny texture of the metal fan blades, parts of the yellow shading are erased to make highlights and the darker tones are strengthened with colour overlays.

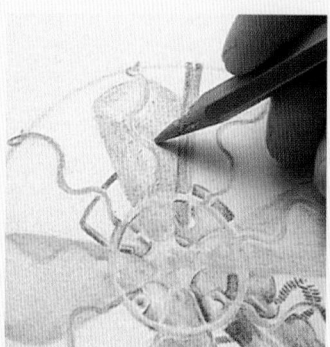

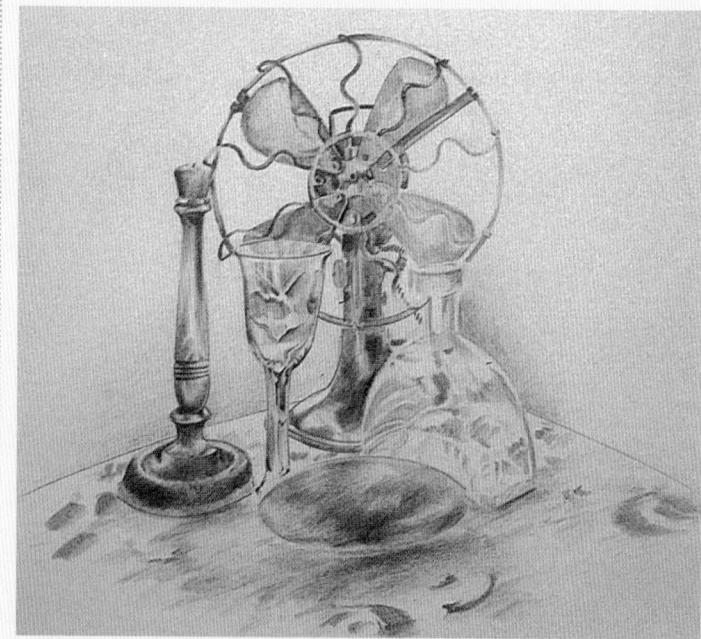

▲**10** Similar techniques are applied to bring up the surface qualities of the glass and wood. Soft shadows shaded in behind the objects add depth to the composition.

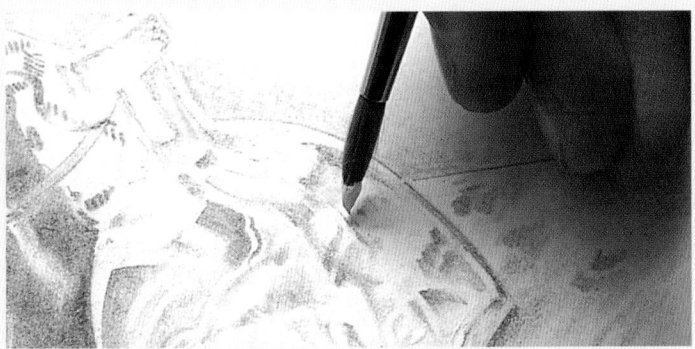

▲**11** The strongest highlights on the glass are brightened with opaque white gouache, delicately painted in with a pointed sable brush.

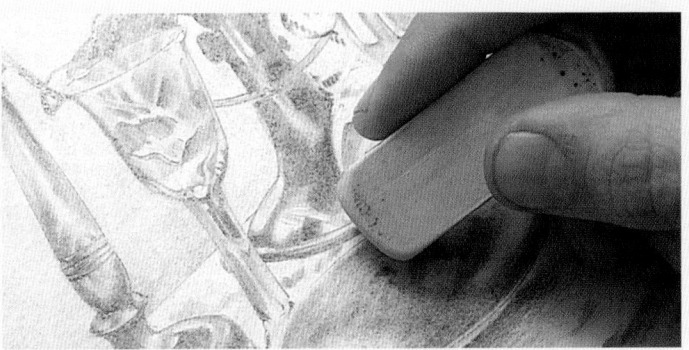

▲**12** Finally, a plastic eraser is used for burnishing the colour on the glossy and reflective surfaces to enhance the smoothness of the tonal and colour gradation.

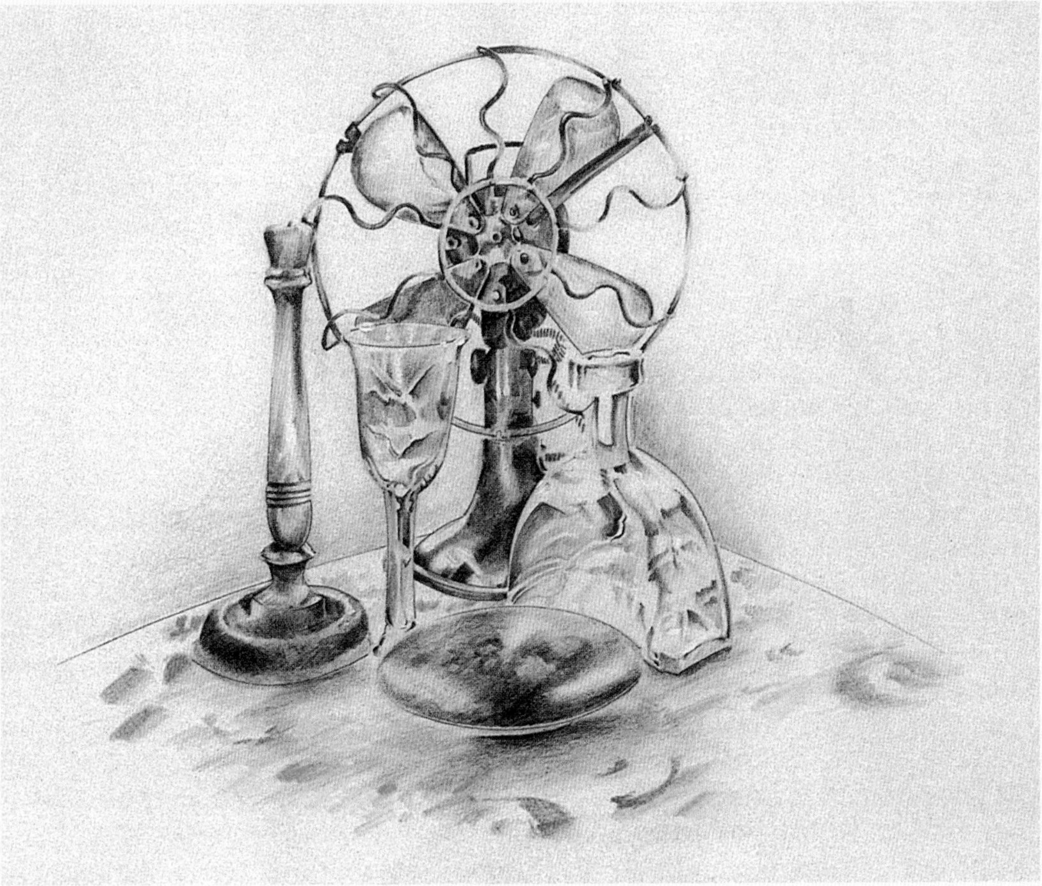

STUART ROBINSON ▶
STILL LIFE
The combination of a smooth paper surface and closely worked shading of the pencil colours produces a highly finished image which gives a clean, naturalistic description of the objects' forms and textures.

Nature

This range of natural subjects provides a wealth of interest for the artist, from the brilliant colours of garden flowers to the elaborate foliage forms of tropical plants; from the familiar elegance of the family cat to the impressive physical presence of a wild beast. For coloured pencil drawing, there is a particular fascination in the range of natural colours and textures in plants and animals.

▼ ANGELA MORGAN
PRIMULAS
The delicate colours of these primulas have been well captured here. The flowers stand cleanly out on the white ground and have been rendered exactly. The white of the paper is used for the white of some of the petals.
• MIXING PENCILS

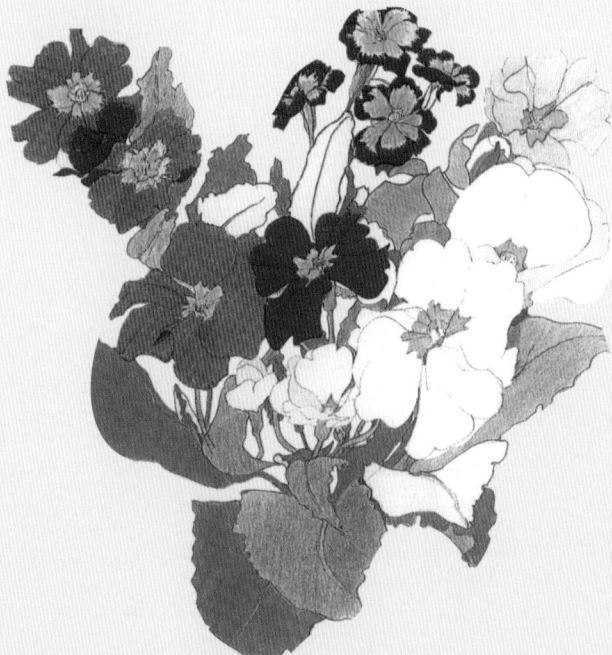

Quite ordinary subjects can be interpreted very creatively with pencil drawing techniques, while more exotic imagery challenges your inventiveness in matching the incidental brilliance of nature's forms and colours with your own deliberate technical skill.

Sources of imagery

Cut flowers and growing plants are accessible subjects. You can buy flowers specially for drawing, cut them from your garden or study them in the wild. You can find your subjects in a public park or specialized botanical garden – large greenhouse displays are a wonderful source of colourful and unusual flower and foliage arrangements. Just about everyone has an immediate response to the natural beauty of plants, which adds to the pleasure of drawing them. Their range of colours enables you to exploit to the full the wonderful potential of your "palette" of coloured pencils. Shapes and textures ranging from the most delicate to the most bold and dramatic exercise the accuracy of your observation.

The animal kingdom is obviously a less accessible resource, although the range, from tiny jewelled insects to huge creatures such as big cats and other larger mammals certainly means that the animal theme contains something for everyone. It is extremely difficult to study any kind of animal in the wild, so photography is an important reference medium. But there are other sources of detailed information. Household pets are rarely obliging about posing, but because you spend a lot of time around them, there are plenty of opportunities to draw.

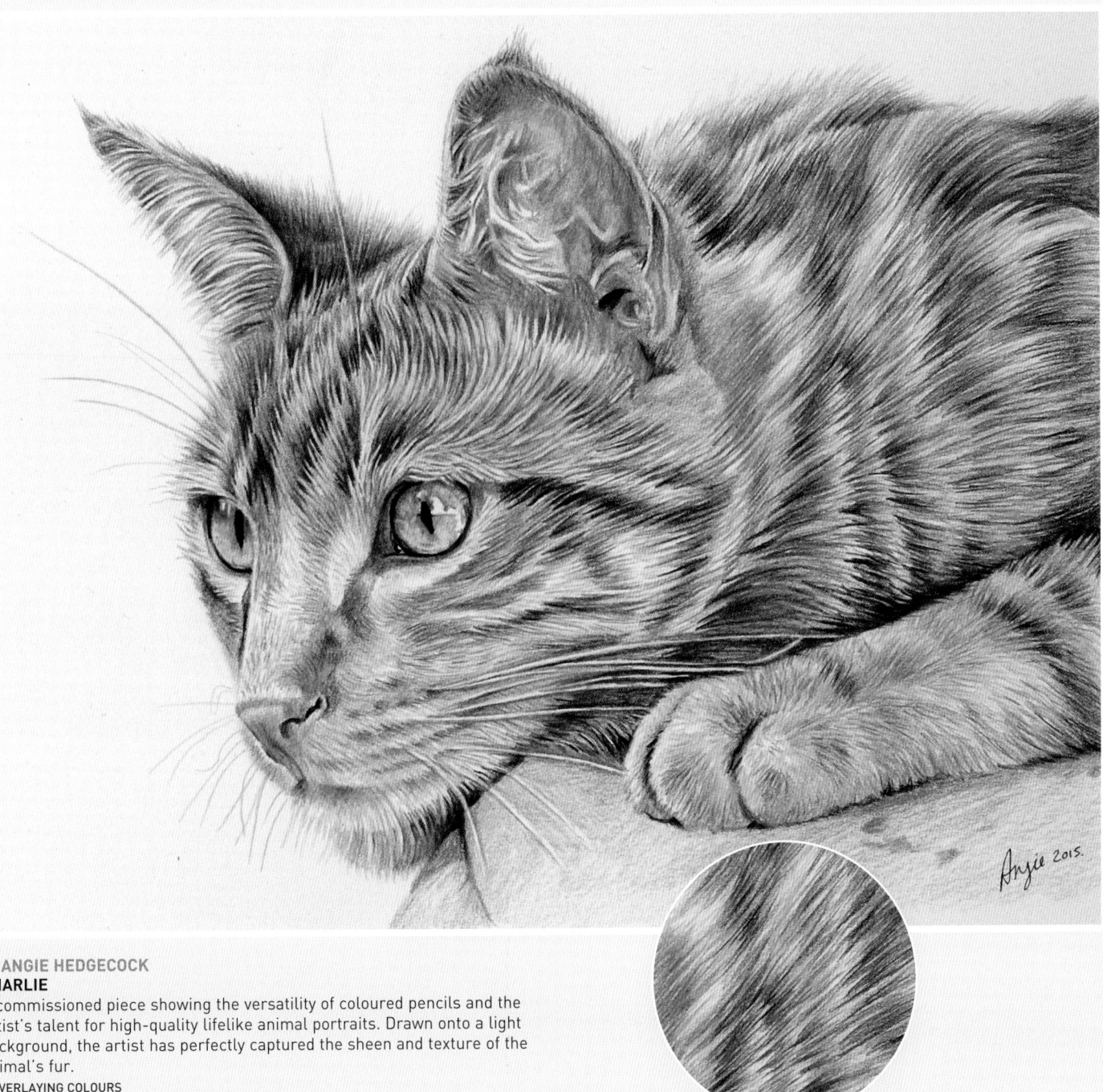

▲ ANGIE HEDGECOCK
CHARLIE
A commissioned piece showing the versatility of coloured pencils and the artist's talent for high-quality lifelike animal portraits. Drawn onto a light background, the artist has perfectly captured the sheen and texture of the animal's fur.

• OVERLAYING COLOURS

Flowers and Foliage

Probably the ideal subject for the beginner learning to work with coloured pencils, flowers have such brilliance and variety in their shapes, colours and textures that they remain a most popular subject even among highly experienced artists. They are well suited to studies in any painting or drawing medium, but perhaps especially to coloured pencils because their complex forms and rich colour variations are contained at a scale that enables them to be observed in close detail.

However, because many flowers have precise and intricate structures, this does not mean that a drawing must be equally elaborate. A free, bold interpretation can be just as successful as a detailed nature study. Flowers provide a vehicle for experimentation with technique, which you can adapt to reveal different impressions of similar subjects, or to investigate the vast natural variety of flower types. You can choose to work with cut flowers, pot plants or garden flowers, according to convenience, and many subjects will be long-lasting enough to provide hours of work from a single selection.

Foliage

Leaves are just as various and appealing as flowers, although at first sight their colour properties may seem less rich in scope. However, part of the skill of working in coloured pencils is learning to control subtle nuances of colour and to form complex colour blends and mixtures by building up and overlaying your range of individual hues. The subtle changes of hue and tone within the range of foliage greens provide an excellent means of developing and testing your skills in this direction: hatching, shading and stippling are all potentially valuable techniques, and in studying the intriguing shapes and textures of different kinds of leaves, you can learn to exploit the full range of your pencils' line qualities.

Indoor plants are ideal subject matter, especially as many foliage houseplants are tropical and sub-tropical species with strong, fluid shapes. The colours of variegated leaves also add to the variety of your resources. Outdoor locations – gardens, parks or the open countryside – provide plenty of inspiration. When working outdoors position yourself close to the subject so you can study the detail; if you wish to bring specimens home to work from, make sure there are no local restrictions on gathering plant material from the wild.

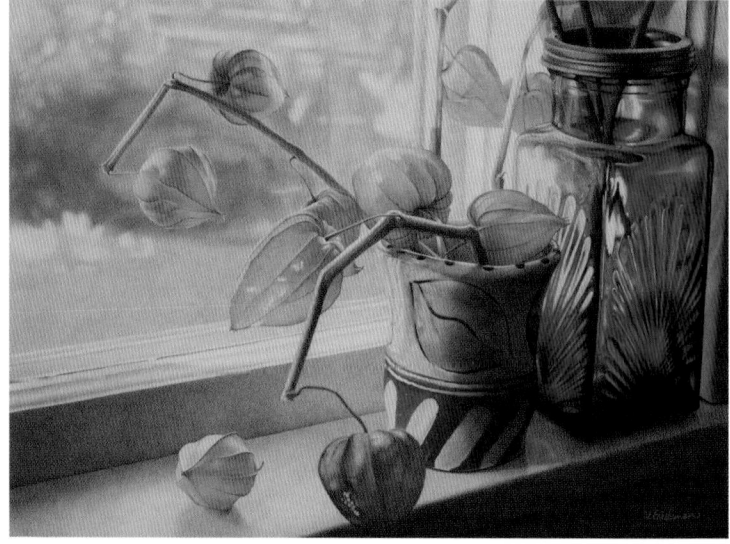

▲ **DEBORAH FRIEDMAN**
THE TRANSPARENCY OF SUMMER
A highly detailed and textured still life that uses a selection of blues and oranges for its main subject, with elements of the study highlighted with flashes of white on the glass vase and windows. As you look to the background you can see that the artist has picked out portions of the garden that increase the depth of perception.
• BURNISHING
• SHADING
• SOLVENTS

▲ **GARY GREENE**

BACK PETALS

In this painting, Gary Greene reveals the beauty of a gerbera from close up and behind. The subtle colour gradations along the length of each petal are achieved by applying layers of colour.

• OVERLAYING COLOURS
• BURNISHING

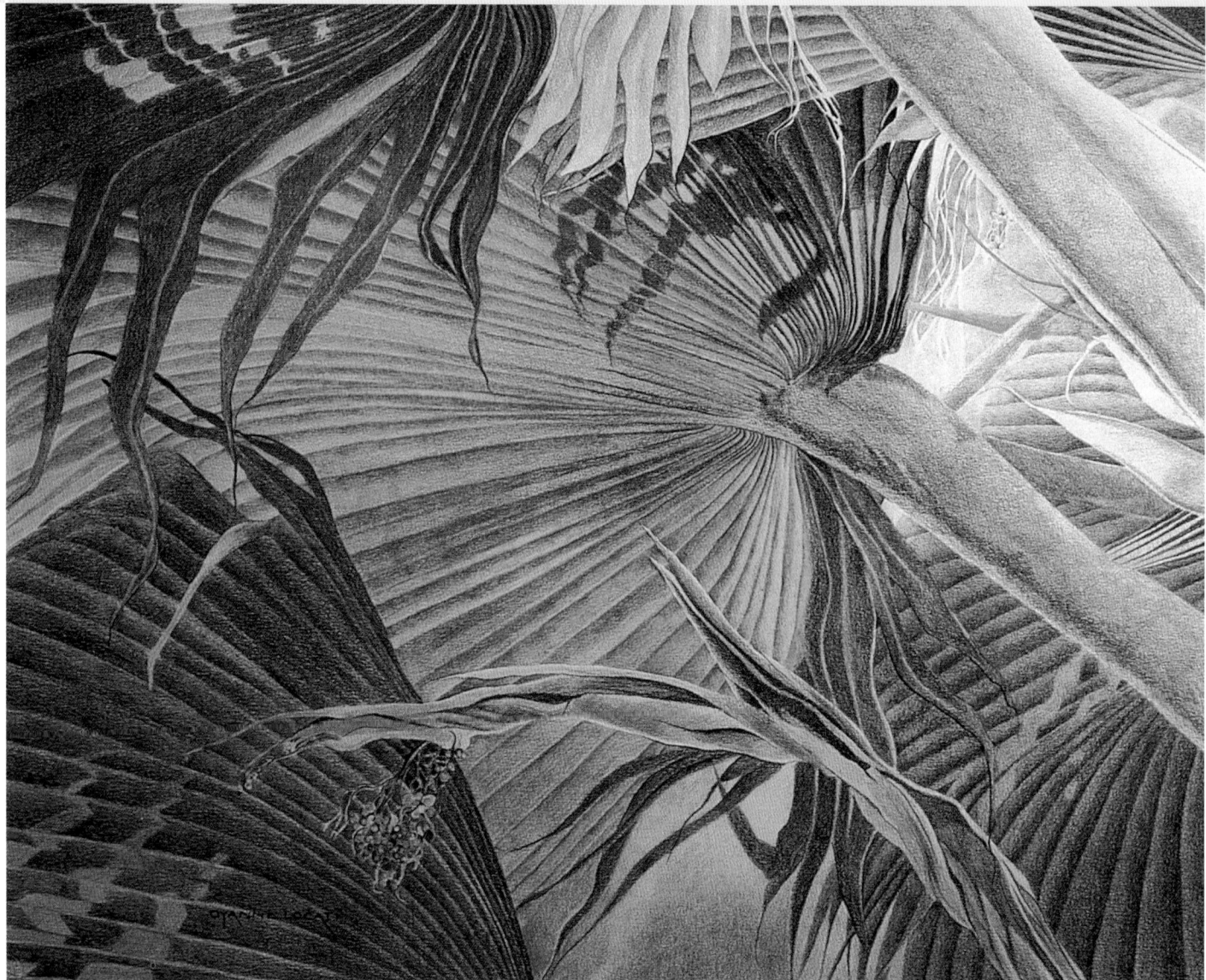

▲DYANNE LOCATI
THE PALM JUNGLE
The effectiveness of an image with strong graphic qualities like
this relies as much on close observation and accurate drawing
as on the techniques of applying pencil colour. Even shading has
been carefully built up to fill the shapes and form subtle tonal and
colour gradations. The grainy texture of the paper allows the
applied colours to "breathe", adding sparkle to the rendering.
• GRADATION
• PAPER GRAIN EFFECTS
• OVERLAYING COLOURS

GRAHAM BRACE ▶
AUTUMN CARPET
The artist is fascinated by patterns created by natural forms.
Here, the fallen leaves of autumn have clearly caught the artist's
keen eye for spotting a natural pattern. This piece was created
using watercolour pencils alone.
• FIXING
• BURNISHING

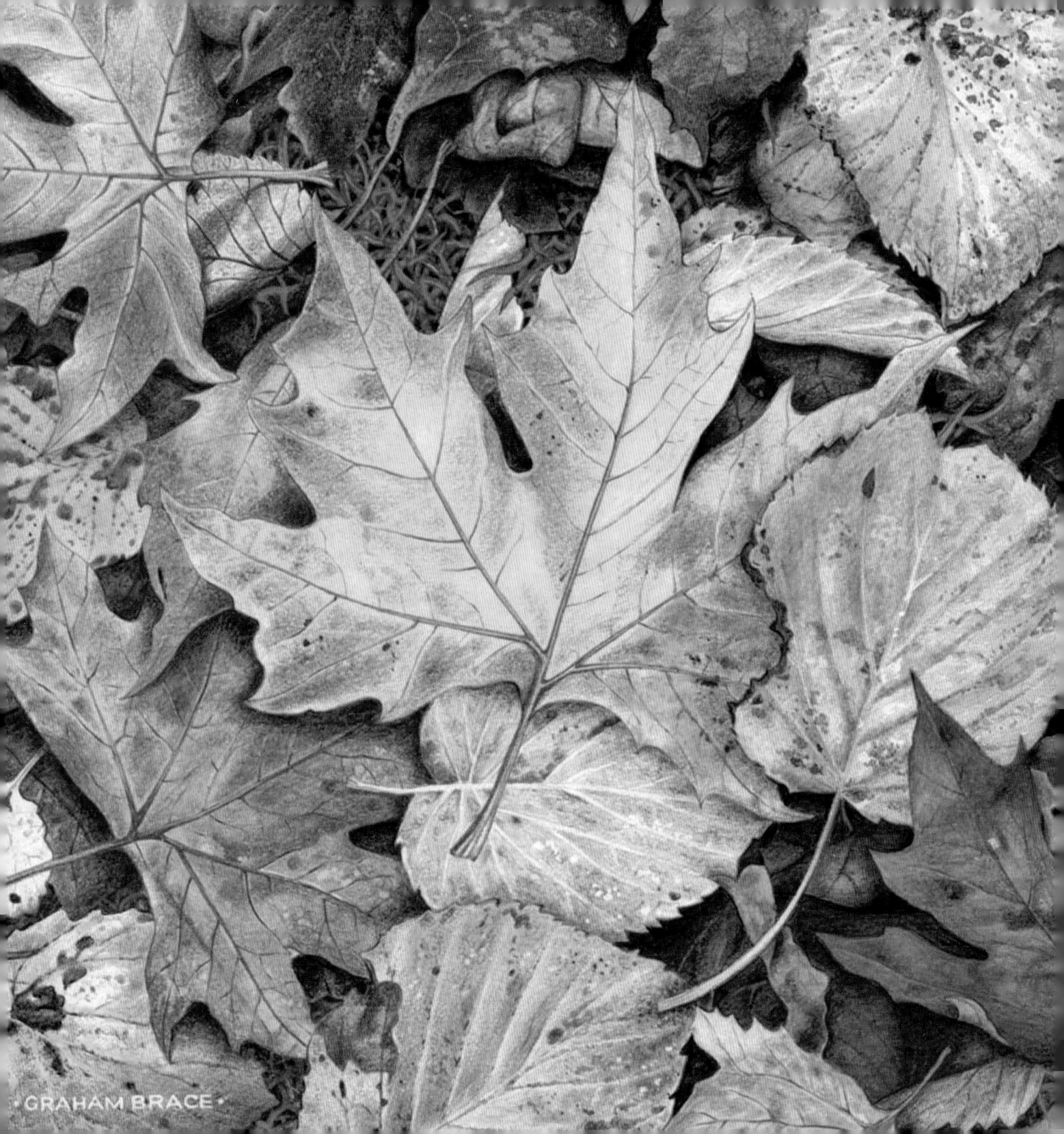
GRAHAM BRACE

▼ ELIZABETH AUBREY
PRIMULA AICULA
The soft texture of the
primula's purple petals
is perfectly captured here.
• GRADATION

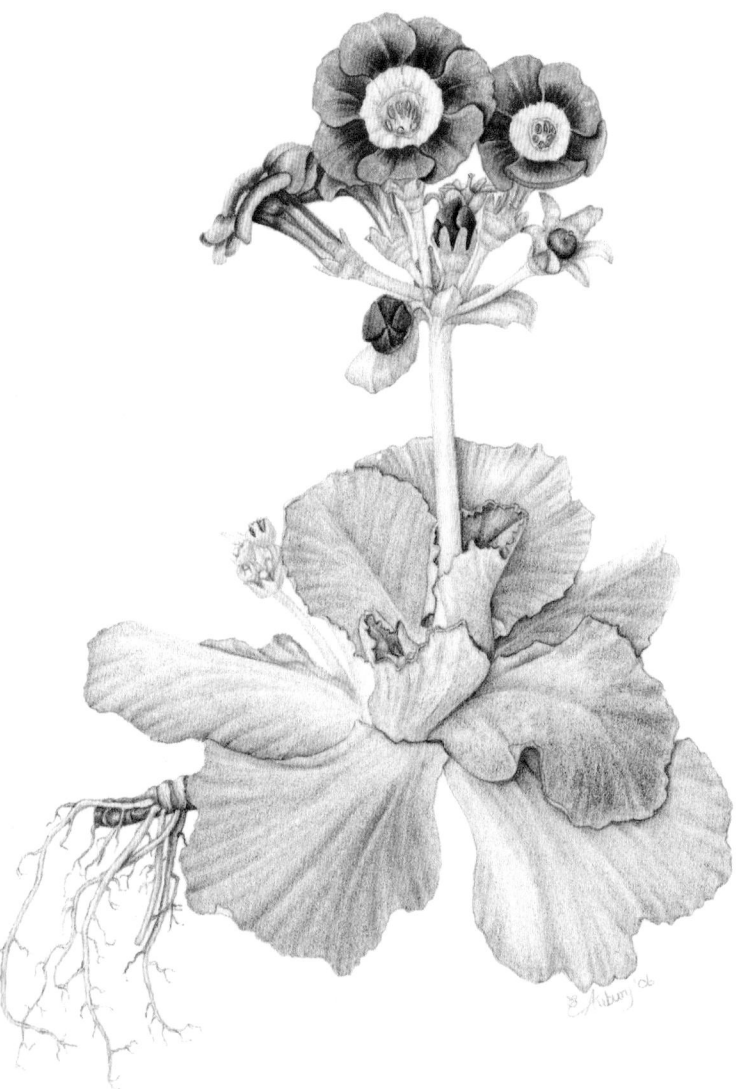

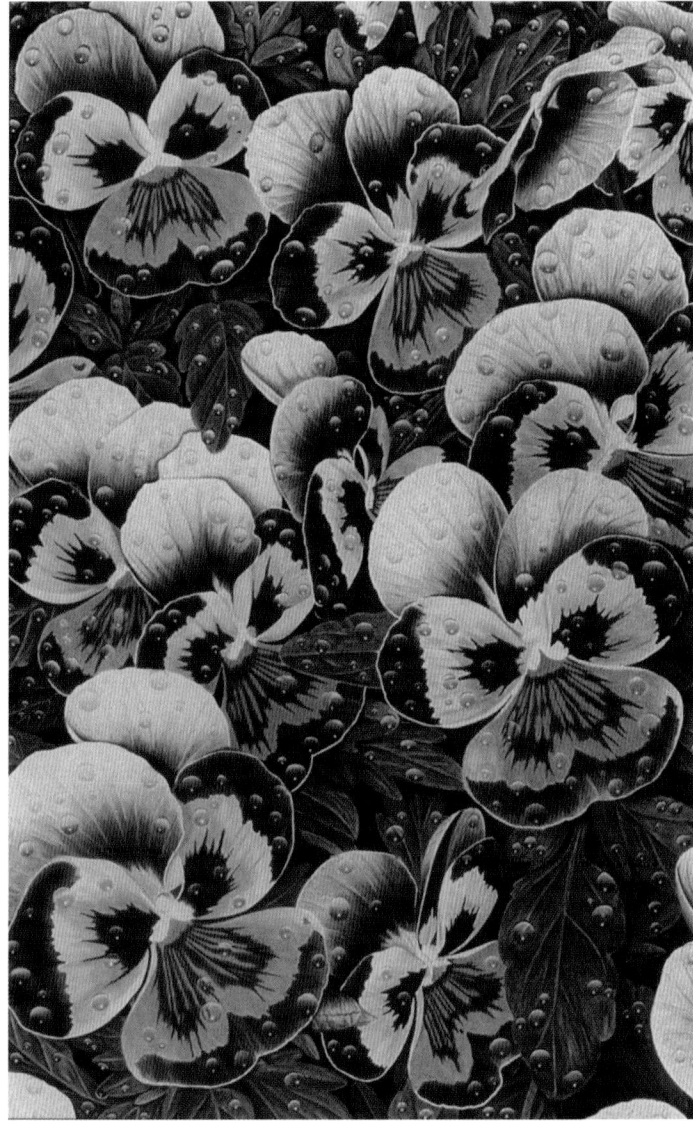

▲ GARY GREENE
PANSIES
The colour clarity that pencils provide is well exploited in this
drawing of vivid pansies covered with jewel-like dewdrops. The
three-dimensional realism of the shapes and textures is due to
careful gradations of colour and tone that model the petals, leaves
and drops of water very precisely. The pinpoint white highlights
are crucial to the effect of glistening dew.
• GRADATION
• HIGHLIGHTING

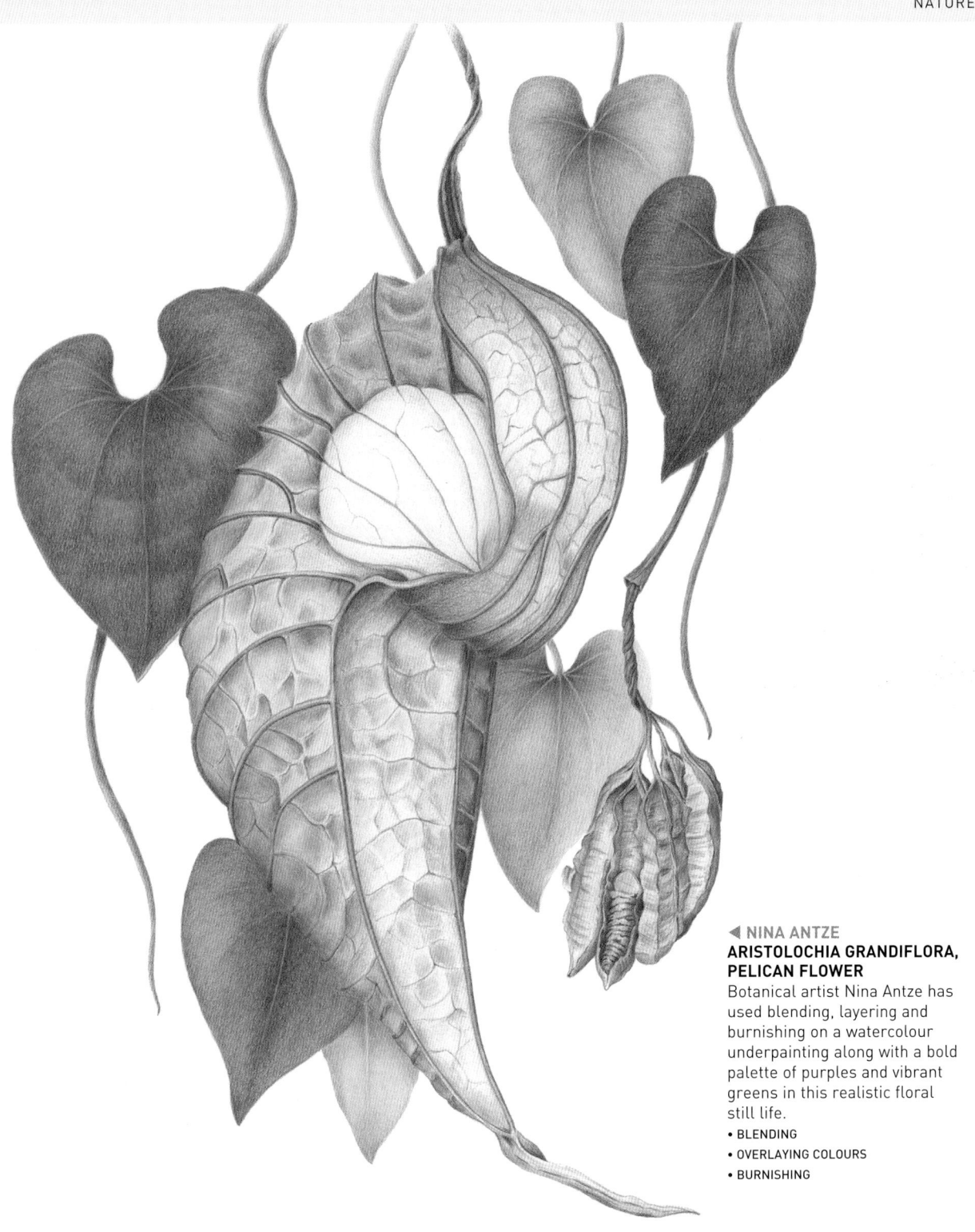

◄ NINA ANTZE
ARISTOLOCHIA GRANDIFLORA, PELICAN FLOWER
Botanical artist Nina Antze has used blending, layering and burnishing on a watercolour underpainting along with a bold palette of purples and vibrant greens in this realistic floral still life.
• BLENDING
• OVERLAYING COLOURS
• BURNISHING

Container Plants

Plants grown in containers are cultivated for their ornamental qualities, so you should have no trouble in finding an attractive composition, whether from a single specimen or a group of plants. As the leaves and flowers are growing, rather than cut materials, the shapes and forms are unlikely to change at all within the time you need to complete a drawing.

The background to a container plant will form an important aspect of your composition, unless you are making the kind of detailed botanical study usually drawn on a flat, untreated background. Consider the colours and textures that surround the plant and its container, if necessary moving the plant or placing something underneath it, to provide a sympathetic complement to its form and detail. Natural textures such as wood, canework or stone provide interesting surface qualities that do not compete visually with the plant. Alternatively, however, you could choose to make a colourful, semi-abstract composition by including patterned fabrics and containers that create a busy background.

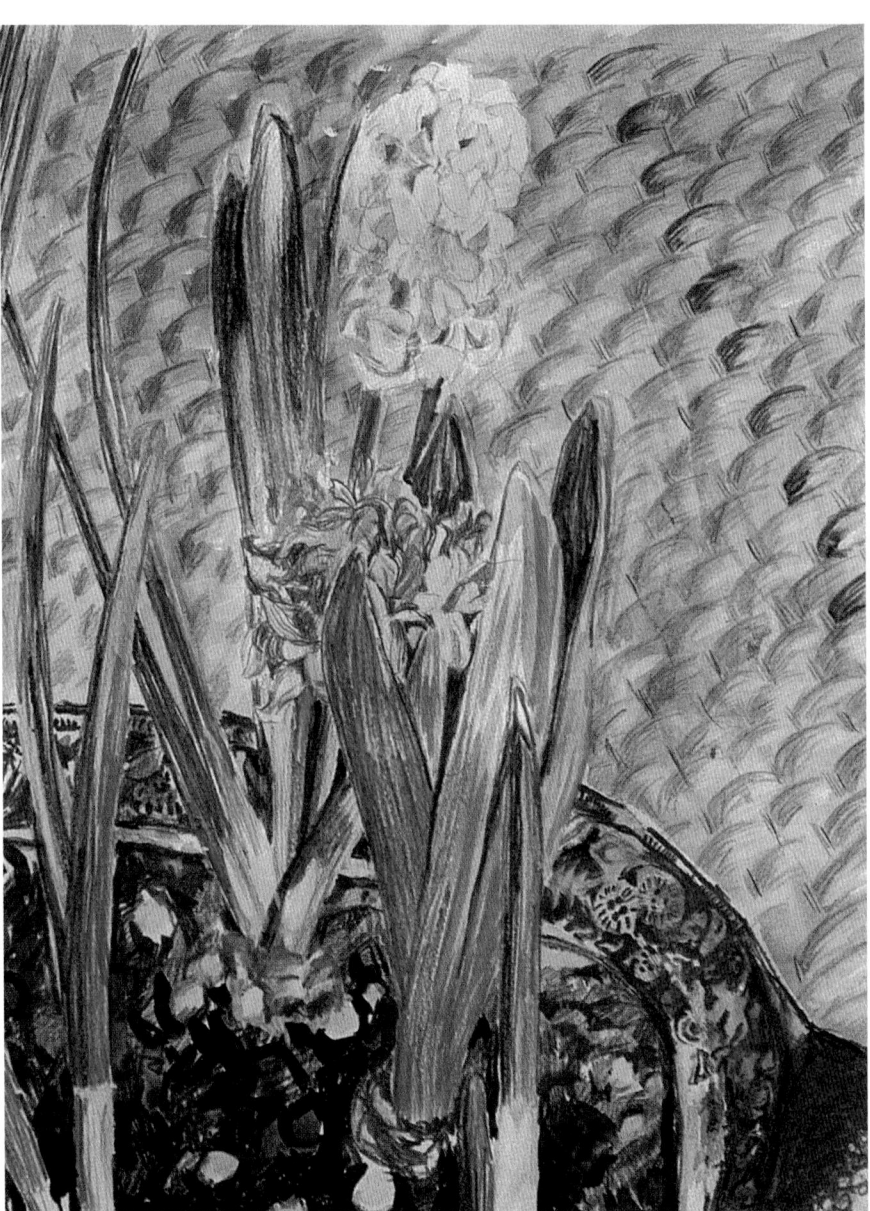

▲ HELENA GREENE
HYACINTHS
The pencil lines have a strong presence in creating the framework of this drawing. They provide distinctive contours and hatched tones, with the watercolour washes forming a subtle complement.
• LINE QUALITIES

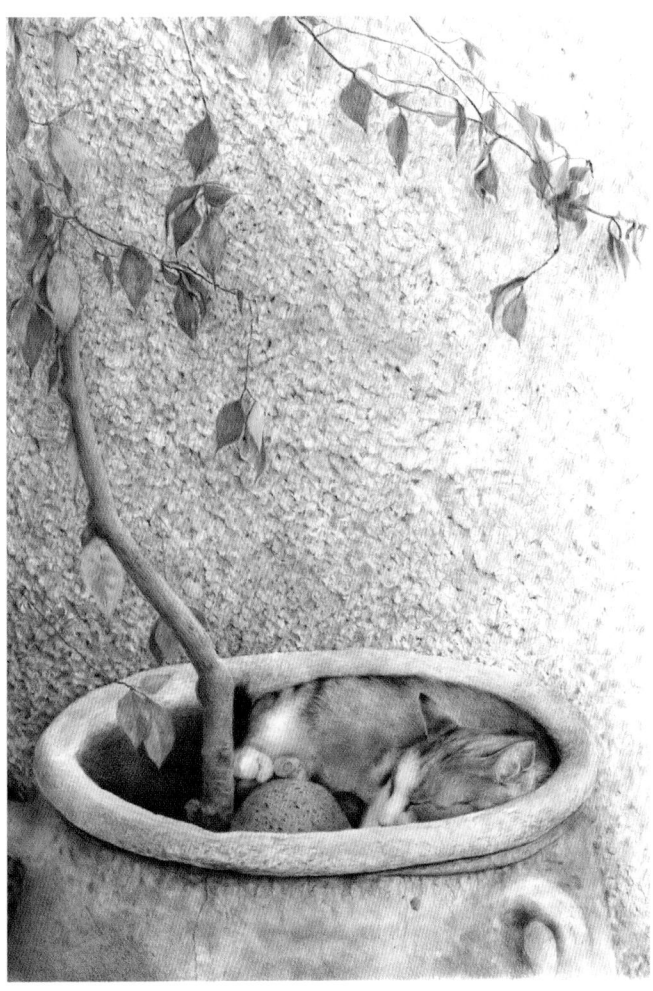

▲ SUSAN BRINKMANN
GREEK CAT
The artist uses a highly detailed pencil technique to capture this scene. The markings on the cat's fur and the texturing on the background wall and on the container are minutely realized.

• OVERLAYING COLOURS
• BLENDING

▼HELENA GREENE
CYCLAMEN
Paint and pencil are a valuable combination for interpreting plants and flowers, giving a wide range of textural qualities that can be matched to aspects of the individual subject. The background is treated simply to focus the eye on the detail of the plant.

• DRAWING INTO PAINT

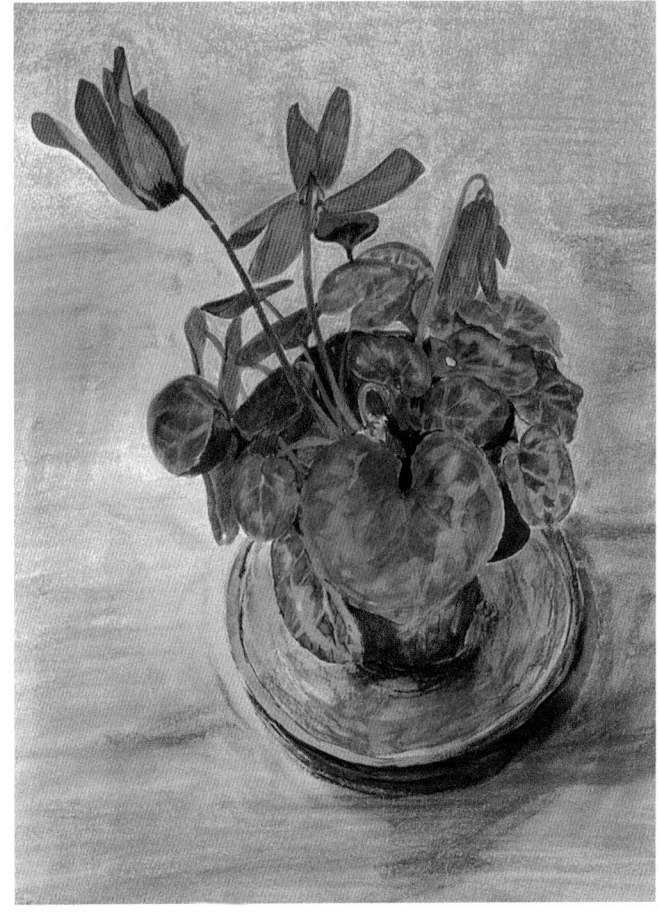

Animal Studies

Animals are not natural models and many artists find it difficult to deal with them because of their constant movement. But they have considerable appeal as drawing subjects, both through the associations we make with images of different kinds of animals and because of their range of forms, colours and textures that we can study as purely visual problems to be solved by applying particular skills and techniques.

It takes patience to complete useful "life studies" of animals; frequently a pose lasts only seconds, and anyone who sets out to draw an animal will become familiar with the frustration of having to abandon a drawing at a promising stage because the model has changed the pose or wandered away. For this reason, photographic reference is commonly used; ideally, this can be combined with direct observation, so that the elements of form that appear imprecise in a photograph can be adjusted from real knowledge of the subject.

This is easy enough if you are drawing domestic animals; more difficult with wild subjects, when photographs are essential sources. It is useful to collect a library of images, even if you base your drawing on one particular shot, as you will then have alternative reference for details that may not be clearly seen in a single photo.

Technical studies, as in the tradition of natural history illustration, need not include a portrayal of the animal's environment. However, if you do choose to give your subject a realistic location, pay as much attention to its detail as you do to the animal itself, otherwise the image may appear unconvincing.

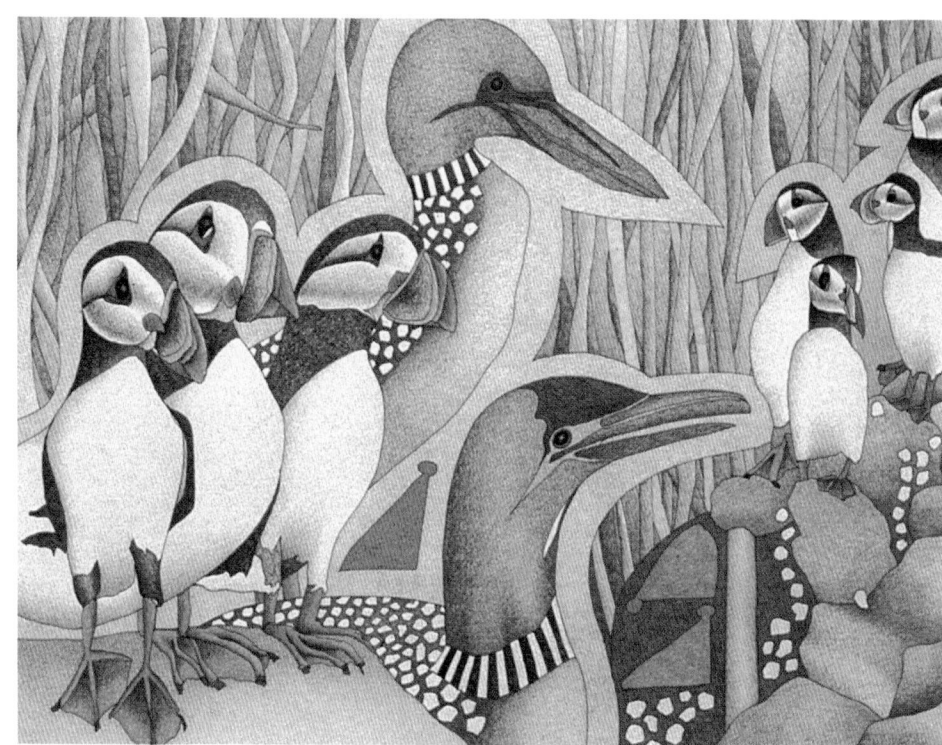

▲ PATTI MCQUILLIN
LOONS AND PUFFINS
This unusual, somewhat stylized study graphically explains the forms and patterns of the birds. By flattening the shapes and working within clear outlines, using an economical amount of tonal modelling, the artist combines detailed observation with a personalized descriptive sense.
• FILLING IN
• GRADATION

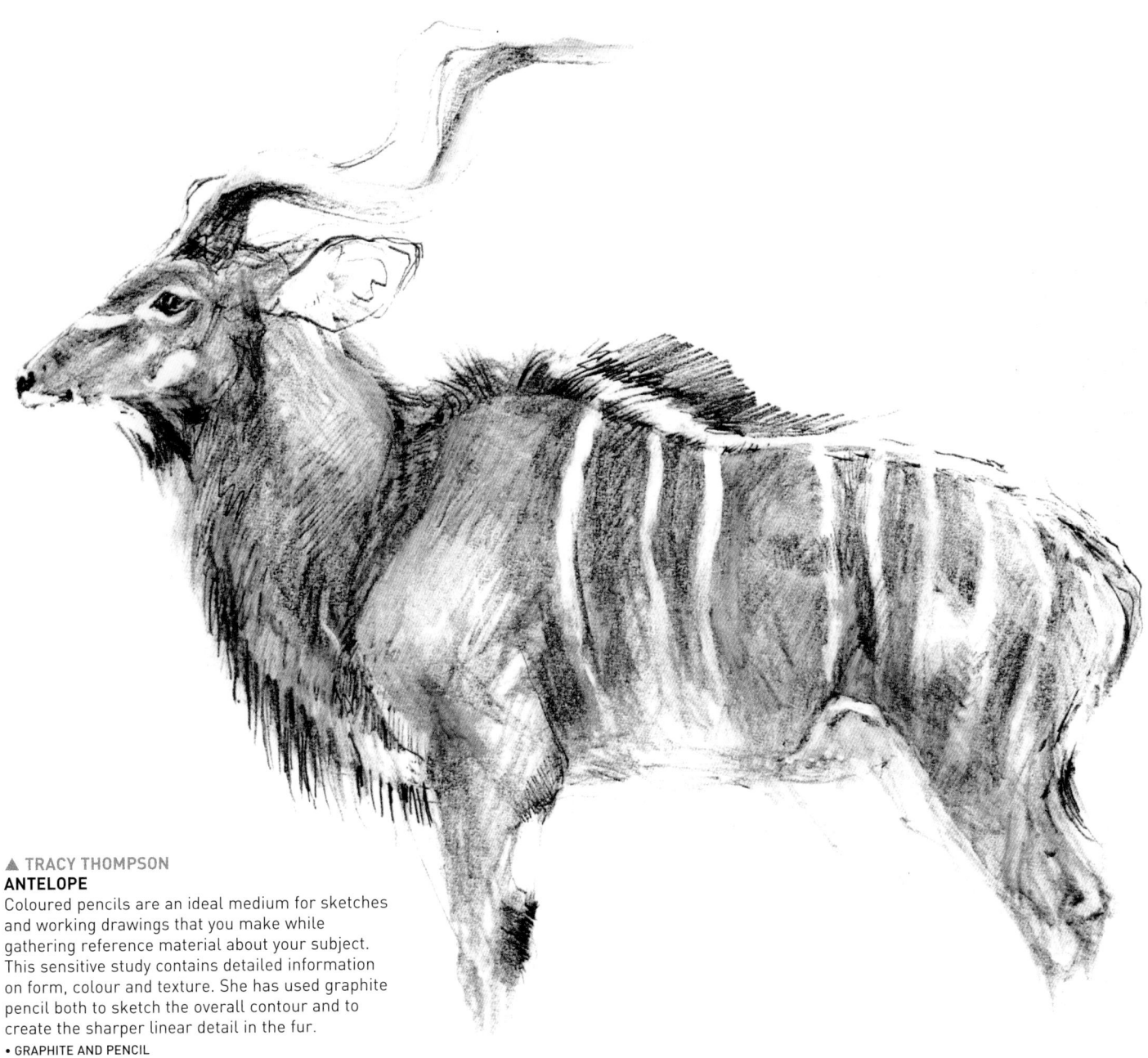

▲ TRACY THOMPSON
ANTELOPE
Coloured pencils are an ideal medium for sketches
and working drawings that you make while
gathering reference material about your subject.
This sensitive study contains detailed information
on form, colour and texture. She has used graphite
pencil both to sketch the overall contour and to
create the sharper linear detail in the fur.

• GRAPHITE AND PENCIL

• SKETCHING

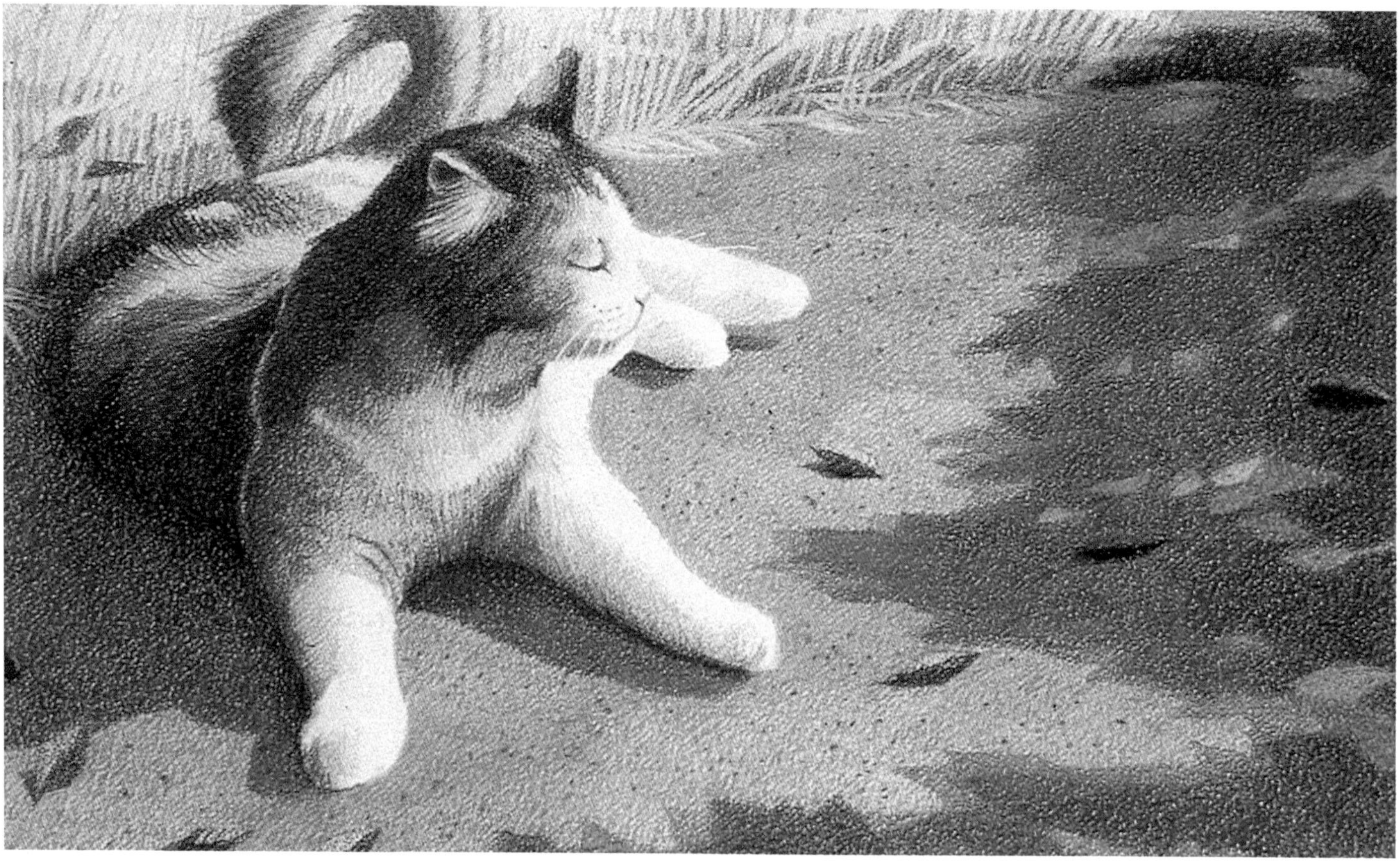

▲ LAURA DUIS
WARMING UP
Controlled shading is used
throughout this image to build
up the colour values over the
heavy paper grain. The technique
appears very consistent, producing
a unified surface, but there are
subtle variations in the directions
of the pencil strokes that model
form and texture. The colour
changes are beautifully
orchestrated to create the
warm summer light.
• BLENDING
• OVERLAYING COLOURS

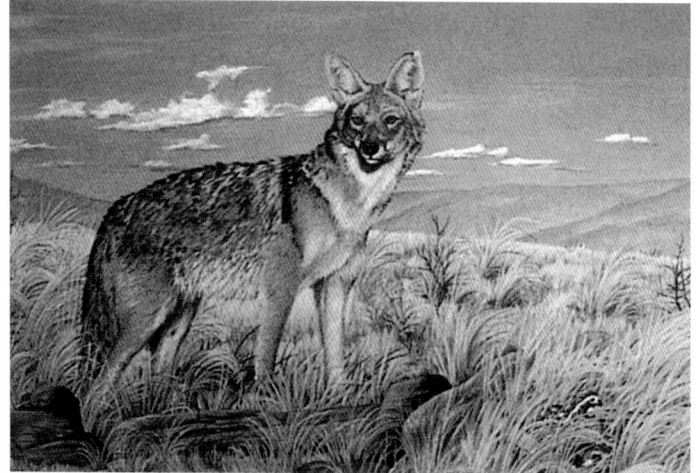

◄ DON PEARSON
COYOTE AND QUAIL
This is a classic presentation of an
animal in its environment, using
the natural camouflage of the
coyote's colours to key the overall
palette. The tones and textures
are carefully managed to ensure
that the animal stands out from
its surroundings. By contrast, the
quail is drawn half-hidden in the
grass, but its pattern is a means
of identification.
• LINEAR MARKS
• SHADING

ANGIE HEDGECOCK
GYPSY
A commissioned piece showing the brilliant results that can be achieved if using a limited palette. In this case the colours are primarily made up of whites, blacks and browns. Drawn onto a light background and with fine pencil detail, Gypsy's personality shines through.
- BLENDING
- ERASER TECHNIQUES
- HIGHLIGHTING

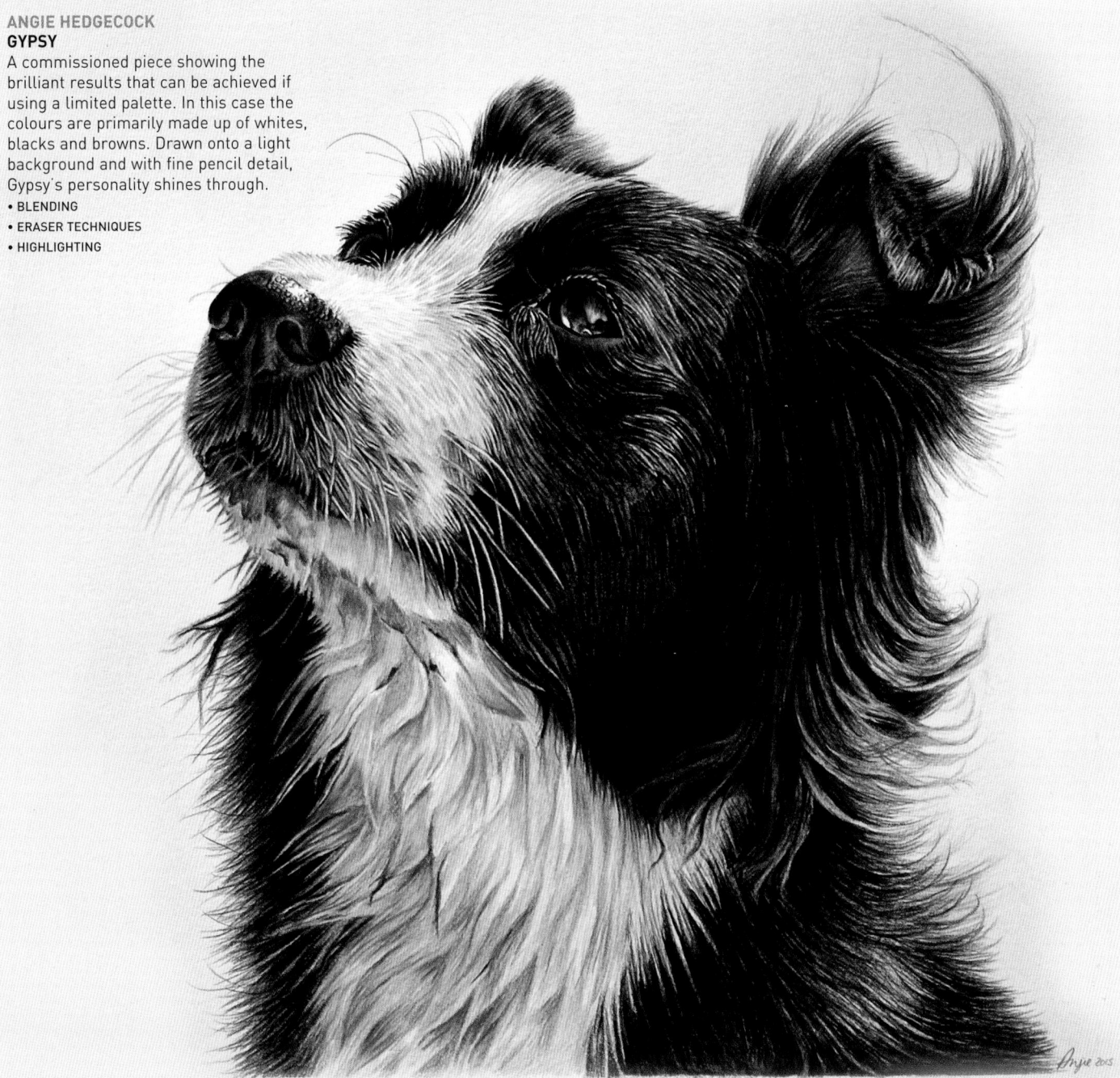

CAT DEUTER ▶
COPPER

Cat Deuter takes her inspiration from nature and all that it encompasses. She is particularly interested in the study of landscapes and animals. Cat uses both coloured and graphite pencils to bring her work to life. This horse portrait lives and breathes.

• COLOURED PAPERS
• BLENDING
• GRADATION

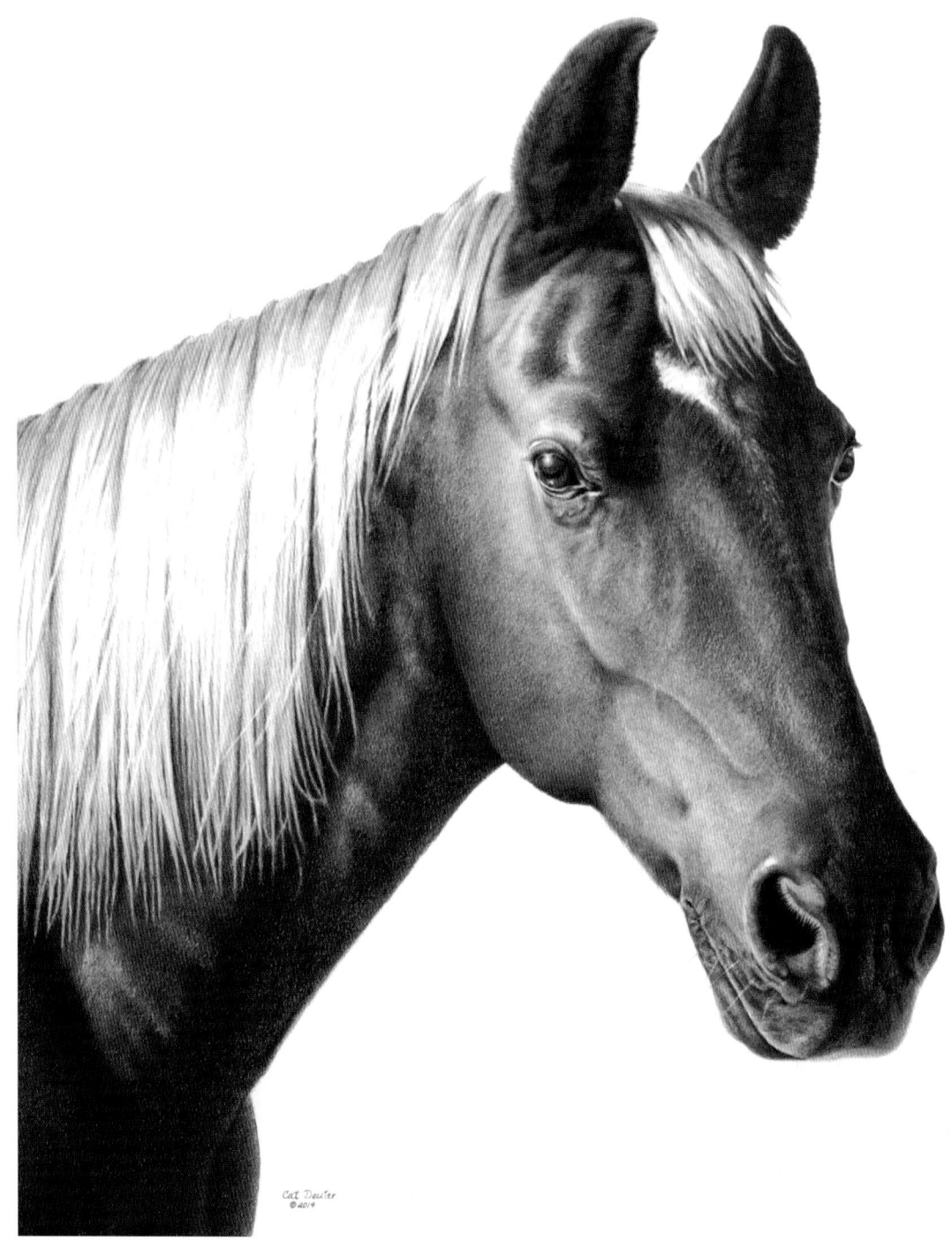

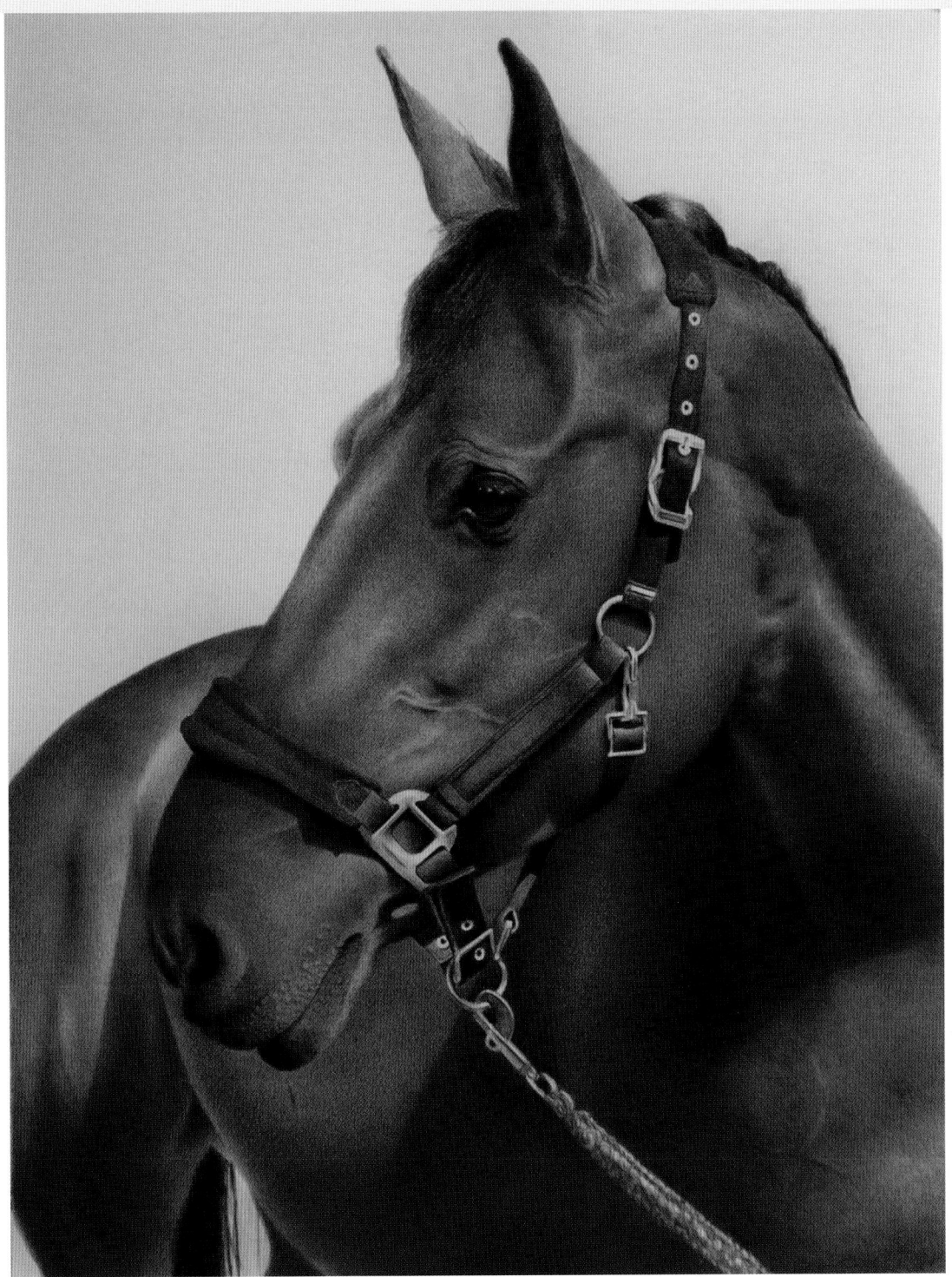

◄ **SUSAN BRINKMAN**
HORSE
Far more than a
photorealistic portrait of
a beautiful and powerful
animal, Susan Brinkman
has imbued her creature
with soul.
• BURNISHING
• BLENDING

Pattern and Texture

Sometimes it is the overall impression of a particular animal that suggests its suitability as a drawing subject – the grandeur of an elephant or lion, for example; sometimes the personal association, as with a family pet – but in pure visual terms, the variety of patterns, textures and colours that different types of creatures display also makes them fascinating as a resource for detailed study.

Small-scale creatures such as butterflies, insects and fish, which carry intricate, bright-coloured patterns, lend themselves particularly well to the delicacy that you can achieve working in coloured pencils. Fine linear marks and subtle hatching and shading can be closely controlled to elaborate the detail. In larger creatures, often the colours and markings are more muted and subtle, but again the linear nature of coloured pencils aids the depiction of such features as fur or bristles and folded or wrinkled hides.

Don't lose sight of the fact that these patterns and textures also reflect the underlying forms of the animals. You need to be responsive to small shifts of colour and tone that trace an animal's structure and contour at the same time as describing its surface feel.

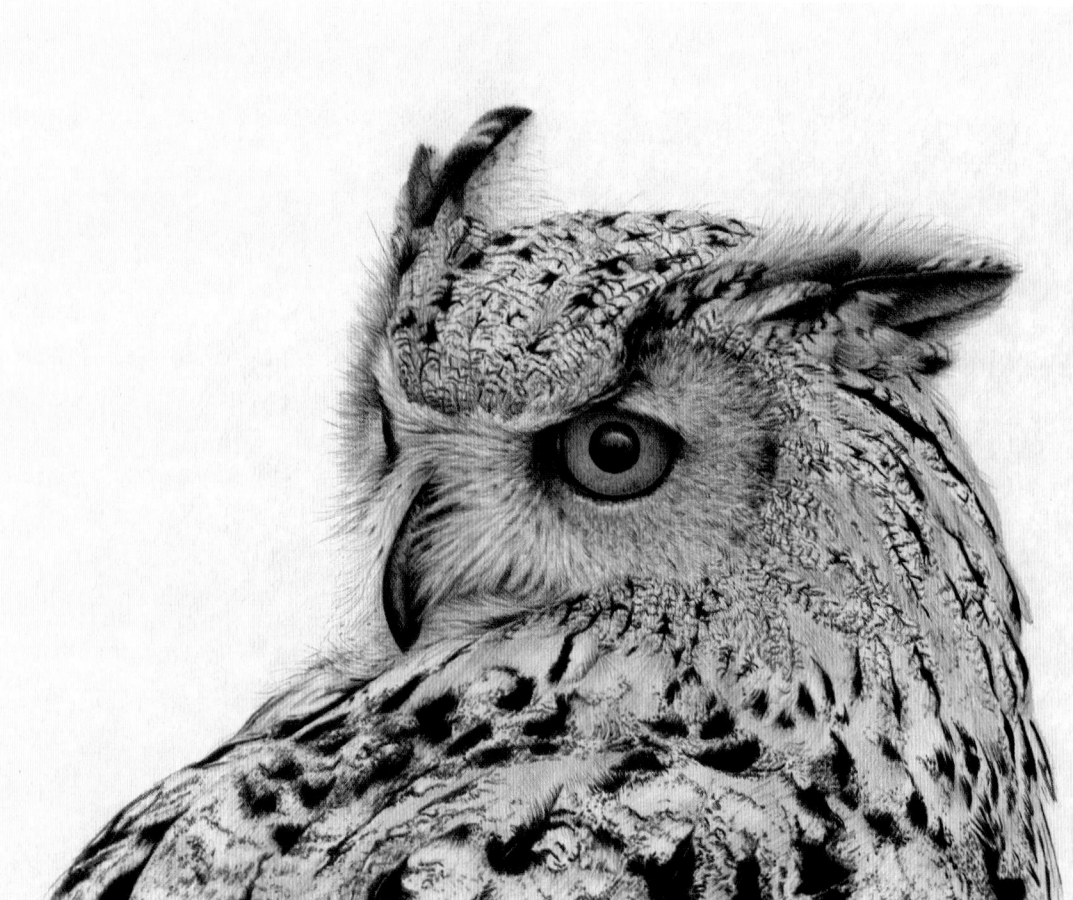

▲ KAREN COULSON
SIBERIAN EAGLE OWL
A characteristic pose and the muted colour scheme and patches of shading on the owl's plumage perfectly capture the essence of this graceful bird. The viewer is drawn to the orange eye in the centre of the portrait.
• HATCHING
• BURNISHING
• SHADING

CAROLYN ROCHELLE ▶
BARNABY
Shading is an extremely versatile technique and, using it, the artist has here conveyed the glossy surface of the dog's coat, the rougher fur on the head and legs and the variations of colour and tone.
• GRADATION
• SHADING

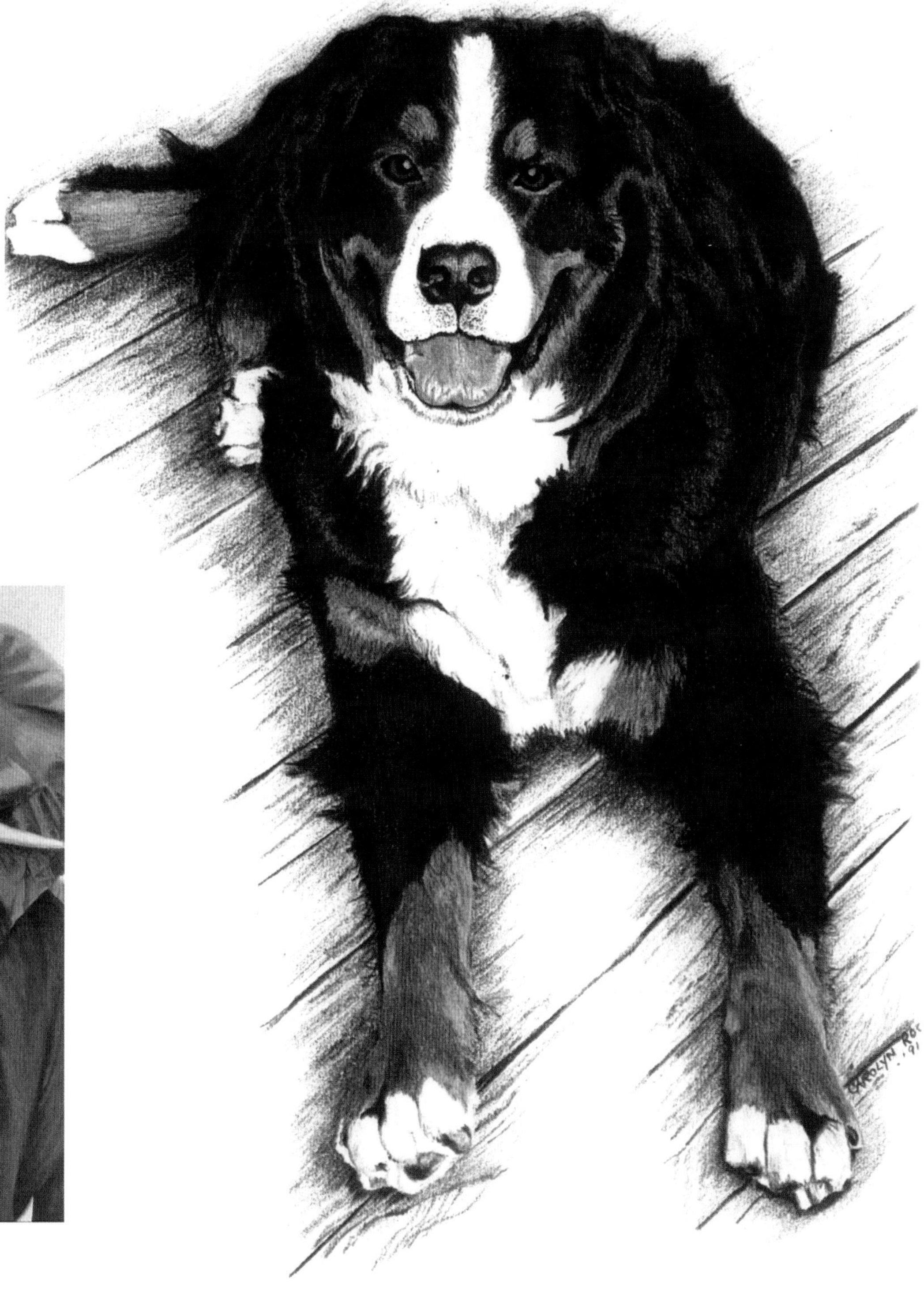

▼ MICHELE BROKAW
THE ROGUE
At 100 x 70 cm (40 x 28 in), this is a relatively large format for a coloured pencil drawing. The size has enabled the artist to give bold treatment to the rugged trunk and rippling ears by layering colour overlays and blends.
• BLENDING
• OVERLAYING COLOURS

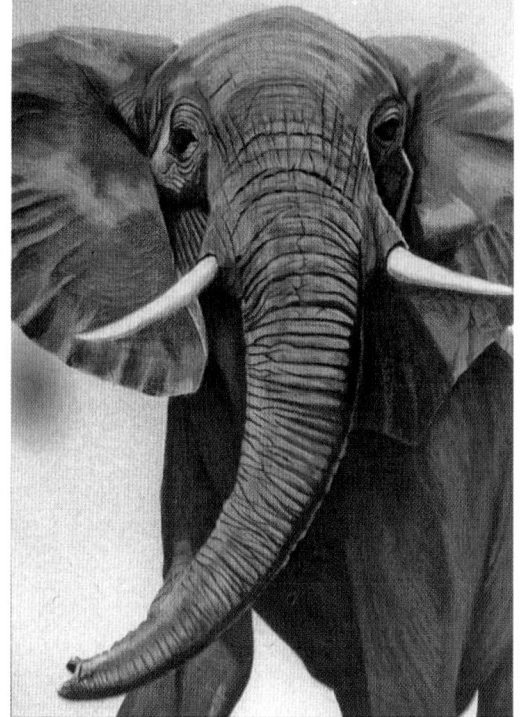

Animal Movement

There are different ways of conveying a sense of movement two-dimensionally, in animal or human subjects.

One way depends on the composition of the image – you choose a "snapshot" pose that conveys the essence of a movement sequence, creating a characteristic contour with internal rhythms and tensions. Another way has more to do with technique – you use the marks of your pencils very actively, to create a network of lines and colour areas from which the moving form emerges; in this case, the viewer does not necessarily see the whole creature in focus, but still gains an impression of its solid form. Another suitable technique in this context is line and wash, which effectively conveys form and movement.

You can produce very interesting drawings by observing a moving animal directly and tracing the lines and shapes that you see on paper. You need to develop a quick response and be unconcerned about creating a "realistic" portrait.

If you prefer a more methodical approach towards a detailed image, you will need to use photographic reference to "freeze" the image. Many magazines and books contain excellent wildlife photography that does the job for you – but be careful not to become stuck in the mode of merely reproducing someone else's image; use your skill in pencil techniques to interpret, rather than copy, the picture. With some subjects you can take the photographs yourself; this has the advantage that at the same time you can directly observe the animal's typical patterns of movement, perhaps also making sketches to use as reference for full-scale finished works.

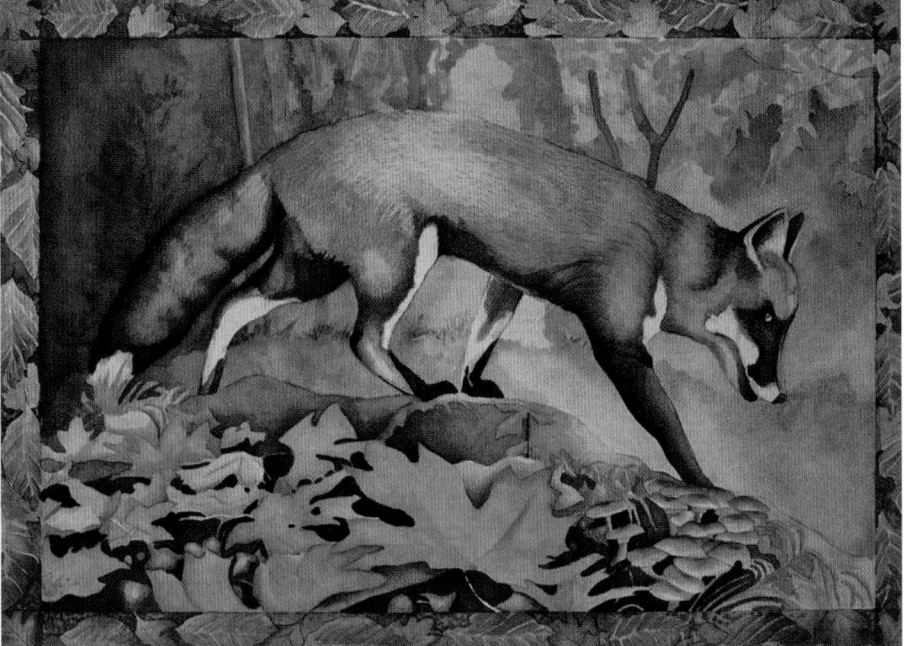

▲STEVE TAYLOR
FOX IN AUTUMN
Most of the modelling and atmospheric description is created here with watercolour, subtly modified with water-soluble coloured pencils. The movement is expressed by the fluid lines of the fox – the angle of its body and the downward thrust of the head, as well as the more obvious motion of its legs and paws. The artist frequently uses decorative borders as a way of edging and enhancing the main image. The leaf shapes in the border relate to, but do not copy, the similar detail within the frame.
• SOLVENTS
• WATERCOLOUR AND PENCIL

FRANK DE BROUWER ▶
HORSE AND RIDER
The gestures of the artist's hand and arm can be seen from the rhythms of this drawing, giving it a sense of physical movement additional to that implied by the subject. The variations of line – emphatic black coloured pencil over more tentative, shifting graphite pencil marks – enhance the vitality. The non-naturalistic primary colours that provide the mid-tones between black and white are also enlivening.
• LINEAR MARKS
• LINE QUALITIES

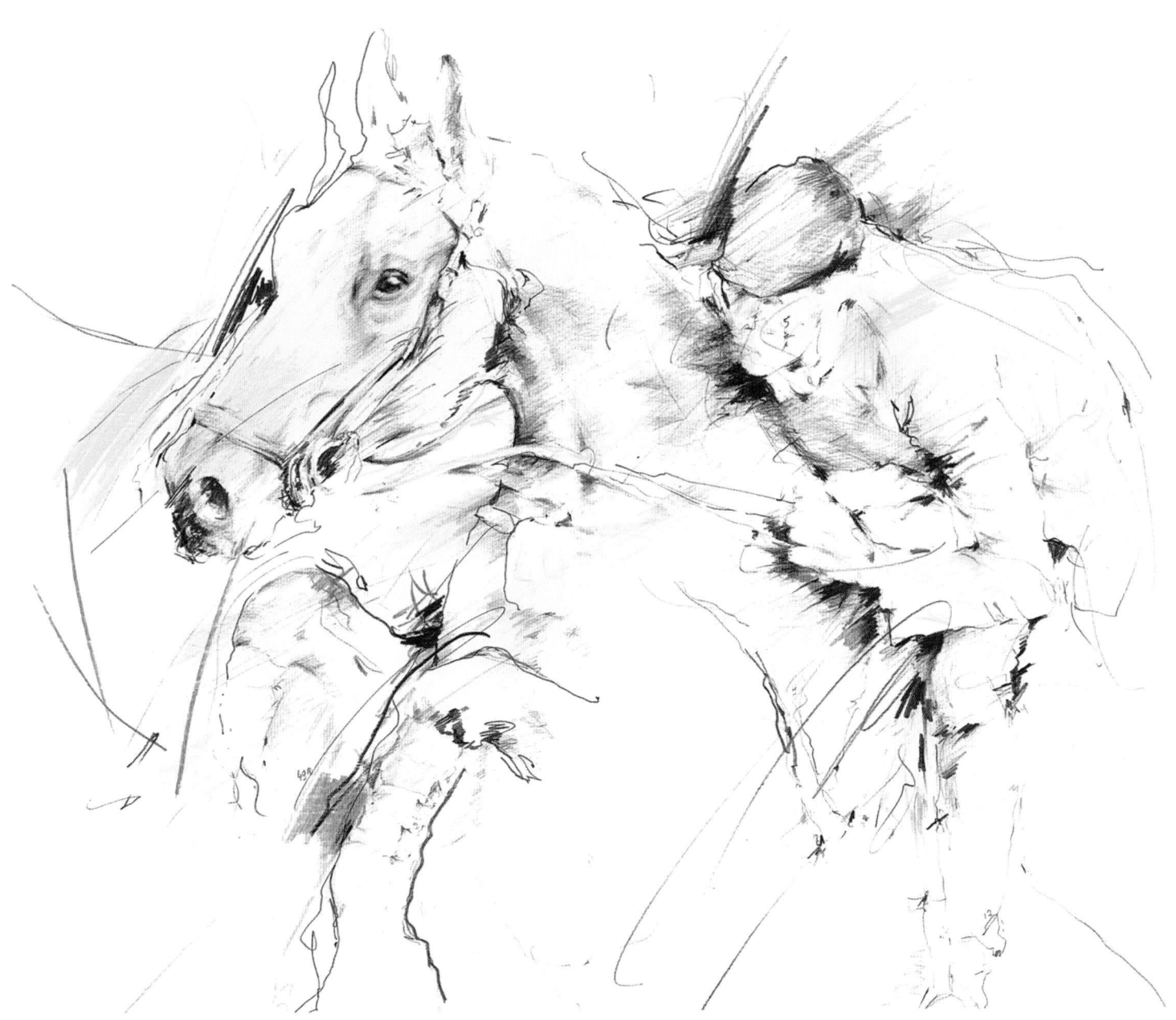

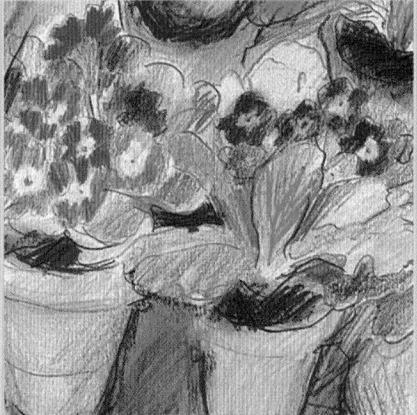

Nature

The fresh beauty of flowers

Jane Strother

One of the most pleasurable aspects of drawing flowers and foliage is their fresh colour and textural variation, which enables you to make the most of your coloured-pencil "palette" and the versatile mark-making capacities of this medium.

Jane Strother's demonstration is drawn on a relatively large scale so that each item in the massed flower group can be freely described. Her pencil initially fluidly travels the contours of the subjects, then she uses solvent to spread and rub the dark tones and, finally, combines drawing and painting techniques to build up richness and texture.

This is not a precise portrait of the plants and garden tools, as the shapes are loosely realized rather than exactly drawn. Tight shading and subtle gradations of tone and colour would produce a very different, probably no less striking result.

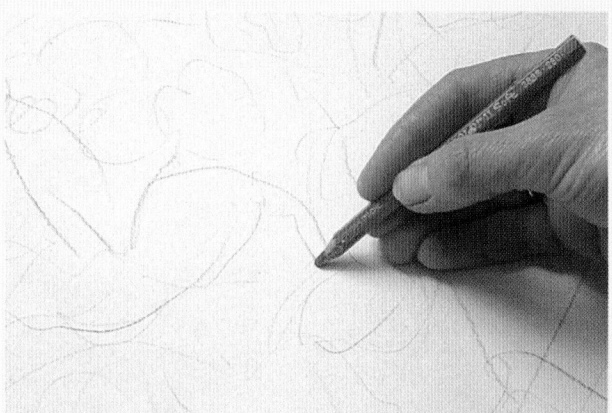

◀**1** The outlines of the composition are first lightly sketched in red, using a soft-leaded water-soluble pencil to create a gentle, grainy line.

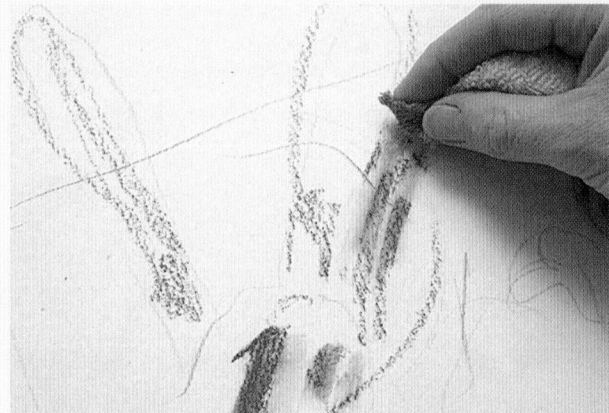

◀**2** A purple pencil is used to block in the areas of darkest tone, including cast shadows. The colour is rubbed with a rag dampened with white spirit to make loosely scrubbed washes.

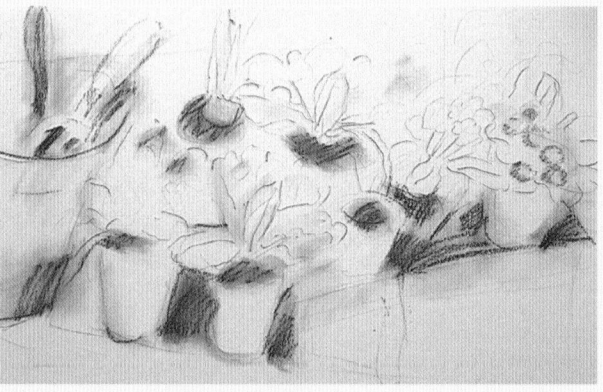

◀**3** The same treatment is applied right across the paper to give the line drawing depth and tone. Further line work is drawn over the top, putting in leaf and flower shapes.

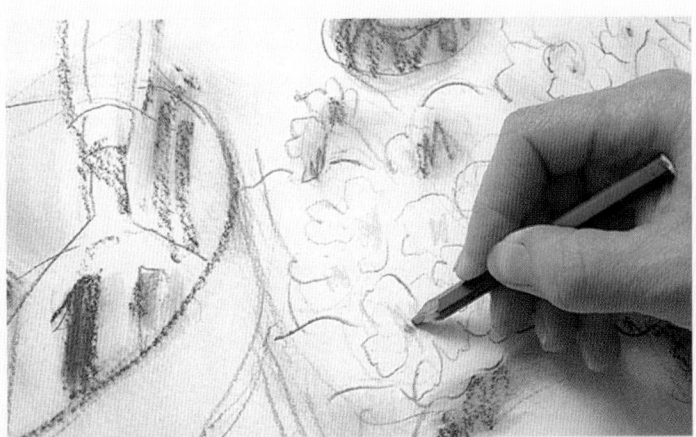

◀**4** The artist gradually builds up the colour detail, using green, yellow and red pencils to shape and colour the flowers.

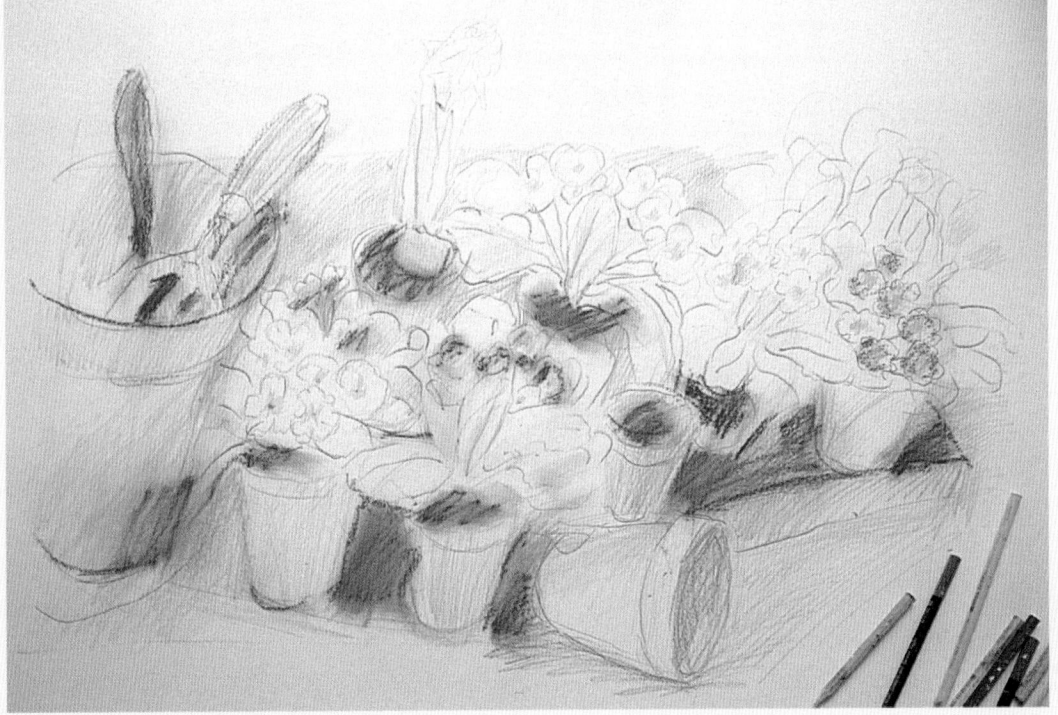

◀**5** Mid-tones are roughly blocked in with free shading and hatching, using terracotta and yellow ochre pencils. Lighter tones are added – pink and yellow.

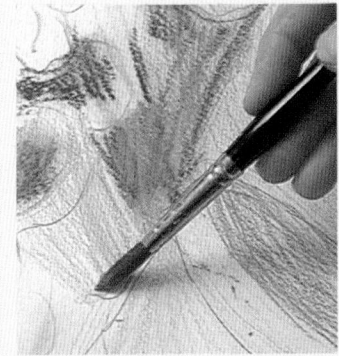

▲**6** A soft sable brush wetted with clean water is passed over the drawing within some of the solid shapes, to dissolve and spread the colour until it resembles a watercolour wash.

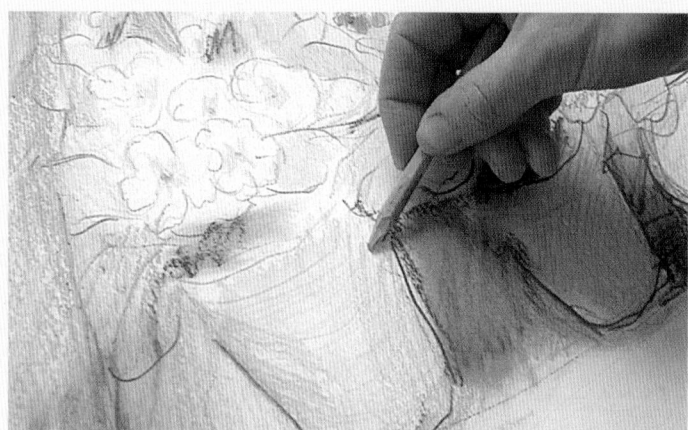

◀ **7** The intensity of tone and colour is gradually developed by overlaying hatched lines, taking care to avoid the areas that must remain highlighted.

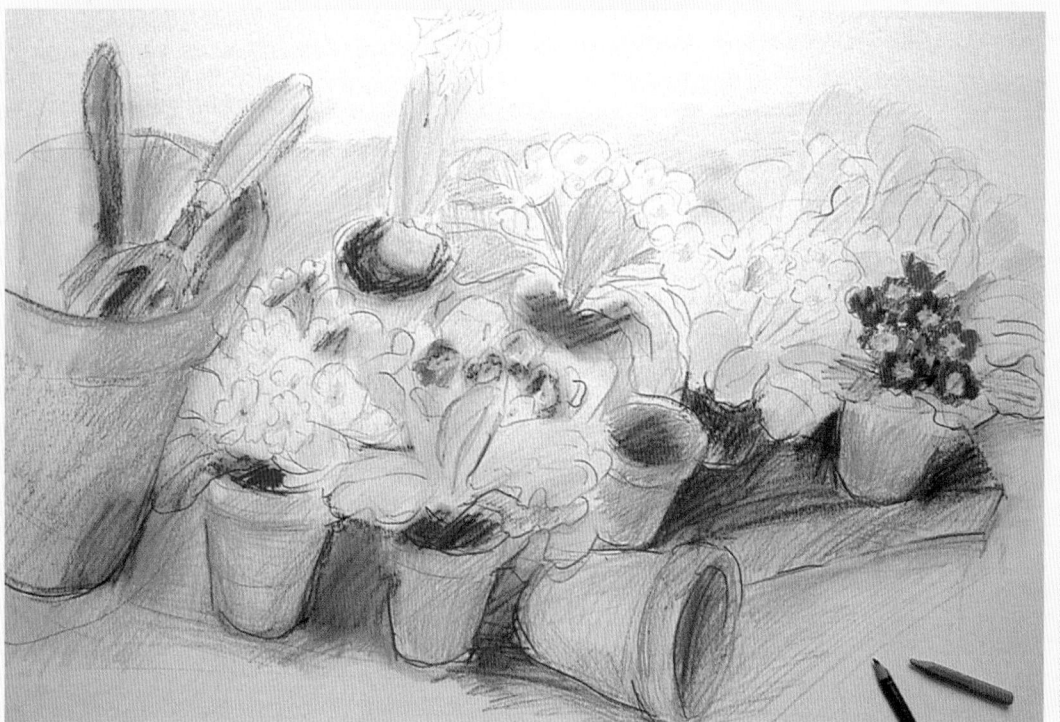

▲ **8** The process of working back and forth into different parts of the image produces a richer, more detailed effect overall.

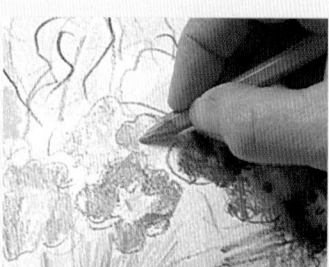

▲ **9** The flowers that have not yet been fully described are coloured more strongly, then the wetted brush is used again to merge some of the pencil marks.

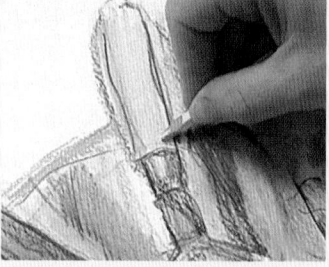

▲ **10** Pale tones on the garden tools enhance the modelling of the shapes. This colour on the handle is heavily hatched with broad lines.

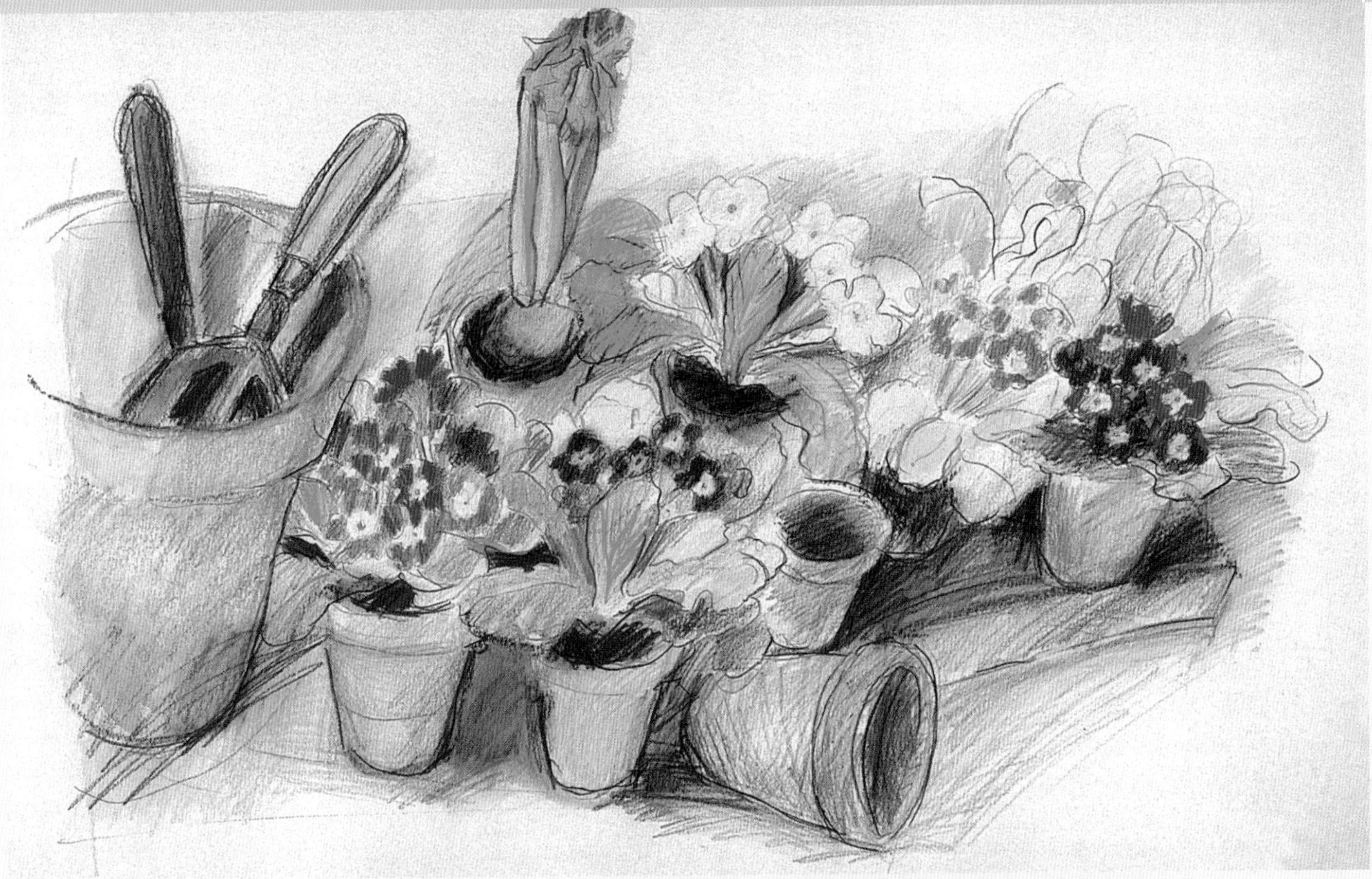

▲ JANE STROTHER
PRIMULAS
In the finished rendering, the active pencil lines give the image vitality and contrast effectively with the smoother, all-over textures of the rubbed and brushed colours. The detail (right) shows the degree of surface interest that has evolved through the layering of the mixed techniques.

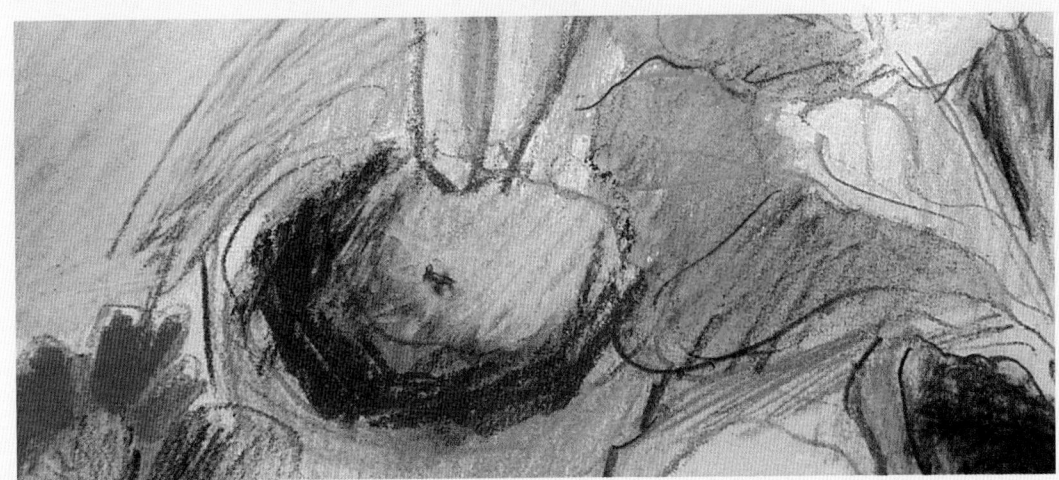

People and Portraits

The human figure is considered by many artists to be the most important and enduring of the major themes in art. There can be no doubt that figure compositions have indeed provided a great wealth of interpretive material, from traditional life studies and posed portraits to images of incidental human activity in a wide variety of situations and contexts.

Other people are continually fascinating as a subject for drawing and painting; associative and narrative elements are always implied in imagery that includes figures, but there are also many interesting visual considerations – the variety of human shapes and forms, the subtle colouring of skin and hair, the colourful detail of clothing and accessories.

Composition and technique

Figure studies range from the life-class nude to quick sketches of individuals to detailed and elaborate renderings of figure groups, sometimes requiring equally detailed attention to the background setting. Photographic reference plays an important part if your subjects are drawn from daily life; some artists collect a library of pictures, from magazines and newspapers, showing different poses and activities, styles of clothing and different backgrounds. Individual elements from different photographs can be combined to create a single composition. Other artists tend to collect more personally selective reference material by taking their own photographs of likely subjects.

If you work from live subjects, you need to develop a facility for quick sketching and a keen eye for essential details. The way you pose and light your model depends on the mood and character you wish to give the portrait. A linear, sketchy portrait does not need dramatic lighting effects, but a strong directional light will aid the tonal study of a face.

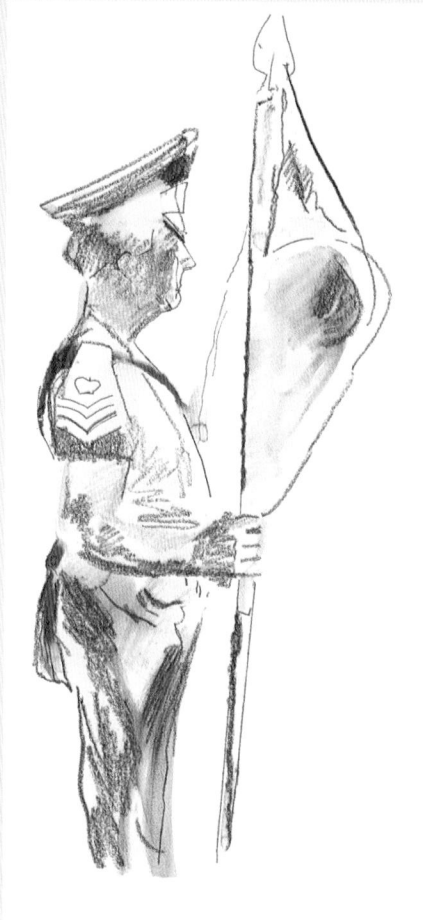

◀ **LINDA KITSON**
C/SGT BURTON
Official war artist during the Falklands Conflict, Linda Kitson uses a sketchy drawing technique to capture the descriptive features of her subject.
• LINEAR MARKS

MAX TEN BOSCH ▶
COUPLE
Sensitive contour drawing underpins a bold use of linear techniques and rapid colour shading. These techniques create a drawing of exciting texture that conveys the appearance and mood of its subjects. Overall, the gestural qualities of the pencil marks are freely laid in, but the right kind of precision just where it is needed builds a sympathetic portrait. The dark lines and tones gain subtle variation from the interplay of graphite pencil with black and grey coloured leads.
• CONTOUR DRAWING
• LINEAR MARKS
• LINE QUALITIES
• SHADING

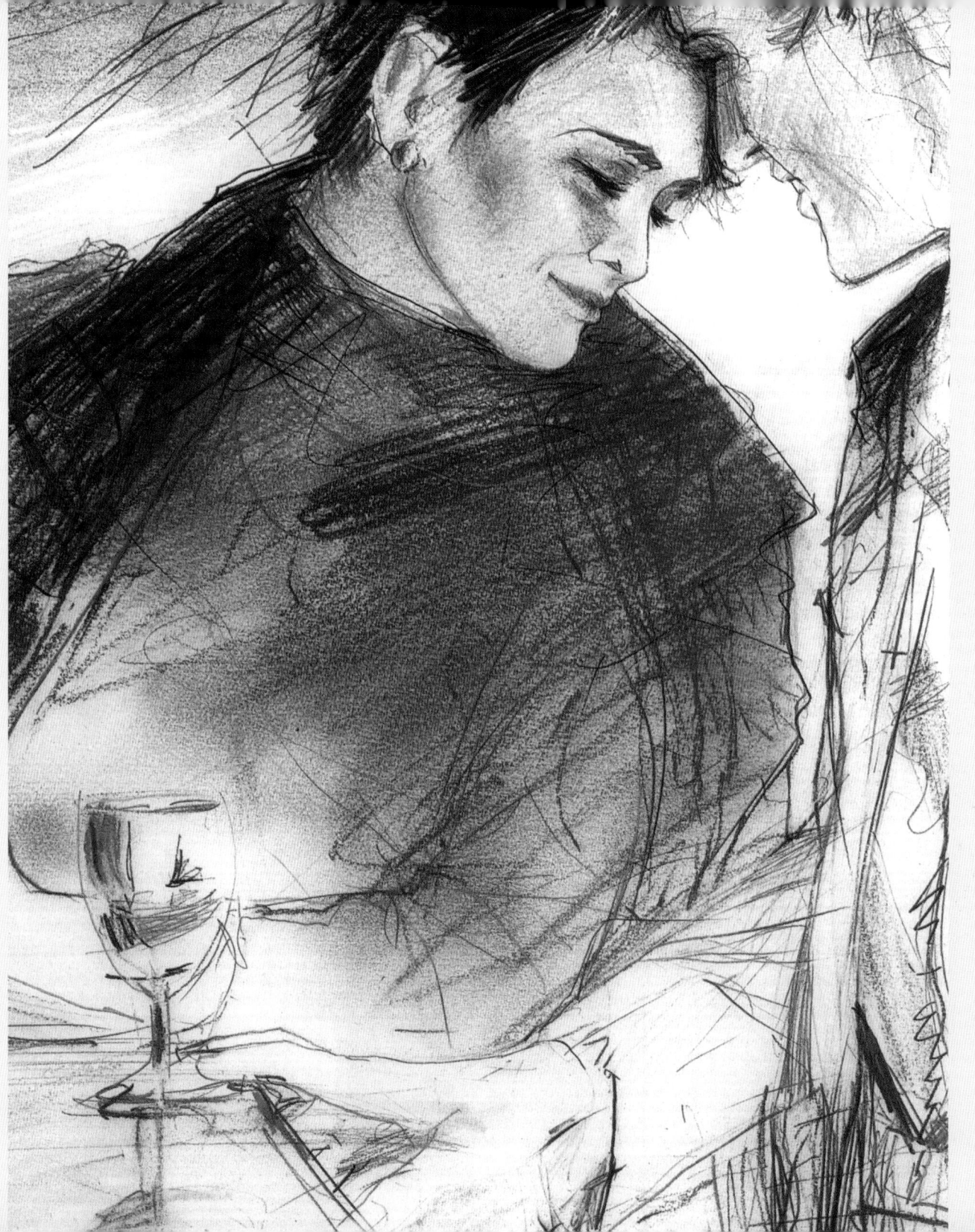

Individuals

The sense of an individual is not necessarily conveyed by a distinct likeness, as in a portrait, but by what seems to be a convincing, characteristic pose or gesture. The viewer does not know who the subject is, but can recognize a particular reality in the representation.

Coloured pencil has an excellent range for figure drawing of all kinds. Depending on whether you decide to create quick reference sketches, to work in detail from life or to interpret photographic reference, you can use a form of rapid linear notation or more elaborate methods of building up detail. The techniques of pencil drawing provide considerable versatility in the surface qualities that you can employ – as well as varying your technical approach, consider the surface values you can obtain by combining different types of pencil textures.

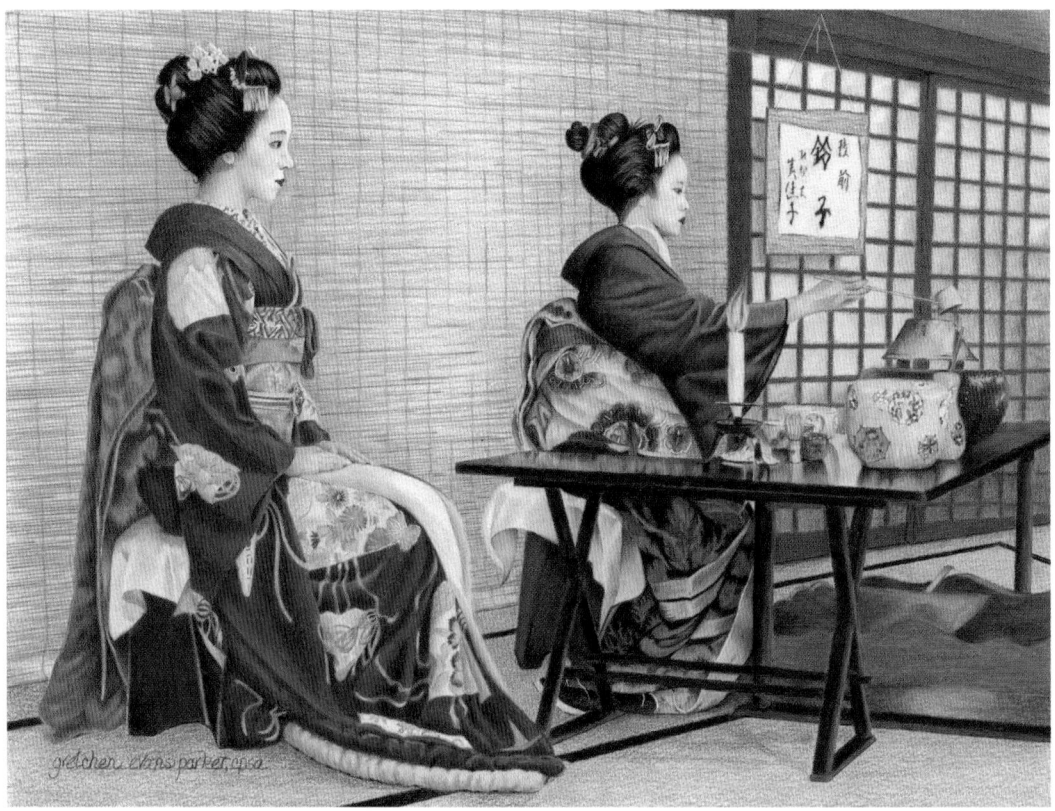

▲GRETCHEN EVANS
PARKER APPRENTICE
This portrait has captured the relationship between mentor and apprentice geisha. A sense of motion is achieved through the artist's shading on the apprentice's kimono and hands. Burnishing colours creates the illusion of shine on both the silk kimonos and the enamelled table-top. Impressed line is a simple way to depict the delicate string supporting the sign hanging in the background.
• BLENDING
• BURNISHING
• CONTOUR DRAWING
• FILLING IN
• FROTTAGE
• IMPRESSING

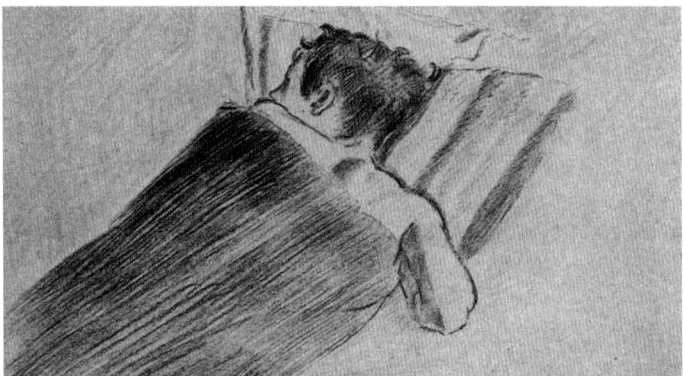

◀JEFFREY CAMP
SLEEPING FIGURE
The sense of an individual does not necessarily come from the face – posture, body shape and characteristic features such as hair colour and texture help to build the impression. These elements are very telling in this unusual figure study.
• CONTOUR DRAWING
• HATCHING

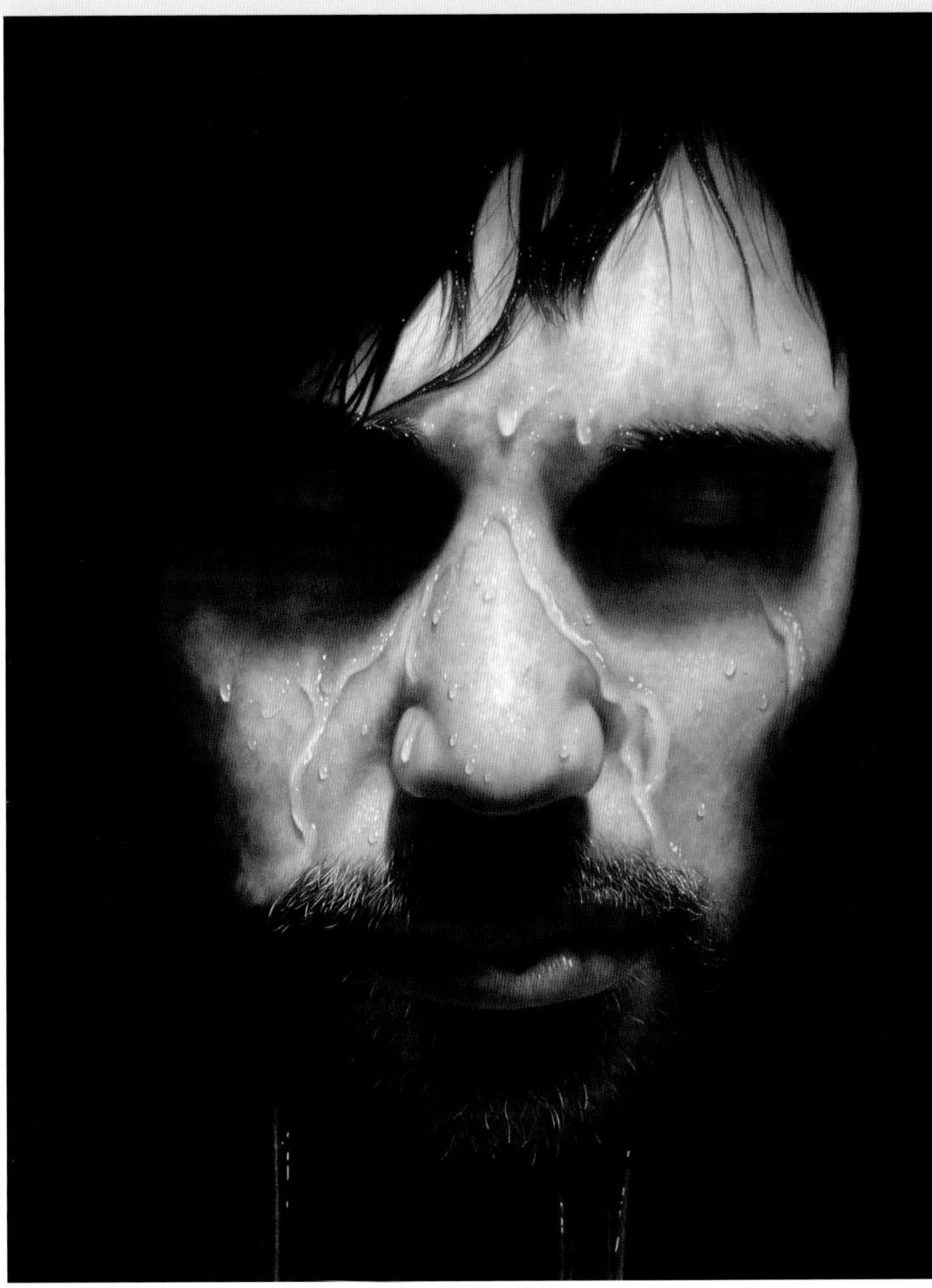

◀ **JESSE LANE**
AFTER THE STORM
Jesse Lane used light layering
and stippling to build up colour
until the drawing became
burnished. She started with a
black area on white paper to
judge values. The beard was
done by scratching in thin
highlights with a scalpel blade.
Some hairs were drawn with
black pencil.
• OVERLAYING COLOURS
• STIPPLING
• SGRAFFITO

Children

Young children have distinctive characteristics that need to be observed and rendered carefully, to give the subjects of your drawings a childlike quality. The facial features of children, smaller and less boldly formed than in adults, also occupy a smaller proportion of the head; typically, the brow is high and cheeks and chin rounded; skin texture and colouring are relatively smooth and uniform. The head is quite large in relation to overall body height, as compared to the proportions of an adult figure.

These are physical characteristics common to children in early stages of development, but there are plenty of signs of individuality in both appearance and behaviour. The eyes are often a striking and expressive feature; clothing and hairstyle also reflect personality; the activities children engage in and the accessories they introduce into work and play provide a variety of visual material for constructing a composition.

It can be difficult to work from life with a child model, as all untrained models find it difficult to hold a pose and a child, especially, will soon find it boring and uncomfortable. If you are making a study of a particular subject, you can sketch unobtrusively while the child is occupied with his or her own concerns; but it is unlikely you will get time to complete a whole, detailed composition. Photography is often a vital resource for the artist working with children and ideally you should take your own shots rather than rely on found images.

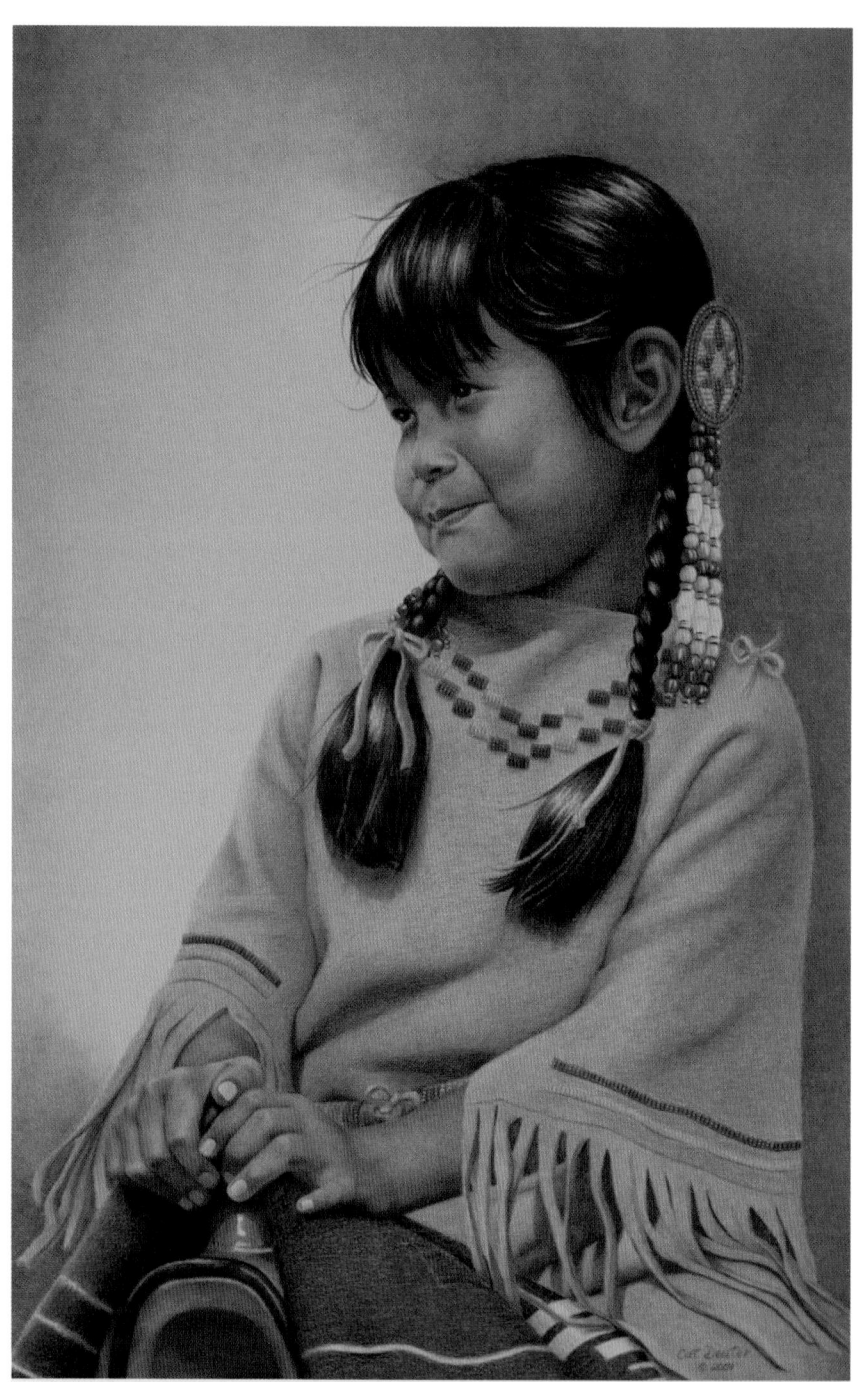

CAT DEUTER ▶
RAVEN HAIR
Cat Deuter captures the spirit and imagination of the American West in her closely worked coloured pencil drawings. This intimate portrait of a young girl shows an amazing level of detail.

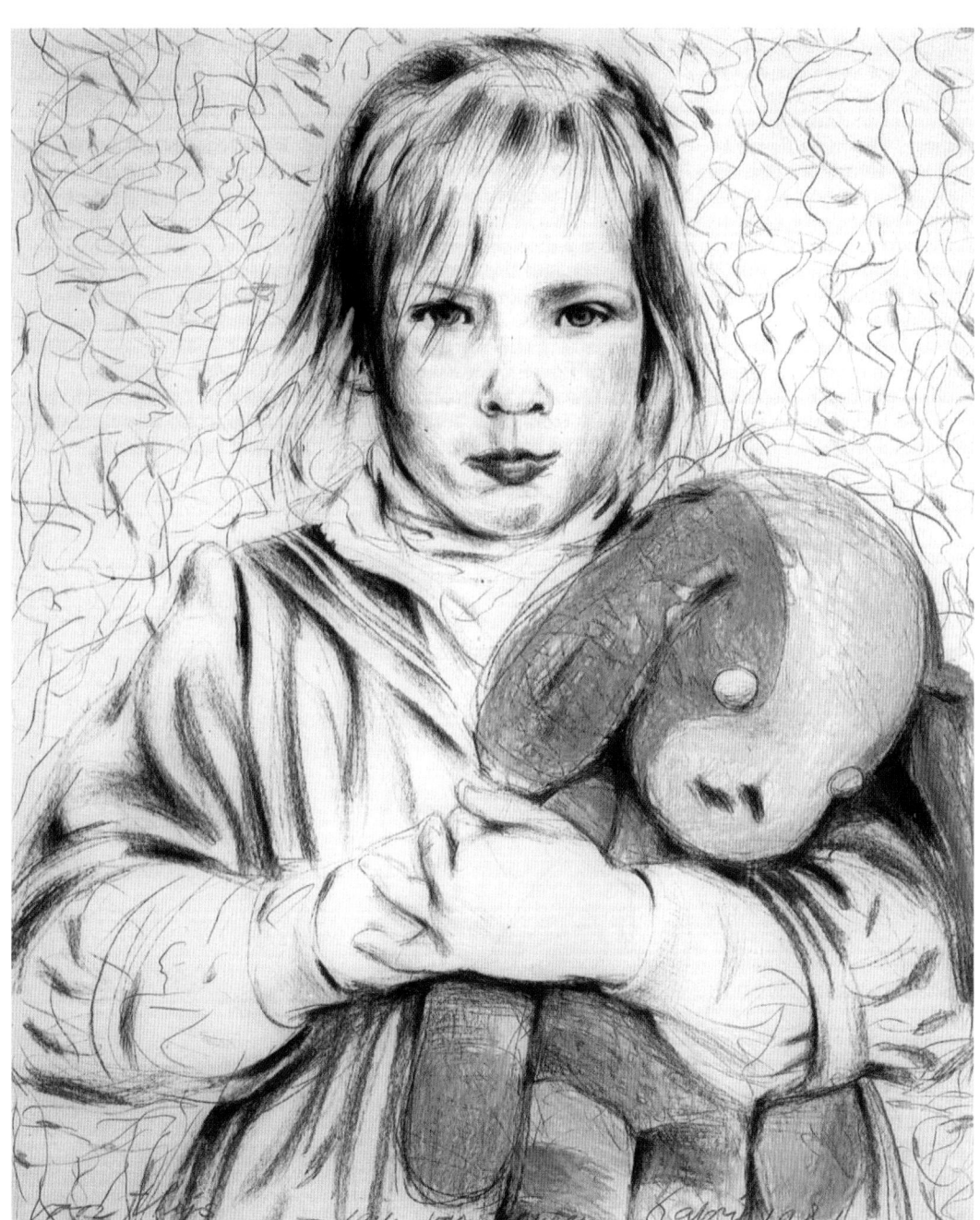

◄ ERIK VAN HOUTEN
CHILD STUDY
A direct frontal pose typically has a confrontational mood, but here this is made ambiguous by the child's posture, which seems to draw back slightly from the viewer, and the cuddly toy she clutches, as if in need of a friend. Her face, though, is strongly drawn, with decision and clarity in those features which form the important focal points of a portrait – the eyes and mouth. Varied strands of colour in the hair and skin enliven what is essentially a monochromatic rendering of the child subject, to which the unreal, bright colours of the toy form a striking contrast.

• LINEAR MARKS
• SHADING

Life Studies

This traditional element of art training has been adapted to all manner of styles and techniques in drawing and painting. The nude figure is used as a vehicle for objective study of form and proportion, yet the tendency for both artist and viewer to identify with a human subject means that it is difficult to maintain a strictly objective response.

If you attend a life class, you may find that you are asked to focus on a different aspect of form and technique in each session: for instance, using line only to trace the contours of the figure; employing a restricted palette of neutral tones to model form with light and shade; using colour as a method of "coding" various kinds of information about the figure. This helps you to acquire a discipline of visual analysis, and the same kind of systematic examination of a subject can be applied to other themes – a still-life group or vase of flowers, for example – if you haven't a human model to work from. The "live" element of life drawing is important; there is little value in working from photographs, which tend to flatten and distort the forms.

If you cannot get someone to pose for you formally, you might try sketching figures on the beach or at a swimming pool where, first, you can see details of bodies and limbs and, secondly, you may find people adopting fairly still poses for some length of time – while sunbathing, for example. Be careful not to be intrusive when selecting and studying your subjects.

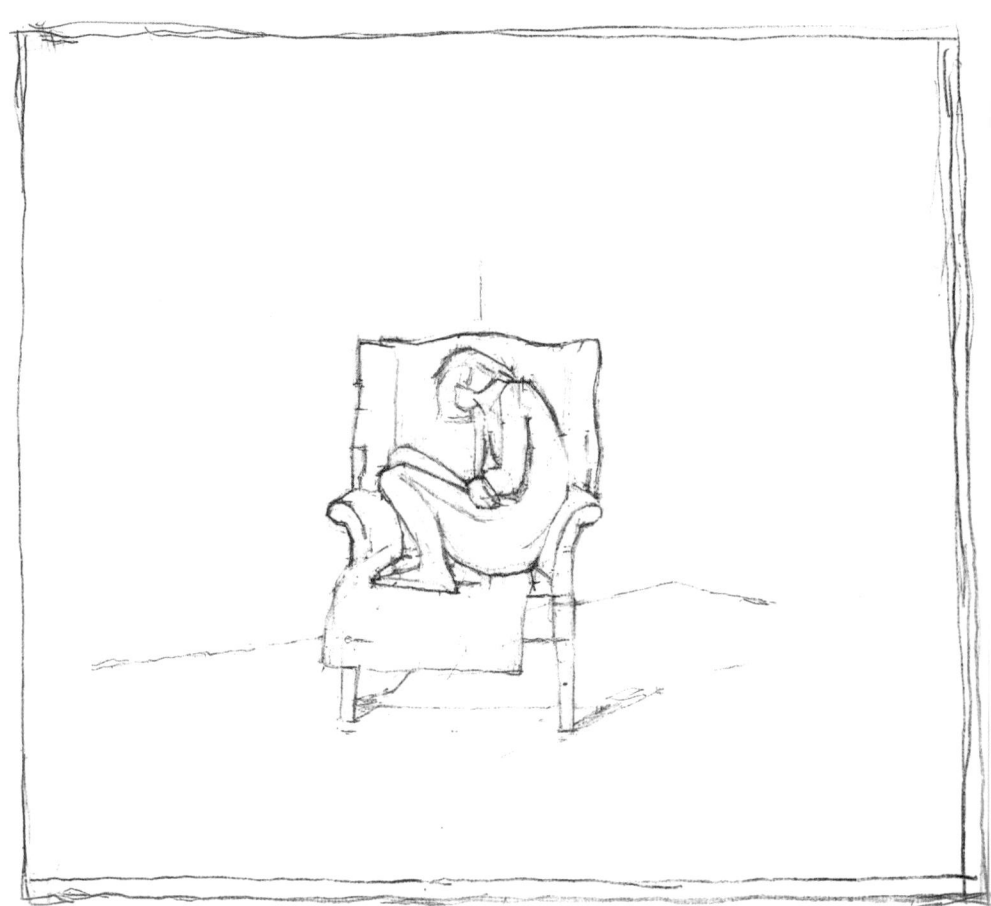

▲ EUAN UGLOW
LIFE DRAWING
Colour is not always a decorative or naturalistically descriptive element in drawing. It often has a structural function, helping to define space and form. In this study, colour is systematically applied to the contours of the figure, chair and interior space, to indicate particular elements of the compositional framework: blue represents the edges between the most distant parts of the subject; green defines butting forms and shadows; on the figure, the deep red stands for distant forms curving away – the mid-toned red defines the middle distance and orange the nearer elements; yellow lines show slight but significant changes of contour within the form.
• CONTOUR DRAWING

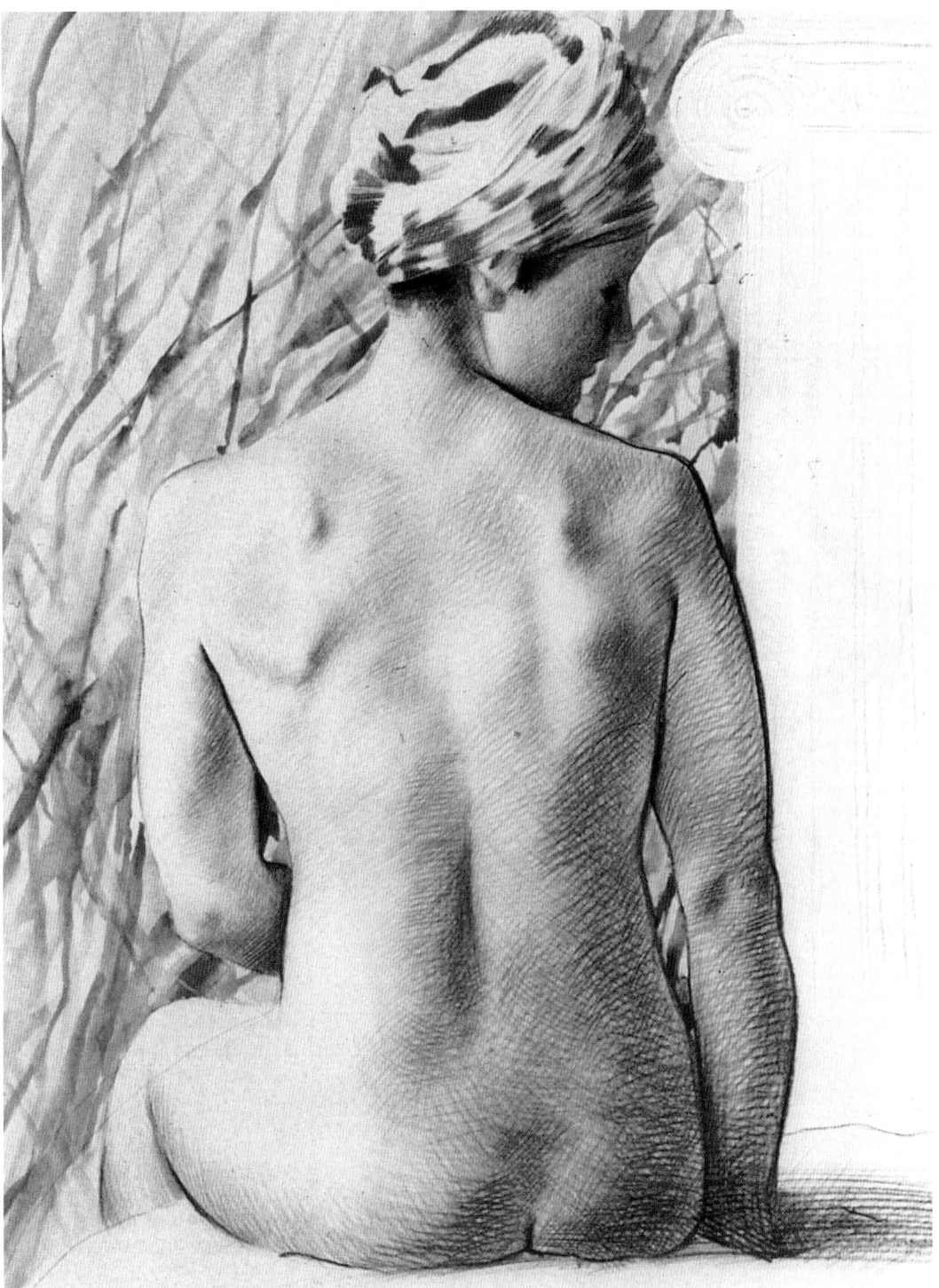

◀ ADRIAN GEORGE
TURBANED NUDE
There is a direct visual reference here to the classical painting of a turbaned bather by the French artist Ingres (1780–1867). The pose and setting have been adapted, but there is the same emphasis on the smooth contour in both the linear outlining of the figure and the modelled curves and hollows of the body. The marbled background consists of light trails of watercolour.
• HATCHING
• LINE QUALITIES

Movement

A sense of movement is inherent in many figure poses, and can be underplayed or emphasized by the artist's choice of technique and method of arranging the composition. The drawing can be treated as a "still picture" of a person engaged in a particular activity or sequence of motion, so that it becomes a cleanly focused and detailed description of a split-second event. Or the active qualities of the pencil marks can be contrived to enhance the sense of movement and the background can be treated in a way that also suggests the figure's motion through the surrounding space.

Pictorial devices that suggest movement include fluid or repetitive line qualities, vigorous hatching, and subtle soft-focus blending of tones and hues. As well as studying the ways artists have expressed various kinds of activity and movement in the examples on these pages, look for different approaches throughout this section on figure drawing and also at the feature on animal movement on pages 146–147.

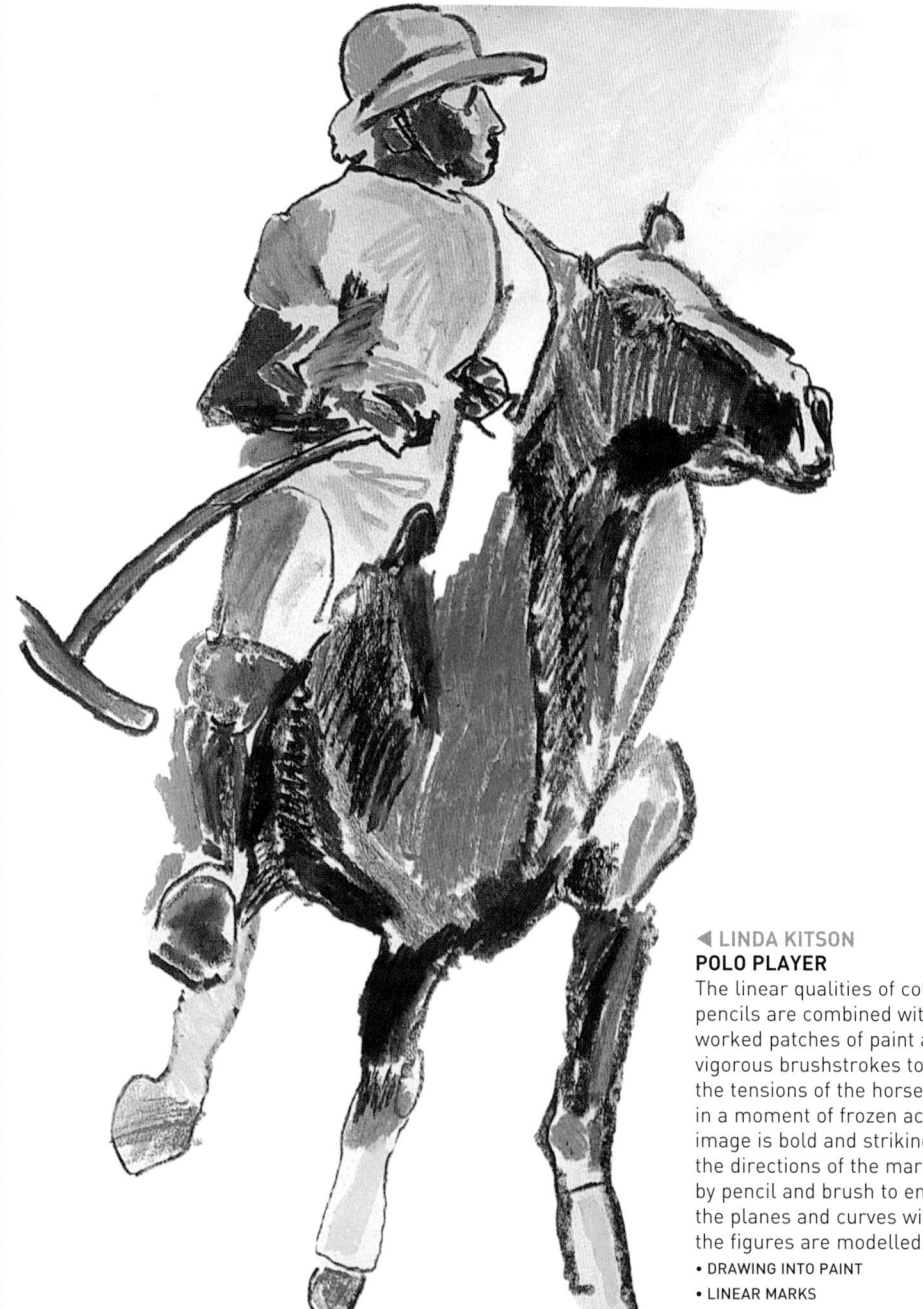

◀ LINDA KITSON
POLO PLAYER
The linear qualities of coloured pencils are combined with loosely worked patches of paint and vigorous brushstrokes to show the tensions of the horse and rider in a moment of frozen action. The image is bold and striking, using the directions of the marks made by pencil and brush to emphasize the planes and curves with which the figures are modelled.
• DRAWING INTO PAINT
• LINEAR MARKS
• LINE QUALITIES

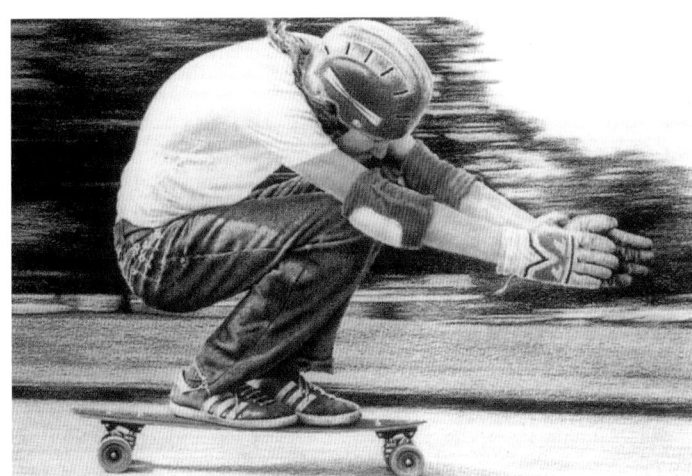

◀ CHRIS CHAPMAN
SKATEBOARDER
The sense of movement is cleverly suggested here by blurring the background, but making the figure very sharp and well defined. An important aspect of conveying motion is the visible contrast between movement and stillness, but here the real relationship has been reversed. Close shading and complex colour overlays are used to create a heightened realism.

• BLENDING
• GRADATION
• SHADING

PRISCILLA WADSWORTH ▶
EDDIE LACY
Every tiny detail in this work is achieved first by drawing: the stitched line on the ball, the powerful muscles in Lacy's arms, the holes in the sports shirt are drawn and then filled in with coloured pencil. In this drawing you get a sense of the sheer power of the subject and his direction of travel.

• FILLING IN

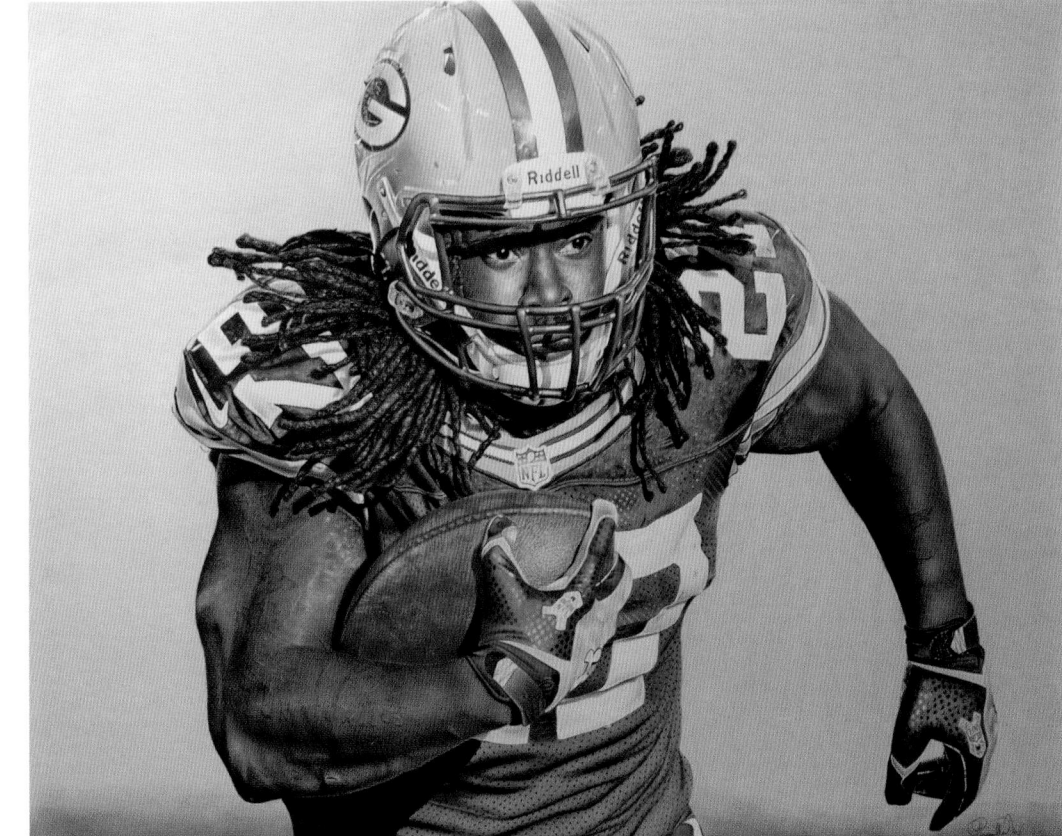

Environment

The location of an individual person or group of people is often an important aspect of a figure composition, giving logic to the poses and sometimes suggesting an ambience that gives the artist a cue for selecting a particular technique or style of rendering. It is not always necessary to include the background elements in great detail, but it is frequently appropriate to indicate the nature of the setting, to add to the descriptive or narrative effect of the image.

The way you render the space that a figure occupies can also imply a mood. A crowded interior space, for example, can be made to seem enclosing by selecting a viewpoint that draws in the perspective and by using a technique that conveys particular qualities of light and atmosphere. However, it is also possible to construct an impression of space, volume and relative distances with economical means. A few lines properly judged can indicate the shape of a room or the open space of an outdoor setting.

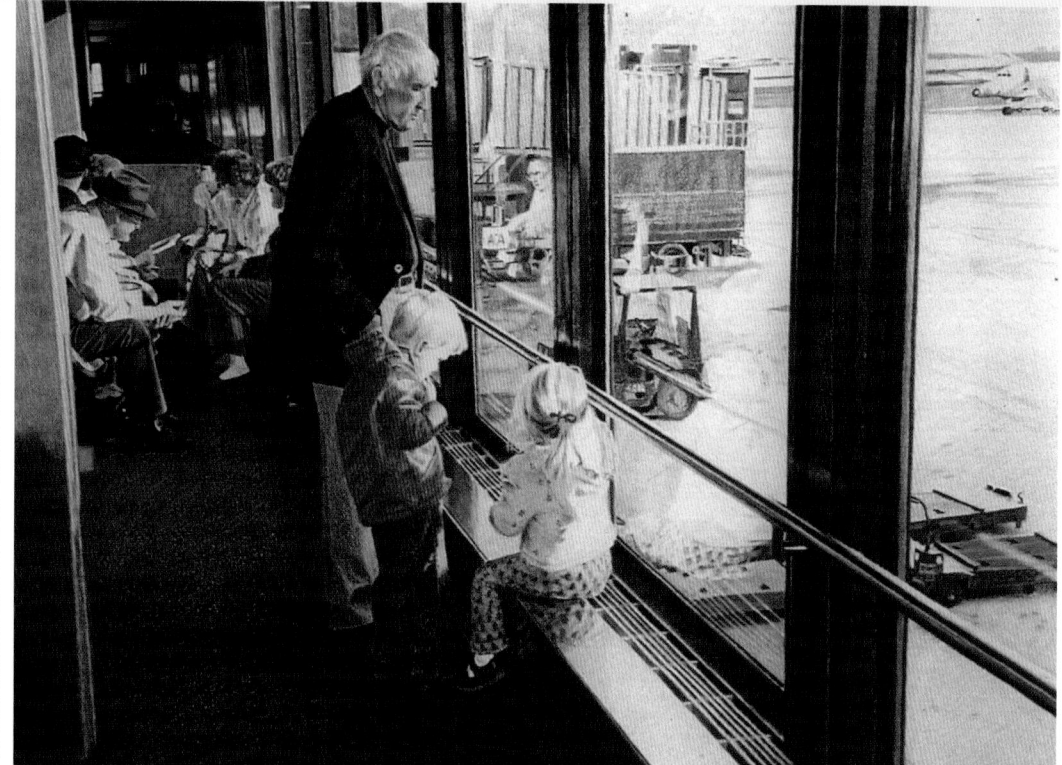

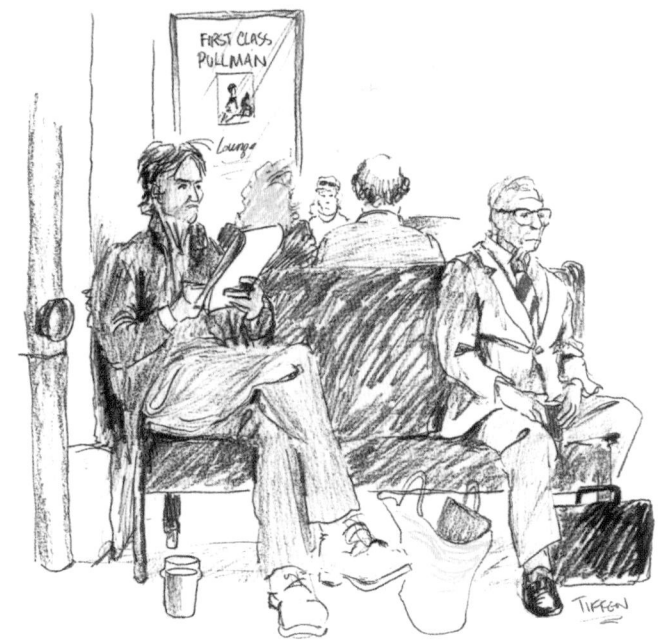

▲ SHERI LYNN GOYER DOTY
SALT LAKE INTERNATIONAL AIRPORT
This sensitive study pulls together the different elements of the subject by means of a consistent, controlled drawing technique. The heavy grain of the paper creates surface interest, helping to define the individual textures, from fabrics to concrete.
• SHADING
• PAPER GRAIN EFFECTS

◄ ANDREW TIFFEN
WAITING ROOM
The bold, sketchy quality of the pencil marks and open contour of the image give vitality to this everyday subject. The strong colours are allowed to stand out clearly, defining separate shapes without overlays or blending.
• HATCHING
• SKETCHING

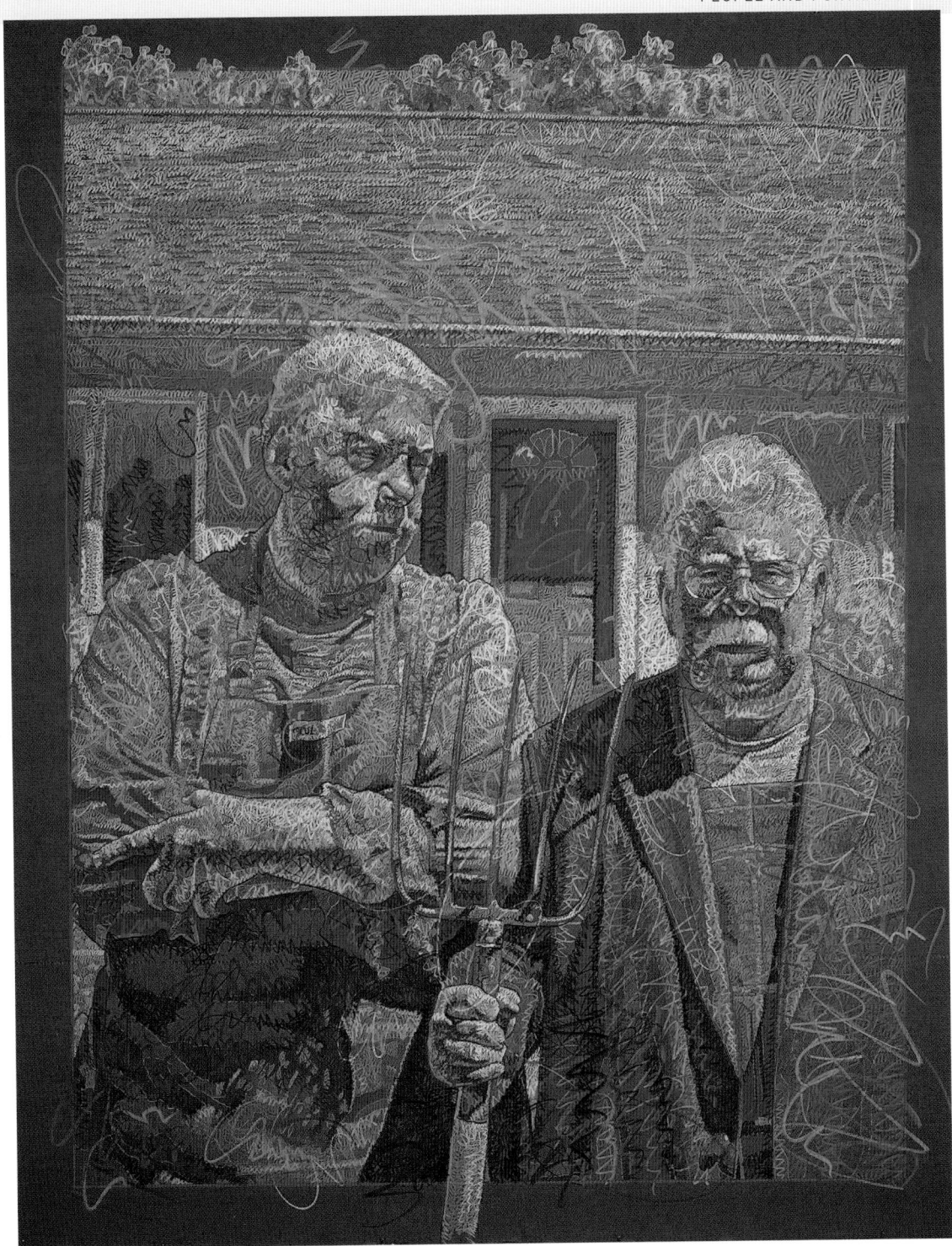

JOHN SMOLKO
AMERICAN ELECTRIC
"American Eclectic" was
created with a variety of
scribble lines ranging from
controlled marks to very
spontaneous expressionistic
lines. The work was inspired
by Grant Woods' "American
Gothic" and incorporates
contemporary issues that are
at the forefront in American
society. With the help of two of
his neighbours, John Smolko
was able to achieve a dynamic
interpretation of a slice of life
in the United States.

- HATCHING
- LINEAR MARKS
- SHADING

Expressive Portrait

Ideally, a portrait expresses something about the sitter as well as making a visual record of the individual. There are various ways of endowing a portrait with expressive character, deriving from both the composition of the drawing and the techniques you apply.

In selecting a pose, you need to decide on the angle of view – showing a person full-face tends to create a confrontational aspect, while a slightly turned pose can seem mysterious or mischievous. You can focus on face and head only, or include part or all of the body, so that the subject's physical shape and posture contribute to the mood of the image.

Different approaches to tone and colour can vary the expressive qualities of the rendering. A tonal study gives emphasis to the modelling of form and features. Colours need not be strictly realistic; to enhance the impact of the portrait you can play up faint nuances, such as warm lights and cool shadows in skin tones, or exaggerate the contrasts of hue and tone to construct a more colourful interpretation.

The kinds of marks you make also contribute to an individualistic portrait; soft shading and subtle gradations can be organized in ways that create a photographically realistic effect; or you can use more vigorous techniques such as hatching and linear marks to emphasize both structural and surface characteristics.

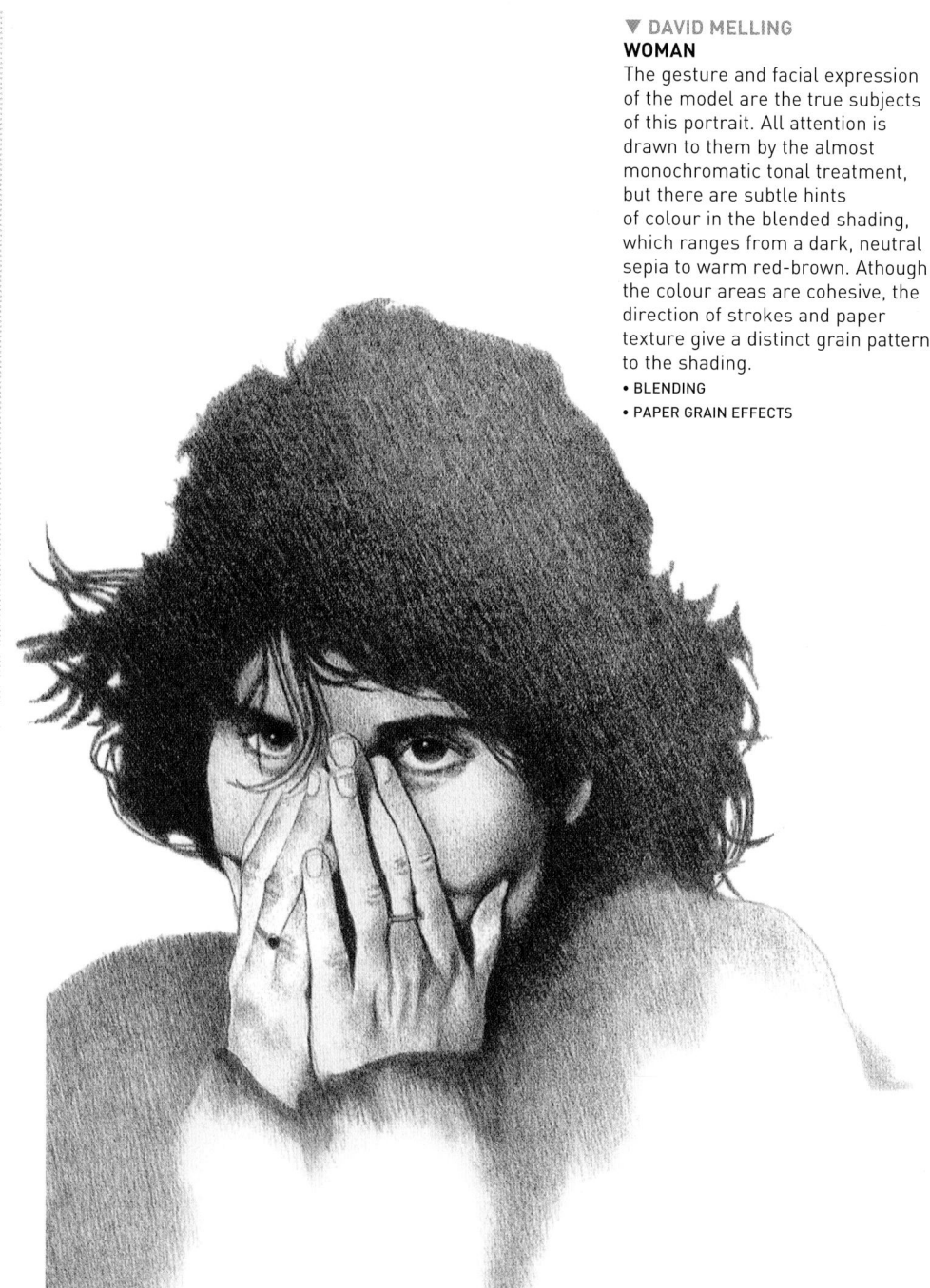

▼ **DAVID MELLING**
WOMAN
The gesture and facial expression of the model are the true subjects of this portrait. All attention is drawn to them by the almost monochromatic tonal treatment, but there are subtle hints of colour in the blended shading, which ranges from a dark, neutral sepia to warm red-brown. Athough the colour areas are cohesive, the direction of strokes and paper texture give a distinct grain pattern to the shading.
• BLENDING
• PAPER GRAIN EFFECTS

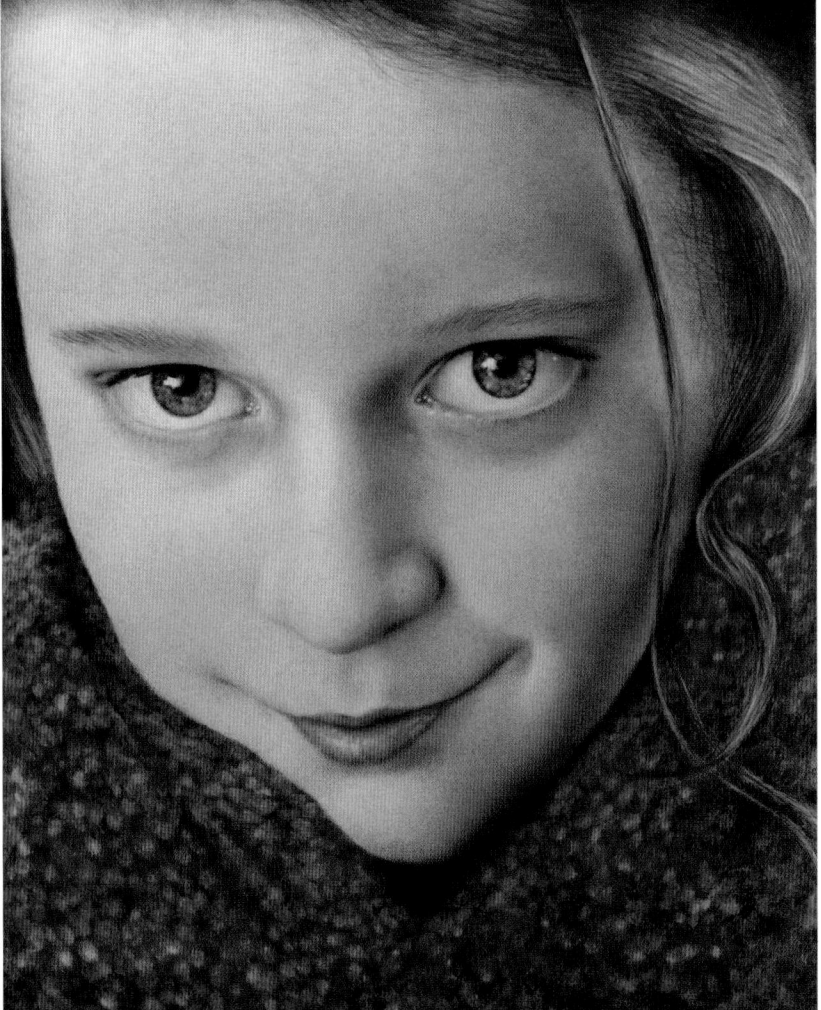

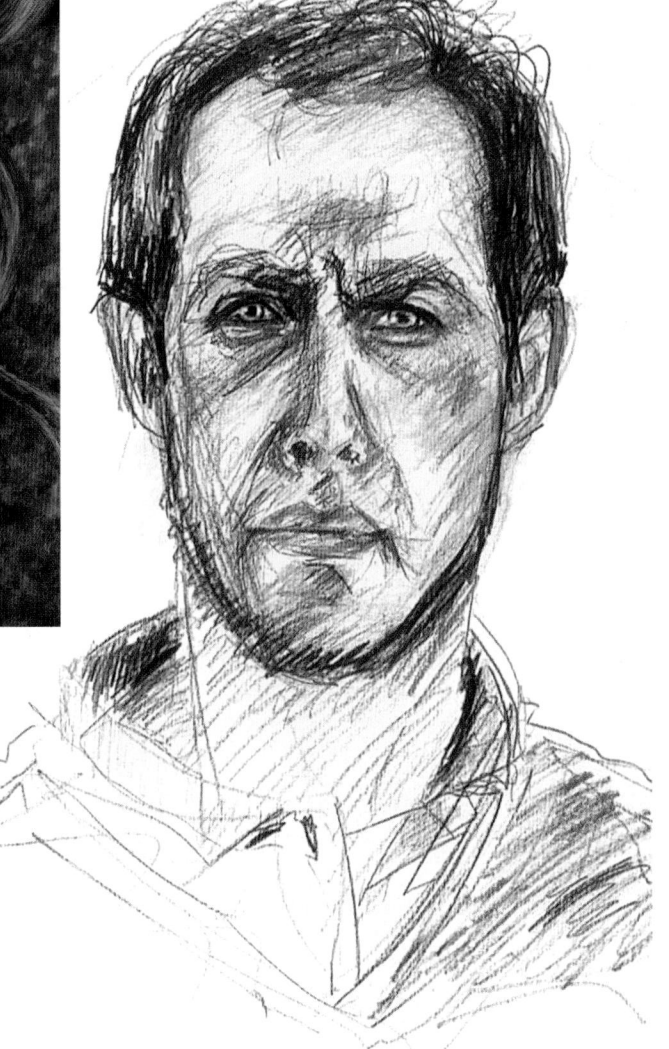

◄ SUSAN BRINKMANN
VERA
Many overlaid colours create a soft, almost translucent effect in the skin. The artist used not only pinks, but also reds, browns, greys, blues and purple. The drawing was created on an easel, so as to be able to stand close to it for fine details, and at a distance for a good overview.
• OVERLAYING COLOURS

JOHN TOWNEND ►
SELF-PORTRAIT
The strong contrast of black and red, further enlivened by the complementary contrast of green shadow areas, presents a powerful, almost aggressive study of the face. The mood of the portrait is emphasized by the busy activity of the pencil marks, weaving over and around each other to describe form and texture.
• LINEAR MARKS
• OVERLAYING COLOURS

Full-length Portraits

In a full-length portrait the subject's body and clothing provide certain kinds of descriptive detail that reduce the emphasis on facial characteristics as a means of creating a likeness. Typically, however, the head and face remain the most closely focused element of the image, whereas in other kinds of figure studies the model may be portrayed in an anonymous way.

When you compose a full-length portrait, consider how your viewpoint can help to construct the mood of the image. Generally, you expect to be roughly at a level with another person, so a high or low viewpoint creates an unusual tension between subject and viewer.

The most commonly used angle of the head in portraiture is a three-quarter view; in the full-length portrait this can be echoed or counterpointed by the posture of the body.

On the other hand, you can choose a more dramatic frontal pose or a clear-cut profile. It is not necessary to include a full background; as in the examples shown here, you can briefly suggest the surroundings to give the figure a context and balance the pose.

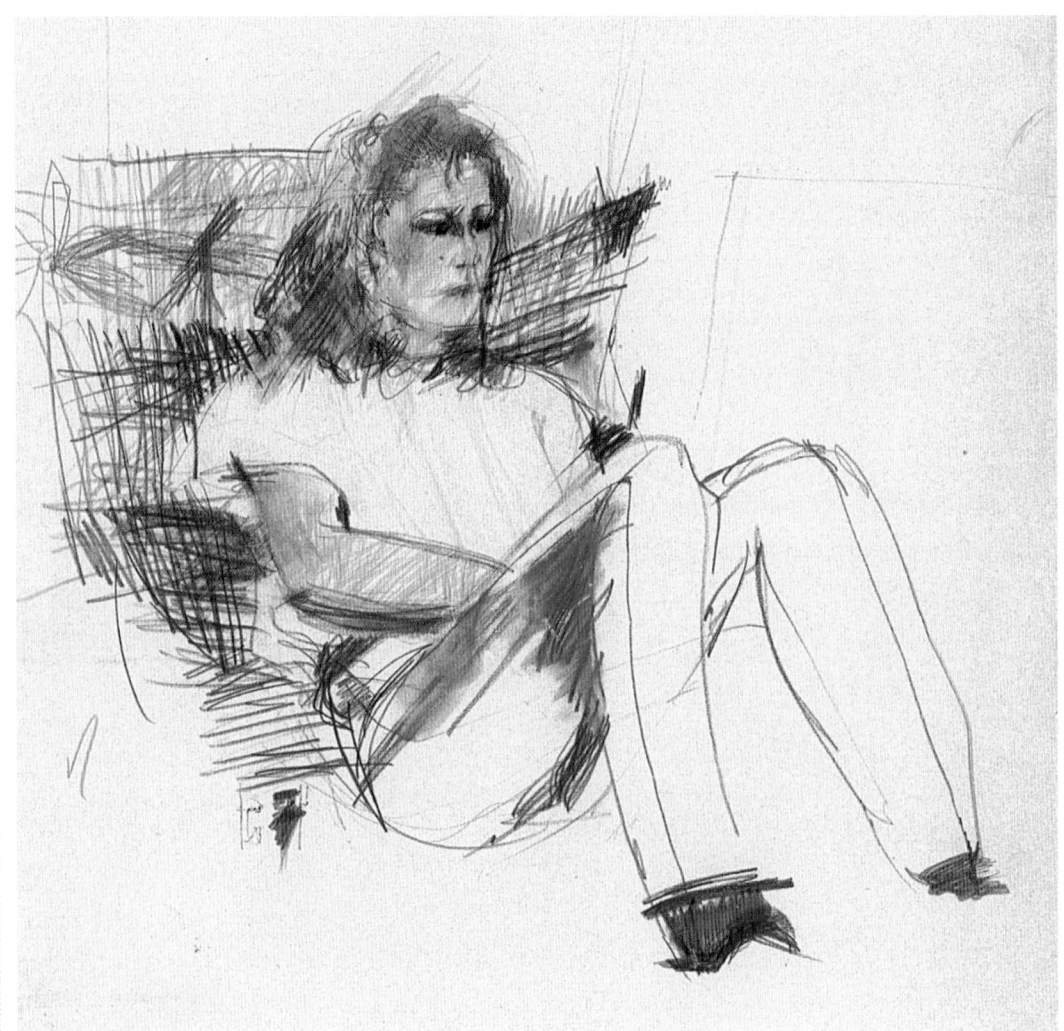

▲ KAYE SONG TEALE
GIRL IN BLUE JEANS
Both the pose of the figure and the facial expression suggest a rather downbeat mood, but the pencil marks and colours are, by contrast, extremely lively.
• CONTOUR DRAWING
• LINEAR MARKS

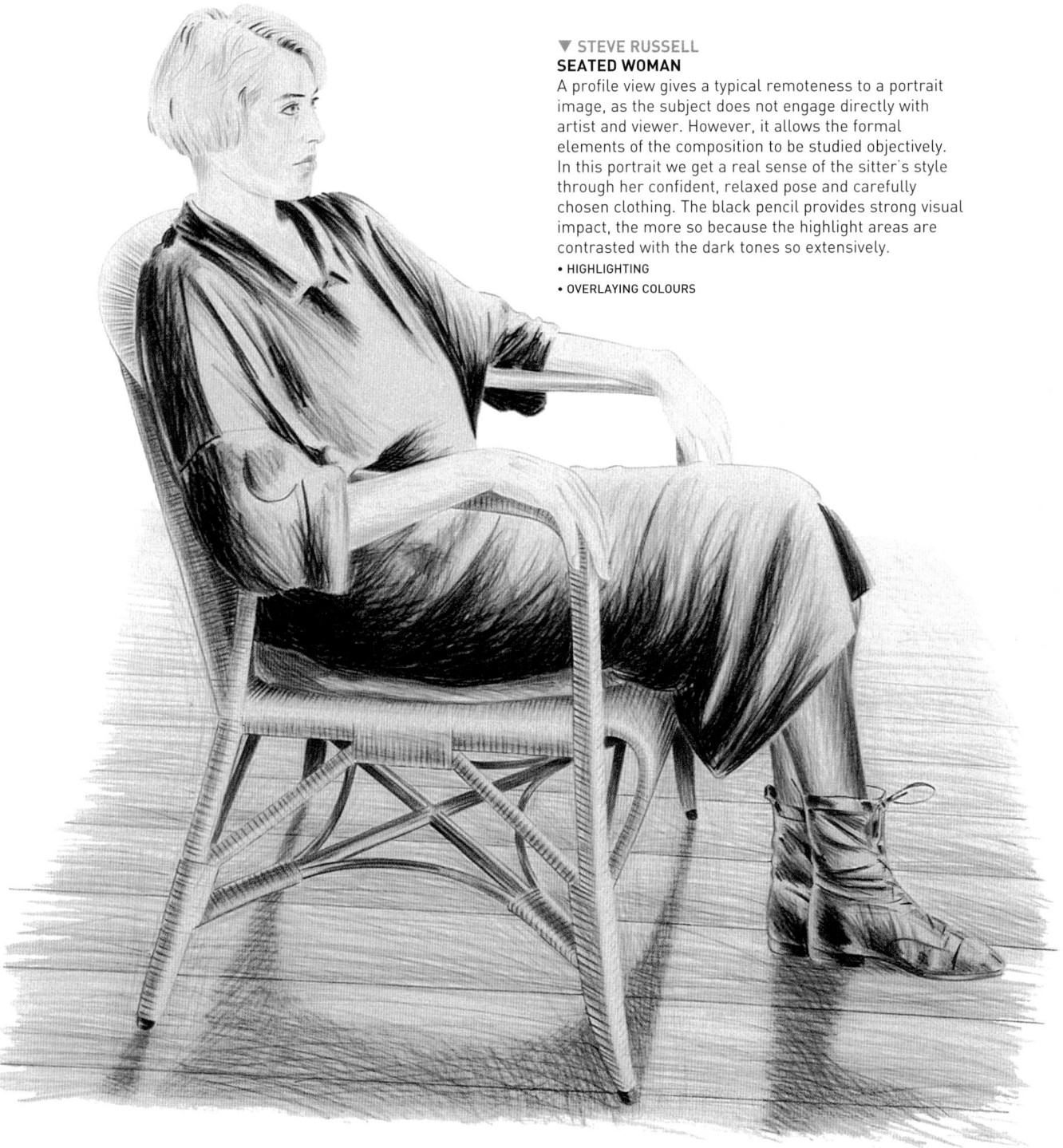

▼ STEVE RUSSELL
SEATED WOMAN
A profile view gives a typical remoteness to a portrait image, as the subject does not engage directly with artist and viewer. However, it allows the formal elements of the composition to be studied objectively. In this portrait we get a real sense of the sitter's style through her confident, relaxed pose and carefully chosen clothing. The black pencil provides strong visual impact, the more so because the highlight areas are contrasted with the dark tones so extensively.

• HIGHLIGHTING
• OVERLAYING COLOURS

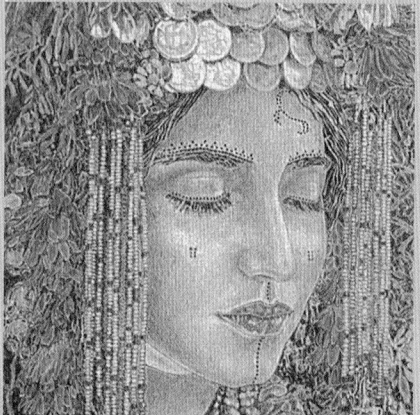

People
Two approaches to the same subject

Tracy Thompson

This demonstration shows two versions of the portrait drawing that illustrate very different ways of using the medium. The artist was commissioned to create the work using only water-soluble coloured pencils. She developed techniques that enabled her to use the pencil colour inventively – drawing with the pencil leads both dry and wet, brushing the colour into washes on the paper surface and softening the sharpened pencil leads in a palette to turn their pigments into a kind of gouache-like "paint". The first version of the coloured pencil drawing is worked in a very free way so that the image has the spontaneity and movement of a rapid sketch, even though the composition was carefully worked out beforehand. In the second version, drawn on a heavy watercolour paper, the artist has emphasized the strong graphic qualities of the subject but has also devised techniques that give a vibrant, painterly finish to the colour work.

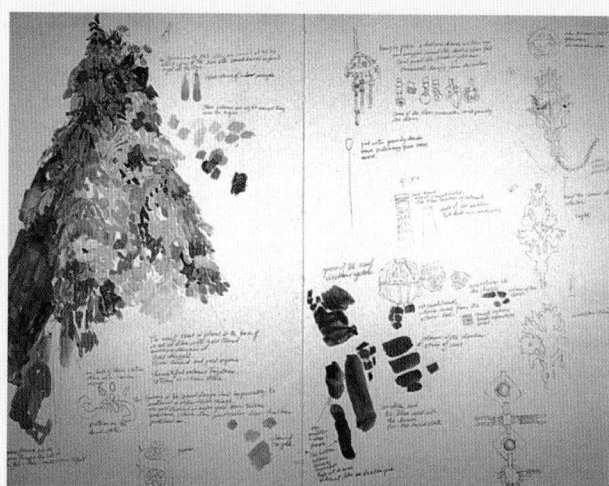

Sketchbook drawings
The detail of the bride's headdress was originally recorded in the artist's sketchbook, using watercolour and pencil to make a colour study and notation of individual elements in the elaborate decoration.

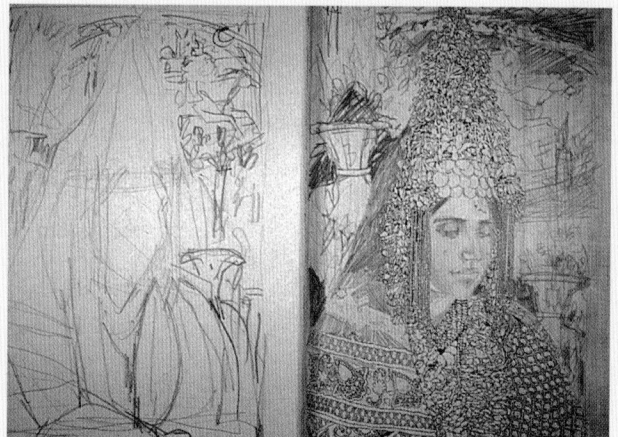

Working drawings
Before beginning the coloured pencil studies, a rough pencil sketch was made to plan out the composition (left), followed by a more intricate working of the actual shapes and patterns (right).

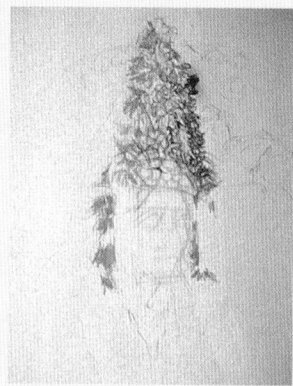

Free colour drawing
▲1 The basis of the portrait is roughly blocked in with line and light shading in appropriate colours. The artist begins to work into the detail of the headdress, initially establishing the larger shapes within the pattern.

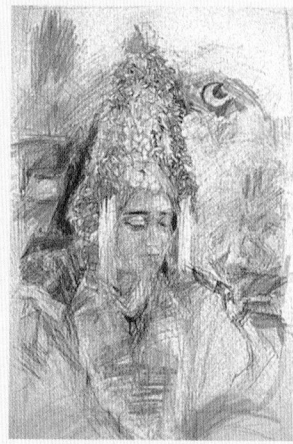

▲2 Gradually the colours are freely introduced all over the image area to develop the general impression of the figure. In places, the water-soluble pencils have been brushed over to create loose washes.

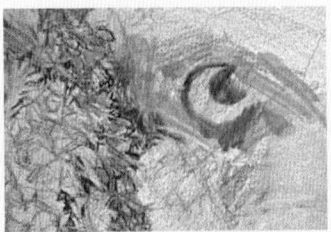

▲ **3** This detail shows the variety of marks already achieved by using the pencils wet and dry, and incorporating light brushstrokes into the rhythms of the drawing.

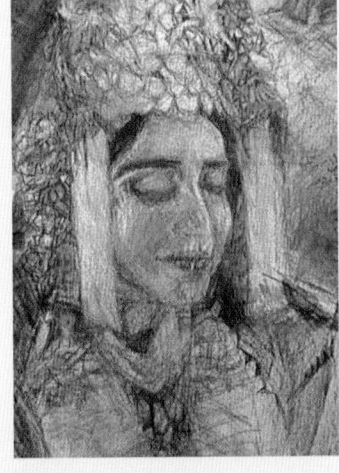

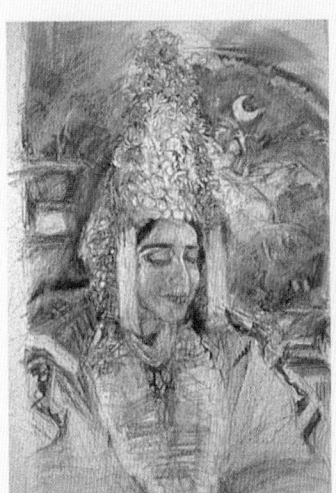

▲ **5** The colour overlays and pencil textures provide rich surface qualities, and tonal values are used more strongly to model the face and hair.

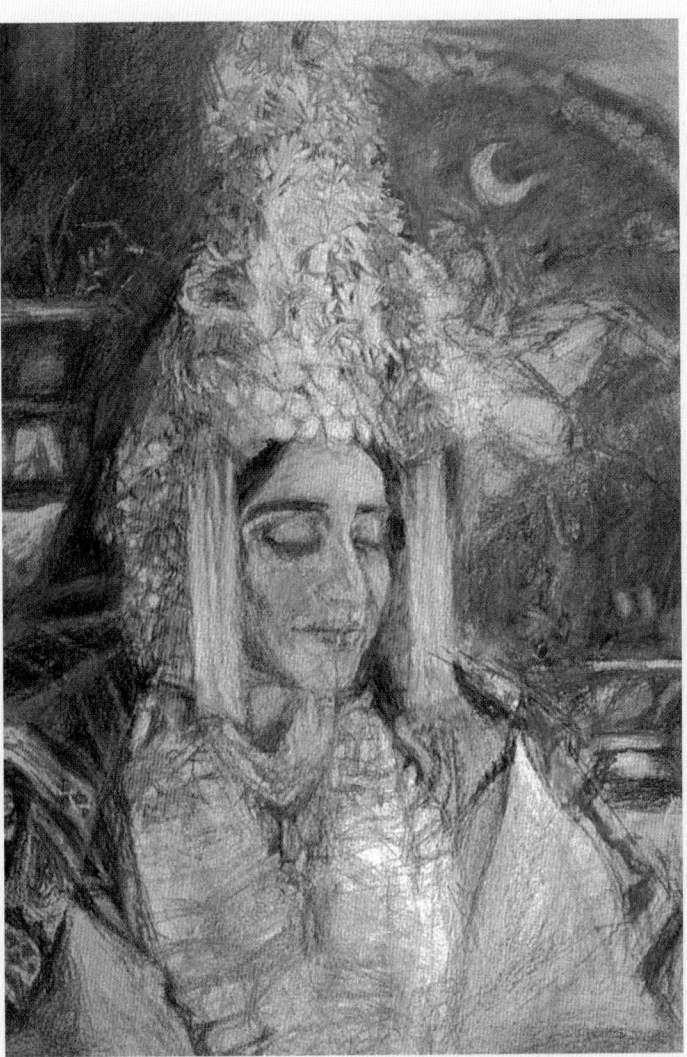

▲ **4** In the final stage of blocking in, all the colour areas are broadly defined and the linear pencil marks create a loose indication of the image's complexity.

▲ **6** The artist increases the range of tones and colours to add depth to the background. Although the interest focuses on the figure, all areas of the drawing are very active and expressive due to the dense combination of shading, linear marks and brushed colour.

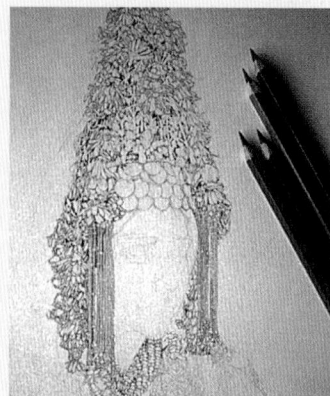

Final version

▲**1** The detailed study is intended to have a more graphic, elaborate effect, with areas of flat colour contained within strong outlines and contours. The initial drawing is made in line only, at first drawn faintly, then strengthened with crisp, dark tones.

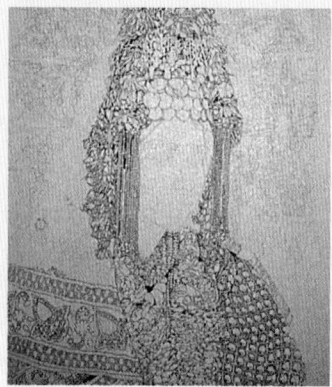

▲**2** The coloured outlines are varied according to the colours with which the shapes will be filled. Contrasting colours are often used, such as purple for the shapes of the orange flowers and green lines for the rose-petal garland, which will be coloured pink.

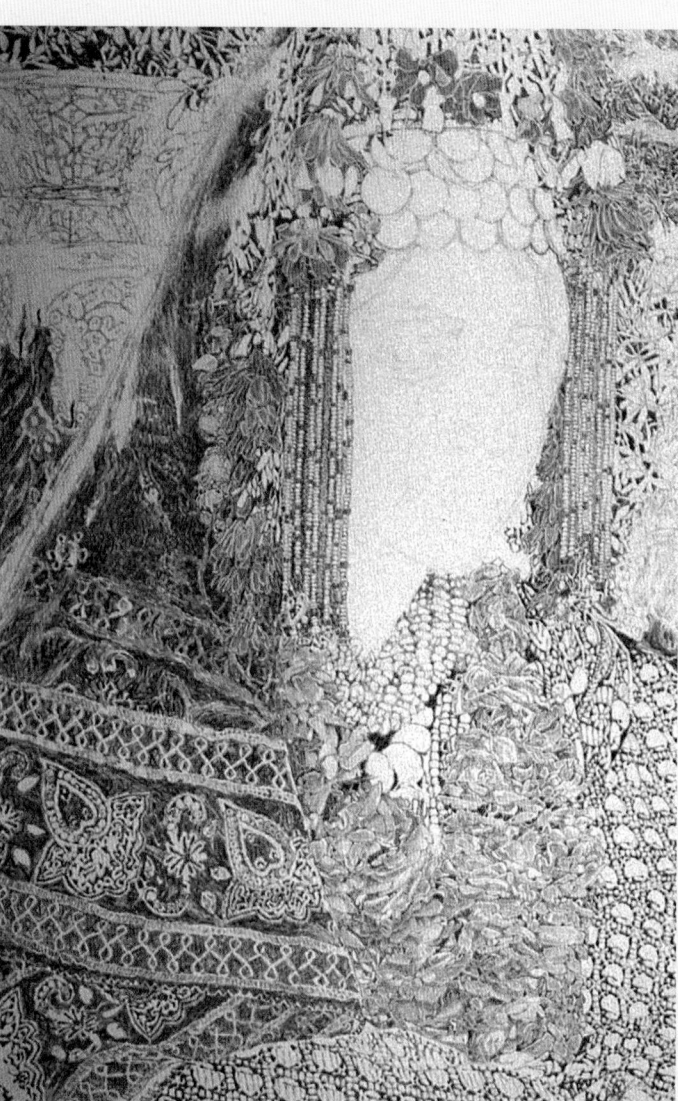

▲**3** Although the keylines strictly define the colour areas, the artist introduces gradations of each colour within the shapes to create a rich interpretation of the textures and patterns.

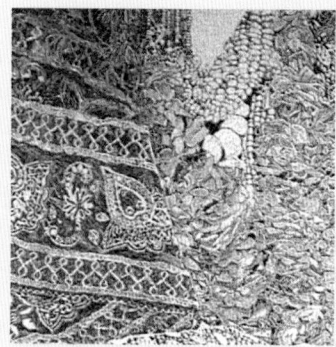

▲**4** The detail shows more clearly how certain colours have been graded in tone and intensity to create depth. The blue patterned fabric is lit up with many touches of other colours – greens, purples and pinks.

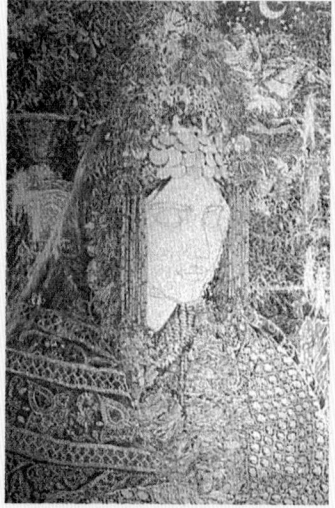

▲**5** Gradually the intricacy of the image is developed. The artist varies the pencil techniques, using the colour wet and dry so that the elaboration of the drawing's surface matches the complexity of the subject.

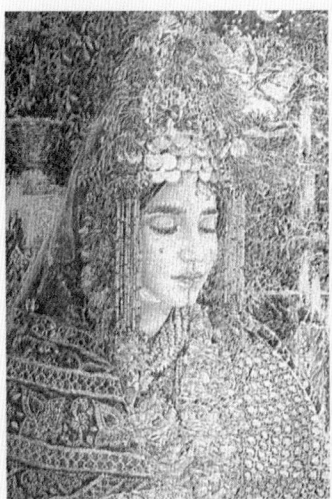

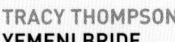 **6** The face is modelled with light washes of colour, spreading the pigment from the pencil leads with a dampened brush. Gentle shading increases the depth of tone, then, over the washed areas, the linear detail is drawn precisely with sharpened pencil tips.

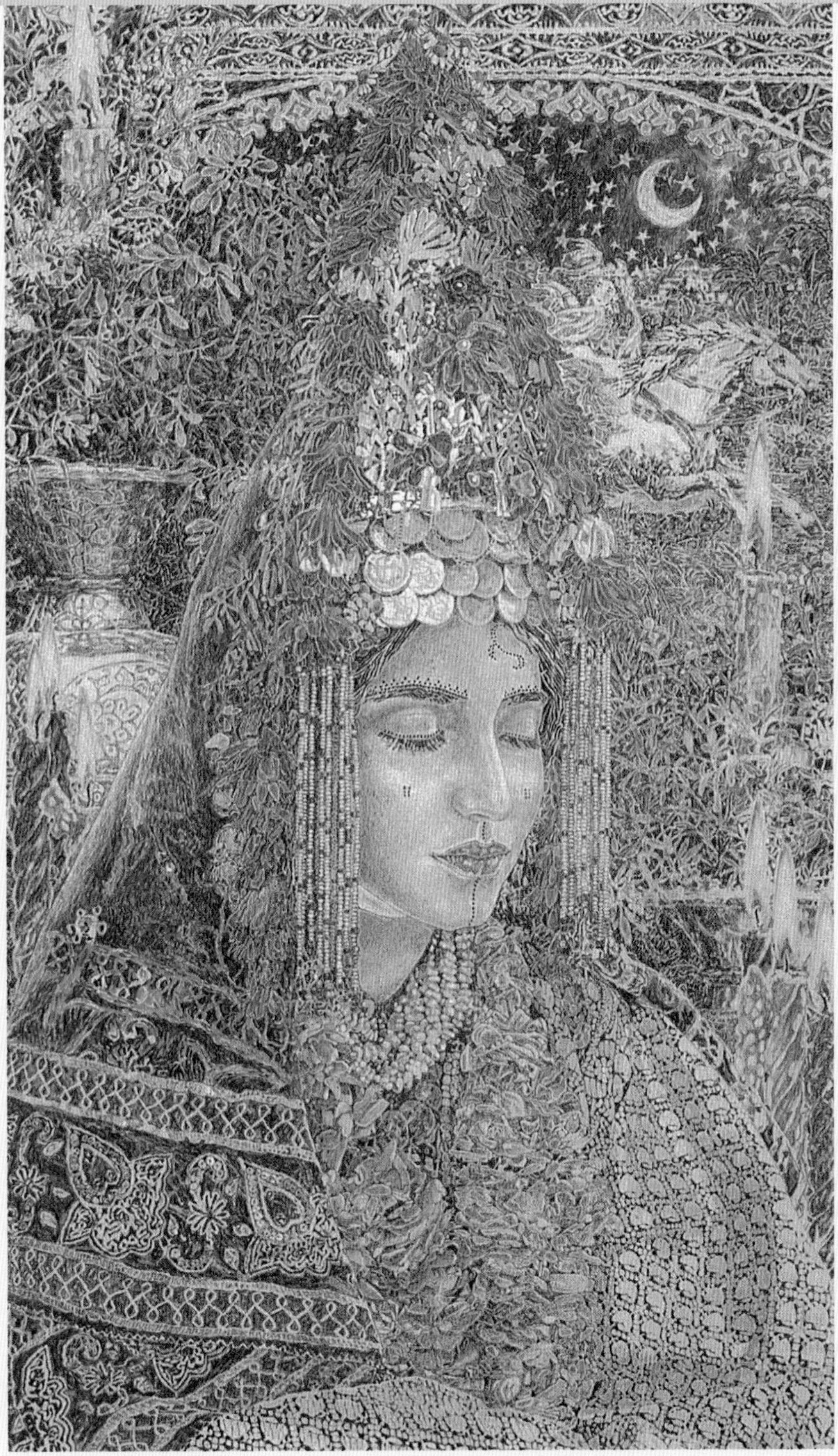

TRACY THOMPSON
YEMENI BRIDE
The drawing that initially was constructed as a flat, graphic pattern is alive with variable colours and lights, all worked delicately into the detailed patterning. Additional highlighting has been achieved by two methods: wetting and lifting the colour with a brush or softening the pencil leads with water to obtain an opaque colour "paste", painted onto the surface.

Index

A

abrasive paper 18
animal movement 146–147
animal studies 138–143
Antze, Nina 135, 25
atmosphere 94–95
Aubrey, Elizabeth 134
Auerbach, Frank 100, 50
Averill, Pat 22, 109

B

Barbier, Wilfred 87
Belcher, Pamela 97, 86, 35, 63
Bishop, Michael 99
blending 26–27
    blending with chalky pencils 26
    blending with waxy pencils 27
blocking in 30–31
Brace, Graham 132, 95, 7, 33
Brinkmann, Susan 137, 143, 165
Brokaw, Michele 145
brushes 9
buildings 96–97
burnishing 38–39
    effects of burnishing 38

C

Callahan, Gloria 107, 38, 11, 120
Camp, Jeffrey 88, 154
cardboard 19
cartridge paper 15
chalk pencils 9
    blending with chalky pencils 26
Chapman, Chris 161, 41
Cheese, Chloë 99, 119

children 156–157
collage 74–75

colour
    blind impressing over colour 57
    building up colour shading 40
    colour charts 17
    colour gradation 35
    colour studies 90–91
    impressed coloured line 56
    mixed hues 41
    mixing colours 37
    using local colour 49
coloured papers 14, 16–17
    drawing on coloured paper 16–17
    making colour charts 17
    range of colours 16
coloured pencils 7
    materials 8–9
container plants 136–137
contour drawing 48–49
    monochrome drawing 48
    using local colour 49
Coulson, Karen 144
craft knives 9
crosshatching 28

D

dashes and dots 36–37
    directional strokes 36
    feathered strokes 37
    irregular spacing 37
    mixing colours 37
    scribbled dots 36
    ticks 36
Davis, John 122

De Brouwer, Frank 146
decorative objects 110–111
    pattern qualities 110
Delmastro, John 85
Dennis, Jo 91, 92
Deuter, Cat 142, 156, 43
distance 88–89
dots 36–37
Doty, Sheri Lynn Goyer 162
Duffy, Mathilde 27
Duis, Laura 140

E

Edidin, Barbara Vicki 121
environment 162–163
ephemera 112–113
erasers 9
    eraser techniques 52–53
Evans, Gretchen 110, 154
Evans, Ray 101, 99
expressive portraits 164–165

F

facades 98–99
filling in 32
    edge qualities 32
    free shading 32
    working to an outline 32
fixing 79
    applying fixative 79
flowers and foliage 130–135
    foliage 130
    fresh beauty of flowers 148–151
foodstuffs 114
form 29

form and surface detail 124–127
Friedman, Deborah 115, 130
frottage 62
    materials for frottage 62
    textured glass 63
    textured wallcovering 62
    wood grain 62
fruits 120–121
full-length portraits 166–167

G

George, Adrian 159
gouache, white 9
gradation 34–35
    colour gradation 35
    tonal gradation 34
graphite pencils 9, 66–67
Greene, Gary 131, 116, 46, 134
Greene, Helena 137, 136, 114, 123, 92, 117
groups 114–119
    foodstuffs 114

H

handling pencils 12–13
    conventional grip 12
    overhand grip 13
    underhand grip 13
hard pencils 9
hatching 28–29
    constructing form 29
    crosshatching 28
    free hatching 28
    varying the texture 28
Hayward, Sara 110, 73, 96, 121, 109
Hedgecock, Angie 129, 141
highlighting 46–47

Holmes, David 95, 91, 89
Hughes, Jane 113, 119

I

impressing 56–57
    blind impressing 57
    blind impressing over colour 57
    impressed coloured line 56
individuals 154–155
ink and pencil 68

K

Kitson, Linda 152, 160
kneaded erasers 9
knives 9

L

landscape 86
    colour studies 90–91
    light and atmosphere 94–95
    shapes and textures 92–93
    sketching in coloured pencils 86
    space and distance 88–89
Lane, Jessie 155
life studies 158–159
light 94–95
    space and light 102–105
line and wash 69
line qualities 44–45
    calligraphic, directional line 44
    firm, unvariable line 44
    repetitive line 44
linear marks 20–21
    aggressive gestural lines 21

broken shading 21
flourished movement 21
grainy loops 21
multi-directional, open shading 21
random scribble 21
slanted scribble 21
Locati, Dianne 132
Ludden, Rita D. 117

M

masking 64–65
    loose masking 64
    using masking film 65
    using masking tape 65
masking tape 9
materials 8–9
McQuillin, Patti 138
Melegari, Carl 106, 108, 93
Melling, David 164
mixing pencils 42–43
    types of coloured pencil 42
Morgan, Angela 128
movement, animals 146–147
    people 160–161

N

nature 128–129
    animal movement 146–147
    animal studies 138–143
    container plants 136–137
    flowers and foliage 130–135
    fresh beauty of flowers 148–51
    pattern and texture 144–145
    sources of imagery 128

O

O'Neill, Jean Ann 96, 112
objects 106
    decorative objects 110–111
    domestic objects 108–109
    form and surface detail 124–127
    fruits 120–121
    groups 114–119
    selecting your subject and
    technique 106
    table settings 122–123
    toys and ephemera 112–113
overlaying colours 40
    building up colour shading 40
    mixed hues 41

P

paper grain effects 14
    cartridge paper 15
    coloured papers 14
    pastel paper 15
    textured papers 14
    watercolour papers 15
pastel and pencil 70–71
patch correction 80–81
pattern 110, 144–145
Pearson, Don 140
Pease, Mike 94
pencil sharpeners 9
people and portraits 152–153
    children 156–157
    composition and technique 152
    environment 162–163
    expressive portrait 164–165
    full-length portraits 166–167

individuals 154–155
life studies 158–159
movement 160–161
two approaches to the same
subject 168–171
plastic erasers 9

R

Robinson, Stuart 124–127
Rochelle, Carolyn 145
Russell, Steve 91, 167

S

scalpels 9
Schoemmer, Barbara 19
sgraffito 60–61
shading 22–25
    broken shading 21
    building up colour shading 40
    combining different qualities 24
    free shading 32
    heavy, directional shading 24
    lightweight, even shading 24
    multi-directional, open shading 21
    open shading 24
    shaded gradations 24
shapes 92–93
sketch pads 9
sketching 50–51
    sketching in coloured pencils 86
Smolko, John 163
solvents 54–55
    using a marker blender 55
    using spirit solvent 54
    using water-soluble pencils 55

space 88–89
    space and light 102–105
squaring up or down 78
Stanton, Philip 67, 123
stippling 33
Stone, Tess 118
Strother, Jane 29, 148–151, 14, 123,
    151, 114
surface detail 124–127

T

table settings 122–123
Takeuma 51
Taylor, Leslie 49
Taylor, Steve 146
Teale, Kaye Song 166
techniques 11
    blending 26–27
    blocking in 30–31
    burnishing 38–39
    collage 74–75
    coloured papers 16–17
    contour drawing 48–49
    dashes and dots 36–37
    eraser techniques 52–53
    filling in 32
    fixing 79
    frottage 62–63
    gradation 34–35
    graphite pencil 66–67
    handling pencils 12–13
    hatching 28–29
    highlighting 46–47
    impressing 56–57
    ink and pencil 68
    line and wash 69

line qualities 44–45
linear marks 20–21
masking 64–65
mixing pencils 42–43
overlaying colours 40–41
paper grain effects 14–15
pastel and pencil 70–71
patch correction 80–81
sgraffito 60–61
shading 22–25
sketching 50–51
solvents 54–55
squaring up or down 78
stippling 33
textured grounds 18–19
tracing 76–77
transparent supports 82–83
watercolour and pencil 72–73
white line 58–59
Ten Bosch, 152
textured papers 14
textured grounds 18–19
    abrasive paper 18
    cardboard 19
    drawing on gesso 19
textures 92–93, 144–145
themes 85
    landscape 86–95
    nature 128–151
    objects 106–127
    townscape 86, 96–101
Thompson, Tracy 139, 171
Tiffen, Andrew 162
Topley, Will 41
torchons 9
Townend, John 105, 88, 93, 165,
    102–105, 90

townscapes 86, 100–101
    buildings 96–97
    facades 98–99
toys 112–113
tracing 76–77
    tracing method 76
    transfer papers 77
    using transfer paper 77
transparent supports 82–83

U

Uglow, Euan 158

V

Van Der Krooy, Luc 101
Van Houten, Erik 157

W

Wadsworth, Priscilla 161
water-soluble pencils 9
    using water-soluble pencils 55
watercolour and pencil 72–73
watercolour brushes 9
watercolour papers 15
wax pencils 9
    blending with waxy pencils 27
white line 58–59

Credits

Quarto would like to thank the following artists for supplying images for inclusion in this book:

Antze, Nina, www.pcquilt.com, pp.25, 135
Aubury, Elisabeth, UKCPS, p.134l
Auerbach, Frank, pp.50r, 100
Averill, Pat, www.pat872.wix.com/pat-averill-artist, pp.23, 109b
Barbier, Wilfrid, www.wilfridbarbier.com, pp.5tl, 87
Belcher, Pamela, CPSA, www.pamelabelcher.com, pp.35, 63, 97
Bishop, Michael, p.98
Bosch, Max Ten, p.153
Brace, Graham, www.grahambrace.com, pp.6, 33, 86, 95t, 133
Brinkmann, Susan, www.susanbrinkmann.nl, pp.10, 137l, 143, 165t
Brokaw, Michele, CPSA, p.145b
Callahan, Gloria, www.gloriacallahan.com, pp.38, 107, 120b
Camp, Jeffrey, pp.88b, 154b
Chapman, Chris, pp.41b, 161t
Cheese, Chlöe, pp.99b, 119l
Coulson, Karen, www.karencoulson.co.uk, p.144
Davis, John, p.122
De Brouwer, Frank, p.147
Delmastro, John, www.j54dell.wix.com/john-delmastro, p.90
Dennis, Jo, pp.91bl, 92bl
Deuter, Cat, www.catdeuterart.com, pp.43, 142, 156
Duis, Laura, CPSA, p.140t

Eddin, Barbara, CPSA, p.121t
Evans, Ray, pp.99t, 101t
Friedman, Deborah, www.dlfriedman.com, pp.115, 130
George, Adrian, p.159
Goyer Doty, Sheri Lynn, CPSA, p.162
Greene, Gary, www.ggart.biz, pp.5tr, 46, 116, 131, 134r
Greene, Helena, pp.92r, 114t, 117t, 123br, 136, 137r
Hayward, Sara, pp.73r, 96b, 109t, 110, 121b
Hedgecock, Angie, www.pencilportraitartist.co.uk, pp.2, 129, 141
Holmes, David, pp.91br, 95b
Houten, Erik Van, p.157
Hudson, Mark, p.89
Hughes, Jane, pp.113, 119r
Kitson, Linda, pp.152, 160
Krooy, Luc Van Der, p.101
Lane, Jesse, p.155
Locati, Dyanne, CPSA, p.132
Ludden, Rita D., CPSA, p.117b
McQuillin, Patti, CPSA, p.138
Melegari, Carl, pp.93b, 106, 108
Melling, David, p.164
Morgan, Angela, p.128
O'Neill, Jean Ann, pp.96t, 112t/b
Parker, Gretchen Evans, CPSA, CPX, www.gretchenevansparker.com, pp.4, 110, 154t
Pearson, Don, CPSA, pp.140b
Pease, Mike, CPSA p.94
Robinson, Stuart, pp.124–127
Rochelle, Carolyn, CPSA, p.145r

Russell, Steve, pp.91t, 167
Schoemmer, Barbara, p.19
Smolko, John, www.smolkoart.com, p.163
Stanton, Philip, pp.67, 123t
Stone, Tess, p.118
Strother, Jane, pp.14, 29, 114b, 123bl, 148, 151
Takeuma, www.k5.dion.ne.jp/~s-tkm231, p.51
Taylor, Leslie, p.49b
Taylor, Steve, p.146
Teale, Kaye Song, p.166
Thompson, Tracy, pp.139, 168–171
Tiffen, Andrew, p.162b
Topley, Will, 41t
Townend, John, pp.88t, 90, 93t, 102–105, 165b
Uglow, Euan, p.158
Wadsworth, Pricilla, p.161b
WhoAreYou, www.shutterstock.com, p.20